Confucianism and Democratization in East Asia

For decades, scholars and politicians have vigorously debated whether Confucianism is compatible with democracy, yet little is known about how it affects the process of democratization in East Asia. In this book, Doh Chull Shin examines the prevalence of core Confucian legacies and their connection to civic and political orientations in six Confucian countries: China, Japan, South Korea, Singapore, Taiwan, and Vietnam. Analyses of the Asian Barometer and World Values surveys reveal that popular attachment to Confucian legacies has mixed results on democratic demand. Whereas Confucian political legacies encourage demand for a nonliberal democratic government that prioritizes the economic welfare of the community over the freedom of individual citizens, its social legacies promote interpersonal trust and tolerance, which are critical components of democratic civic life. Thus, the author argues that citizens of historically Confucian Asia have an opportunity to combine the best of Confucian ideals and democratic principles in a novel, particularly East Asian, brand of democracy.

Doh Chull Shin is Jack W. Peltason Scholar in Residence at the Center for the Study of Democracy at the University of California, Irvine. He is the founder of the Korea Democracy Barometer and a cofounder of the Asian Barometer. His recent books include *The Quality of Life in Confucian Asia* (2010); *How East Asians View Democracy* (2008); *Citizens, Democracy, and Markets around the Pacific Rim* (2006); and *Mass Politics and Culture in Democratizing Korea* (Cambridge 2000).

Confucianism and Democratization in East Asia

DOH CHULL SHIN

Center for the Study of Democracy
University of California, Irvine

CAMBRIDGE
UNIVERSITY PRESS

CAMBRIDGE UNIVERSITY PRESS
Cambridge, New York, Melbourne, Madrid, Cape Town,
Singapore, São Paulo, Delhi, Tokyo, Mexico City

Cambridge University Press
32 Avenue of the Americas, New York, NY 10013-2473, USA

www.cambridge.org
Information on this title: www.cambridge.org/9781107631786

First published 2012

Printed in the United States of America

A catalog record for this publication is available from the British Library.

Library of Congress Cataloging in Publication data
Sin, To-ch'ol.
Confucianism and democratization in East Asia / Doh Chull Shin.
p. cm.
Includes bibliographical references and index.
ISBN 978-1-107-01733-7 (hardback) – ISBN 978-1-107-63178-6 (paperback)
1. Democratization – East Asia. 2. Democracy – East Asia. 3. Confucianism and state –
East Asia. I. Title.
JQ1499.A91S56 2012
320.95–dc23   2011027737

ISBN 978-1-107-01733-7 Hardback
ISBN 978-1-107-63178-6 Paperback

CONTENTS

v

Acknowledgments

This book has been in the making for three years, beginning in September 2008 when the Woodrow Wilson International Center for Scholars in Washington, DC, invited me to write it. During this three-year period, a number of institutions and scholars helped me complete the research reported in the book and present all the research findings clearly and coherently. I would like to gratefully acknowledge my intellectual and other relevant debts to these institutions and individual scholars.

The book is based on public opinion surveys conducted by two large-scale research programs that monitor and compare the cultural and institutional dynamics of democratization across countries in East Asia and other regions. I am deeply indebted to Yun-han Chu, Larry Diamond, and Andrew Nathan who designed and coordinated the Asian Barometer surveys in thirteen Confucian and non-Confucian East Asian countries, and to Ronald Inglehart and Christian Welzel who directed the fifth wave of the World Values Surveys in fifty-seven countries throughout the globe.

The Woodrow Wilson International Center for Scholars awarded an international fellowship that enabled me to spend nine months in an ideal setting and prepare the first draft of the book manuscript. At the center, I enjoyed the gracious hospitality of Robert Hathaway and Steven Lager-feld. The Korea Foundation, the Korea University International Center for Korean Studies, and the University of Missouri endowed chair in Korean studies provided financial support for analyzing public opinion surveys and for preparing all the materials presented in this book. The Center for the Study of Democracy at the University of California, Irvine, provided what I needed at the final revising stage.

Daniel A. Bell kindly read all the core chapters of the book and helped me to broaden and deepen my understanding of Confucianism and avoid many factual and interpretative errors and oversights. Russell Dalton, Pippa Norris, Dorie Solinger, Christian Welzel, and two anonymous reviewers also kindly read chapters and provided me with valuable comments and suggestions for revision. I am also indebted to Dana Cha, Peter Chereson, and Nick Spina who prepared materials for the first two chapters, and Nisha Mukherjee who proofread the final draft.

Many ideas and themes presented in this book benefited from exchanges and discussions with numerous colleagues who have conducted empirical, philosophical, or theoretical research on Confucianism and democratization and with students who enrolled in my graduate seminars on democratization and East Asian politics. They include: Robert Albritton, Michael Bratton, Joseph Chan, Myung Chey, HanSeung Cho, Aurel Croissant, Guo Dingping, Edward Friedman, Christian Haerpfer, Baogang He, Kenichi Ikeda, Takashi Inoguchi, Jiho Jang, Byong-Kuen Jhee, Hong-Cheol Kim, Jiyoung Kim, Kwang-Jin Kim, Kwang-woong Kim, Sungmoon Kim, Sunhyuk Kim, Wang Sik Kim, Hans-Dieter Klingemann, Hsin-Chi Kuan, Wai-Man Lam, Jae Chul Lee, Joon-Beom Lee, Junhan Lee, Xiaoting Li, Robert Mattes, Ian McAllister, Jose Alvaro Moises, Leonardo Morlino, Chong-min Park, Lingling Qi, Benjamin Reilly, Richard Rose, the late Tianjian Shi, Huoyan Shu, Ming Sing, Anna Sun, Ern-Ser Tan, Mark Tessler, Rollin Tusalem, Jack Van Der Slik, Zhengxu Wang, Bridget Welsh, and Xinzhong Yao.

I am most grateful to three individuals. Conrad P. Rutkowski has been a true friend and wonderful colleague during my entire academic life. As he did with my earlier books, Conrad read all versions of the manuscript more than once and identified many alternative viewpoints and perspectives for me to consider. Youngho Cho, my last Ph.D. student, selflessly spent months creating all the tables and figures, proofreading the entire text, and preparing the book's index. Anita Harrison thoughtfully edited the final version of the entire text and helped me to improve it not only stylistically, but also substantively. She is the most brilliant copy editor with whom I have ever worked.

Cambridge University Press has been an indispensable source of encouragement and support for this book project. I would like to especially thank Robert Dreesen and James Dunn for bringing this book to the readers in an attractive format and in a timely fashion.

My deepest debt is due my wife, Haelim. Her patience, understanding, and support have been the foundation of my academic and family life. I dedicate this book with affection, love, and gratitude to her and our two children, Sueme and Eugene.

Introduction

We live in a monumental era for the advancement of democracy. For the first time since its birth in ancient Greece more than two and a half millennia ago, democracy no longer remains confined mostly to socioeconomically advanced countries of the West. Instead, it has become a global phenomenon for the first time in human history. As a set of political ideals as well as political practices, democracy has finally reached every corner of the globe, including the Middle East and North Africa, the two regions known as the most inhospitable to it (Corby 2011; Haerpfer et al. 2009; Huntington 1991; McFaul 2002; Shin 1994, 2007).

Almost everywhere on earth, democracy has emerged as the political system most favored by a large majority of the mass citizenry (Diamond 2008a; Heath et al. 2005; Mattes 2007).[1] More notably, according to Freedom House (2010), the family of democratic states has expanded from 40 member countries to 116 since 1974, when the third wave of democratization began to spread from Southern Europe. Democracies currently account for 60 percent of the world's independent states. Even economically poor and culturally traditional societies, such as Benin and Mali in Africa, have been transformed into functioning liberal democracies. Growing demands from ordinary citizens, along with increased pressures and inducements from international communities, have turned the third wave of democratization into the most successful diffusion of democracy in history.

---

[1] According to the latest wave of the World Values Surveys conducted in fifty-seven countries during the period of 2005–8, more than nine out of ten people (92%) rated democracy favorably on a 4-point scale ranging from "very good" to "very bad."

The Third Wave of Democratization in East Asia

The third wave of global democratization reached the shores of East Asia more than ten years after it hit Southern European countries. Over the past two decades, beginning with the 1986 overthrow of the Marcos regime in the Philippines, this wave has transformed seven of the thirteen autocracies in the region into democracies (Diamond 2011; Shin 2008). These seven are Indonesia, Mongolia, South Korea, Taiwan, Cambodia, the Philippines, and Thailand. Of these countries, three – Cambodia, the Philippines, and Thailand – have since reverted into nondemocracies because their people and political leaders were unable to resolve political differences peacefully through the process of democratic politics. Other countries in the region resisted the wave and have yet to hold free and competitive elections. Included in this group of autocracies are China, the largest and most populous country and the core state of Confucian civilization, and Singapore, a city-state known as the world's richest non-democracy. Even with the recent return of the Philippines to democratic rule, nondemocracies outnumber democracies by a substantial margin of ten to six.[2]

The six democracies in East Asia today include one second-wave democracy, Japan, and five third-wave democracies: Indonesia, Mongolia, South Korea, the Philippines, and Taiwan. Despite growing experience with democratic politics, all five third-wave democracies in the region have failed to become truly functioning liberal democracies (Kaufman et al. 2007; Shin 2008). Although many third-wave democracies in Europe became consolidated within the first decade of democratic rule, new East Asian democracies remain defective or nonliberal in character even in their second or third decade of existence (Chang et al. 2007; Cheng 2003; Croissant 2004; Shin 2008). In view of the slow pace of democratic regime change and its limited liberal expansion, it is fair to conclude that in the region as a whole the movement toward democracy is stagnating. Of all the regions of the world, East Asia remains one of the most resistant to the third wave of democratization.

Why does a region blessed with rapid economic development remain cursed with democratic underdevelopment? Why have so many countries in this region, unlike their peers in other regions, failed to join the powerful wave of global democratization? Why have nearly half the countries

---

[2] According to Freedom House's (2010) survey of electoral democracies, Thailand is rated as one of ten East Asian nondemocracies, along with China, North Korea, Malaysia, Singapore, Brunei, Vietnam, Laos, Burma, and Cambodia.

that joined the third wave been unable to sustain democratic rule, making the third wave of democratization more like an ebb-and-flow tide than a surging wave? Why have all the new and old democracies in East Asia, unlike many of their peers in the West, failed to improve the quality of their democratic governance? These questions have yet to be addressed adequately in the literature on democratization in general or that on East Asian politics in particular.

Confucian Legacies and Democratization

East Asia is a region infused with the core values of Confucianism. These Confucian values, once promoted as "Asian Values," have historically been used to prioritize and justify the rights and duties of individual citizens and to define the power and authority of their political leaders (Bell 2006; Bell et al. 1996; Compton 2000; Pye 1985; Tu 1996a). Together with the distinct makeup of the region's political institutions and their practices (Reilly 2008), these values have led to political order and economic welfare being top national development goals.[3] These values have also ushered in delegative democracy with power concentrated within the executive branch (Im 2004; O'Dwyer 2003).

Accordingly, many scholars and policy makers have turned to the region's Confucian legacies in an attempt to explain the slow pace of democratic progress in East Asia. For decades, they have vigorously debated whether those cultural legacies have served to deter the emergence of liberal democracy in the region, been neutral forces, or been advantageous to democracy (Bauer and Bell 1999; Emmerson 1995; Huntington 1996; Moody 1996; Tamney 1991; Weatherley 1999). Yet little consensus exists about the relationship between Confucian cultural legacies and a lack of democratic political development in East Asia.

Lee Kuan Yew (1998) and other proponents of Confucian Asian Values, for example, have claimed that Western-style liberal democracy is neither suitable for nor compatible with the Confucianism of East Asia, where collective welfare, a sense of duty, and other principles of Confucian moral philosophy run deep in people's consciousness (Barr 2000; Huntington 1996; Y. Kim 1997; Pye 1985; Zakaria 1994). These proponents advocate a benevolent and paternalistic form of governance as a

---

[3] As discussed in Chapter 3, it is the supreme goal of Confucianism to build *datong shehui*, a community of grand harmony or unity in which people live in peace and prosperity.

viable alternative to a liberal democracy that is based on the principles of Western individualism.

In contrast, Kim Dae Jung (1994), Amartya Sen (1999), and many other advocates of liberal democracy have denounced the Confucian Asian Values Thesis as a politically motivated attempt to legitimate authoritarian rule and have rejected it as anachronistic and oppressive (Bell 2006; Bell and Hahm 2003; Hahm 2004). Francis Fukuyama (1995b) also rejects the portrayal of Confucianism and democracy as antithetical doctrines. However, Fareed Zakaria (2003) argues that democracies in Confucian Asia are likely to remain "illiberal democracies" because elites and ordinary citizens are reluctant to embrace and observe the fundamental tenets of constitutional liberalism.

Theoretically, despite decades of argumentation and debate, no systematic effort to date has been made to recast the Asian Values Thesis as a theory seeking to unravel the cultural dynamics of democratization. As a result, its claims linking Confucian cultural legacies to democratic underdevelopment in historically Confucian East Asia (defined in Chapter 1) have yet to be evaluated in view of congruence theory and other recent theoretical advances in the study of democratic cultural development.

Empirically, little systematic effort has yet been made to determine how Confucian values and norms actually affect the building of democratic nations in Confucian East Asia. To date, only a handful of studies have empirically explored – from the perspective of ordinary citizens in the region – how Confucianism affects the process of democratizing authoritarian rule (Blondel and Inoguchi 2006; Chang et al. 2005; Dalton and Ong 2006; Fetzer and Soper 2007; Kim 2010; Nathan and Chen 2004; Park and Shin 2006; Welzel 2011). These studies offer only a partial account of the complex relationship between Confucian legacies and the democratization among the mass citizenries of historically Confucian countries.

Conceptually, these empirical studies are based on narrow or thin conceptions of Confucianism and democratization. They often equate Confucianism with authoritarianism or familism, and democratization with the embrace of democracy as the preferred regime. *Theoretically*, these studies are also weak in that they search exclusively for a direct link between Confucian and democratic orientations, neglecting to examine indirect relationships through engagement in civic life, which Alexis de Tocqueville (2000 [1835]) once called "the schools of democracy."

Methodologically, these studies have relied on techniques of quantitative analysis that merely allow estimating the level or amount of a specific

Confucian or democratic property; as a result, they provide little information about how the various legacies of Confucianism and the divergent dimensions of democratization interact with one another in *qualitatively distinct patterns*. Moreover, these studies have examined only one country or a few in historically Confucian Asia or one or a few dimensions of Confucian and democratic orientations. Most do not adequately compare this region with other Asian and non-Asian regions to determine whether Confucianism is a truly regional phenomenon confined to East Asia (the development and spread of this phenomenon is discussed in Chapter 1).

Although these studies point in a valuable direction, neither singly nor together do they conclusively settle the age-old debate over the compatibility or incompatibility of Confucianism and democracy (reviewed in Chapter 2). This book is designed to resolve this debate empirically by analyzing how Confucian political and social norms encourage or discourage the mass citizenries of historically Confucian Asia from becoming members of a civic community and citizens of a democratic state. It is also designed to resolve the debate theoretically by evaluating the claims and counterclaims of the Asian Values Thesis in view of a variety of theories that have been recently advanced.

The empirical work that follows covers six of the seven countries in this region – China, Japan, South Korea (Korea hereafter), Singapore, Taiwan, and Vietnam – with the exception of North Korea. These countries are compared with one another and with those in other regions to highlight intraregional and interregional differences and similarities in the extent to which the masses are attached to the principles and practices of Confucianism and democracy; these comparisons also reveal different patterns in which those values and practices relate with one another in the minds of ordinary citizens.

From the Perspective of the Mass Citizenry

What constitutes democratization? Who promotes it and how? The existing literature on third-wave democracies generally agrees that democratization is a highly complex transformation that involves multiple actors and agencies, including political institutions and processes, civic associations and groups, and individual citizens and their political leaders (Boix and Stokes 2003; Bunce 2000, 2003; Diamond 2008a; Geddes 1999; Karl 2005; McFaul 2002; Rose and Shin 2001; Whitehead 2002). The same literature also agrees that the mass citizenry significantly shapes the pace and trajectories of the democratization process (Alagappa 2004; Bermeo 2003; R. Collier 1999; Newton 2001; Norris 2002; Tusalem 2007).

On a conceptual level, democratization is a multidimensional phenomenon because it involves the establishment of both democratic ideas and practices and the disestablishment of whatever came before. *Institutionally*, democratization typically involves a transition from authoritarian rule to a political system that allows ordinary citizens to participate on a regular basis and to elect their political leaders. *Substantively*, it involves a process in which electoral and other institutions consolidate and become increasingly responsive to the preferences of the citizenry.

Culturally, it is a process in which ordinary citizens dissociate themselves from the values and practices of authoritarian politics and embrace democracy as "the only game in town." As Robert Dahl (1997), Terry Karl (2000), and Juan Linz and Alfred Stepan (1996) note, the process of democratizing a political system involves much more than the installation of representative institutions and a democratic constitution; as discussed in greater detail later, these elements are the "hardware," but there is much citizen "software" that must also be in place.

Finally, democratization is a multilevel phenomenon because it involves ongoing interactions between individual citizens and institutions of their political system. On one level, the transformation must take place in individual citizens, and on another level, it must take place in institutions of the political regime that rule them. At the regime level, democratization refers to the extent to which authoritarian structures and procedures transform into democratic ones and in the process become responsive and accountable to the preferences of the mass citizenry (Dahl 1971). At the citizenry level, the extent to which average citizens become civic-minded and convinced of democracy's superiority constitutes democratic change.

Of these two different levels of democratization, this study of democratization in Confucian East Asia chooses to focus on what takes place in individual citizens because of the notable Freedom House finding that ordinary people shape the actual process of democratic transition and consolidation. According to a recent worldwide study by Freedom House (Karatnycky and Ackerman 2005), among fourteen countries in which ruling elites drove the transition from authoritarian rule, only 14 percent have become liberal democracies, whereas 50 percent have reverted to nondemocracies. Among the countries in which the transitions were driven by *strongly active* civic coalitions, not just active civic coalitions, 75 percent became liberal democracies, and only 6 percent emerged as nondemocracies. A comparison of these figures reveals that the incidence of becoming a liberal democracy posttransition is more than five times higher for countries with strong civic coalitions, whereas the incidence of reverting to authoritarian rule posttransition is more than eight times higher for those with strong ruling elites. Evidently, the mass citizenry plays a crucial role in lasting democratization.

What mass citizens think about democracy is also known to affect the process of democratic governance. Institutionally, a political system can become democratic with the installation of competitive elections and multiple political parties. These institutions alone, however, do not make for a fully functioning democratic political system. As Richard Rose and his associates (1998, 8) aptly point out, these institutions constitute nothing more than "the hardware" of representative democracy. To operate the institutional hardware, a democratic political system requires "software" that is congruent with the various hardware components (Almond and Verba 1963; Eckstein 1966). Both the scholarly community and policy circles widely recognize that what ordinary citizens think about democracy and their reactions to its institutions are key components of such software.

To build an effectively functioning democracy, moreover, people have to develop "the social ability to collaborate for shared interests" through norms and networks of civic engagement (Putnam 1993, 182; see also Nuyen 2002; Tan 2003b). They also have to develop the political ability to appreciate the virtues of democracy and then must commit themselves to those. Therefore, civics and politics constitute two distinct arenas in which individual citizens can contribute to the building of an effective democracy.

Conceptualization

This study is designed to examine the effects that Confucianism has on the democratization process at the level of individual citizens. To examine these effects, I chose democratic citizenship as a central conceptual tool and define it in broad terms from a Confucian communitarian perspective (S. M. Kim 2010). In this perspective there is no duality between the private and public spheres of life; instead, the two life spheres are seen as interdependent, and obligations and responsibilities to one's community are crucial components of citizenship (Nuyen 2002).

This perspective derives from the Confucian ethic that individuals are not autonomous but are social beings defined and refined through their relationships with others and with their communities. Therefore, rights, duties, and responsibilities must be defined not in terms of the individual but in terms of the relationship between the individual and his or her community (Fox 1997). Citizenship is always a reciprocal and social idea; it requires both a strong sense of solidarity and active participation in social networks in which rights and responsibilities are mutually supportive (Park and Shin 2006; Putnam 1993).

This broad and deep notion of citizenship, which Charles Tilly (1996) characterizes as "thick citizenship," contrasts sharply with the liberal notion of "thin" citizenship in which a citizen's responsibilities are minimal and subordinate to any concern about rights. In the liberal democracies of the West, citizenship refers primarily to the right of autonomous individuals to pursue freely their conceptions of the good life. In such an atomized vision of human existence, there is little room for self-interested individuals to reflect about the importance of community in terms of their social responsibilities and role. As Xinzhong Yao (1999, 34) points out, "freedom without responsibility would result in the collapse of the social network and in the conflict between individuals and between individuals and society." To avoid such conflicts, early Confucians advocated civic life as a crucial component of citizenship in the belief that any polity, either democratic or nondemocratic, cannot be sustained without citizens caring for each other and their community.

Following this civic tradition of Confucianism, in this study I define the two central terms of Confucianism and democratic citizenship broadly. I define Confucianism both as a system of social ethics endorsing a particular way of private and public life and as a system of political ethics advocating a particular system of government. As a code of social ethics, Confucianism refers to the norms prescribing proper interpersonal relationships with people we know and with strangers (discussed in Chapter 3). As a code of political ethics, Confucianism refers to the principles defining the relationship between rulers and the ruled (discussed in Chapter 4). I also define democratic citizenship more broadly than citizens' cognitive competence or sophistication about democratic politics; I look at the processes through which they begin to engage in civic life and become committed to the ideals and practices of democratic politics.

Civic life plays a vital role in educating people about the art of democratic politics (Putnam 1993). Therefore, I examine how Confucian social ethics affects the way in which people in Confucian Asia engage with their fellow citizens *behaviorally* and *psychologically* and how these ethics affects how people in Confucian Asia become members of a civic community. Specifically, I measure civic engagement in psychological terms – how civic-minded are people – and behavioral terms – how they interact with other people. Because traditional political values influence how people orient themselves to or away from the democratization process (Inglehart and Welzel 2005; Nathan and Chen 2004; Putnam 1993), I examine how Confucian political ethics affects the ways in which people react to the process *cognitively* and *affectively* and become democrats, with a small "d." Specifically, becoming a democrat requires both an accurate understanding of democracy as a distinctive system of government and unconditional endorsement of it as the preferred regime structure and policy-making process.

In a nutshell, this study aims to offer a comprehensive account of the roles Confucianism plays in making democratic citizens by investigating its effects on the civic and political life of individual citizens. To analyze its effects on civic life, I chose civic engagement as a key conceptual tool and examine it in both behavioral terms – for example, joining voluntary associations – and psychological terms, for example, placing trust in other people. To analyze its effects on political life, I chose democratic commitment as a key conceptual tool and examine its cognitive and affective characteristics in terms of understanding democracy as a distinct political system and embracing it as "the only game in town."

Databases and the Methods of Analysis

Do Confucian cultural legacies really matter in the process of building nations of democratic citizens in East Asia? To address this general question adequately, I needed to perform two types of comparative analyses. The first compares countries within the region of historically Confucian East Asia to determine whether these legacies still remain pervasive and prevalent throughout the region. The second compares countries in the Confucian region with those in non-Confucian Asia and other regions to determine whether Confucianism represents a unique system of ethics confined to the former. To perform both types of comparative analyses, I assembled two sets of multinational public opinion surveys as the main empirical base for our study: the Asian Barometer Surveys (ABS) and the World Values Surveys (WVS).

The second wave of the ABS was conducted during the 2005–8 period in six Confucian Asian countries – China, Japan, Korea, Taiwan, Singapore, and Vietnam – and six non-Confucian Asian countries:

Cambodia, Indonesia, Malaysia, Mongolia, the Philippines, and Thailand.[4] This wave of the ABS consisted of batteries of questions tapping attachment to four principal Confucian legacies – familism, communitarianism, paternalism, and meritocracy – as well as civic engagement and orientations to democracy and its alternatives. To supplement the items on interpersonal trust asked in this second wave of the ABS, I selected one item tapping affective trust from its first wave, which was conducted in only four countries – China, Japan, Korea, and Taiwan – during the 2001–3 period. These two waves together allowed a comparison of Confucian and non-Confucian countries within East Asia.

The fifth wave of the WVS was conducted during the 2005–8 period in fifty-seven countries, including five Confucian Asian countries – China, Japan, Korea, Taiwan, and Vietnam – and three non-Confucian Asian countries: Malaysia, Thailand, and Indonesia.[5] For our purpose of cross-regional analysis, I classified the fifty-seven countries into seven major cultural regions – the democratic West, South Asia, the Middle East, East Asia, Latin America, ex-communist West, and Sub-Saharan Africa – by collapsing into two zones – democratized West and ex-communist West – the five cultural categories of Western culture constructed by Ronald Inglehart and Christian Welzel (2005).[6] From the WVS fifth wave, I selected two sets of questions, one tapping the Confucian way of life featuring hierarchism and collectivism and the other, a set of four items, tapping divergent conceptions of democracy and other types of regimes.

The WVS enabled an exploration of whether the people of Confucian East Asia are distinct from their peers in other regions in how they prefer to live their lives and whether they understand and think about democracy in different patterns. Yet the limited number of questions posed by both the ABS and the WVS to tap key Confucian social and political values and norms made it difficult to analyze this and other research questions fully. Due to this limitation, I had to choose a specific pair of questions for each of those values and norms.

I used both quantitative and qualitative methods to analyze the items selected from the ABS and WVS. To conduct quantitative analyses I relied

---

[4] Detailed information on sampling methodology, fieldwork procedures, and questionnaires is available from http://www.asianbarometer.org.

[5] Detailed information on sampling methodology, fieldwork procedures, and questionnaires is available from www.worldvaluessurvey.com.

[6] These five cultural categories are: non-English-speaking Protestant West, English-speaking West, non-English-speaking Catholic West, ex-communist West, and ex-communist East.

on the simplest tools of univariate, bivariate and multivariate statistical analyses. Specifically, I used percentages and standardized regression coefficients as the principal tools of those analyses for two reasons. First, complicated statistical techniques such as those of factor and cluster analyses are not popular among the scholars and policy makers who have been key contributors to the Confucian Asian Values Thesis debate. Second, because these scholars and policy makers have little experience with the more complex statistical techniques, it is difficult for them to interpret results based on them. Given these considerations, I opted for the simplest quantitative methods of constructing composite indexes of Confucian and democratic orientations and of analyzing their relationships with percentages – statistically adjusted and unadjusted – and standardized regression coefficients (*beta*).

In addition to examining quantitative differences in those orientations, I analyzed their qualitative differences by means of a typological analysis, as performed in Chapters 3, 7, and 8. I considered jointly responses to the different dimensions of Confucianism and democracy and constructed distinct types of Confucian and democratic attachments. To address the increasingly important questions of who contemporary Confucians are, who committed democrats are, and how they are distributed throughout Confucian Asia (Shin 2011; Sun 2009; Yao 2001), I compared the types of these attachments across standard demographic categories – gender, age, education, and family income. In addition, I reported the entire sets of these demographic data so that advocates and critics of the Confucian Asian Values Thesis may interpret them from their own perspectives. In each Confucian country, these data can also be used as a benchmark for trend analysis in the future.

To estimate the effects of categorical independent variables, such as types of culture and regime, on citizen conceptions and embrace of democracy, I used multiple classification analysis (MCA). MCA, unlike any other technique of multivariate analysis, is capable of displaying the effects of independent variables with multiple categories on the dependent variable both before and after adjusting for the effects of all other independent variables (Andrew et al. 1973). Comparing the adjusted values of the dependent variable across the categories of an independent variable allows us to determine how each particular category of the independent variable – for example, the Confucian hierarchical way of life and the democratic and nondemocratic types of regime – matters in the democratization process relative to all other categories; for example, the individualistic culture of the West.

Central Themes and Organization

Part I of this book examines the evolution of Confucianism and Confucian East Asia, offering a comprehensive review of the theoretical and empirical literature that deals with Confucianism as an influence on democratization. Part II explicates the notion of Confucianism as a way of life and as a system of government, and it examines popular attachments to the Confucian hierarchical way of life and the Confucian model of paternalistic meritocracy. Part III focuses on the Confucian social ethics of familism and communitarianism and examines their effects on civic engagement and the norms of interpersonal trust and tolerance. Part IV examines Confucian political and social ethics as influences on popular conceptions of and support for democracy and its alternatives.

Chapter 1 begins with a brief account of how Confucianism has been transformed from a scholarly tradition confined to the literate segment of the Chinese population into an international cultural movement reaching every population segment in six historically Confucian countries. The discussion then moves to the characteristics of private and public institutions that these countries share and the similar patterns of thinking and associating among their citizens.

Chapter 2 first reviews the various theoretical claims and counterclaims on Confucianism as an influence on democratic politics and synthesizes them into three intellectual camps, which focus on their incompatibility, compatibility, or convergence, respectively. Then it critically reviews a handful of public-opinion-based studies designed to determine the nature of the linkage, and it identifies these studies' conceptual and theoretical limitations.

Chapter 3 first introduces the key norms of Confucian social ethics and conceptually distinguishes the Confucian culture of hierarchism from individualism, egalitarianism, and fatalism on the basis of the cultural typology proposed by anthropologist Mary Douglas (1978, 1999). To identify the upholders of these four types, the study considers two dimensions of culture, group and grid – (1) ties to the family and friends and (2) adherence to the Confucian principles of *ren* (benevolence) and *li* (propriety). Analyses of the WVS, which asked a pair of questions to tap each cultural dimension, reveal that the Confucian hierarchical way of life is not favored by a majority in any of the five countries surveyed – China, Japan, South Korea, Taiwan, and Vietnam. In fact, more people have embraced an egalitarian or individualist way of life. Equally notable is the finding that Confucian Asia as a whole is more individualistic than any of the four other non-Western cultural zones including Latin America.

Chapter 4 introduces the two core Confucian principles of good government, paternalism, and meritocracy, and contrasts those with the principles of liberal democracy. Analyses of the second wave of the ABS conducted in six Confucian countries reveal that those fully attached to both Confucian principles do not constitute a majority in any of the six historically Confucian countries. Yet a great deal more people still remain more attached to than detached from those Confucian principles. Moreover, people in nondemocratic countries remain far more deeply attached to Confucian principles than do people in democratic countries, and even within democratic countries, the highly attached are far more numerous in the new democracies of Korea and Taiwan than in the old democracy of Japan. These findings clearly suggest that democratic political experience lessens popular attachment to Confucianism more strongly than the latter deters the former. Further analysis of the ABS also suggests that popular affinity for a government of moral meritocracy is not a phenomenon confined to Confucian Asia; in contrast, it is more pervasive throughout the non-Confucian region than in the Confucian region of Asia.

Chapter 5 first explores the Confucian notion of civil society as a complementary and cooperative model of civic engagement with the state. Then it contrasts this notion of civil society with the Western liberal model that values competitive and antagonistic relationships between a civil society and the state. Analyses of the ABS conducted in the six Confucian countries reveal that, in the informal sphere of face-to-face personal contact, people in Confucian Asia prefer the Confucian communitarian model of interdependent and cooperative relationships. In contrast, in the formal sphere of joining voluntary associations and groups, they prefer the liberal model of independent and competitive relationships. This indicates that people in Confucian countries are far more liberal in formal intergroup relations than in informal interpersonal relationships. When the preferred models of informal and formal associations are considered together, those exclusively attached to the Confucian communitarian model outnumber those attached to the Western liberal model. The attachment to the Confucian model has significant practical effect on how people associate with other people informally and formally.

Chapter 6 begins with an explication of the original notion of Confucian familism and discusses its potential for inhibiting trust of strangers and thus for producing a low-trust society. Analyses of the ABS conducted in the six Confucian countries reveal that their citizens no longer remain fully devoted to the graded love or trust advocated in Confucian family-centered ethics. They are becoming nations of cognitive or knowledge-based trust. Mainly because most people are still reluctant to trust strangers, however, five of the six countries remain low-trust societies.

In striking contrast, those willing to tolerate people with different views constitute a majority in every country. Accordingly, there is a large gap between the willingness to tolerate and to trust throughout the entire region of Confucian Asia. This regionwide pattern of failing to uphold fully the two core civic norms of trust and tolerance is also found in non-Confucian Asia. More notable is the positive net impact of Confucian familism on a willingness to tolerate and trust other people. This finding, which runs counter to what is known in the literature (Fukuyama 1995a; Tan and Chee 2005), suggests that Confucian familism is not an amoral familism that favors the family at the expense of all other associations; instead this tradition seems to foster positive feelings toward all people.

Chapter 7 focuses on the *cognitive* dimension of democratic commitment and analyzes it in terms of the distinct patterns in which people in Confucian Asia understand democracy and the specific terms in which they conceive of it. In all five Confucian countries surveyed in the fifth round of the WVS, more than two-fifths remain ill informed or *partially informed* about the practices of democratic politics and their differences from those of military and theocratic rules. Only a small minority of one-third is *well informed* about each set of practices, democratic and authoritarian. Confucian East Asia is the only region in the world in which nearly one-quarter of its people are either *partially informed* or *uninformed* about democracy. Of the six regions outside the democratized West, however, people in this region are the most likely to define democracy accurately in terms of free elections and civil rights. Yet analyses of the ABS reveal that people in Confucian Asia consider security and equality in economic life far more essential to democracy than political freedom. Such substantive conceptions of democracy accord with the Confucian notion of good government (discussed in Chapter 4), which emphasizes the welfare of people over their freedom to participate in the political process.

Chapter 8 analyzes the *affective* dimension of democratic commitment by means of a fourfold typology of political regime orientations. Considering together popular reactions to democracy and its alternatives, in principal and in practice, I discerned four distinct types of citizens: nondemocrats, nonliberal democrats, liberal democrats, and the politically indifferent. Analyses of the ABS reveal that, in all six Confucian countries, large majorities embrace democracy as the preferred type of political regime (or democracy-in-principle), but do not endorse democracy as the preferred method or process of daily governance (or democracy-in-practice). As a result, liberal democrats – those who embrace democracy at both the regime and political process levels – do not constitute a majority in any of the six countries. Within the region as a whole, more people prefer nonliberal democracy to liberal democracy.

Regardless of the extent to which people uphold the Confucian political legacies of paternalism and meritocracy, they prefer to live in a democracy rather than in any of its alternatives. Moreover, regardless of the type of political system in which people live, attachment to Confucian political traditions deters them from embracing liberal democracy and encourages them to favor nonliberal democracy. These findings do not support the central claim of the Asian Values Thesis that Confucianism is not compatible with any type of democracy at all, yet they do support its claim that Confucianism is incompatible with liberal democracy.

Chapter 9 first highlights the key findings on the prevalence of Confucian political and social legacies and critically evaluates the implications of those findings for each of the incompatibility and compatibility claims of the debate over the Confucian Asian Values Thesis. Then it recasts the Asian Values Thesis within the framework of Harry Eckstein's (1966) congruence theory and critically evaluates its limitations as a cultural theory of democratic underdevelopment. Finally this chapter examines the implications of our research findings for the three prominent pairs – early socialization vs. adult learning, cultural values vs. institutional experience, and modernization vs. indigenization – of competing theories of cultural democratization.

One central message of this chapter is that both advocates and critics of the Asian Values Thesis have failed to understand that democratic development requires both democratic and nondemocratic orientations among the citizenry and that the relationship between Confucianism and such political orientations are of a reciprocal nature. For example, although the Confucian legacies of paternalistic meritocracy discourage people from embracing liberal democracy, the longer that people experience democratic regime, the less likely they are to adhere to those legacies. In Confucian East Asia today, democratic regime experience influences cultural democratization far more powerfully than Confucian political legacies. Another central message is that a powerful wave of liberal democratization is not likely to surge and sweep through the entire region of historically Confucian East Asia for many years to come.

Significance of This Study

This book contributes to the study of Asian politics and democratization by addressing a central theme in the literature in several unique ways. Substantively, this book investigates the forces advancing and impeding democratization in six historically Confucian countries from the perspective of ordinary citizens, who play a crucial role in the process (Booth and Seligson 2009; Bratton et al. 2005; Inglehart and Welzel 2005; Rose et al.1998; Shin 2007; Welzel 2009). While exploring these forces, the book improves on the existing literature by settling with research-driven conclusions the age-old debate regarding the compatibility or incompatibility of Confucianism and liberal democracy.

Conceptually, this book offers a broader view than the literature of both the legacies of Confucianism and the notion of democracy. Both the theoretical and empirical works in the literature on democratization in Confucian East Asia have focused only on one or a few of the authoritarian or democratic upshots of Confucianism. All of the empirical studies have been based on a narrow conception of democracy that deals merely with its structural characteristics; consequently, these empirical studies have failed to take into account citizen views of the processes that keep democratic politics operating on a daily basis. Unlike these studies, the research reported in this book broadly conceptualizes both Confucian legacies and democracy as multidimensional and multitiered phenomena. Such full conceptualizations of the two key variables allow for a comprehensive and balanced analysis of their relationship by examining how citizens' attachment to several Confucian legacies affects their engagement in civic life and commitment to democratic politics both as an ideal and as a viable form of government.

The driving *theory* of this book is that regime type matters significantly in the process in which Confucian legacies affect the region's democratization at the level of individual citizens. This book offers the first systematic effort to examine those impacts across all the democratic and authoritarian regimes in Confucian Asia, except for North Korea. It compares these impacts in the three democratic countries of Japan, Korea, and Taiwan with those in the three nondemocratic countries of China, Singapore, and Vietnam. This comparison allows for a determination of how regime type matters in the process of cultural democratization and whether the experience of democratic rule promotes the development of democratic political culture in Confucian Asia, as predicted by the theory of democratic learning (Anderson and Dodd 2005; Mattes and Bratton 2007; Peffley and Rohrschneider 2003; Rohrschneider 1999; Rose and Mishler 2002; Rose, Mishler and Haerpfer 1998).

Methodologically, by combining the methods of quantitative and qualitative analyses, this book seeks to offer a more accurate and nuanced account of how Confucian legacies shape the contours of subjective democratization taking place in the minds of ordinary citizens. More often than not, these citizens react differently to the various characteristics of each of these two phenomena both in magnitude and in kind. By considering their qualitatively different reactions to these two phenomena, the book identifies not only different types of Confucian upholders but also the democratic or nondemocratic form of government that each type of upholders prefers most and least. In all historically Confucian countries, for example, upholders of paternalistic meritocracy are found to be least supportive of liberal democracy while most supportive of non-liberal democracy.

Analytically, the book performs two modes of comparative analysis: intraregional and interregional. The six historically Confucian countries in East Asia are compared with each other to identify the ones that remain the most and least Confucian, and the ones that have been the most and least successful in promoting democratic political culture. In addition, four standard demographic characteristics – gender, age, education, and income – are considered together to identify the particular population segments that are most and least attached to Confucianism and those that are most and least committed to democracy in Confucian Asia today. Finally, the countries in the Confucian region are compared as a whole to those in non-Confucian Asia and all other regions of the world to determine whether Confucianism is a truly regional phenomenon confined exclusively to China and its neighboring countries.

In short, this book offers the most comprehensive and balanced test of the age-old debate over whether Confucian values and norms are compatible with the liberal form of democracy practiced in the West. In addition, it addresses a number of questions dealing with the various aspects of cultural and political changes in East Asia from the perspective of ordinary people.

PART I

CONFUCIANISM AND CONFUCIAN EAST ASIA

The Evolution of Confucian East Asia
and Its Cultural Legacies

Over the past three decades, East Asia has been the most successful region of the world in expanding its economy, recovering from financial crises, and enhancing the quality of its citizens' lives (Fukuyama 2011; Izvorski 2010; Shin and Inoguchi 2009; World Bank 2000, 2003). As a result, it has received a great deal of attention from the global scholarly community and policy circles (Dupont 1996; Hira 2007; C. Kim 2010; Miller 2006). Within the scholarly community, the region is often viewed as a model of socioeconomic and political modernization that is more harmonious, kinder, and gentler than the capitalist liberal democratic model of the West (Bell 2008a; Rozman 2002; Tu 2000). Among policy makers, East Asia is increasingly regarded as a region of powerhouses contending for global superiority (Huntington 1996; Rozman 1991b; Scher 2010).[1]

What distinguishes East Asia from the other parts of Asia, the world's largest continent? Do the countries of East Asia share a cultural heritage or some historical experience that ties or unites them into a cohesive whole? Do they have similar patterns of organizing public and private institutions? Do their citizens exhibit any distinct patterns of thinking or action? The answers to these and other related questions depend on

---

[1] As of June 2010, the five East Asian countries of China, Japan, Taiwan, South Korea, and Singapore, as well as China's special administrative region of Hong Kong, together hold 46 percent of the world's foreign exchange reserves, totaling $1,008,392 million. Their combined holdings are nearly seven times larger than those of the Euro zone, and thirty-six times larger than those of the United States. Further information can be retrieved from http://en.wikipedia.org/wiki/List_of_countries_by_foreign_exchange_reserves.

how the term "East Asia" is defined. Although the term has been used for centuries, there is considerable ambiguity regarding its meaning. As a result, *East Asia* does not always refer to the same collective among and across different professional communities and intellectual circles.

The Notion of Confucian East Asia

The most common definitions of the term "East Asia" have to do with either the geographic or geopolitical lineage of countries or their cultural and historical ties. Geographically, East Asia refers to the eastern part of Asia, which comprises the two subregions of Northeast Asia and Southeast Asia. Northeast Asia covers the greater China area including Taiwan and Hong Kong, the Korean peninsula, Japan, and Mongolia. Southeast Asia stretches from Burma in the west to the Philippines in the east, and from Laos in the north to Indonesia in the south. Geopolitically, Southeast Asia consists of the ten members of the Association of Southeast Asian Nations, organized to promote economic prosperity and political stability. According to this geographic definition, therefore, East Asia encompasses sixteen countries with a great deal of cultural diversity and without much shared political history. This broadly conceived notion of the region is increasingly popular in business and diplomatic communities, yet it represents a significant departure from how the term "East Asia" has been used historically (Dent 2008).

Historically, the term has been used most often to identify the sinic cultural sphere for which China has served as the core state (Huntington 1996). Therefore, as culturally defined, "East Asia" refers to a subregion of the geographically defined "East Asia"; Chinese characters have been a major part of the writing system in this subregion, but more importantly, the teachings of Confucius, Mencius, and their followers have for centuries served as the cultural and institutional foundations of public and private life. Cultural East Asia, or historically Confucian East Asia, consists of China, Japan, North and South Korea, Singapore, Taiwan, and Vietnam, all countries in which Confucian ethics has been "the source of inspiration as well as the court of appeal for human interaction at all levels" for a thousand years (Tu 1986, 1).

For the region's educational and civil institutions, Confucian traditions, especially those of moral education and meritocratic governance, have been foundational in all of the historically Confucian East Asian countries. In accordance with the Confucian doctrine of universal education and with Confucian texts,[2] these countries have established government schools and private academies. Within these schools, the five Confucian Classics have served as the core curriculum of moral education.[3] In accordance with the Confucian notion of meritocracy, moreover, all the historically Confucian East Asian countries except Japan have instituted a system in which prime ministers and other government officials are selected through competitive merit-based examinations. It would be hard to overstate the influence the Confucian ethical system has had in shaping the way Confucian East Asians think about the world in which they live and their relationships with other people (Yao 2001, 326).

For example, in interpersonal communication many East Asians still use family terms, such as brothers, sisters, and uncles, to express personal affection or respect for other people (Bell 2008a; Tu 2000). They also rely on Confucian terminology to engage in moral reasoning and to define and evaluate their own roles, as well as those of their political leaders (Hwang 1998). Throughout the region, "the Confucian values such as the importance of the family, the respect for learning and education, and the emphasis on order and harmony remain significant" (J. Chan 2008a, 114). For all these reasons, Tu Weiming (1993, 149), one of the most influential Confucian scholars, notes that regardless of their religious beliefs, people in Confucian East Asia "seldom fail to be Confucian," and Confucianism is also more formidable, pervasive, and unifying as a political, social, economic, and spiritual influence than any of the Abrahamic religions, whether Judaism, Christianity, or Islam.

The dynamics of Confucianism, both in principle and in practice, can be understood from two contrasting perspectives: historical and spatial. Confucianism can be viewed as a historical phenomenon that has undergone a great deal of transformation or reformulation over time, as evidenced by the rise of scholarly movements known as classical Confucianism, neo-Confucianism, and new Confucianism (Yao 2000, chap. 2) and political movements such as imperial Confucianism, reform Confucianism, elite Confucianism, mass Confucianism (Rozman 1991c), spiritual Confucianism, politicized Confucianism, and popular Confucianism

---

[2] The core principle of this doctrine is to make education available to students from all classes (*Analects* 15:39).

[3] The five Confucian Classics are *The Book of Changes, The Book of History, The Book of Rites, The Spring* and *Autumn Annals*, and *The Book of Poetry*.

(Liu 2007).[4] It can also be viewed as a regional phenomenon or as an international movement that spread from China to its neighboring states and the territories settled by the Chinese (Rozman 1991a, 2003; Tu 1993). The reformulation of Confucian values and norms and the dissemination of those values and norms are two of the main concerns of this chapter.

How did Confucianism, which began as a scholarly tradition in the Central Plain of mainland China, turn into a cultural movement affecting the way of life of ordinary people in a sizable region of Asia? In this chapter, I first offer a historical account of how Confucianism evolved in China over a period of more than two millennia and how it spread from China eastward and westward to five other countries: Japan, Korea, Singapore, Taiwan, and Vietnam. I then identify and discuss the characteristics shared by these Confucian countries' institutions and the patterns of thoughts and behavior common among their citizens.

The Historical Evolution of Confucianism in China[5]

In historically or culturally Confucian East Asia, Confucianism permeates every aspect of daily life; it shapes people's preferences, priorities, and values, and it prescribes the proper modes of conduct and interactions with others (Rozman 2002, 15). Confucian values and norms have maintained a powerful hold in the region since their emergence more than two thousand years ago and have remained entrenched within East Asia's history and culture while other competing ideologies have come and gone. The values of filial piety, respect for authority and learning, and self-cultivation through education have combined and given rise to a regional political culture unique to China and its neighbors. Tracing the historical, regional, and sociological aspects of Confucianism's origins and their eventual dominance in East Asian society is essential for understanding the role Confucian norms play in those countries today (Yao 2000).

Confucianism originated from the teachings of Confucius, which were based on historical examples dating back to the beginning of the Zhou Dynasty (1045–256 B.C.E.) half a millennia before his birth. At its inception in the 4th century B.C.E., it represented one of several scholarly

---

4 Other categories of Confucianism, such as liberal Confucianism, left Confucianism, political Confucianism, economic Confucianism, educational Confucianism, and social Confucianism, are discussed in Bell (2008b) and Tucker (2003).

5 Various stages of the historical evolution are more fully discussed in Tu (1993, 150–5), Tucker (2003, 7–13) and Yao (2000, 4–12).

traditions.[6] A few generations after his death, his students and their followers were able to organize "archaic and archaizing practices" into a *loosely structured* belief system and to establish it as the dominant tradition in the Chinese scholarly community (Nylan 2008, 86).

After it became the dominant intellectual force, it expanded to the ruling circles to become the official ideology of the imperial state. From the elite circles of rulers and scholars, it spread to all other segments of the mass citizenry to become a cultural movement embracing all of China. Finally, Confucian scholarly and political traditions spread from China to other countries to become the mainstream of their cultural and political movements.

Undoubtedly, Confucius was the founder of Confucianism, but all of the ideas of Confucianism did not originate with him. Confucius was quoted in *The Analects* (7:1) as a transmitter of values and norms[7] that first appeared during the Shang dynasty (1766–1050 B.C.) and the succeeding Zhou dynasty (1000–256 B.C.). This suggests that the Confucian tradition had begun even before Confucius was born (J. Chan 2008b, 113). However, Confucian concepts were neither clearly articulated nor systematically organized until the turbulent Hundred Schools period when Confucius, a scholar who lived his entire life (551–479 B.C.) in China, combined a range of historical beliefs into one somewhat coherently organized system of ethics. Observing the chaos and strife surrounding him at the time, Confucius promoted social harmony, benevolence, propriety, duty, the family, and rituals as crucial for establishing a community of grand harmony called *datong shehui*. He used poetry, governmental decrees, and historical documents to frame his vision, making it much easier for his successors to preserve his ideas (Berthrong 1998).

The teachings of Confucius did not receive much recognition within scholarly circles before or even at his death. Nor did his teachings receive immediate attention, much less acceptance, in government circles. However, some thirty to fifty years after his death, his students and their followers were able to distill the essential components of his teachings into a document called *The Analects of Confucius*. Between the time of his death and the middle of the Han dynasty (206 B.C.–226 A.D.), Confucianism was only one of many competing schools of thought in ancient China. Of all these schools, Buddhism, Taoism, Mohism, and Legalism

---

6 These traditions include Buddhism, Taoism, Legalism, and Mohism.
7 In *The Analects* (7:1), Confucius is quoted as saying, "I transmit but do not innovate; I am truthful in what I say and devoted to antiquity."

presented the greatest obstacles to the doctrine's rise during the Warring States Period (480–221 B.C.). It was only through the efforts of Confucian scholars such as Mencius (371–289 B.C.) that Confucius's works survived and eventually found devoted adherents within the Chinese government (Berthrong 1998).

Mencius's tireless promotion of Confucian ideals helped fortify the belief system, gain supporters, and protect Confucianism against constant attacks by alternate ideologies. Confucian values faced their greatest threat during the Qin dynasty (221–207 B.C.), when Emperor Qin labeled Confucius "subversive" and ordered that all his books be burned. To establish Legalism as the state's ruling ideology, Legalists attempted to destroy all other philosophies, including Confucianism, by proclaiming them illegitimate. In the aftermath of Legalist attacks, Confucian values integrated with government laws and morphed into a codified set of values and beliefs. As a result, Confucianism took on a substantially more authoritarian character than is found in the original teachings of Confucius and Mencius. This authoritarian tendency, which strengthened in later dynasties, was often equated exclusively with Confucianism by its critics.

One of the most important developments in Confucianism's history was when Emperor Wu of the Han dynasty (156–87 B.C.), under the advice of scholar-official Dong Zhongshu (179–104 B.C.), established Confucianism as an official state ideology and put new institutional hardware in place to support it. Emperor Wu established the system of civil service examinations and founded the Imperial University to educate the children in the royal household and other students as well. Confucian classics were used as texts to educate these students and recruit government officials. As a national orthodoxy, Confucianism helped provide for a stable political order.

Confucianism's privileged position within the Chinese government proved to be short-lived, however, as the Han dynasty's eventual decline was accompanied by the dramatic rise of Buddhism and Taoism. Alternative philosophies and religions became so popular throughout the region that Confucianism, as a scholarly tradition and a political ideology, nearly disappeared from Chinese society altogether in the post-Han period; what likely saved Confucianism from eradication was the Confucian classics' continued status as the chief source of learning for scholars. Confucian ideas were saved from obliteration by leaders of the Song dynasty (960–1279 A.D.), who merged classical Confucian values with spiritual metaphors drawn from Buddhism. The most important figure in Song

Confucianism was Zhu Xi, who created a core Confucian curriculum for the civil service exams, which remained in existence until the early twentieth century.[8] To convey basic Confucian principles to ordinary people, neo-Confucian reformers introduced new institutions such as village compacts and charitable schools (Ebrey 1991, 82).

Neo-Confucianism addressed citizens' desire for spirituality, while reinforcing the societal and political ideas of Confucius's original works. It quickly gained prominence throughout China and established a hold on Chinese intellectual and societal life, which persisted until the country's political transformations in the twentieth century (Tu 2000). After the fall of the Qing dynasty in 1911, political reformers and liberal intellectuals became increasingly critical of Confucian traditions as a hindrance to China's modernization (Yao 2000, 252). During the Cultural Revolution (1966–76), Red Guards vilified Confucius and persecuted followers of his teachings at the behest of Mao Tze-tung, chairman of the Chinese Communist Party (Zhang and Schwartz 1997). Inside China today, Confucius is enjoying a renaissance as party leaders extol him as the country's best teacher and most popular ambassador to the world (Ho 2009).[9]

This brief historical account makes it clear that, since the death of its founder in 470 B.C. at the age of 73, Confucianism's principles and practices have changed a great deal. It first took hold as a school of thought or a scholarly tradition and was later transformed into a ruling ideology of the imperial state. Then it was gradually expanded into a cultural movement taken up by the families of ordinary people and the schools of local communities, where its values and norms were able to persist "even when the winds had shifted at higher levels" (Bell 1996, 20; see also Rozman 1991a, 47; Tu 1993).

Conceptually and practically, therefore, Confucianism expanded from a one-dimensional phenomenon confined to the literate segment of the Chinese population to a multidimensional and multilevel phenomenon reaching all echelons of the population, including scholars, government officials, and ordinary peasants (C. Cheng 2002).[10] It also expanded from

---

[8] Four books comprise this core curriculum: *Great Learning*, *The Mean* (or the Doctrine of the Mean), *The Analects* (Analects of Confucius), and *Mencius* (Book of Mencius).

[9] As of July 2010, the central government of China has set up more than 316 Confucius Institutes in 94 countries to promote Chinese history and culture (http://en.wikipedia.org/wiki/Confucius_Institute).

[10] According to Joseph Chan (1999, 213), Confucianism is a multilevel phenomenon encompassing philosophical thought, political ideology, actual state policies and practices, and a way of life. In my study, I consider each of these characteristics as constituting

a local movement, confined to northeast and central China, to a national movement embracing every corner of the country.

The Spread of Confucianism in East Asia

Although Confucianism originated in mainland China, its influence has certainly not been limited to one country or one region.[11] Centuries of foreign occupation, intercultural communication, and civilian migration helped Confucian ideas spread to several neighboring nations; Korea, Japan, Vietnam, Taiwan, and Singapore remain the most profoundly Confucian states in East Asia today. The development of Confucianism within these countries took different paths in response to each one's native customs and traditions; as a result, Confucianism developed into a truly international and cross-cultural tradition (Elman 2002, 10). To understand the rise of Confucianism as a regional phenomenon, one must explore the various developmental paths it followed in the different countries. The following section studies Confucianism's historical and sociological spread in each of the five neighboring nations mentioned earlier.

Korea

Unlike in China, where Confucianism evolved as a native tradition, Confucianism in Korea began as an imported system of beliefs and values that was in conflict with the Korean way of life. Accordingly, the process of Confucianization proceeded differently in Korean society from the way it did in China (Haboush 1991, 85). In China, Confucianism initially began in the private sphere of scholarly life and then migrated to the public sphere of governance. In Korea, it began within a small circle of scholar-officials in government and spread to the common people. Through several eras of vigorous government sponsorship and social legislation, Confucianism became accepted as the only legitimate ideology

---

a distinct dimension, not a level, of Confucianism, and equate its levels exclusively with the geographic sites – local, national, and regional – where its activities took place.

[11] Matteo Ricci (1552–1610), an Italian Jesuit, started to report on the thoughts of Confucius at the end of the sixteenth century, and then Father Prospero Intorcetta published the life and works of Confucius into Latin in 1687. Their works were known to have influenced Voltaire, Francois Quesnay, and other thinkers of the Enlightenment (Yao 2000, 1–2).

of a truly civilized moral order and was ingrained in both the private and public spheres of life.

Korea shares a border with China and has long been influenced by its larger neighbor's cultural institutions and political practices. Confucianism first arrived in Korea in 108 B.C., when Emperor Wu of the Chinese Han dynasty colonized the northern section of the country. Koreans became familiar with Confucian ideals during this time, although its influence remained largely confined to the country's north. Korean resistance to the Chinese led to the founding in the north of an independent state called Koguryo (37 B.C.–668 A.D.). Its rulers did not adopt a Chinese-style centralized bureaucratic state, although they adopted Chinese writing.

It was not until the Three Kingdoms period (57 B.C.–668 A.D.) that Confucianism began to establish itself as a major force within all of Korean society. The first step was the establishment of formal Confucian academies in Korea, which occurred as early as 372 A.D. Then, four centuries later in 788, the government of the United Silla, which became China's vassal state in 668, introduced a state examination system, which was based entirely on knowledge of the Confucian Classics (Berthrong 1998). The United Silla's examination system, unlike the one in China, was not fully meritocratic; it was open only to children of aristocrats (Haboush 1991, 87). As a result, government positions were awarded mostly by birth and family connections, not by merit alone. At this time, the ruling elite still favored Buddhism over Confucianism.

During the Koryo dynasty (918–1392), the process of Confucianization remained for the most part confined to the public spheres of government bureaucracy and the educational system. Taking the Chinese Tang government as its model, the Koryo dynasty adopted a civil service examination system to staff its bureaucracy of civilian and military officials. In addition, the state established national and regional schools to train future bureaucrats. As in the United Silla, these exams and schools were open only to descendants of Silla aristocrats. As a result, Confucianization in Koryo society served to perpetuate the existing rigid class system and had little effect on the life of commoners; Confucianism was monopolized by a small circle of ruling elites.

With the advent of the Yi dynasty (1392–1897), called Choson, Confucianization expanded in both scope and depth. In the belief that "a Confucian revolution" would transform Korea into "a truly civilized moral order," the dynasty founders replaced Buddhism with Confucianism as the state ideology (Haboush 1991, 85). Of the two opposing schools of neo-Confucianism,[12] they adopted Zhu Xi's brand of Confucianism as the official ideology of the Korean state and implemented a wide-ranging array of laws. In addition to refashioning the structure and process of government, the legislative measures, which were issued in the form of edicts, aimed to remove the influences of non-Confucian native customs, in particular Buddhism and shamanism. The reforms were also meant to reshape the public and private spheres of life among the entire population in accordance with the Confucian ethos.

In the wake of these reforms, a nationwide public education system was established primarily for the purpose of training bureaucrats in the newly adopted neo-Confucian political ideology. To become bureaucrats in the national or local levels of government, both children of aristocrats and those of commoners were required to take civil service examinations after attending schools that used Confucian texts as a core curriculum. In accordance with the Confucian governing principles of benevolent government, moreover, the Censorate and the petition system were formally established to keep the government accountable both horizontally and vertically.[13] Most notably, the throne and the bureaucracy were required to advance, argue, and justify their decisions by using Confucian rhetoric (Haboush 1991, 95). Even with all these reforms, the fundamental structure of the aristocratic/bureaucratic hybrid system remained intact (Robinson 1991, 206).

Culturally, the establishment of Confucianism required drastic reshaping of gender roles. No longer were commoners or members of the *yangban* elite class permitted to follow such traditional customs as equal inheritance between the two genders, female property ownership, the remarriage of widows, and uxorilocal marriage, a tradition in which the man moves to the woman's home to live. Instead, Koreans were forced to adopt the Confucian norms of patrilineality and patriarchy, embodied in ancestor worship and exogamy.[14] In each village, moreover, all male members, including slaves, were asked to join in a community compact, a self-regulating organization, and regularly discuss Confucian norms of

---

[12] There were many competing views within the neo-Confucian community. The two best known were called Zhu Xi's school of principles and Wang Yang Ming's school of mind or intuition.

[13] More detailed accounts of these two institutions can be found in Mo (2003) and Haboush (2002).

[14] Ebrey (1991) discusses these norms in the context of China.

interpersonal life and have their behavior judged by those norms (Deuchler 2002). In short, the Choson dynasty fundamentally transformed the structure of family life and broadened the contours of civic engagement by even including slaves in social networking.

By the mid-seventeenth century, Korea had become the most thoroughly Confucianized state in East Asia (Tu 1993, 180), even surpassing China. Korean neo-Confucians came to view themselves as being more faithful to Confucianism than members of any other nation (Deuchler 1992). The growing strength of socioeconomic modernization and the arrival of Christianity, however, worked together to gradually weaken Confucianism's hold on Korea, causing the ruling ideology to lose a great deal of influence throughout the nineteenth and twentieth centuries.

Confucian ideals were strengthened once more at the end of the twentieth century, as numerous Koreans began to express a renewed desire to understand Confucian teachings. Even if Confucianism is no longer an officially mandated way of life in Korea, its fundamental values continue to play a large role in shaping social life in Korean society today. As Byong-Ik Koh (1996) points out, very few Koreans today declare themselves to be Confucians, but all Koreans are Confucians because they practice the basic Confucian rituals and subscribe to Confucian values.

Japan

Confucian ideas arrived in Japan not directly from China, as occurred in Korea, but from the early Korean kingdom of Paekche (18 B.C.– 660 A.D.). Wang In, a well-known Korean scholar, traveled to Japan during the fifth century for the sole purpose of educating Japanese leaders in Confucian ways. He came to Japan with a copy of *The Analects* and another Chinese document called *Thousand Character Classic*, and he used these materials to illustrate Confucianism's fundamental ideas. At this time, Japanese leaders were struggling to build a stable state and found Confucian political doctrine useful in consolidating their rule.

The *Seventeen Article Constitution* attributed to Prince Shotoku (573–621) is known as the first document testifying to Confucian influence among the government circles of ancient Japan. The document, which begins with a quote from *The Analects*, emphasizes harmony in social relations and loyalty to rulers. Despite its strong appeal within the government, Confucianism was not as readily accepted by ordinary people, who remained strongly attached to a conglomerate system of beliefs that drew from Buddhism, Taoism, and Shintoism.

Between the seventh and tenth centuries, Japan attempted to establish a centralized political system with an emperor at its head and a corps of Confucian mandarins or bureaucrats on the model of the Chinese Tang dynasty (618–907). This political system, known as the *ritusuryo* system, sought to build a harmonious society of hierarchical social relations and obligations. It even attempted to enforce the Confucian *handen* system of equal land distribution and made some effort to impose Confucian family and kinship values and practices. It also established a government college for the training of future bureaucrats on the basis of Confucian classics. Yet it never adopted the Chinese-styled civil service examination system based on merit. Because government offices were meted out according to birth, rather than earned by merit, the centralized bureaucratic system failed to work as properly and efficiently as it did in Tang China and Yi Korea.

There is little doubt that the *ritusuryo* reforms helped Confucianism establish a substantial place in Japanese society. Yet Confucian ideas underlying these reforms were often overshadowed by those of Buddhism and increasingly become incompatible with social realities and the age-old practices of native family life. As a result, the Confucian-inspired system of a centralized bureaucracy slowly lost the capacity to function and completely broke down in 1185. Because the native tradition successfully circumvented the implantation of the imposed Chinese system, Japanese society during this Heian period (794–1185) failed to be Confucianized as fully as Korean society during the Yi dynasty was (Collcutt 1991, 124).

Intermittent periods of war and instability weakened Confucianism's influence in Japan over the next 500 years. Although it persisted, it was largely confined to a few noble families, Zen Buddhist monks, and some provincial warrior families (Collcutt 1991, 127). In the Tokugawa era (1600–1867), the doctrine's ideals began to regain serious traction in Japanese society. Under the influence of neo-Confucian philosopher Fujiwara Seika (1561–1619), Tokugawa Ieyasu, the founder of the Tokugawa Shogunate, turned to neo-Confucianism, attracted by the idea that harmony could be maintained by a reciprocal relationship of justice between a superior who is benevolent to a subordinate and a subordinate who is obedient to a superior and who observes propriety.

Because an emphasis on mass obedience to the authorities was well suited to the Shogun's desire to maintain a stable political and social order, the *bakuhan* or military government of the Shogunate adopted neo-Confucianism as its official guiding philosophy. In 1790, the Shogunate issued the Kansei Edit declaring neo-Confucianism as the official philosophy. The purpose of this law was to forbid the teaching or propagation of "heterodox" studies, which meant anything in disagreement with the teachings of neo-Confucianism.

With the support of the ruling elite, Confucianism became more widely accepted throughout Tokugawa society than ever before. Hayashi Razan (1583–1657) directed an imperial academy and led a dynasty of neo-Confucian philosophers in the Tokugawa court in transmitting the general philosophy of neo-Confucianism to the Tokugawa government. Following the Shogun's lead, daimyo (fief lords) built schools that ingrained students with the moral virtues from Confucian classics and trained them to observe the norms guiding the five cardinal relationships.[15] Private academies also offered a Confucian-based education to commoners. In rural communities and towns, reading and writing schools known as *terakoya* used a textbook that advocated Confucian virtues. The Samurai community also began to adopt Confucian moral ideals as house codes. A few daimyo even practiced Confucian funeral rituals and other rites, although no daimyo imposed full-scale Confucianization, as Yi did in Korea. These developments enabled Confucianism's spread throughout Tokugawa Japanese society (Berthrong 1998).

Nonetheless, Confucianization in Tokugawa Japan yielded quite different results from what was noted in Korea and Vietnam (discussed next). Unlike these two countries, Japan never experienced direct Chinese rule, nor did the country adopt the civil service examination system based on Confucian texts. Whereas soldiers were at the bottom of the hierarchy in Chinese governments, they constituted the ruling elite in Japan. Because Confucianism was merely an official philosophy, not the ideological orthodoxy, of the government, other belief systems were allowed to coexist with Confucian doctrine in the ruling ideology (Collcutt 1991). The Confucian doctrine of rule by men was not adopted as the overriding principle of government; instead, laws and administrative methods were often favored as means to institute the rule of law.

In addition, the Japanese system of social ethics, unlike the Chinese system, did not emphasize the importance of the family and blood ties in establishing networks of kinship relations (Hiroshi 1996, 120–1; F. Hsu 1998, 62–8). Because such relations often extended beyond blood ties, the Japanese ethical system was more group oriented than the Chinese system.

---

[15] Five cardinal relations are those between a ruler and the ruled, between husband and wife, between parents and children, between older and younger brothers, and between friends.

Of the two Confucian virtues of loyalty and filial piety, the Japanese system placed more emphasis on loyalty to rulers and to the group than filial piety to parents. In Japan, it still is the group, not the family, that matters most in social life (Yamashita 1997, 155; see also F. Hsu 1998). On the whole, Japan was much less of a Confucian society than China and Korea. Still, the Japanese developed the Confucian tradition in many unique ways to suit the conditions of their society.

In the wake of the Meiji restoration in 1868, all schools were reorganized along Western lines, and the core of their curricula shifted from Confucian moral education to practical knowledge and skills, which could be useful in modernizing the country. The Meiji leaders, however, used Confucianism to legitimize their rule and maintain order by forcing the Japanese people to passively accept their authority. Confucian ideals became so rooted in Japanese politics during this time that loyalty to the emperor was mandated by law (Hahm 2004). The authority of the rulers was dealt a serious blow when Japan was defeated in World War II, however, and usage of Confucian ideals to legitimize governmental behavior became less common. Currently Japanese citizens follow a variety of belief systems; Buddhism and Shinto are particularly popular. However, Confucian thought will likely remain an influential aspect of Japanese life well into the future.

Vietnam

Whereas the three countries already discussed are typically regarded as quite comparable from a cultural perspective, Vietnam's location in Southeast Asia and its distinct history often preclude any discussion of its similarities to other countries in historically Confucian Asia. However, we should not overlook the impact of Confucianism on Vietnamese society. It is an important part of the cultural environment in which the Vietnamese have lived for millennia (P. Doan 2002; T. Doan 2002).

The Confucian tradition has long influenced Vietnamese life in both the public and private spheres. Confucian ideas first arrived in Vietnam in 118 B.C. when Emperor Wu of the Han dynasty formally occupied the country's northern provinces. Chinese forces quickly entrenched themselves in the region, and Vietnam remained under China's direct control for more than one thousand years. However, the seeds of the rebellion of the Vietnamese against foreign rule were planted then. During the period of Chinese domination, Vietnamese monks and elites slowly adopted Confucian beliefs as their own, mirroring the initial support for

Confucianism demonstrated among elites in Korea and Japan. Ordinary Vietnamese, however, were less receptive to Confucian ethics than were their leaders. Because Confucianism was not a religion, they were attracted to Taoism and Buddhism to fulfill their religious needs. After Vietnam became independent from China in 939 A.D., the influence of Confucianism grew. As Vietnamese kings and aristocrats struggled to bring order to their unruly kingdom, they embraced the Confucian philosophy emphasizing social harmony and political order. In Hanoi in 1070, Confucianism was officially recognized with the dedication of Van Mieu (the Temple of Learning) to Khong Tu (Confucius). Five years later, in 1075, civil service examinations in the Confucian classics were introduced. In 1076, the first Vietnamese University was established next to the Temple of Confucius. For the first time in the history of Vietnam, Confucianism began to share a place at the royal court with Buddhism. In 1253, the government established the Institute for National Studies to teach the classical books of Confucius. During this period of national unification, ordinary Vietnamese also began to respond to Confucianism favorably, because they no longer viewed it as the belief system of their Chinese invaders.

In 1404, the Chinese reconquered northern Vietnam, but their rule was short-lived; the Vietnamese patriot Le Loi defeated the Chinese in 1427. The Le dynasty, which lasted 380 years, replaced Buddhism with Confucianism as the official ideology of the state and established a Confucian model of a centralized bureaucratic government with merit-based civil service examinations (Huy 1998). Beyond the political and ideological arenas of public life, the government carried out reforms to Confucianize family life and private education. In 1663, the Le court published "The Forty-Seven Rules for Teaching and Changing," which called for family members to abide by filial piety and other Confucian norms of family life. Confucianism also served as the foundation of the country's educational system until the French occupied the entire country in 1885. Throughout Vietnam, Confucian classics and ethics were taught even at the elementary school level. In the nineteenth century, to be educated meant to be learned in the Confucian classics.

With the introduction in the late nineteenth century of civil service examinations and a Western system of modern education under French colonial rule, Confucianism lost its dominant influence in the public sphere as a ruling ideology and a system of government. These reform measures produced a new generation of political and intellectual leaders who were not immersed in Confucian learning (Tran 2009). In both family and social life, however, Confucianism remained influential in the thinking and behavior of people from all walks of life. In Vietnam even today, people are encouraged to fulfill the five duties, which originated from the Confucian notion of the five cardinal human relationships.[16]

Nonetheless, it should be noted that even during the Le dynasty, the Vietnamese did not follow many of the Confucian tenets, especially those concerning the patriarchal family system, which the government promoted to "gain a better control of the countryside" (Whitmore 1984, 306). For example, the Confucian norm that "when the father dies, the mother should obey the children" was not practiced. Another example concerns the property rights of women. In the Confucian system of patriarchy, the family property belongs to the husband because he is the patriarch of the family unit. Women in Vietnam, unlike their peers in China and Korea, were allowed to inherit property along with their brothers and to manage the family property jointly with their husbands.

More notably, the Confucian norm of loyalty took on a different meaning in Vietnam, being understood in broad and impersonal terms. In China, Korea, and Japan, the reach of this norm was always confined to rulers and other personally known people. In Vietnam, it was extended to encompass the entire nation of the Vietnamese, including unknown fellow citizens. Moreover, for many Vietnamese, love of or loyalty to their nation weighed more heavily than love for members of the family and other people known to them (Duong 2003, 296). For this reason, many Vietnamese were willing to sacrifice their lives in the wars to drive out the French and American foreign invaders from their land.[17] Even in the process of governing, they did not rely on the Confucian principle of virtuous leadership. Instead, they preferred the rule of institutions and laws over the rule of virtuous men, as did the Japanese (Cima 1987).

On the whole, Confucianism, as an alien system of social and political ethics, never evolved in Vietnam into the monumental force that it was in China and Korea. As the country gradually expanded toward the south, it incorporated several new ethnic groups, increasing its

---

[16] These five duties or obligations are (1) *nhan*, love and humility; (2) *nghia*, right actions in expressing love and humanity; (3) *le*, observation of the rites or rules of ceremony and courtesy; (4) *tri*, the duty to be educated; and (5) *tin*, self-confidence and fidelity toward others.

[17] Neil Sheehan (1989) argues that villages-based Confucian rituals help explain why the Vietnamese were successful in repelling the American invasion.

heterogeneity and producing a plurality of ideas that prevented Confucian norms from becoming established as the nation's dominant belief system. Years of French occupation and the introduction of ideas from Europe also weakened the doctrine's strength, increasing the number of philosophical alternatives to Confucianism. However, although Confucianism's sociocultural roots in Vietnam were never as deep as those in China and Korea, Confucian norms do persist and have been regaining greater influence on the country's cultural and intellectual spheres since the country was reunified (P. Doan 2002).

Taiwan

The historical path that brought Confucianism to prominence in Taiwan has not been as long or complex as those observed in Korea, Japan, and Vietnam. Confucian values and norms were first brought to Taiwan in the early seventeenth century, when a large group of ethnic Chinese immigrated to the small island from China's mainland. The Chinese arrivals quickly established themselves as a legitimate and powerful community, easily overpowering the island's native Austronesian population.[18] Chinese influence became so strong in Taiwan that mainland China formally annexed the territory in 1683 (Thurston 1996). The Confucian beliefs brought by the Chinese gradually supplanted indigenous ideas in the island. In Taiwan, therefore, Confucianism's spread was made possible by the arrival and eventual dominance of foreigners in a new land.

Unlike in Imperial China, however, Confucianism never served as a state ideology in Republican Taiwan, and its state institutions were not built on the Confucian principle of ethical meritocracy. Instead, they are under the hegemonic rule of the Kuomintang or Nationalist Party, which is based on the organizational principles of Leninism. Consequently, the political legacy of Confucianism as a model of governance was never as powerful as in China, Korea, or Vietnam (King 1996). Yet, its legacy as a way of life remains as strong as in those countries, as evidenced by the prevalence of family-based medium-sized enterprises, the importance of affect-based interpersonal networks, and the active involvement of the state in the economy (Gold 1996).

Singapore

Singapore's location along several international trading routes has helped the island become a truly international community, as passing ships

---

[18] Austronesian people share a common descent from ancient Mongoloid aboriginal peoples of Oceania and are known to be found in Taiwan 6,000 years ago.

brought both goods and residents of foreign countries into Singapore in search of work. Immigrants arrived from a variety of lands, but the number of Chinese migrants exceeded all others, and eventually the Chinese formed a majority of the island's population. Descendants of these migrants still dominate Singaporean affairs today, although the island is also host to a substantial number of Indians and Malays. Singapore has never been formally occupied by China, nor have Confucian beliefs ever been officially mandated or enforced by governmental authorities (Englehart 2000). However, the Confucian belief system has still managed to shape Singaporean society, because descendants of the ancient Chinese have largely preserved the Confucian traditions of their ancestors. Most Singaporeans with a Chinese heritage remain "Confucian to some extent in their thinking and behavior" (Kuo 1996, 301).

Singapore is a small city-state in which citizens with Chinese ancestries constitute more than three-quarters of the population, and Chinese is one of the official languages. Many Chinese Singaporean families view Confucianism as indigenous, not alien, and still uphold its traditional family values. There is a system of private Chinese schools in Singapore in which Confucianism is a component of the core curriculum, and many Chinese Singaporean families send their children there. In other public schools, traditional Confucian family values and other Confucian virtues are also taught, although those are no longer part of the required religious knowledge course (Wong 1996).

Recently the government has made a conscious effort to develop a new national creed by promoting Confucian values as the four core shared values of Singapore 21, a vision of the Singapore of the 21st century: (1) community over self, (2) the family as the basic building block of society, (3) the resolution of major issues through consensus instead of contention, and (4) racial and religious harmony and tolerance.[19]

Although this government-sponsored Confucian movement was promoted as a means "to revive traditional values to counter the perceived evils of Westernization" (Kuo 1996, 304; see also Wong 1996, 287–8), many non-Chinese Singaporeans perceived it as a campaign merely to promote Chinese culture. Consequently, it failed to turn into a truly nationwide movement and achieved limited success in reviving traditional values. However, it did sensitize the Chinese Singaporeans to the positive

---

[19] Prime Minister Goh Chok Dong announced "Singapore 21: A Vision for New Era" in his June 5, 1997, speech to the Parliament, which adopted the aforementioned four Confucian values as the nation's shared values on January 15, 1991.

values of their Confucian heritage, and those values were then incorporated into the moral education curriculum of primary and secondary schools.[20] In addition, in Singapore today, children are required by law to remain filial to their parents, and authorities are allowed to "punish and fine" children who do not take care of their parents. Confucianism still has a strong, if unstated, hold on Singapore.

Patterns of Confucianization

As indicated by this brief history, Confucianism's spread throughout East Asia has been characterized by several key elements. In China, Korea, Japan, and Vietnam, the formal curriculum of the education system and the selection process of government officials required elites to internalize Confucian values and norms first and, having done so, to propagate Confucianism to commoners to realize the potential political benefits of mass indoctrination. These commoners, however, were less enamored with Confucian norms than were the elites, and so the elites had to overcome civilian reluctance to accept Confucianism. This was done through instruction in Confucian academies, and thus Confucianism was transmitted from the top down until it permeated every level of society.

This vertical process of Confucianization did not occur in Taiwan and Singapore, the two countries settled predominantly by Chinese immigrants. These immigrants brought the virtues of Confucianism with them; they were eager to preserve their Confucian beliefs in their new homes and were also willing to support the ruling elite of a paternalistic meritocracy. Thus there was no need for the government to impose the doctrine from above, as in the other three countries: Taiwan and Singapore represent a horizontal model of Confucianization.

Another important element of Confucianism's spread throughout East Asia was its emphasis on education. In public and private schools, Confucian texts constituted the core of their curriculum, and students were taught to think of themselves not as unique individuals but as interconnected units in complex interpersonal networks (Rozman 1991b). Fulfilling the roles required of such networks brought such rewards as social recognition, and these rewards reinforced students' commitments to Confucianism. It was through this blend of instruction and societal relations

---

[20] The government withdrew the ethics curriculum after a few years because it failed to achieve the stated goals.

that Confucianism became not only a historical but also a regional phenomenon in East Asia (Tu 2000).

Finally, it should be noted that Confucianism has been neither a missionary tradition nor an exclusive religion. As a highly secular belief system that aims to solve practical problems (Li 2008a), it was highly adaptable to local cultures. These adaptations have produced various reformulations of classical Confucianism, which, however, were all based on different interpretations of the same Confucian classics; the differences in interpretations arose from the different contexts in which Confucian scholars lived.

Confucian Legacies in East Asia Today

Although Confucianism developed in various ways throughout East Asia, all the East Asian nations with a Confucian heritage share several cultural characteristics. This section discusses these commonalities across East Asian countries, beginning with an analysis of how three institutions – the family, the state, and the educational system – are organized. I focus on these three institutions because in all of the countries they have served as the principal channels and mechanisms through which Confucian values were planted and took root (Rozman 1991b, 33). Having examined these three institutions, I then move to an analysis of how individual citizens perceive of, think of, and associate with other people.

The Family

The family occupies a special place in Confucianism (Slote and De Vos 1998); it is regarded as the basic unit of social life. Of the five cardinal relationships venerated in Confucianism, three – the relationship between father and son, the relationship between husband and wife, and the relationship between brothers – concern members of the family. As further expounded in Chapter 6, the family is viewed as the forum in which all humans learn to live virtuously and dutifully, because it is in their families that humans observe the proper rites of conduct through interactions with their elders, superiors, subordinates, and peers. In historically Confucian societies, filial piety and other family-related norms dictate people's roles not only in private relationships but also in public life (Tu 1996a).

By and large, people throughout the region still view family as their preeminent priority and grant familial obligations precedence over all other commitments, including legal obligations to the state (Bell 1996). People in both capitalist and communist countries are expected to put the welfare of their families far ahead of their personal ambitions and needs, and those who place their own desires over the good of their family members are considered selfish and uncaring. People in Confucian East Asia expect to practice self-sacrifice for their families' benefit and are taught they should be willing to endure short-term difficulties to improve their families' futures. According to Confucian ethics, people are not free, and should not seek to be free, from such family responsibilities; consequently, freedom is not a primary concern or virtue in traditionally Confucian societies (Li 1997, 187).

This suppression of personal interest for familial gain seems illogical and confusing to many Westerners, because, although those in the West provide for family members to some degree, individual success is often more important than collective gain (Rozman 1991b). Familial devotion is so deeply ingrained in East Asia that parents often spend their evenings not on personal affairs but instead helping their children study and succeed in school. Parents often sacrifice much of their free time and financial resources because their actions are seen as setting the foundation for familial success in the future (Bell 1996).

Interactions among family members in Confucian East Asia are guided by a series of strict, hierarchical norms based on age and gender. Children are expected to respect and obey their parents at all times, remaining loyal and unquestioning well into adulthood. Citizens are also taught to care for their aged parents, a sociological trait that has produced a proliferation of multigenerational households throughout the region. Adults in East Asia are well aware of the continued devotion expected of them and are loath to allow their parents to enter retirement homes, which in their view would equal abandonment. This aspect of Confucian culture, known as filial piety, remains so important in East Asian thought that laws in China and other countries require young people to provide financial support to their parents after marrying (Bell 1996).

The preeminent role afforded to families within Confucian thought has produced a system of "familism," in which the family unit transcends individual family members in importance. In this system, people have a fear of bringing collective shame on their relatives through their own personal actions (Lee and Hsiao 2010; Rozman 1991b). Because a person's identity is viewed as the product of familial relations and family-centered networks of personal relations, the person's behavior reflects on everyone with whom he or she is related.

In all East Asian countries except North Korea, there is little doubt that Confucian familism has contributed to the development of their economies by favoring the creation of family businesses of various sizes that require close cooperation among nuclear family members and extended relatives. The most prominent of these businesses are small- and medium-sized firms in Taiwan and Hong Kong and large conglomerates known as *chaebul* in Korea. These family businesses have developed gradually and become the backbone of Asian capitalism, which is often called *network capitalism*. In this way, familism has supported economic growth; however, it has negative economic consequences as well. Because this system emphasizes the good of the family over the good of the community or any other collective unit, familism fosters high levels of nepotism and corruption, two defining characteristics of crony capitalism (Fukuyama 1995a; Lingle 1997).

The State

From the family, we turn to the state. There are three broad categories of states: predatory, developmental, and regulatory. In *predatory states*, the type heavily concentrated in Africa, rulers extort taxes in their own interests, while providing minimal government services (Diamond 2008b). The defining characteristic of *developmental states* is a push for national prosperity and public welfare (Johnson 1982; Woo-Cumings 1999); to achieve these long-term goals, government agencies collaborate closely with private enterprise in formulating industrial policies and fostering technological modernization. In this respect, developmental states contrast sharply with *regulatory states*, such as the United States, in which private enterprises, not government agencies, are the primary drivers of economic development and technological modernization. Within regulatory states, the government intervenes in markets only when enterprises deviate from the governmental regulations guiding their activities.

The Confucian doctrine that government should actively promote the economic welfare of the people has provided a "great symbolic resource" for the establishment of developmental states in Confucian East Asia (Tu 2000, 203). All six historically Confucian countries, including Vietnam, have been able to establish and sustain the developmental state apparatus for all or most of the past five decades. As is widely known in the political economy literature, their economic planning agencies are highly centralized and are given the authority to intervene in various domains of public life. Protected from interference from voters and their representatives, these economic planning agencies were able to play a crucial role in transforming Japan, Korea, Taiwan, and Singapore into economic powerhouses at the fastest rates ever recorded in human history (Evans 1995; Wade 1990).

In these Confucian societies, ruling elites and economic experts were afforded a great deal of power and influence to intervene extensively in national economic development, while the mass citizenry was excluded from the policy-making process. Although such extensive governmental intervention might seem dangerous to Western champions of liberal democracy and private enterprise, East Asian leaders consistently enjoy widespread public support for their actions because "strong government with moral authority... is acclaimed a blessing" (Tu 1996a, 26). For decades, proponents of the developmental state were able to maintain societal support because mass citizenries liked the result: East Asia's recent rapid modernization. With centralized authority and close ties among politicians and business tycoons, the government played an instrumental role in producing explosive financial gains that brought several countries out of poverty (Tu 2000).

In addition to fostering support for government intervention in economic affairs, the Confucian tradition of a welfare state, as discussed further in Chapter 4, has had a major impact on popular attitudes concerning the boundaries between private and public spheres. Western liberalism stresses privacy and freedom from excessive state intervention; anything else is denounced as unchecked authoritarianism. East Asians hold far more permissive attitudes and are much less apt to view their personal lives as distinct from their roles in society. Residents of historically Confucian countries do not have a fear of powerful leaders, and they are rarely infused with Western thought or agree with the drive to limit government. This may explain why citizens in nations such as Singapore are so willing to tolerate frequent invasions of their privacy; the Confucian tradition views such governmental acts not as *invasive* but as *benevolent* and essential for state security. Thus East Asians are likely to grant more power to government authorities than Westerners would ever dream (Tu 1996a).

Why did political leaders in Confucian East Asia embrace the notion of the developmental state, whereas leaders in other regions preferred being the heads of predatory states? Why did Japan's Meiji reformers, China's Deng Xiaoping, Korea's Park Chung Hee, Taiwan's Chiang Ching-kuo, and Singapore's Lee Kuan Yew choose national prosperity and public welfare as their most important goals? Why did their citizens support them in their efforts to become the caretakers of their respective states? The Confucian legacy of meritocratic leadership provides the answer to these questions concerning the successful creation and management of developmental states throughout East Asia (Tu 1993, 220; see Mahbubani 1995).

One of the Confucian values often identified with the developmental state is the notion that the government exists solely for the welfare of the people (Hood 1998). Political leaders in agreement with this view are supported in their focus on national development and can use this rationale to direct government intervention in economic affairs for the goal of maximizing the welfare of the citizenry.

Another Confucian value that provides support for the developmental state is deference to authority/respect for hierarchy. Citizens who uphold this value are willing to respect and support their political leaders, whether freely elected or not, and to make personal sacrifices as long as their leaders are perceived to be serving their nation's best interest. In both of these principles – that government exists for the welfare of the people and the respect for authority – one sees traces of Confucian familism with its emphasis on paternalistic and hierarchical values. These values support the two defining characteristics of the developmental state: centralization of policy-making authorities and active intervention in the marketplace.

Schools

Respect for education and learning is perhaps the most striking characteristic of Confucianism. More than any other teaching, the Confucian emphasis on universal education distinguishes Confucius and his followers from other prominent philosophers and religious thinkers (T. Lee 2000). Early Confucians believed that all humans are not only inherently good but also morally perfectible; that is, they are capable of becoming fully virtuous people (a point discussed further in Chapter 3). Accordingly, Confucius and his disciples stressed the importance of educating people and rejected the categorization of human beings as good or bad, bright or dull, for the purpose of education (*Analects* 15:39).

For followers of Confucian teachings, therefore, hard work or continuous effort matters far more than innate abilities for learning. Only through hard work can individuals maximize their abilities and attain moral perfectibility (Stevenson and Stigler 1992). For this reason, Confucius claimed that "the practice of benevolence depends on oneself alone, and not on others" (*Analects* 12:1) and "No sooner I desire it than it is here" (*Analects* 7:30). For the same reason, Confucius characterized those who "make no effort to study even after having been vexed by difficulty as the lowest" (*Analects* 16:9).

In all historically Confucian societies, therefore, public education works from the belief that how much students achieve depends more on how hard they work than on their innate abilities. This *effort-based model* of educating children contrasts sharply with the American *ability-based model*, which often discourages students from working hard by suggesting they will be as successful as their innate intelligence allows them to be.

It should also be noted that Confucius was the first educator who advocated the democratic principle of universal education and who emphasized education as one of the most important governmental functions (T. Lee 2000). To promote meritocratic rule, his followers established the tradition of selecting government officials through competitive merit-based examinations called *keju*, which in China lasted almost 1,300 years, from 606 to 1905 A.D. To pass these imperial examinations, candidates had to memorize a vast amount of classic Confucian texts without making much effort to cultivate the ability to critically evaluate the theses presented in the texts or to propose alternative viewpoints (T. Kim 2009). In historically Confucian countries even today, students are known to engage in rote learning and to neglect any topic outside the examination syllabus (Yung 2010).[21] Test-oriented schooling and memory-based learning together with the exam-based selection of the civil servants undergird the Confucian education system in practice.

As discussed earlier, these educational practices were later exported to China's neighbors, especially Korea and Vietnam, where the educational systems were also designed to recruit civil servants immersed in Confucian classics. In short, all historically Confucian countries including Japan were left with a strong legacy of education as an important conduit for upward mobility.

In these countries even today, teachers and students approach education mainly from the perspective of employment and upward mobility. Consequently, schools are geared to prepare students for various kinds of examinations and tests for professional certificates; they have content-oriented and test-driven curricula. At the same time, parents spend a large proportion of their family income to send their children to "cram schools," which offer various academic and non-academic courses. By placing more emphasis on effort than innate intelligence (Stevenson and Stigler, 1992), this system of exam-oriented schooling has produced a

---

[21] Some Confucian critics, such as Huang Zongxi (seventeenth century), were known to be critical of exams because they exclusively tested rote memorization.

literate and disciplined workforce that has allowed for the rapid industrialization of the agrarian economy – but it is often blamed for failing to
produce Nobel Laureates and innovative scientists.

Patterns of Thinking and Behaving
Being influenced by Confucian education for centuries, people in historically Confucian countries think about and see the world differently
from the way people in the West do (Yao 1999, 315). As Tu Weiming (2000, 199) notes, "The Confucian insistence on the importance of
equality rather than freedom, sympathy rather than rationality, civility
rather than law, duty rather than rights, and human-relatedness rather
than individualism may appear to be diametrically opposed to the value-
orientation of the Enlightenment."

According to the social psychologist Richard Nisbett (2003), East
Asian civilization, which arose from Confucian cultural traditions, has
long emphasized social harmony over pluralism and interpersonal duties
over individual rights. It contrasts sharply with Western civilization,
which grew out of an Aristotelian tradition valuing individual identity
and personal agency. The divergent influences of these two cultural traditions have led to stark differences in how people in historically Confucian
Asia and people in the West think about the world.

In the Confucian tradition, every person is seen as an interdependent
part of a collective, not as an autonomous and independent individual,
as further discussed in Chapter 3. In such a world, every aspect of human
life is relational, and interpersonal relationships take precedence over
individual expression. The emphasis on the context and nature of such
relationships has shaped the cognitive development of people in historically Confucian societies. According to Nisbett (2003), they are more
likely to see the world holistically than its parts separately, and they
pay more attention to the environments and relationships of the world's
components than Westerners who tend to focus on selected, discrete
objects.

Such a holistic mode of perception motivates Confucian East Asians
to explain events in broad terms. East Asians do not believe that events
occur in isolation but rather are embedded in a meaningful whole. When
explaining events, therefore, they do not focus exclusively on specific
happenings as Westerners do, but instead tend to cast a broad net that
includes the surrounding environment. Unlike Westerners who seek to
understand the world analytically and exclusively in terms of categories,
East Asians find meaning holistically and integrally by examining the

various relationships among the world's various components (Nisbett 2003, chap. 5; Tu 2000, 201).

This mode of comprehending events is often called circular reasoning or correlative thinking. It contrasts strikingly with logical or causal thinking, which is commonplace in the West (Hall and Ames 1995). Correlative thinking does not make use of any principle to guide either deduction or induction; instead, it makes use of analogies or metaphors to highlight the similarities between the phenomenon under observation and what is already known. Relying on such metaphors and images rather than precise observations and in-depth analyses, correlative thinking is known as a nonlogical method of inquiry. Instead of identifying actual causes, it conveys how various phenomena are associated with one another or differentiated from each other (Hall and Ames 1995, 125).

In the Confucian tradition, moreover, the ultimate end is to establish a peaceful and prosperous community on the basis of harmonious relations among its members (Li 2006). "All parts should be ordered in mutually supportive ways to achieve the ethical ideal" (Chan 2008a, 123). This emphasis on social stability and interpersonal harmony over other values has discouraged people in historically Confucian East Asia from engaging in the practice of criticism and argumentation. Whereas Plato and Aristotle never stopped challenging and rejecting the thoughts of their predecessors, Confucius and his followers always admired and emulated their forerunners. Consequently, these early Confucians left the legacies of equating alternative viewpoints with destructive thoughts and of discouraging any perspective challenging the mainstream school of thought or ideology. These legacies have slowed the development of *critical thinking* among the masses in the region. According to Bell (2008a, 107), college professors in China even today do not expect their students to examine the world critically until age forty or so.

Another consequence of holistic thinking is the tendency of people in Confucian societies to see no duality between the spheres of public and private life and no separation between public and private morality (Hall and Ames 2003, 137). Because they view these two life spheres as connected closely with one another, they become both public and private at the same time. As a result, they do not separate the purely impersonal process of rational deliberations from the personal process of forming affection; instead, they tend to think rationally and affectively at the same time (Nuyen 2002, 135). This pattern of thinking is known as heart-mind, and it contrasts sharply with that of the West that typically assigns affect or emotions to the private sphere of life and rationality to the public life sphere. In short, there appears to be no such thing as purely rational thinking in the Confucian tradition.

Like patterns of thought, patterns of speech in Confucian societies are quite different from what is typical in Western societies where languages are little differentiated by social status, age, and gender. Among people in Confucian societies, for example, there is one notable trait in the way they communicate with each other: Depending on the particular role they play, they can choose one of three forms of addressing the hearer in the audience (plain, polite, and honorific) and one of two different forms of referencing the speaker (humble and neutral). These forms of addressing and referencing, when combined, result in many different patterns of communicating, including one of combining the honorific address form for the hearer and the humble form of self-reference (Yum 1988, 382).

More importantly, the Confucian values of interpersonal harmony and interdependency are known to prohibit self-assertion in verbal communication (S. Cheng 1990; Yum 1988). In Confucian tradition, self-assertion is often equated with a form of aggressiveness that threatens the harmony and cohesion of their group. Many East Asians are highly conscious of how their communications might make someone else feel and tend to be reticent and deferential in expressing their personal opinions, especially to strangers whose viewpoints are unknown to them.

Whereas Westerners want to express their true feelings and let others "take it or leave it," Confucian Asians prefer to withhold their feelings and not risk offending someone. Consequently, whereas Westerners take pride in claiming, "What you see is what you get," people in East Asia draw a distinction between the *façade self* and *inner self*, a concept the Japanese articulate with the dichotomous terms of *tatemae* and *honne* (Bachnik 2007). Of the seven cultural regions covered in the latest round of the World Values Surveys, historically Confucian East Asia is the region with the least assertive people. Chapter 7 discusses this finding in greater detail.

Confucianism has also produced a unique pattern of associational life. This system of ethics provides an elaborate moral code for relationships among people who know each other. However, it offers only a few guidelines for relationships among people who are not at the least acquainted, except for the Golden Rule, which instructs the individual to treat others as he or she would like to be treated (Li 2008a, 183). As A. T. Nuyen writes, "There are no free-floating rights and responsibilities, only those that arise from being a parent, a teacher, a civil servant, a general or a prince" (2002, 134). Moreover, the most important moral and political obligations, such as filial piety and loyalty, are conceived in terms of specific relations among people who know each other. When a conflict occurs between specific and universalistic obligations, such as filial piety and benevolence, the former prevail (O'Dwyer 2003, 44).

Moreover, the Confucian norm of graded or graduated love requires adherents to assess the ties connecting them to a person and to express greater love to those with closer ties.[22] Accordingly, people in historically Confucian societies do not feel obliged to treat all people equally. In determining how to interact with someone, they look as much at their familial or other personal ties as at their formal ties, such as membership in a political organization (Bell 2008a, 27; Chan 2003, 247).

Such a pattern of voluntary association is known as *particularistic social networking* (Tu 2000, 211), as opposed to *universalistic social networking*, which is commonplace in the West. In universalistic networking, the norms of equality and fairness apply uniformly to all others, whether a close relative or a complete stranger, and outweigh personal ties as an influence on interpersonal relations. As a result, there is not much need in associational life for people to distinguish between those who do and those who do not have personal ties with them.

In contrast, in particularistic social networking, in-group members, or those with personal ties, are often distinguished from out-group members for preferential treatment. Confucian norms such as filial piety, loyalty, and reciprocity require a favorable treatment of in-group members. At the same time, those norms make it difficult to distinguish between the private and public spheres of interpersonal life, and as a result, social exchange tends to be based on ascriptive ties, connections, and favors, but not contractual principles. This model of particularistic social networking is bound to discourage generalized bonding among people without personal ties and to encourage corruption and nepotism (Pye 1999; Rozman 2002).

Summary and Conclusions

Democratization in East Asia can be studied from a variety of disciplinary perspectives or professional interests. For this study, I chose a cultural perspective because Confucianism is the most pervasive heritage of historically Confucian East Asia and to understand Confucianism one is required to "engage with East Asian societies in respectful ways" (Bell

---

[22] According to this principle of graded love, obligations to the family should always take priority over all other obligations (Hall and Ames 2003).

2008a, xi). To offer a comprehensive account of the role Confucianism has played in the region, I examined the tradition as a historical and regional phenomenon. Historically, I treated Confucianism as the result of an evolutionary process and examined how its principal doctrines and practices evolved into a system of social and political ethics. Regionally, I explored how those doctrines and practices spread across countries on China's periphery to form one of the distinct cultural zones in the world.

More than two millennia ago, Confucius first organized ancient beliefs and practices into a loosely structured system of ethics to enable people in warring states to live in a harmonious and peaceful community as their forefathers once did. The scholarly tradition he established solely for the literate segment of the population in Central China first expanded into the ideological and institutional instruments of the ruling elite. It then expanded into a cultural movement reaching all the segments of the population in all of China. The historical process of transforming the Confucian scholarly tradition into a cultural movement accompanied the process of reinterpreting classical Confucianism as an ethical or philosophical ideal and reformulating it as daily political and social practices.

While such reformulations were taking place within China, Confucianism was becoming a regionwide phenomenon, spreading to China's adjacent territories. It was first exported to Korea and Vietnam, then to Japan, and finally to Taiwan and Singapore. In Korea and Vietnam, which China occupied and directly ruled for an extended period of time, Confucianism began as an imposed ruling ideology and centralized bureaucratic institution. Although Confucianism eventually permeated both the public and private spheres of the Korean people, its teachings of patriarchy and patrilineality never took hold in Vietnam. In Japan, which did not come under China's direct rule, even the ruling ideology was never exclusively Confucian. Nor was its system of centralized bureaucracy based exclusively on merit, as was the case in Korea and Vietnam. Whereas the intellectual and political elite spearheaded the process of Confucianization in Korea, Vietnam, and Japan, the immigrant masses from motherland China helped establish Confucianism as a dominant belief system in Singapore and Taiwan. Across these five countries there was a great deal of variation in the process of Confucianization and in its consequences.

Yet for all these national differences, China and the five other historically Confucian countries share similar patterns of institutional performance and a similar mode of citizen thinking and behavior. Institutionally, the family remains the foundation of social life, and education in prestigious schools is exalted (Tu 2000). The state institutions in all these countries, whether democratic or nondemocratic, are highly centralized and intrusive, especially in the management of economic affairs. In contrast, individual citizens tend to perceive their living environment holistically and reason about its dynamics circularly. In communicating and associating with other people, they tend to refrain from being assertive, and they engage in particularistic networking according to the Confucian norm of graded love. The Confucian tradition is still powerful in supplying norms or standards for individual citizens and their family, community, and government to observe.

Where once, classical Confucianism provided the institutional "hardware" for an aristocratic meritocracy – hardware that included the imperial court, the rule by virtuous men, and civil service examinations based on Confucian classics – these relics of Confucianism have long been washed away by the waves of modernization, globalization, and Westernization (Yao 1999). Consequently, Confucianism no longer serves as a system of social classes and political power. As a way of life or culture, however, its surviving values and norms affect both public and private life in a myriad of direct and indirect ways. These Confucian cultural legacies, therefore, have to be taken into consideration to attain a sophisticated understanding of the historically Confucian region, as Xinzhong Yao (2000, 277) suggests.

In recent decades, there has been a revival of public interest in Confucius and Confucianism in China and other East Asian countries (Bell 2008d; *Economist* 2007; Fan 2007; Ho 2009; Lam 2008; Yao 2001). In China, for example, more than ten million copies of Confucius's *Analects* have been distributed across the country,[23] and Confucian academies have recently been built to educate young children in the classics of Confucianism. More notably, the ruling Chinese Community Party has also recently begun to teach the Confucian classics in its schools (Bell 2008c).

In Taiwan and Vietnam, Confucius has been honored as the greatest teacher, and his birthday has been celebrated as Teacher's Day. In South Korea, more than twenty universities have begun to offer courses in Confucianism. In North America, Europe, and Australia as well, more and more universities and colleges are offering courses to examine Confucianism from a variety of disciplinary perspectives. Even UNESCO held a conference to celebrate the 2,540th birthday of Confucius. Once reviled, Confucius and Confucianism are now becoming culturally fashionable.

---

[23] This figure refers to the number of copies of Yu Dan's (2009) interpretation of *The Analects*.

A renewed consciousness of the shared Confucian heritage among ordinary people and its growing popularity among scholars in East Asia and elsewhere have recently rekindled and reshaped the age-old debate over its compatibility or incompatibility with democratic politics (Ackerly 2005; Bell 2006, 2009b; Dallmayr 2009; He 2010; S. M. Kim 2008; Li 2009; Tan 2003a, 2009). On the one hand, the new wave of Confucianism has raised questions concerning the character of contemporary Confucians and their distribution across the different segments of the population in each and all of the historically Confucian countries (Bell 2008c; Cheung et al. 2006; Sun 2009; Yao 2001). On the other hand, it has encouraged social scientists and political leaders to identify the particular sets of Confucian social and political ideas and practices that would facilitate or hinder the process of democratization in the region (Bell 2009a; Crowell 2005).

What does this newly emerging wave of mass Confucianism imply for the process of establishing and consolidating the institutions of democratic politics and for building a democratic political culture among the mass citizenries of East Asia? My analyses of the Asian Barometer and World Values Surveys, which are reported in six substantive chapters, are intended to address some of these newly emerging concerns of the scholarship on Confucianism from a social scientific perspective. Before I present these results, I review in the next chapter the theoretical debate and empirical research on the various role Confucian norms and values play and can play in the process of democratization.

2

The Confucian Asian Values Thesis

Theoretical Debate and Empirical Research

More than three decades have passed since the third wave of democratization began spreading from Southern Europe to all other regions of the world in the mid-1970s. In the wake of this wave, most or all of the countries in East, Central, and Southern Europe and in Latin America have been transformed into democracies (Diamond 2011; Haerpfer et al. 2009). In historically Confucian East Asia, where the institutional, cognitive, and behavioral legacies of Confucianism are prevalent, however, the same wave produced only two new democracies – South Korea (Korea hereafter) and Taiwan – and failed to democratize four other nondemocracies: China, North Korea, Singapore, and Vietnam. Moreover, of the two nascent democracies, Taiwan remains a "flawed" democracy even after more than two decades of democratic rule (Economist Intelligence Unit 2010), and Korea has recently moved backward from "free" to "partly free" in press freedom rankings (Freedom House 2011).

Despite all the unprecedented achievements in socioeconomic development and globalization in the region over the past three decades, Confucian East Asia today remains one of the few regions in the world in which nondemocracies prevail over democracies. To explain a lack of democratic development in the region, many scholars and political leaders have promoted Confucian values as Asian values (Tamaki 2007) and have vigorously debated their influence on the democratic transformation of authoritarian regimes in the East Asia region from a variety of disciplinary and ideological perspectives.

In this chapter, I first examine and synthesize conflicting claims and counterclaims on the actual and potential role of Confucian legacies on democratization and attempt to unravel the gist of the Confucian Asian Values debate from a theoretical perspective. Then I review empirical studies to identify their limitations as empirical tests of those claims and counterclaims and to determine what needs to be done to reassess the ongoing debate empirically in a fuller fashion. Finally, I explore why there has been so much debate over the compatibility or incompatibility between Confucianism and democracy.

The Theoretical Debate

Scholars studying Confucianism and democracy generally espouse one of three perspectives. Those in the first camp conceptualize democracy procedurally and Confucianism nonliberally; they argue that the ethical principles of Confucianism, both political and social, are fundamentally incompatible with the principles of liberal democracy (Huntington 1996; X. Kang 2006; Li 1997; Pye 1985). In stark contrast, those in the second camp define democracy substantively and Confucianism liberally, and they interpret the principles of Confucianism as analogous to democratic values (De Bary 1998b; Hsu 1975; Tu 2002). Those in the third camp suggest that Confucianism and democracy can be adapted to form a hybrid system that is suitable for historically and culturally Confucian societies. They either define democracy procedurally and Confucianism liberally, or they define democracy substantively and Confucianism nonliberally (Ackerly 2005; Bai 2008; Bell 2006; Hahm 2004; Hall and Ames 1999; S. M. Kim 2008, 2011; Tan 2003a, 2007). Of these three contrasting perspectives, the Incompatibility Thesis is known as orthodoxy (Nuyen 2000, 133).

The Incompatibility Argument

Proponents of this interpretation focus on the overall character of Confucianism and its prime concern as a system of social and political ethics, and they characterize its fundamental principles as undemocratic or antidemocratic (Pye 1985). Specifically, they interpret Confucianism as a system of social and political ethics that emphasizes the collective good, hierarchical social relations, and meritocratic rule by the wise and virtuous. As such, its ethical system is fundamentally different from the liberal ethical system of the West, which places priority on individual freedom and rights and on mass participation and competition in the political process. In short, Confucianism and democracy have two distinct and incompatible value systems (Chan 1999; Li 1997, 1999).

The Incompatibility Thesis reflects a comprehensive analysis of Confucianism as a system of both social and political ethics and offers a critical assessment of the relationships between its social and political values and those of democracy. In a recent literature review, Baogang He (2010, 20) argues that Confucianism represents "a political order in which the rule of the gentleman prevails, where duty is central, political inequality is taken for granted, moral concern overrides the political bargaining process, and harmony prevails over conflict."

Confucian political order, therefore, "conflicts with a democratic political order in which the rule of law prevails, rights are central, political equality is taken for granted, the political bargaining process overrides moral consensus, and conflict is seen as a necessarily normal condition of political life." To put it differently, the fundamental values that serve as prerequisites for democracy, particularly the values of freedom, equality, and pluralism, are incompatible with the Confucian key values of duty, responsibility, and loyalty (Li 1997, 187; Nuyen, 2000, 135).

Many scholars and political leaders subscribe to the Incompatibility Thesis. Samuel P. Huntington is the most outspoken of these scholars, claiming that classical Confucian thought is inherently antidemocratic and that Confucian democracy is a contradictory term (1991, 30).[1] Confucian-influenced societies are inhospitable to democratization because the Confucian heritage promotes the group over the individual, authority over liberty, and responsibilities over rights, and it offers no institutional protection of individual rights against the state (Huntington 1991, 24; 1996, 238). Former prime minister of Singapore, Lee Kuan Yew, and several other East Asian leaders also have espoused the idea that the dominance of Confucian Asian values in those states precludes any emergence of Western liberal democracy (Zakaria 1994). Critics, on the other hand, maintain that state leaders in Confucian East Asia have used Confucian doctrines to justify illiberal or nonliberal policies (Brennan and Fan 2007).

What specific principles of Confucianism and democracy are most incompatible with one another? Supporters of the Incompatibility Thesis point to the qualifications of rulers and the role of the ruled in the political process as two discordant areas. In democracy, which is a form of collective self-rule, people rule themselves directly or indirectly through

---

[1] Huang (1997) and Kang (1999) offer highly critical assessments of Huntington's scholarship on Confucianism.

the election of their representatives. In Confucianism, only those capable of discharging the responsibility of governing are allowed to serve as rulers (*Analects* 4:14). It is the moral elites – the wise and virtuous – who are charged with ruling the state. Confucius and Mencius emphasized ordinary people as "the root of the state," meaning their interests are paramount (*Mencius* 7B:14), but neither talked about self-rule, as discussed in Chapter 4. Nor did they support the direct participation of the masses in the decision-making process. Therefore, "Confucianism does not contain any fundamental democratic values or principles, such as political equality or popular sovereignty" (J. Chan 2007, 191).

According to early Confucians, only morally upright people called "exemplary persons" and sages, not the masses, have the capacity to grasp the Way (ethical living) and put it into practice. The common people are incapable of governing themselves and thus should not be entrusted with governance. Instead, they ought to be made to follow virtuous leaders as "the grass bends to the wind" (*Analects* 12:19). In short, the Confucian political world is a hierarchical political order in which the common people remain in a passive role.[2]

Moreover, classical Confucianism equates good government with a paternalistic meritocracy in which the relationship between rulers and masses is analogous to that between parents and children (Murthy 2000). As mother and father to the people, moral elites make decisions concerning their welfare. Although the Confucian government of moral meritocracy allows for some degree of popular consultation, dissent, and remonstration, it is, at best, a form of guardianship (J. Chan 2007, 187). This indeed is a stark contrast to the Western notion of democracy as government by the people, which requires their participation in policy making.

The second set of incompatible principles concerns the proper relationship between rulers and the ruled. Confucius and his followers promoted an organic notion of the state in which the family serves as a model. As in the family, therefore, the state's structure and process are *hierarchically organized*. Political powers are typically concentrated into the hands of a prime minister or a president (or emperor), which contrasts sharply with Western democratic state structures in which powers are divided among branches of government (Robinson 1996; Subramaniam 2000).

---

[2] Tu (2002, 6) challenges this view, arguing that "[i]n the Mencian tradition, *min* (the common people) is absolutely not a passive element to be manipulated by rulers."

Moreover, in Confucian government, ordinary citizens must exhibit proper conduct and loyalty to their political leaders, although it is not blind loyalty (Hahm 2001; S. Lee, 2001; Mahbubani 1995; Pertierra 1999). For example, the norms of *zhong* (loyalty) and *li* (propriety) stress obedience to authority and discourage any behavior that undermines political stability. As Chenyang Li (1997, 185–6) points out, Confucian norms of loyalty and propriety make it impossible for ordinary people to express their interests in the process of policy making and to challenge government policy.

In the past, East Asian political leaders, especially in China, Korea, Singapore, and Taiwan, often invoked Confucian values stressing national unity and welfare to legitimize their oppressive authoritarian rule as benevolent and inherently necessary (X. Kang 2006). Rulers in such situations embody O'Donnell's (1994) conception of "delegative democracy," characterized by the entrenchment of political power within the executive branch. In delegative democracies, citizens are technically allowed to vote, but every decision of any importance is made by executive leaders and is imposed on society from above. This system is clearly antithetical to Western democracy, which rests on the existence of competing ideas – political debates and political contestation – which are essential for preventing any type of authoritarian ruler from assuming control. In this regard, then, historical Confucian values certainly appear to be antithetical to democratization and liberalization.

On the proper role that the state ought to play for the people, Confucianism and liberal democracy are also in conflict. As mentioned earlier, in Confucianism the state, like the family, is a paternalistic institution in charge of the welfare of its members. It is supposed to fulfill parental functions. In principle, therefore, there is no limit to what it should do to ensure the welfare of the people by promoting economic prosperity, political stability, and social harmony. It has the authority to intervene in the economic as well as moral affairs of its citizens if such interventions are deemed necessary for the welfare of the people (Bai 2008, 24; O'Dwyer 2003, 45). Such an interventionist state runs counter to a liberal democratic state, which is morally neutral and does not intervene in economic and private affairs (J. Chan 2007).

The final irreconcilability between Confucianism and Western democracy discussed here focuses on the role *virtue* plays in Confucian politics. Confucianism deems virtue to be far more important than formal political institutions in governance, stressing the need for moral leadership rather than institutional safeguards against official misbehavior. For example,

Confucius portrayed virtuous leaders as the North Star, because all are expected to turn toward them in search of enlightenment (*Analects* 2:1). As Shaohua Hu (1997) notes, there is a major shortcoming in such a Confucian notion of political leadership. What should be done when morality fails?

Although Confucianism's optimistic notion of leaders embodying virtue would be useful for societies in which leaders always place national welfare above their own, the ideology provides no clear mechanism for resolving conflict when they fail to do so (Fukuyama 2011; Nuyen 2000). Small agrarian communities emblematic of Chinese life during Confucius's era no longer exist. In large urbanized and industrialized societies where values continue to shift (Inglehart 1997; Inoguchi 2007), a morality in flux alone cannot motivate leaders to do what is right and avoid doing wrong. To ensure that political leaders and institutions work on behalf of the people, Confucian countries must guarantee that the rule of law is upheld. For those who view Confucianism and Western democracy as fundamentally irreconcilable, it is strict adherence to the rule of law, not virtuous political leaders, which historically Confucian societies urgently need to become well-functioning democracies.

The Compatibility Argument
The establishment of democratic institutions and processes in historically Confucian East Asia has not been an easy process. Yet those institutions and processes are firmly established in three – Japan, Korea, and Taiwan – of the seven countries in the region. Moreover, throughout the region, an increasing number of ordinary citizens and political leaders are championing democracy (Chu et al. 2008). In fact, former Korean president Kim Dae Jung (1994) maintained that Confucianism would enable the region to expand democracy beyond Western standards. Former Taiwanese president Lee Teng-hui (2006) argued that Confucian doctrine is capable of moderating the excesses of individualism and addressing other shortcomings of democracy by enhancing both the welfare of individual citizens and the groups of which they are a part.

Some scholars argue that Confucianism contains "democratic seeds" and that these seeds can serve as the very foundation of sustainable democracy in Confucian East Asia (De Bary 1998; Shils 1996; Tu 1966c; see also Hsu 1975, chap. 9; Murthy 2000; Xu 2006; Yung 2010). According to Joseph Chan (2007), four leading Confucian scholars coauthored *Manifesto to the World on Behalf of Chinese Culture* in the 1950s and advocated the compatibility thesis.[3] They examined Mencius's notion of the heavenly mandate and other Confucian principles of social and political order, emphasizing their compatibility with principles of democratic government. The prominent aspects of Confucianism that are often considered reconcilable with democracy are political accountability, equality, dissent, tolerance, and social participation.

The similarity most often noted by scholars proposing a compatible relationship concerns *political accountability*. Although Confucianism clearly values societal order and civilian loyalty to the state, its basic tenets never condone a ruler's arbitrary action against the ruled. Instead, a ruler's accountability to the people is at the core of those tenets. At the root of such accountability are two principles of government: *minben* (people as the root) and the Mandate of Heaven. The *minben* principle holds that "the people are of supreme importance" (*Mencius* 7B:14) and that the ruler ought to take care of their welfare. The Mandate of Heaven holds that people's acceptance or consent is the basis of legitimate rule. Although neither of these principles fully meets the definition of democracy as government by the people, both are in accord with its definition as government for the people. The Confucian practice of selecting government officials by public and open examinations can be viewed as an institutional alternative to the free and competitive elections of political leaders (Nuyen 2000, 143).[4]

Political constraint of leaders is also present in both Confucianism and democracy. Although the Confucian belief in a Mandate of Heaven grants leaders considerable authority, such power is fully contingent not only on continued ethical leadership but also on continued support from the people as a whole. Confucian governance is a form of political stewardship conferred on the elite after they are deemed appropriately wise and virtuous. Moreover, as God's representatives on Earth, Confucian leaders ought to respect public opinion before making important decisions, just as do leaders of democratic states (Hsu 1975). The following passage emphasizes the importance of listening to the people's opinion:

When your close attendants say of a man that he is good and wise, that is not enough; when everyone says so, then have the case investigated. If the man turns out to be good and wise, then and only then should he be given office.... When

---

[3] These four scholars are Carson Chang, Tan Junyi, Xu Fuguan, and Mou Zongsan. Albert Chen (2007) reviews their analyses of the linkage between Confucianism and democracy.

[4] Another Confucian institution of accountability is the Censorate of the Choson dynasty (1392–1920). For further details, see Mo (2003).

all your close attendants say of a man that he deserves death . . . when everyone says so, then have the case investigated. If the man turns out to deserve death, then and only then should he be put death. In this way it will be said, "He was put to death by the whole country." Only by acting in this manner can one be father and mother to the people (*Mencius* 1B:7).

In short, Confucian leaders are expected to remain cognizant of public demands; provide for the national welfare; and maintain liberty, equality, and impartiality (Murthy 2000). If a leader fails to remain accountable to his subjects, his citizens need no longer respect his rule. In this regard, Tu Weiming (1994) notes that, although state leaders do enjoy a great deal of power in historically Confucian East Asia, their authority is often checked by the citizens, who remain attached to the Confucian notion of government for the people. He further argues that in Confucianism there is a ritual tradition that has a constitutional function by requiring everyone to observe social norms and political rules (2002, 9).

The characteristics expected of an ideal Confucian leader are quite similar to those associated with leaders of democratic polities. As Shaohua Hu (1997) points out, both Confucianism and democracy oppose the despotic behavior of political leaders, and both belief systems promote the right and ability of the people to remove malevolent leaders from power. If leaders use their positions for personal gain rather than for the promotion of the national welfare, citizens of both Confucian and democratic states are fully justified and authorized to replace those rulers with better qualified leaders. Democracy might emphasize the protection of personal liberty from governmental oppression to a greater degree than Confucianism, but both doctrines still maintain that citizens deserve leaders who are accountable to the populace.

A similar concept of accountability is evidenced in Confucianism's tradition of *remonstrance*, in which a country's residents maintain open dialogue with leaders on pressing issues. According to Keqian Xu (2006), early Confucians viewed governance as an act of mutual commitment on the part of rulers and the ruled. According to *Mencius* (4A:20), the real responsibility of the ruled to the ruler includes "rectifying the evils in the ruler's heart." "Having obtained the confidence of his prince, one may then remonstrate with him. If he have not gained his confidence, the prince will think that he is vilifying him" (*Analects* 19:10).

These Confucian ideas of the people's responsibility to criticize author-ity and dismiss unresponsive leaders are similar to the democratic political practices of conducting competitive elections and impeaching those lead-ers peacefully. When King Hsuan of Ch'i asked about ministers, Mencius

(5B:9) replied, "If the prince made mistakes, they would remonstrate with him, but if repeated remonstrations fell on deaf ears, they would depose him." The divine obligation of political leaders to serve and follow the people in Confucian societies can be therefore viewed as equivalent to the Western rule of law – if either is broken, leaders must be held responsible for their actions (Ackerly 2005).

In addition to the domain of political accountability, Confucianism and democracy are deemed to have similar views of *equality*. All Confucians believe in the equality of human beings (*Analects* 17:2, 15:39; *Mencius* 6A:7). For this reason, Confucianism emphasizes universal education for citizens from all walks of life and equal opportunity for political appointment. The Confucian ideal of universal education is compatible with the principle of democratic citizenship that requires the development of an informed citizenry (Collins 2008; Herr 2010).

Although not all citizens possess the abilities needed to become political leaders, everyone has an opportunity to take merit-based civil service examinations and to be appointed as a government official. Citizens in Confucian societies, as in democratic societies, are expected to respect the rights and personal sovereignty of others, because all residents of a country are equally integral components of their national network. These norms certainly parallel democracy's emphasis on equality and opportunity, indicating that, although East Asian societies today might not always actualize such values, Confucianism can be used to foster such democratic behavior.

A closer inspection of historical Confucian documents shows that *tolerance* of diverse ideas is also encouraged by the doctrine. The very concept of *harmony* incorporates diversity and the tolerance of diversity, as Confucius (*Analects* 13: 23) admonishes: "Exemplary persons value harmony but not conformity; petty persons value conformity but not harmony." In the ideal world of Confucianism, harmony refers to the blending of diverse ideas, not the elimination of opposing views. As Bell (2008c, 120) aptly points out, it is "harmony in diversity" that is sought after, although uniformity and conformity are often championed in practice.

In principle, it is unnecessary to sacrifice pluralism to attain societal harmony, because harmony presupposes the existence of diverse views and can be achieved by blending those views. Healthy societies are possible only when individuality and harmony enhance one another, benefiting both the individual and the nation (Collins 2008; Nuyen 2000). The Confucian idea of social harmony and the historical practice of tolerating multiple religions can promote the Western liberal tradition of tolerating and combining diverse interests to help the state advance (Fukuyama 1995b).

Emphasizing the importance of order and stability, Confucianism seems inherently in opposition to liberal democracy's championing of political contestation. Yet, several scholars suggest that *dissent*, which can be expressed through the practice of remonstration, is a fundamental element of Confucian values (Ackerly 2005; Collins 2008; Tan 2003b). In principle, the Confucian notion of *dao* or ethical living allows people to speak out against any injustice or malice that transgresses basic human values. Communal problems can be solved only when all citizens participate in a democratic fashion, challenging existing ideas when necessary to ensure that the optimal outcome is reached (Hsu 1975).

In practice, however, Confucianism permits popular opposition only when such actions do not incite political mayhem or rebellion (Hall and Ames 1999). Order and harmony are qualities sought above all else by all Confucian states, and national peace should not be disturbed. In both Confucianism and democracy, however, dissent can be an important component of political procedure, although its expression is much more restricted in the former.

A final domain of compatibility between Confucianism and democracy concerns the issue of *societal participation*. Societal participation is certainly a hallmark of traditionally democratic societies, for Western liberalism rests on the notion of the people choosing leaders and shaping policies through free and fair elections. Although widespread participation might not seem as emblematic of Confucianism, Confucian values still certainly promote robust civil societies, especially through the provision of equal and mandatory education by the state (Bai 2008; S. M. Kim 2010; Madsen 2002). In Confucian East Asia, education has always been one of the most fundamental ways in which individuals fully develop themselves, and an intellectually advanced population is apt to be more willing to place demands on state leaders (Yung 2010).

According to William de Bary (1998a), moreover, classical Confucianism espouses the virtues of democratic civil society, including the benefits of free political discussion and open criticism of those in power to the extent to which it can be compatible with democracy. Edward Shils (1996) goes even further and argues that Confucian values of trustworthiness, reciprocity, civility, and tolerance are not only compatible with but also indispensable to the development of democratic civil society.

Strong civil societies have long played a role in East Asian history and culture, with the most prominent civic movements found in Korea.

Although it is difficult to identify the exact time when societal organizations emerged in Korea, scholars suggest that such groups first gained traction during the Choson dynasty of the early nineteenth century (Cho 1997). Because the Korean national identity was facing serious threats from Chinese and Japanese mercantilists at the time, progressive intellectuals formed independent associations designed to prevent foreign influences from eroding traditional norms. In Korea's case, civil society was created to preserve the nation's very identity. Korea's civil society also relied on the Confucian tradition of remonstrance, providing citizens with a greater opportunity to communicate with political elites than in China and Japan. Contemporary Korean scholars argue that the emerging civic movements during the Choson dynasty were the first instances of state capitulation to popular demand anywhere in East Asia (Cho 1997).

It is important to note that the similarity between Confucianism and Western democracy promoted by scholars in this school of thought is concerned primarily with *societal*, rather than *political*, participation. Civic organizations have a long history in East Asia and often serve as a mediating factor between the state and the family. Confucianism's historical view of political participation is less established, given that, as described earlier, citizens are expected to remain content and loyal if their state's leader behaves virtuously and responsibly. Thus widespread political participation is a much more recent phenomenon in the region and is not as closely attuned to Confucian ideals as is societal participation.

In short, the Confucian ideas of benevolent government, the duty consciousness of the elite, and the right of the people to remonstrance and revolution are all consistent with democratic demands for civility, impartiality, and public accountability. For this reason, Tu Weiming (1996c, 546) concludes that "democracy with Confucian characteristics is not only imaginable but also practicable."

The Convergence Argument

In the scholarly works reviewed so far, there is a tendency to evaluate the relationship between democracy and Confucianism as dichotomous – Confucian values are perceived as either compatible or incompatible with democracy. Such dichotomous perceptions often overlook the similarities between the two phenomena and fail to take note of their potential to overlap, in which case their relationship actually becomes much more complex, with each being transformed by a host of other factors. When they focus exclusively either on the democratic or undemocratic Confucian values, scholars are likely to ignore the intricacies of the relationship between Confucianism and democracy and overlook the areas of their potential linkage as well.

An increasing number of scholars have recently begun to note that Confucianism and democracy can be reformulated in such a way to build new and hybrid regimes throughout the region (Bai 2008; Bell 2006; S. M. Kim 2008, 2010; Y. Kim 1997; Tan 2003a). On the one hand, proponents of this perspective perceive traditional Confucian values of order and efficiency as helpful for building stronger democracies, because such norms promote societal stability and cooperation. On the other hand, they recognize that the introduction of democracy into East Asia can encourage the growth of liberal thought and self-reliance, while still respecting the Confucian ideals of the common good and mutual responsibility. This final section surveys scholarly work on possible *convergences* between Confucianism and democracy and evaluates ways in which each might build on the other to create new forms of governance.

Although democracy and Confucianism clash on several significant points, many scholars have identified elements of each doctrine that can benefit both. One of the most prominent linkages between the two doctrines concerns the Confucian conception of human rights (de Bary 1991; J. Chan 1999; Freeman 1996; Tu 2002). The Confucian principles of benevolence and reciprocity stress humanism, or consideration of other people in society. In East Asia today, governmental leaders might find it desirable to limit certain liberties to maintain political power, but they can reformulate these principles of humanism to promote democratic government for the people, not just by the people. Confucianism could also be used to strengthen existing democracies in East Asia. Yung-Myung Kim (1997), for example, points out that the Confucian emphasis on societal order and respect for authority might indeed enhance the survival of burgeoning democracies.

Institutionally, what features might a fusion of Confucian and democratic governance possess? Daniel A. Bell (2006) argues that government solely by the people is inappropriate for historically Confucian societies, because democratically elected representatives might not be fully able to assess the long-term consequences of their decisions. He proposes instead a system combining Confucian ideals of government by intellectual elites with liberal ideals of electoral accountability of government to its citizens, using both traditional and modern institutional frameworks. More specifically, his model of Confucian democracy consists of two chambers of policy makers – a lower chamber elected by the people and an upper chamber selected on the basis of competitive examinations. Shielded from the demands of voters concerned with their short-term interests, the upper chamber would be able to serve the interests of the people as a whole. Bell's ideal upper chamber would also be able to protect unpopular individuals and vulnerable minorities from the verdicts of majorities in the lower house (Bell 2006).

It is entirely possible that Confucian values might be used to amend the less desirable aspects of Western liberal democracy. Confucian norms can remedy problems such as rampant individualism and lack of commitment to family and community. Democracy, when forged with Confucian ideals, could produce a uniquely regional system that combines the principle of government by the people with that of government for the people. Sor-hoon Tan (2003a) proposes such an alternative to liberal democracy in *Confucian Democracy*. Tan argues that, unlike a liberal democracy that operates under the constraints of interest groups, Confucian democracy is capable of promoting both individual freedom and the common good. To put such a notion of Confucian democracy into practice, however, Tu Weiming (2000, 211) points out that we have to find out how Confucianism can be democratized and how democracy can be Confucianized. This is because "the present institutional forms of Asian Confucianism and Western democracies are sufficiently distinct to preclude a marrying of the two" (Hall and Ames 2003, 124).

Ensuring the mutual existence of liberal democracy and Confucianism in East Asia, therefore, requires a great deal of effort, but scholars in this third and final school of thought believe that such goals are entirely achievable. Electoral democracy and Confucian practices both possess some innate flaws, and arriving at a convergence between the two may be the best way to prevent any future problems. Sor-hoonTan's promotion of Confucian democracy and Daniel A. Bell's notion of a legislature based on both democratic principles and Confucian ideals serve as important theoretical steps on the path to implementing such systems. It is difficult to predict the developmental passage that democratic governance will take in East Asia, but the growing convergence between history and modernization will certainly be an interesting and dynamic journey.

Empirical Studies

How does Confucianism affect democracy? Can Confucianism accommodate democratic politics? To date, the debate on the relationship between Confucianism and democracy has been mostly conjecture and lacks empirical validation, although it has helped identify the important components that underlie each of the three theories of their relationship. Remaining largely speculative, without empirical support, theoretical interpretations need to be tested against the patterns of the relationship that actually exist in the minds of the people of historically Confucian societies.

Scholars have only recently begun to use public opinion data from East Asia to assess the impact of Confucian values on the democratization process taking place among individual citizens. The Asian Barometer Surveys, the World Values Surveys, and other national public opinion surveys, such as the Korea Democracy Barometer (Shin 1999), have asked for citizens' opinions on traditional Confucian values such as family values, conformity, communalism, deference to authority, and strong leadership. However, these studies have not reached consensus on whether people in historically Confucian Asia hold unique cultural values and how those values affect their reactions to democracy.

Do people in the region hold characteristically or uniquely Asian or Confucian values as compared to people in non-Confucian Asia or those in the West? To explore this and other related questions, Jean Blondel and Takashi Inoguchi (2006) analyzed the Asia-Europe Surveys conducted in nine countries in Europe and nine countries in East and Southeast Asia during summer 2000.[5] Their analysis of the interregional surveys revealed that the political cultures of East Asian and European regions differ in degree. Those differences, however, "are not large enough to allow for the conclusion that the countries of East and Southeast Asia hold 'Asian Values' which are pitched against the 'Western Values' of Western European countries" (Blondel and Inoguchi 2006, 63).

A recent analysis of the third and fourth waves of the World Values Surveys (WVS) by Russell Dalton and Nhu-Ngoc Ong (2006, 102) also revealed that "acceptance of authority is not sharply different between these East Asian nations and a set of established Western democracies around the Pacific Rim." They found more variation in authoritarian orientations among Confucian Asians than among their peers in other regions. These findings run counter to the Incompatibility Thesis that holds that respect for authority is significantly greater in Confucian Asia.

[5] The eighteen countries surveyed are Japan, South Korea, China, Taiwan, Singapore, Malaysia, Indonesia, Thailand, and the Philippines from East and Southeast Asia and the United Kingdom, Ireland, France, Germany, Sweden, Italy, Spain, Portugal, and Greece from Western Europe.

Zhengxu Wang and Ern-Ser Tan (2006) factor analyzed the same WVS and found that Confucian East Asians hold some common values and beliefs that are different from those held by non-Confucian Asians; however, these researchers are not fully in agreement with the central claim of the Asian Values Thesis that Confucian East Asia constitutes a distinct cultural zone (see also Wang 2008). They claim that Confucian Asians are more inclined toward a vision of good government featuring a paternalistic state that provides for the people and in which strong leadership is conducive to effective governance.

So Young Kim's (2010) more recent analysis of the World Values Surveys IV and the Asian Barometer Surveys I and II, however, revealed little difference between Confucian Asians and non-Confucian Asians in their orientations to two of four Asian Value dimensions: communalism and work ethic. In the two other dimensions, authoritarianism and familism, however, they differ significantly. Contrary to what is expected from the Incompatibility Thesis, Confucian Asians are significantly less attached to the norms of familism and authoritarianism than non-Confucian Asians. This finding challenges the central claim of the Confucian Asian Values Thesis.

Most recently, Christian Welzel (2011) analyzed the latest, fifth wave of the World Values Surveys to determine whether people in Confucian East Asia are significantly different from people in non-Confucian Asia and regions of the West in endorsing human rights and liberal democracy. In upholding both the emancipative values of the Western Enlightenment and the liberal notion of democracy, Confucian Asians trail the citizenries of the West, but they lead non-Confucian Asians; however, their deficit in relation to the West is merely one of degree, not one of category.

Does attachment to Confucian values deter people from embracing the values of democratic politics? Russell Dalton and Nhu-Ngoc Ong (2006) examined how social authority orientations in six historically Confucian countries affect popular support for democracy. Their analysis of the WVS revealed no strongly significant relationship between the two variables. Contrary to what is expected from the Incompatibility Thesis, a belief in parental respect, obedience, and deference to authority is not a powerful force deterring people in those countries from supporting democracy.

By contrast, Yu-Tzung Chang, Yun-han Chu, and Frank Tsai (2005), and Yu-Tzung Chang and Yun-han Chu (2007) found that, among the people in China, Taiwan, and Hong Kong, Confucian family values detract significantly from popular support for the democratic values of political freedom and equality. Among South Koreans, Chong-Min Park and Doh Chull Shin (2006) also found that adherence to the Confucian norms rejecting adversarial politics detracts from support for democracy. These negative relationships between Confucian and democratic values support the Incompatibility Thesis. By contrast, Joel Fetzer and J. Christopher Soper (2007) found that, among the Taiwanese, placing a value on family loyalty actually increases support for democracy and women's rights. This finding that Confucianism strengthens support for human rights confirms the Compatibility Thesis.

All in all, the results of these empirical studies are not consistently supportive of any of the three contrasting theories discussed earlier. The direction and magnitude of the relationships between Confucian and democratic values vary considerably from one study to another and from one country to another. These differences are largely due to the divergent conceptions of the two variables and the divergent measurements of selected components of each variable.

For all these differences, these studies are alike in failing both to consider all or most of the core norms and values of Confucianism and to examine their distribution throughout the entire region of historically Confucian Asia. As a result, they provide little information about the extent to which people in the region as a whole are attached to all those norms and values. Equally little is known about the particular population segments that are most and least attached to Confucianism.

In addition, previous studies have all failed to examine the effects of Confucian cultural legacies on both the civic and political dimensions of cultural democratization. In studying these legacies' effects on the political dimension, moreover, they failed to consider both the cognitive and affective dimensions of democratic political orientations. Theoretically also, they made no serious effort to estimate the influence of democratic or authoritarian rule on adherence to Confucianism. The extant empirical literature on Confucianism provides neither a comprehensive nor balanced account of its linkage with cultural democratization.

Summary and Conclusions

Decades of theoretical debate and empirical research on Confucian political culture and East Asian democratization have failed to produce much agreement on the relationship between Confucianism and democracy as a system of political ideas. Theoretical, philosophical, and empirical research efforts have generally taken one of three interpretations: *compatibility*, *incompatibility*, and *convergence*. Those in the *compatibility* camp reject the portrayal of democracy and Confucianism as antithetical doctrines. Instead, their interpretations reveal numerous shared values and traditions. Categorizing Confucianism as inherently opposed to liberalism disregards a number of pro-democratic values and norms that can promote the goals of liberal democracy, such as elite accountability, citizen dissent and equality, the formation of civic groups, and pluralism.

In striking contrast, those in the *incompatibility* camp posit that the Confucian principles of ethical meritocracy and paternalism run counter to fundamental democratic values and principles, including those of popular sovereignty, political equality, and individual rights (J. Chan 2007). Moreover, Confucian interpersonal norms, especially of loyalty (*zhong*) and appropriateness (*yi*), do not allow people to make political choices for themselves democratically as the democratic norms of individual rights and freedom do (Li 1997). A third group of scholars pursues a middle ground, acknowledging that, although Confucianism and democracy might not be innately compatible, some characteristics of the two systems can still be reformulated to create uniquely hybrid systems in the region.

Clearly, the two doctrines of Confucianism and democracy espouse vastly different value systems and governmental structures. Any relationship between them therefore would seem to be inherently problematic. Yet, as reviewed earlier, conceptions about the compatibility of Confucianism and democracy do not lend themselves to such clean-cut conclusions. Indeed, scholars have vigorously, and often convincingly, debated both the compatibility and incompatibility of Confucianism and democracy.

Why is there so much debate and division over the compatibility between Confucianism and democracy, and why has the debate persisted for so long? To begin with, disagreements originate over which *concepts* of Confucianism and democracy should be used in analyses and how they should be conceptualized. Divergent conceptualizations of Confucianism and democracy have contributed to different interpretations of their relationships (J. Chan 2007; Collins 2008; S. Hu 1997; Xu 2006).

Democracy has been conceptualized procedurally as government by the people or substantively as government for the people. Similarly, Confucianism has been conceptualized liberally in terms of benevolence, reciprocity, and other humanistic values or nonliberally in terms of conformity, duty, loyalty, and other authoritarian values. Those who define democracy substantively and/or Confucianism liberally tend to promote the *pro-democratic* argument of compatibility (de Bary 1991; L. Hsu 1975; Tu 2002). Those who conceptualize democracy procedurally and/or Confucianism nonliberally tend to advocate the *antidemocratic argument* of incompatibility (Huntington 1996; X. Kang 2006; Li 1997). Those who define either democracy procedurally and Confucianism liberally or democracy substantively and Confucianism nonliberally are likely to subscribe to the convergence argument (Ackerly 2005; Bell 2006; Hahm 2004; Tan 2003a, 2007). Such divergent conceptualizations are at the heart of the compatibility debate and have spurred conflicting perspectives in political and philosophical research.

From this ongoing debate, two conclusions can be drawn about Confucianism as an influence on democracy. First, Confucianism, like all other political and religious doctrines, is multivocal, containing both pro-democratic and antidemocratic elements (Stepan 2000). Depending on the properties that one considers most essential or fundamental to democracy, therefore, Confucianism can be viewed as more antidemocratic than pro-democratic or as more pro-democratic than antidemocratic. However, a more accurate view is to characterize the entire system of Confucian political ethics or doctrine as supporting a semi-authoritarian or semi-democratic hybrid regime, instead of calling it either an exclusively pro-democratic or exclusively antidemocratic regime, as Samuel Huntington does.[6] This is because government becomes fully democratic only when it works by the people and for the people in parallel.

In addition, Confucianism constitutes a general system of thought capable of comprehending and addressing a variety of human concerns and problems in addition to those dealing with government. It offers a critical perspective on the serious problems that many liberal or procedural democracies of the West face these days. Its emphasis on the need to protect the economically disadvantaged and to develop a strong sense of community enables it to serve as a counterbalance to excessive individualism and highly limited electoral democracy (Tu 1996c). When integrated with the procedural form of democracy, therefore, Confucian democracy may be able to offer a communitarian alternative to Western liberal democracy, which can be a more generous, kinder, and gentler democracy (Ackerly 2005; Fox 1997; S. M. Kim 2008; Tan 2003a, 2007; Tu 2000).

---

[6] Collier and Adcock (1999) offer a balanced review of the debate on the merits of dichotomous versus continuous measures of democracy.

PART II

UPHOLDING CONFUCIAN LEGACIES

3

Confucianism as a Hierarchical Way of Life

In the West, for centuries Confucius has been known as the founder of Confucianism, but interestingly, in China where he was born in the small feudal state of Lu and lived his entire life (551–479 B.C), there is no term equivalent to Confucianism (Tu 1998a, 3), nor is there any corresponding term in any of the other East Asian countries where he has been honored and respected as the most influential philosopher and teacher for more than two thousand years. In the sixteenth century, an Italian Jesuit priest, Matteo Ricci, coined the term "Confucianism" after he Latinized the name "Kong Fuzi" to "Confucius" and introduced to Europeans Confucius's teachings and those of his disciples. Subsequently, Confucianism influenced Voltaire and other European Enlightenment thinkers (Creel 1949, chap. 15; Mungello 1991; see also Collins 2008).

In the West, Confucianism was introduced as China's traditional system of social ethics, which Confucius, Mencius, and their students explicated in the works known as the Confucian classics (Yao 2000, 47–67). The most important of these works are *The Analects* of Confucius, a collection of conversations, questions, and answers between Confucius and his students, and the seven books of Mencius (371–289 B.C.), who was a principal interpreter and defender of Confucius's teachings. For the past two thousand years, the ideas presented in these two Confucian classics and others, including *The Great Learning* and *The Doctrine of the Mean*, have been subjected to different applications and interpretations (Tan 2003a, 7). As a result, Confucianism as a concept has taken on a variety of meanings in different places and at different times (Nosco 2008, 21; Tu 1994, 146–9; see also C. Cheng 2002).

Indeed, Confucianism refers to a wide variety of principles and practices that are neither homogeneous nor monolithic (Nosco 2008; Tu 1986). In an attempt to categorize its diversity, scholars have divided Confucianism into several pairs of subtypes. The pair of "classical Confucianism" and "neo-Confucianism" highlights how its meaning has changed over time. In contrast, the pairs of philosophical and political Confucianism, and idealistic and naturalistic Confucianism, highlight the substantive differences in its meaning (W. Chan 1963). Classical Confucianism is further divided into the subcategories of traditionalism and moralism (Yao 2000).

Although there are clearly different interpretations of Confucianism, there is a general agreement in the scholarly community that it is not a religion; instead it is a system of ethics dealing exclusively with the affairs of this world.[1] As a system of ethics, it has deeply influenced life in East Asia for more than two thousand years. As discussed in Chapter 1, its influence as a guide to private and public life is still evident in China, Taiwan, Hong Kong, Japan, Korea, Singapore, and Vietnam, a group that comprises historically Confucian East Asia. It is for this reason that "a picture of China and East Asia which takes no account of Confucianism is partial and superficial" (Yao 2000, 277). In these and other Confucian-influenced societies in Asia, moreover, Confucianism is increasingly recognized as a living tradition capable of moderating the undesirable consequences of democratization, marketization, and globalization (Bell 2008a; Yao 1999).

In this study, I define "Confucianism" as a general system of social and political ethics that Confucius, Mencius, and their followers advocated to build a moral community of *datong shehui* (grand harmony or unity) in which people can live a happy and worthy life. As a system of social ethics, Confucianism sets forth an ideal culture or a way of life that people ought to practice to live virtuously (Bell 2008c, 113–15). As a system of political ethics, Confucianism refers to a model or system of government that aims to build a community of harmony and peace (M. Dawson 1942; L. Hsu 1975). A detailed account of this community is provided in the following passage from *The Book of Rites* (*Li chi*), a collection of essays that Confucius compiled and edited (L. Hsu 1975, 25; Yao 2001, 53).

---

[1] A few scholars, like Tu Weiming and Xinzhong Yao, interpret Confucianism as a civil religion.

When the Great Way was practiced, the world was shared by all alike. The worthy and the able were promoted to office and men practiced good faith and lived in affection. Therefore, they did not regard as parents only their own parents, or as sons only their own sons. The aged found a fitting close to their lives, the robust their proper employment; the young were provided with an upbringing and the widow and widower, the orphaned and the sick, with proper care. Men had their tasks and women their hearths. They hated to see goods lying about in waste, yet they did not hoard them for themselves; they disliked the thought that their energies were not fully used, yet they used them not for private ends. Therefore all evil plotting was prevented and thieves and rebels did not arise, so that people could leave their outer gates unbolted. This was the age of Grand Unity.

Confucius, Mencius, Xunzi, and other early Confucians considered the breakdown of political order and social harmony to be the most fundamental problem of human life and located its roots in the moral degeneration of human beings. To build a fiduciary or moral community of *datong* in which people would live in peace and happiness selflessly, Confucius and his disciples advocated the ethical cultivation of every member of the community. Their vision of *datong* is predicated on the belief that humans are inherently social beings with moral integrity.

Accordingly, the Confucian ethical system emphasizes the importance of cultivating humanity through entering mutually beneficial relationships with other people. To foster a mutually beneficial social life, the ethical system identifies five cardinal human relationships and prescribes the appropriate norms or virtues that people involved in each of these relationships ought to observe. In addition, the Confucian ethical system recognizes the state as the most important human institution for building a community of grand harmony and offers a model of good government and leadership that can serve to promote the economic welfare and moral and intellectual development of the masses.

In this chapter, I examine the social dimension of the Confucian ethical system as a way of life aiming to promote social harmony and then highlight its differences from three other ways of life. To this end, I first explicate the Confucian notion of human nature as the philosophical foundation of the ethical system that Confucius and Mencius advocated. Then I examine the Confucian way of life in terms of the key principles or virtues that guide personal conduct and promote harmonious interpersonal relationships. I then compare Confucianism with three other ways of life and explore all of their implications for democratic politics. Finally, I compare and contrast the extent to which people in five of the six Confucian East Asian societies – China, Japan, Korea, Taiwan, and

Vietnam – practice the Confucian way of life and compare and contrast the East Asian region with six other cultural zones throughout the globe.

The Notion of Human Nature

What does it mean to be a human being? What should be done to become fully human? These are the two fundamental philosophical questions addressed in the works of Confucius, Mencius, and other early Confucians (Tu 1985, 1999). In the Confucian conception of humanity, the ultimate goal of being human is to become a good or virtuous person who curbs one's ego and serves other people selflessly. According to Mencius, "A man neither benevolent nor wise, devoid of courtesy and dutifulness, is a slave" (*Mencius* 2A:7), and "if he reveres virtue and delights in rightness, he can be content" without being "led astray by wicked world" (*Mencius* 7B:10).

For all early Confucians, the key to living in happiness and peace is to become virtuous. Accordingly, their fundamental concern was to ensure the cultivation of virtuous character traits by the common people and government officials. In the belief that people can become virtuous in character and deed through constant interactions with others, they offered a system of ethics, which contrasts sharply with the *liberal system* of ethics created by Western thinkers of the Enlightenment.

The Confucian ethical system is built on four basic premises concerning human mind and nature (Munro 1969; Scarpari 2003; Shun and Wong 2004). The first premise is that we humans are intrinsically good in nature and are capable of perfecting ourselves through the cultivation of the self. Second, humans are not autonomous individuals, but instead are social beings who belong in relationship with others. The third premise is that humans can cultivate themselves and become fully human only through "entering continuous dialogue with others" and fulfilling mutually complementary roles. Finally, the cultivation of self is the root of social order, and social order is the basis of political stability and universal peace.

The belief that humans are innately good and become better through self-cultivation and moral education is an important feature of Confucianism. Confucius believed that "man is born with uprightness; if he loses high uprightness, and yet lives, his escape from death is the effect of mere good fortune" (*Analects* 6:19). According to Mencius, "There is no man who is not good; there is no water that does not flow downwards" (6A:2). "No man is devoid of a heart sensitive to the suffering of others" (2A:6), and every person is "capable of becoming good" (6A:6).

He further pointed out that all humans possess the "germs" of the four cardinal virtues:

The heart of compassion is the germ of benevolence [*ren*]; the heart of shame, of dutifulness [*yi*]; the heart of courtesy and modesty, of observance of the rites [*li*]; the heart of right and wrong, of wisdom [*zhi*]. Man has these four germs just as he has four limbs.... If a man is able to develop all these four germs that he possesses, it will be like a fire starting up or a spring coming through. If these are fully developed, he can tend the whole realm within the Four Seas, but if he fails to develop them, he will not be able even to serve his parents (*Mencius* 2A:6, 6A:6).

Early Confucian thinkers believed that all humans are born with the potential for goodness and the capacity to fulfill this potential. They also believed that this moral potential is not always fulfilled because the social environment in which people live deters its realization. To emphasize this viewpoint, Confucius said, "By nature men are similar; by practice men are wide apart" (*Analects* 17: 2). In the belief that people's characters become differentiated through the various environments and practices in which they live, he and his followers recognized the importance of spreading education to all segments of the population to facilitate the realization of their moral potential. Mencius, for example, claimed, "Now men possess a moral nature; but if they were well fed, warmly clad, and comfortably lodged, without being taught at the same time, they become almost like the beast" (*Mencius* 3A:4), and "the sole concern of learning is to go after this stray heart" (*Mencius* 6A:11). To fix the stray heart, early Confucians emphasized the importance of cultivating people from all walks of life, from the emperor to the commoner.

In the belief that such cultivation is essential for the development of harmonious relations with others, they also claimed that personal cultivation serves as the foundation of the orderly state, the good society, and the entire world, as suggested in the following passage from *The Great Learning* (1:4):

When the personal life is cultivated, the family will be regulated. When the family is regulated, the state will be in order. When the state is in order, there will be peace through the world. From the Son of Heaven down to the common people, all must regard cultivation of the person as the root or foundation. There is never a case when the root is in disorder and yet the branches are not in order.

As Tu Weiming (1994, 193) notes, the Confucian notion of self-cultivation is therefore grounded in an "anthropocosmic" vision of humanity, which refers to much more than an internal, subjective search for one's own individuality. It is both a multidimensional – mental and physical – and multilevel (individual and collective) phenomenon (Li 2008b). As a multidimensional phenomenon, the process of self-cultivation involves not only disciplining and training the body but also enlightening the mind and the soul. As a multilevel phenomenon, it requires continual participation in ever larger associations, including one's own family, neighborhood, community, and the state, each of which constitutes an environment for learning to be human.

For all early Confucians, self-cultivation through education was not a lonely quest for one's inner spirituality, but instead was a communal act – a collective and collaborative act of continuous interactions with other human beings (Tu 1985). Therefore education has two interrelated purposes. The first purpose is to learn to cultivate virtues and become an upright, moral, and complete person, or a gentleman or exemplary person (*junzi*). The second purpose is to serve other people and the larger community by practicing and extending what is learned. Of these two purposes, the higher one – indeed the ultimate aim of Confucian ethics – is the latter one: aiming to become a civilized member of society in which people help each other (Ng 2009).

In Confucianism, therefore, fulfilling responsibilities to other people takes priority over exercising individual rights. To underline the importance of these responsibilities, Confucius said, "Now the man of perfect virtue, wishing to establish himself, seeks also to establish others; wishing to enlarge himself, he seeks also to enlarge others" (*Analects* 6:28). "The superior man cultivates himself so as to give the common people security and peace" (*Analects* 14:42).

In short, the Confucian system of ethics contrasts sharply with the liberal ethical system of the West in its conceptions of human nature and the good society. The liberal system is one of adversarial relationships in which priority is given to individual autonomy and freedom, allowing individuals to pursue and claim their own interests and rights. In contrast, the Confucian system gives priority to fulfilling social obligations and requires the cultivation of virtuous individuals who help others and are, in turn, helped by others. Whereas the Western liberal system of ethics is built on autonomous individuals and aims to protect their contractual relationships, the Confucian system seeks to develop a community of mutual trust by promoting affective relationships among its members (Rosemont, 2008, 49; Tu 1994, 196–7).

Of the two systems, it is Confucianism that encourages both self-improvement and social responsibility at the same time. In principle, therefore, it can be considered better designed than liberalism for facilitating the building of a humane and just society in which the dignity of each individual is recognized and material goods are equally distributed.

The Proper Way of Life

As mentioned earlier, in Confucianism, humans are viewed as social beings; their cultivation depends on being linked to other fellow humans. Confucius pointed out, "I cannot run with the birds and beasts. Am I not one among the people of this world? If not them, with whom should I associate?" (*Analects* 18:6). Therefore, Herbert Fingarette (1983, 217) proclaims, "For Confucius, unless there are at least two human beings, there are no human beings." Individuals do not exist as single, separate entities but stand in the midst of partly concentric, partly overlapping circles of relationships (Tu 1994, 144). Only through constant communication and interaction with others in these circles can humans overcome selfishness and self-centeredness and become fully human.

In Confucianism, humans, in contrast to other animals, are viewed as social beings who also have moral integrity. Because humans are moral beings, Confucianism insists that their relationships with each other ought to be different from the relationships animals or beasts have with each other. In *The Analects* (2:7), Confucius pointed out, "Today people see filial piety merely as looking after parents, but even dogs and horses look after their parents. If one does not respect one's parents, what is the difference between a man and a dog or a horse?" For the entire range of interpersonal relationships, Confucianism spells out the specific norms or principles of moral behavior that both parties in each relationship must observe in interacting with each other as benefactors and beneficiaries. Only when people fulfill these social obligations can they build a community of *datong* or grand harmony.

What are the important roles people ought to play to build such a community? How should they play these roles? Confucianism identifies these roles and their attendant norms in the context of five cardinal relationships (*wu lun*), a term often used to refer to social life in general. The five relationships and their norms are ruler and subject (benevolence and loyalty), father and son (love and reverence), husband and wife (obligation and submission), elder and younger brothers (seniority and courtesy), and friend and friend (fraternity). When asked to elaborate on the nature of each relationship, Mencius (3A:4) replied, "Between father and son, there should be affection; between sovereign and minister, duty; and between husband and wife, distinction; between old and young, a proper order, and between friends, faith." Mencius and other early Confucians admonished that, when interacting with other people, each individual should carefully evaluate the nature of the relationship and then play the appropriate role required for that relationship.

One of the five Chinese classics of Confucian literature, *Li Chi* (chapter 9), which Confucius compiled, elaborates on the specific ethical codes that should be honored in each of the five relationships:

What are the things which humans consider righteous? Kindness on the part of the father, and filial duty on that of the son; gentleness on the part of the elder brother, and obedience on that of the younger; righteousness on the part of the husband, and submission on that of the wife; kindness on the part of the elders, and deference on that of juniors; benevolence on the part of the ruler, and loyalty on that of the minister. These are the ten things humans consider to be right.

Underlying all five of these cardinal relationships is a notion of reciprocity that requires each person to fulfill his or her responsibility to another (Dallmayr 2004). In each of these relationships, the superior has the duty of benevolence and care for the subordinate, whereas the subordinate has the duty of being obedient to the superior. However, the subordinate's obedience is not unconditional, but is contingent on the superior's observance of his or her duty to be benevolent. When asked whether there is "any one word that can serve as a principle for the conduct of life," Confucius replied "reciprocity" (*Analects* 15: 24), an answer that rejects a hierarchical arrangement featuring one-way obedience.

In Confucian thinking, therefore, power is contingent on the reciprocal act of exerting benevolence: powerful superiors are always required to act with self-restraint and generosity. Accordingly, the norm of loyalty and obedience is not a slavish kind of unconditional allegiance; quite to the contrary, it even entails the duty to remonstrate with one's superiors.

For Confucius and his early followers, each relationship can become *harmonious* only when the two parties involved meet their complementary and mutual role obligations (Li 2006, 2008b). When both parties engage in a mutually beneficial interchange, they will be able to overcome egoism to become authentically human. When each relationship becomes harmonious, the whole community becomes peaceful and orderly. Therefore Confucianism is sometimes characterized as a philosophy of mutuality or an ethical system of reciprocal relations.

However, although it is hierarchical, it is not a system that stresses one-way obedience, such as that of the "three bonds." The ethics of the three bonds, which scholars of the Han Dynasty court propounded to prescribe the subservience of the minister to the king, the son to the father, and the wife to the husband, is "a far cry from the Mencian idea of the five relationships" and "no longer the teachings of Confucius and his disciples" (Tu 1994, 194).

Wu lun, in the original Mencian conception, not only identifies important interpersonal relations but also specifies appropriate norms to observe in the context of those relationships. These behavioral norms or rules are known in Confucianism as "constant virtues" governing how individuals should act and behave in relation to others. These virtues are *ren* (benevolence, compassion, love); *li* (propriety, politeness); *yi* (righteousness, justice); *zhi* (wisdom); *zhong* (loyalty); *xiao* (filial piety); and *xin* (trust). Confucianism holds that, when everyone acts in accordance with these virtues, there is a harmony in the family and society, and peace in the universe.

Of these virtues, *ren* is the most fundamental one in Confucian moral teaching. Confucius defined it as "loving all men" (*Analects* 12: 22). As the virtue of benevolence and humanness, it forms the basis of all the other virtues and embodies the fulfillment of all the responsibilities one should bear for others. It is expressed through treating all other people with compassion and kindness regardless of their rank or class.

"The man of *ren* is one who, desiring to sustain himself, sustains others, and desiring to develop himself, develop others" (*Analects* 12: 2). Confucius summarized the principle of *ren* in this statement, often called the Golden Rule: "Do not do to others what you would not like them to do to you" (*Analects* 12:2, 15:24). Mencius also said: "Try your best to treat others as you would wish to be treated yourself" (7A.4) and "Do not do what you would not do; do not desire what you would not desire" (7A:17). This rule of Confucianism constitutes the ultimate guide to human action.

Unlike *ren*, which defines love as the ultimate end of interpersonal relationships, *li* constitutes the procedural foundation of all virtues as "a body of unwritten constitutional laws founded on an ethical basis" (L. Hsu 1975, 35). It structures authority and hierarchy by articulating the duties and obligations of each person appropriate to his or her status and role and by specifying the courteous and proper mode of meeting those duties and obligations. Whereas *ren* emphasizes love and affection on the part of the superior, *li* stresses respect and reverence on the part of the subordinate. Therefore, *ren* and *li* represent opposing virtues pulling in different directions.

As A. T. Nuyen (2000) notes, however, *ren* and *li* can also act as countervailing forces against each other and thereby produce a dynamic harmony. Benjamin Schwartz (1985, 82) concurs with this assessment, saying, "Without the constant presence of the will to attain *ren* and all its associated virtues, the *li* will remain empty form. Without the structuring and educative effects of *li*, *ren* as the highest ideal of personal excellence cannot be attained." This study uses these two virtues to examine popular adherence to Confucianism in East Asia and elsewhere.

In summary, Confucian ethical doctrine emphasizes the importance of mutually beneficial reciprocal relationships for the cultivation of personal character and the building of a harmonious community. In every interpersonal relationship, loyalty and obedience from those in a lower position are contingent on how those in a higher position fulfill their responsibilities and vice versa. In the Confucian ethical system, therefore, one relational partner's rights are contained within the responsibilities of the other partner in the same relationship (Hong 2004, 57). As a result, individual rights are not realized directly through one's own actions. Instead, those rights are realized indirectly through the action the other relational partner takes. This system of mutual dependence and responsiveness, which links the realization of individual rights with the fulfillment of social responsibilities, contrasts sharply with the Western ethical system that treats those rights and responsibilities separately.

In Confucian-influenced societies, all interpersonal relationships are held together by a multitude of social roles and statuses. When interacting with others of different roles and statuses, individuals have to abide by multiple norms (Tan and Chee 2005). Because different relationships require individuals to take on different roles, they have to be able to adapt their behavior. As juniors, people ought to obey and revere their seniors, and those seniors have the duty to love and care for their juniors. Being morally binding and mutually dependent, these norms are likely to result in the development of strong personal and *particularistic ties*. Such ties, in turn, are expected to forge strong *affective bonds* between the parties (Hahm and Bell 2004).

The multiplicity of norms guiding hierarchical interpersonal relationships and the prevalence of strong affective ties arising from those relationships can be considered the defining characteristics of Confucianism as a way of social life. This particular way of social life or culture featuring relational-centered and affective-based interactions contrasts sharply with that of the individual-centered and cognitive-based interactions in the West (Bell and Hahm 2003).

The Confucian Way of Life in Comparative Perspective

Confucius, Mencius, and other early Confucians all taught that people would be able to live a good life only when they interact closely with other people and abide by a host of civic norms, including those of *ren* and *li*. The proper way of life they advocated for ordinary citizens and government officials is predicated on the premise that humans are inherently social beings and can thus become fully human only through meaningful and appropriate interactions with others. It is therefore different from other ways of life, especially those advocated by John Locke and other liberal thinkers of the West who do not share the same conception of human sociality.

What type of culture does the Confucian way of life represent? How does it contrast with other ways of life known in the democratized West and other regions of the world? This section addresses these questions in terms of a cultural theory known as the *grid-group cultural theory*, which explains how different ways of life maintain or fail to maintain themselves. I first identify four distinct ways of life known as cultural biases or types and then highlight how Confucianism as a cultural type differs from the three other cultural types.

More than thirty years ago anthropologist Mary Douglas (1978) proposed the grid-group analysis as a heuristic tool for identifying cultural diversity and comparing cultures. Since then, political scientist Aaron Wildavsky (1987) and other scholars have collaborated to develop it as a theory explaining how individual citizens and institutions formulate their preferences and act to realize those preferences in the political process (Thompson, Ellis, and Wildavsky 1990). As a unique way of "combining functionalism and rationality," grid-group analysis "takes the theory of 'bounded rationality' a long step forward" (Selle 1991, 122).

Central to grid-group analysis is the notion that viable ways of life are limited and determined primarily by the patterns of sociality or social relations that people choose. In turn, patterns of social relations depend exclusively on the group with which people associate and the norms or rules that direct their interactions with other people in the group. As Aaron Wildavsky (1987) notes, the first dimension of social life called "group" deals with the question of identification (i.e., Who am I?). The second dimension called "grid" deals with the question of behavior (i.e., How should I behave?). By combining these two key dimensions of social life, proponents and practitioners of the grid-group cultural theory have identified four viable ways of life: hierarchism, individualism, egalitarianism, and fatalism, also called reclusivism. Each of these four ways of life corresponds to a different type of culture representing a particular pattern of the values individuals cherish and the choices they make.

In this grid-group cultural theory, "group" stands for incorporation into a bounded group; it thus separates individuals into "those to interact with" and "those not to interact with." According to Mary Douglas (1978, 14), "The strongest effects of group are to be found where it incorporates a person with the rest by implicating them together in common residence, shared work, shared resources and recreation, and by exerting control over marriage and kinship." In other words, the group dimension of social life refers to the strength of attachment to formal or informal associations. It is strong when those associations are tightly knit and penetrate every aspect of a person's life. It is weak when they are loosely organized and allow their members to come and go as they please without any sense of allegiance or loyalty.

The grid dimension of social life stands for regulations or restrictions on individual behavior. According to Douglas (1978, 8), "The term 'grid' suggests a cross-hatch of rules to which individuals are subject in the course of their interaction. As a dimension, it shows a progressive change in the mode of social control." In other words, "grid" refers to the extent to which people are controlled in their interactions with other members of their own groups and the society in which they live. Therefore, grid becomes strong or weak depending on the number of constraints or restrictions placed on individuals' interactions. Grid becomes strong when the rules and regulations directing people are so powerful that there is little room left for freedom and autonomy. It becomes weak when people do not feel compelled to follow rules and regulations.

To what extent are people bounded by the formal or informal groups with which they affiliate? To what extent do they face and comply with external restrictions on their behavior? Grid-group theorists maintain that the answers to these two questions, which deal with the two key dimensions of social life, hold the key to ascertaining a few and yet viable ways of life (Ellis and Thompson 1997; Thompson 2008; Thompson et al. 1990). These cultural theorists also maintain that people formulate different value preferences and priorities as a consequence of their grid and group positions because their way of life constrains what they want

TABLE 3.1. *A Typology of Cultural Preferences*

		Group Incorporation	
		Low	High
Norm	Low	*Individualism*	*Egalitarianism*
Compliance	High	*Fatalism*	*Hierarchism*

and do. Moreover, their way of life becomes viable only when the patterns of their social relations (group) and cultural bias (grid) are mutually supportive of each other.

Table 3.1 displays a typology of four ways of life in terms of the strength of group affiliation and regulation of social relations. When both group affiliation or identification and external regulation or role prescriptions are weak, the lifestyle falls into the cultural type of *individualism*, shown in the upper left quadrant of Table 3.1. Individualism spawns a competitive culture because it places high priority on the individual pursuit of personal rewards. In this culture, people do not highly value personal ties based on family, ethnicity, and other personal characteristics. Society favors a free flow of people from one type of group to another, which may have widely varying characteristics[2] (Lockhart 2001). People are self-interested and seek to live free of others' control; therefore they are free to negotiate with others as they wish and are able to pursue what they think is the best for themselves. They view fairness in social interactions mainly in terms of equality of available opportunity and blame themselves for their failures rather than institutional malfunctioning. In the individualist way of life, there is much competition and little cooperation among people.

Strong group affiliation together with strong regulation entails a second distinct way of life called *hierarchism*, as shown in the lower right quadrant of the culture map in Table 3.1. Unlike individualism, hierarchism values affiliation with groups formed exclusively on the basis of family and other personal ties. It seeks to maintain strong solidarity among group members by placing highly binding prescriptions on their behavior. These prescriptions are justified on the ground that the collective whole is more important than its individual members. Because it assumes that humans are not equal in capacity, hierarchism emphasizes

---

[2] The distinguishing characteristics of individualism and the three other types of culture, which are presented in this section, are heavily drawn from Lockhart (2001).

respect for authority and the observance of historical customs as well as existing rules and regulations. Furthermore, as in Confucianism, hierarchism also emphasizes the need to differentiate roles for different people so that they can live harmoniously by avoiding competition and conflict. Adherents of hierarchism understand fairness in terms of equality before the law and blame disruptions of the peace on those who do not conform to rules and regulations. Critics of hierarchism argue that the immense trust placed in authority poses a serious risk.

Strong group affiliation coupled with weak regulation produces a third distinct way of life called *egalitarianism*, which is shown in the upper right quadrant of the culture typology. Egalitarianism resembles hierarchism in highly valuing close and exclusive ties among group members. Unlike hierarchism, however, it dismisses the need for authority, regulation, and role differentiation because humans are viewed to be broadly equal in their capacity and capable of reaching collective decisions through discussions and consensus among group members. Egalitarians understand fairness in terms of equality of results. Critics of this way of life point out that an unwillingness to endorse authority as a means to resolve internal conflicts is likely to lead to frequent deadlocks.

Finally, the combination of weak group affiliation with strong regulations produces a culture of *fatalism*, as shown in the lower left quadrant of Table 3.1. People in this type of culture are separated from others by imposition or choice. Either way, they are barred from joining groups by the rules and regulations that control social relations, including the various qualifications set in terms of race, money, and education. As a result, they have no close friends to talk to and no incentive to cooperate with others. Social avoidance rather than social interaction distinguishes fatalists or isolates from the adherents of the other three ways of life. For fatalists or isolates, therefore, there is no such thing as fairness. Because they blame their problems on fate or bad luck, they are not motivated to organize or make plans to change their lives.

Grid-group theorists claim that these four distinct ways of life constitute the viable combinations of social relations. They also claim that every society is *multicultural* because each type of culture needs adherents of other types so it can define and defend it against those types (Douglas 1999; Douglas and Ney 1998). If they contain adherents of only one way of life, societies cannot identify and correct their blind spots. In all societies, therefore, adherents of all four different ways of life or types of culture need to be present in varying proportions (Coughlin and Lockhart 1998; Greenstadt 1999).

Of these four culture types, the Confucian way of life corresponds to *hierarchism* most closely. More than anything else, Confucianism as a way of life emphasizes strong group identification and incorporation, especially with the family group, as further expounded in Chapter 6. In the Confucian world, family constitutes the most fundamental unit of social life; all other groups and organizations are treated merely as an extension of family life. Just as the family consists of highly differentiated roles, so do all other groups and organizations, which are ordered hierarchically with superiors and subordinates fulfilling their respective roles. In fulfilling those roles, individuals are required to abide by a variety of norms. Because individuals feel a strong identification with their families and accept strong prescriptions on social relations, Confucianism as a way of life resembles an ideal type of hierarchical culture.

Cultural Preferences and Democracy

In no society do all members value the same things for either their own lives or their country's well-being; neither is there any society in which all members prefer to live in the same way (Halman et al. 2007). Consequently, all four types of cultures discussed earlier are present in every society. Of the four cultural types, which one is most congruent with the principles of democratic politics? What particular mix of cultural types would be most conducive to the performance of democratic political systems? These two questions have been a central theoretical concern of political scientists who study culture in terms of the grid and group dimensions of social life (Thompson et al. 1990; Wildavsky 1987).

Among these scholars there is a general agreement that people of different cultures have different feelings about living in a democracy, and their preference and commitment to democracy vary considerably according to their preferred cultural type. For example, according to Aaron Wildavsky (1987, 2), "Once people decide to live by hierarchical or egalitarian or market relationship, it follows that they will adopt corresponding types of political systems." The more congruent a culture's interpersonal relations are with the power relations defined in democracy, the more strongly upholders of that culture will prefer to live in a democracy and commit themselves to it (Shin et al. 1989, 221).

Democracy is government by the people. Unlike its alternatives, therefore, it allows individual citizens to participate and compete in the political process freely with minimal interference from either other people or government authorities. These democratic principles of free participation and fair competition are congruent with those of individualism, which allow individuals to compete with others free of social prescriptions and to pursue their own interests independent of their group. In contrast, these democratic principles are incongruent with those of hierarchism, which require individuals to follow orders from their superiors and to prioritize the interest of the collective over their own.

However, democracy is not a system of complete freedom and unbridled competition. As practiced around the world today, democracy involves the rule of law and protects those either not represented or underrepresented in the political process. Thus, it needs upholders of hierarchism and egalitarianism to function well. Hierarchs make sure that all the rules and regulations of democratic governance are enforced, whereas egalitarians encourage political leaders to provide for those who are not represented in the political process (Wildavsky 1993).

Even so, cultural theorists claim that citizen preferences for and commitments to democracy are strongest among upholders of an individualist culture because, although the rule of law and protections for the weak are found in democracies, its core principles are freedom and fair competition. Preference for and commitment to these central democratic principles would be weakest among those of a hierarchical culture in which orders come down and obedience flows up. Between individualism and egalitarianism, both of which accept only a minimum level of social control, the democratic principles of freedom and competition are less congruent with egalitarianism because it does not allow for competition among group members. Between individualism and fatalism or reclusivism, both of which reject strong group ties, the democratic principles of freedom and competition are less congruent with fatalism because it accepts a high level of social control that restricts individual freedom. Between fatalism and hierarchism, the democratic principles are less congruent with the former because it encourages people to withdraw from politics.

Of the four cultural types, therefore, individualism is considered most compatible with democracy and fatalism is the least. Democracy cannot survive without upholders of individualist culture, who would demand that competitive elections take place and defeated politicians leave office (Thompson et al. 1990, 256). Yet, again, democracy needs adherents of other cultures to fill its other requirements, as shown earlier and summarized by Wildavsky (1993, 82–3):

The more individualism, the political conclusion would be, the more polyarchy. However, if individualism were dominant over long periods, many citizens might become fatalists, unable to found networks of their own, so that competition would likely give way to some form of control. Therefore without significant elements of egalitarianism to challenge inequality, without hierarchy to inculcate the norm that the parts should sacrifice the whole, and without individualism to legitimize accepting the results of competitive elections, democracy is doubtful.

In short, the survival of a democratic political system depends on the embrace of individualism by the citizenry. Individualists therefore should form the largest group of cultural adherents to ensure the endurance of democracies, especially those newly installed. The good performance of all democracies, however, does not depend solely on the dominance of individualists over other cultural adherents. The quality of democratic governance has more to do with the extent to which individualism, egalitarianism, and hierarchism are balanced. This is the reason why Wildavsky (1993) characterizes democracy as "a coalition of cultures."

The Confucian Way of Life in Practice

How do the contemporary publics of Confucian Asia live their lives? Do they practice a hierarchical way of life and remain hierarchs as Confucius and other early Confucians admonished? Or have they shifted away from the Confucian way of life in the wake of modernization and globalization and become individualists or egalitarians? Are people in Confucian Asia more attached to the culture of hierarchism than are their peers in other regions? This section explores these questions using the latest, fifth wave of the World Values Surveys (WVS) conducted in fifty-seven countries covering all regions of the globe. Included in the surveys are five East Asian Confucian countries: China, Japan, South Korea, Taiwan, and Vietnam.

From the WVS, I selected two pairs of items to measure the two key dimensions of social relations: group and grid. For the group dimension, I selected a pair of items tapping identification with and incorporation into the groups of family and friends, respectively. Together these two groups encompass four of the five cardinal relationships known in Confucianism. The family involves three of those four relationships: the relationship between father and son, between husband and wife, and between elder and younger brothers. Friends as a group cover the fourth cardinal relationship between friends. The only cardinal relationship excluded from consideration is the relationship between ruler and subject.

To measure the strength of family ties, I chose Item V64 that asked respondents how strongly they agree or disagree with this statement:

"One of my main goals in life has been to make my parents proud." To measure the strength of friendship ties, I chose Item V66 that asked how strongly they agree or disagree with this statement: "I put forth a lot of effort to live up to what my friends expect." Responses to these items were measured on a 4-point numerical scale. By summing the values of both responses, I constructed a 7-point index of group strength. Those who scored above the index median of 3.0 are considered highly attached to the group.

To measure the strength of grid or regulation of social relations, I selected a pair of items (V84 and V87) that deal, respectively, with *ren* (benevolence) and *li* (propriety), the two most important Confucian norms guiding social life. Item V84 taps orientations to the norm of *ren* by asking respondents to what extent they are like the person who "helps the people nearby; to take care for their well-being." The second item, V87, taps orientations to the norm of *li* by asking them to what extent they are like the person who "always behaves properly; to avoid doing anything people would say is wrong."

To answer these two items, respondents were allowed to choose one of six response categories ranging from "very much like me" to "not at all like me." To construct a 4-point scale, the lowest three negative categories were collapsed into the fourth lowest category. As done with the two items tapping group strength, I combined the resulting two 4-point scales tapping attachment to the norms of *ren* and *li* into a 7-point index of grid strength. Those who scored above the index mean of 3 are considered highly constrained by the two Confucian norms guiding interpersonal relationships.

For each of the five East Asian Confucian countries, Table 3.2 reports the strength of group ties using the proportions affirming group identification with their family and friends with a positive rating on the 4-point verbal scale.[3] It also reports the proportions identified with neither and both of these two groups, and the proportions strongly identified with each, neither, and both groups. In all five Confucian countries, the majorities are attached to their family, as evidenced by their strong desire to make their parents proud, and they show attachment to their friends by trying to live up to what their friends expect.

---

[3] The main goal of the data analysis here is to identify the most and least prevalent types of culture in each country and compare those across five countries in historically Confucian Asia and across the regions of the world. Accordingly, I excluded nonrespondents when calculating the proportions reported in this chapter.

TABLE 3.2. *Attachment to Family and Friends*

Country	Percent Generally Attached				Percent Strongly Attached			
	Family	Friends	None	Both	Family	Friends	None	Both
Japan	69.9	54.3	24.9	46.4	6.3	1.8	91.8	0.9
Korea	75.8	77.4	9.2	62.4	21.6	14.1	71.2	7.0
Taiwan	85.2	66.2	9.0	58.5	18.3	6.8	78.8	3.9
China	72.6	75.0	12.4	59.6	13.5	8.0	81.9	4.5
Vietnam	92.1	64.3	7.2	65.3	40.0	13.3	58.3	12.5
(Pooled)	79.7	67.9	11.2	59.8	21.0	9.5	74.6	6.4

Source: 2005–8 World Values Surveys.

The size of the majorities attached to the groups of family and friends varies considerably across the five countries. For example, the percentages attached to family vary by 22 percentage points – from 70 percent in Japan to 92 percent in Vietnam. Those attached to friends vary by 23 percentage points – from 54 percent in Japan to 77 percent in Korea. When attachments to family and friends are considered together, Japan becomes the only country in which less than half the population (46%) is attached to both groups. It is also the only country with one-quarter (25%) attached to neither group. In contrast, in Vietnam, nearly two-thirds (65%) remain attached to both groups, whereas less than one-tenth (7%) are unattached to either group. South Korea (Korea hereafter) is another country with more than three-fifths (62%) attached to both groups. In China (60%) and Taiwan (59%), slightly smaller majorities are attached to the two groups.

When the size of majorities attached to each of the two groups is compared across the five countries, there emerge two patterns of group identification. The first pattern involves China and Korea in which slightly more people are attached to friends than to family. In the second pattern, significantly larger majorities are attached to family than to friends. Japan, Taiwan, and Vietnam belong to this pattern. There is no doubt that in Confucian Asia as a whole people continue to feel a primary bond with their family.

A more notable feature of Table 3.2 concerns the proportions *strongly attached* to either and both of the two groups considered. Despite these differences, all five countries are alike in that more people are *strongly attached* to family than to friends. In Taiwan and Vietnam, more than twice as many are strongly attached to family than to friends. Yet, contrary to what is expected from the Confucian ethical doctrine emphasizing

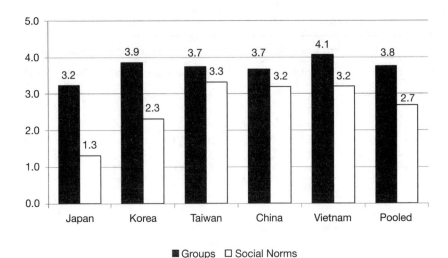

FIGURE 3.1. Levels of Attachment to Groups and Social Norms (on a 7-point scale). *Source:* 2005–8 World Values Surveys.

mutual dependence in all interpersonal relationships, those strongly attached to either family or friends do not constitute a majority in any of the five Confucian countries. In all but Vietnam, they constitute small minorities of less than one-quarter. Only in Vietnam, do as many as two out of five people (40%) feel strongly attached to family. In Japan, fewer than one in fifteen people is strongly attached to either group. In all Confucian countries including Vietnam, moreover, those strongly attached to both groups constitute very small minorities, ranging from less than 1 percent in Japan to 13 percent in Vietnam. In Confucian Asia today, most people no longer feel strong bonds to the people they regularly interact with, including their own family.

Figure 3.1 compares national differences in the overall strength of group ties, which are measured on a 7-point scale. Vietnam registered the highest level of group strength (4.1), followed by Korea (3.9), China (3.7), Taiwan (3.7), and Japan (3.2). These five countries averaged a score of 3.8, which is above the index midpoint (3.0) but more than two points below the score (6.0) registering unqualified attachment. This confirms the earlier finding that people in Confucian Asia remain attached, but not strongly attached to group life.

Of all the Confucian countries considered, Japan registered the lowest level of group attachment. This finding runs counter to the literature on Japanese culture. Within the East Asian Confucian region, Japan has long

TABLE 3.3. *Attachment to the Confucian Norms of Compassion and Propriety*

Country	Percent Generally Attached				Percent Strongly Attached			
	Compassion (*ren*)	Propriety (*li*)	None	Both	Compassion (*ren*)	Propriety (*li*)	None	Both
Japan	47.5	36.4	39.3	24.0	5.7	3.8	91.3	1.3
Korea	52.2	79.2	13.6	45.1	6.7	18.8	78.3	3.8
Taiwan	89.8	82.3	3.3	75.5	24.2	16.0	69.7	9.5
China	88.9	67.6	6.1	62.7	23.9	14.6	67.8	6.5
Vietnam	92.8	80.2	2.9	76.2	17.1	15.4	76.0	8.8
(Pooled)	74.3	69.5	12.8	57.1	15.5	13.9	76.5	6.2

Source: 2005–8 World Values Surveys.

been known as the most group-oriented nation (F. Hsu 1998; Nakane 1970). However, this finding suggests that Japanese culture has shifted toward individualism, an occurrence that supports the idea that people become less group-oriented as they live in a highly democratized and modernized society (Inglehart 1997).

To what extent do people in Confucian East Asia feel constrained by the two most fundamental Confucian virtues or norms of *ren* and *li*? Table 3.3 shows the compliant responses to each and both norms. According to the data reported in this table, most people in most Confucian countries find that these norms still restrict their interpersonal behavior at least to some extent, judging the person who follows those norms at least "somewhat like me." A vast majority of nearly nine-tenths (87%) is compliant with either of the two norms. Only in Japan, the most modernized and globalized country in this region, are people more unwilling than willing to comply with each norm. Japan is the only country in which most people (76%) show an unwillingness to adhere to the two most fundamental Confucian interpersonal norms.

As in the case of attachment to family and friends, the proportions of those compliant with either or both of the two norms vary a great deal from one country to another. The proportions of those at least somewhat compliant with *ren* vary by 45 percentage points, from 48 percent in Japan to 93 percent in Vietnam. The proportions of those at least somewhat compliant with *li* vary by an almost equal margin of 46 percentage points, from 36 percent in Japan to 82 percent in Taiwan. The proportions of those strongly compliant with *ren* vary by 18 percentage points, from less than one-tenth in Japan (6%) and Korea (7%) to nearly one-quarter in

China (24%) and Taiwan (24%). Those strongly compliant with *li* vary by 15 percentage points, from 4 percent in Japan to 19 percent in Korea.

In three of the five countries – China (62%), Taiwan (76%), and Vietnam (76%) – substantial majorities of more than three-fifths are at least somewhat compliant with both norms of *ren* and *li*. In the other two countries – Japan (24%) and Korea (45%) – minorities are equally compliant with both norms. Japan stands out once again as the least Confucian nation. Korea also stands out in that it is the only country where more people are compliant with the norm of *li* than *ren*, and by a large margin of 27 percentage points (79% vs. 52%).

Despite these national differences, all five countries are alike in that those who are strongly compliant with both norms constitute very small minorities of less than one-tenth of their populations. These proportions range from 1 percent in Japan to 10 percent in Taiwan. When all of these findings are considered together, it is evident that the populations of Confucian Asia are far from being highly adherent to the ethical system that Confucius and his followers prescribed for the good life.

To what extent are people in Confucian Asia willing to abide by the two Confucian norms guiding interpersonal relationships? Figure 3.1 reports the mean scores on the 7-point index measuring the overall level of grid strength: Only Taiwan (3.3), China (3.2), and Vietnam (3.2) scored above the midpoint of 3.0. They are followed by Korea (2.3) and by Japan (1.3), which scored significantly below the midpoint. Evidently, there is a great deal of variation in the extent to which people in these Confucian countries remain favorably oriented to the fundamental norms of Confucianism. People in Taiwan, for example, are 1.5 times and 2.5 times more receptive to those norms than their peers in Japan and Korea, respectively.

Once again these findings indicate that these Confucian countries are culturally more divided than united in upholding what Confucius taught concerning how to live a fully human life. It should also be noted that, of the five countries, Japan is the least adherent to the Confucian ethical tradition. This may be the reason why Samuel Huntington (1996) excluded Japan from the sinic civilization zone.

All in all, to what extent do East Asians adhere to the way of life Confucius and early Confucians prescribed as proper? Do they still prefer a hierarchical culture, or are they more in favor of other types of cultures? In Table 3.4, I explore these questions in terms of the four types of culture identified by low and high levels of group identification and grid regulation. As expected from the grid-group theory, East Asians are *highly*

TABLE 3.4. *The Most and Least Preferred Types of Culture*

Country	Types of Culture That Individuals Favor (%)			
	Individualism	Fatalism	Egalitarianism	Hierarchism
Japan	47.7	4.4	41.0	6.8
Korea	27.7	5.3	51.0	16.0
Taiwan	19.8	15.0	31.4	33.8
China	22.0	15.6	30.1	32.2
Vietnam	17.9	7.6	31.2	43.3
(Pooled)	25.5	9.7	37.2	27.6

Source: 2005–8 World Values Surveys.

divided in cultural biases or preferences. None of the four types is favored by a majority of the mass publics in any of the five countries. In the entire region of Confucian Asia, moreover, the most popular cultural type is not the culture of hierarchism that Confucius prescribed. Instead it is egalitarianism, the cultural type that values incorporation into group life but disvalues social control. Even this type is upheld by only a relatively small plurality of less than two-fifths (37%). Fatalism is the least popular of the four culture types, but yet is embraced by a sizable minority (10%). From this finding, it is evident that Confucian Asia is no longer a culturally homogeneous region favoring Confucian hierarchical culture: It is a region of cultural diversity.

Across the five countries in the region, the particular type of culture that people favor most varies considerably. In China, Taiwan, and Vietnam, hierarchism is the most favored. In Japan, the most favored culture is individualism. In Korea, it is egalitarianism. There is also considerable difference across the countries in the extent to which people favor those types. For example, nearly half (48%) the Japanese are upholders of individualism, in comparison to China (22%), Taiwan (20%), and Vietnam (18%). Whereas more than half the Korean people (51%) uphold egalitarianism, less than one-third do so in China (30%), Taiwan (31%), and Vietnam (31%). These quantitative and qualitative differences in how East Asians favor the various ways of life reinforce the finding that East Asia no longer forms a single cultural zone based on the Confucian culture of hierarchical collectivism. Instead, it represents a region in which divergent cultures compete against each other as alternative ways of life.

Nonetheless, careful scrutiny of Table 3.4 reveals that the five Confucian countries are alike in embracing egalitarianism as a favored cultural type, with 37 percent of the population favoring it.[4] In Korea, it is the choice of more than half the population. In the four other countries upholders of this cultural type form the second largest group. By a large margin of 10 percentage points (37% vs. 27%), moreover, egalitarians outnumber hierarchs who practice the Confucian way of life. The preponderance of egalitarians over other cultural adherents attests to the fact that the region has begun to shift away from the Confucian culture of hierarchism.

More importantly, none of the five Confucian countries currently has a majority adherent to individualism, the pattern of cultural composition identified as the most conducive to the development of democratic politics. Individualists are most numerous in Japan, the oldest democracy in Confucian East Asia. In four other countries, they are outnumbered by either egalitarians or hierarchs by more than 10 percentage points. Even in Japan where individualists are most numerous, there is no balance among upholders of each of the three culture types – individualism, egalitarianism, and hierarchism – that is known to be conducive to democratic governance. As compared to the population's more than two-fifths of individualists and egalitarians, hierarchs – who are the most likely to defend the rule of law – constitute a very small minority (7%). In Japan and elsewhere in Confucian Asia today, there is no well-balanced coalition of these three cultures with individualism in the lead.

Finally, of the five countries in Confucian Asia, Vietnam and Japan stand out, respectively, as the most and least Confucian cultural nations. In Vietnam, upholders of hierarchical culture are more than twice as numerous as are those of individualist culture (43% vs. 18%). In Japan, the pattern is reversed; there are seven times as many individualists as hierarchs (48% vs. 7%). Both socioeconomically and politically, Vietnam and Japan are the least and most advanced countries in the Confucian region, respectively. These structural differences suggest that a society's culture shifts to individualism from hierarchism as it becomes democratized and modernized. It should also be noted that Japanese culture is far less hierarchical than any other Confucian country, including Korea and

---

[4] Daniel A. Bell points out that Confucians can be both hierarchical and egalitarian at the same time because they value age and merit, while supporting the equal distribution of opportunities and wealth.

TABLE 3.5. *How the Most and Least Preferred Types of Culture Vary across Cultural Zones*

Cultural Zones	Types of Culture That Individuals Favor(%)			
	Individualism	Fatalism	Egalitarianism	Hierarchism
Dem. West	46.0	20.1	15.1	18.8
Ex-communist West	39.9	22.4	19.1	18.6
South Asia	21.9	12.9	40.4	24.8
Muslim zone	7.1	6.7	28.4	57.4
East Asia	25.5	9.7	37.2	27.6
Latin America	23.9	23.9	22.0	30.2
Africa	10.4	15.5	26.6	47.5
(Pooled)	30.6	17.8	23.2	28.4

Source: 2005–8 World Values Surveys.

Taiwan, which are also politically democratized and socioeconomically modernized.

Comparing Cultural Preferences across Seven Cultural Zones

When the five historically Confucian countries surveyed are considered together, egalitarianism, not hierarchism, emerges as the most prevalent type of culture in Confucian Asia. Does this region then represent a cultural zone different from other zones? To address this question, I compared the cultural zones identified by the earlier analysis of the World Values Surveys by Ronald Inglehart and Christian Welzel (2005). By collapsing their five Western cultural zones[5] into the two zones of democratized West and former communist West, I reduced the number of zones to seven: the long-democratic West, former communist West, South Asia, Muslim countries, East Asia, Latin America, and Africa. For each of these seven zones, Table 3.5 compares the four group-grid cultural types.

One notable feature of this table is that the culture of hierarchism, which early Confucians advocated, is a great deal more popular in other non-Western cultural zones than in Confucian Asia. Excluding the West, only in South Asia is hierarchism less popular than it is in Confucian Asia. In the core Muslim zone (57%), Africa (48%), and Latin America

---

[5] These zones are non-English-speaking Protestant West, English-speaking West, non-English Catholic West, ex-communist West, and ex-communist East.

(30%), upholders of hierarchical culture constitute a majority or plurality. In the core Muslim zone and Africa, nearly or more than one-half of the population is attached to this culture. This cultural type is also the one most favored by people in Latin America. The popularity of this culture in other non-Western cultural zones around the world suggests that it is not a unique cultural characteristic of Confucianism. Instead, it is a cultural characteristic of non-Western traditional societies.

Of the seven cultural zones surveyed, the two cultural zones of the West – old democracies and formerly communist states – stand out as zones of individualist culture. Only in these two cultural zones is individualism most popular, with a plurality of two out of five or more people favorably disposed to it. In all other zones, including Latin America, only one-quarter or less of the population adheres to individualism. In the Muslim zone (7%) and Africa (10%), only one in ten people or fewer are an individualist. This finding makes it clear that individualism is indeed the distinguishing characteristic of the West. It also suggests that Latin America is culturally closer to the non-West than the West.

Confucian East Asia and South Asia stand out from all other cultural zones in favoring egalitarianism: Only in these two regions are egalitarians more numerous than are upholders of any other culture, outnumbering individualists and hierarchs by 10 percentage points or more. In all other regions, in contrast, egalitarians are outnumbered by either or both individualists and hierarchs. Contrary to what is expected from the Confucian tradition and its spread to South Asia, egalitarianism, not hierarchism, is a distinguishing cultural characteristic of Asia today.

What types of culture are currently the most and least popular among people worldwide? In an attempt to address this question, I pooled the respondents of all fifty-seven countries included in the latest, fifth round of the WVS.[6] This analysis of the pooled data reveals that the global population is fairly well divided across the four types. At 31 percent, individualists are most numerous. They are followed by hierarchs (28%), egalitarians (23%), and fatalists (18%). On a global score, the individualist culture of the West is more popular than the culture of hierarchism, which Confucius and his followers prescribed as the proper way of life. Of all non-Western cultural zones, moreover, hierarchism is far

---

[6] The number of respondents to the WVS and ABS varies considerably from one country to another. In pooling their national surveys to estimate regional and global means, therefore, I weighted each country equally.

more popular in the two least modernized zones of the Muslim zone and Africa.

Of the four types of cultural adherents, individualists and hierarchs have the most variance across the cultural zones. The proportions of individualists vary by 39 percentage points, from 7 percent in the Muslim zone to 46 percent in the democratized West. Those of hierarchs vary by a similar 38 percentage points, from 19 percent in the West to 57 percent in the Muslim zone. Egalitarians vary by 25 percentage points, from 15 percent in the democratized West to 40 percent in South Asia. Fatalists vary least, by 17 percentage points, from 7 percent in Muslim zone to 24 percent in Latin America. The variation of fatalists is less than one-half of the cross-zonal differences for individualism and hierarchism. A comparison of these figures suggests that upholders of individualist and hierarchical cultures are most unevenly distributed across the globe today.

Demographic Characteristics of Cultural Adherents

In Confucian Asia, do cultural preferences vary according to demographic characteristics? If they do, which population segments favor most and least each cultural type? Do the cultural types that each population segment favors most and least vary across countries in the region? This section addresses these and other related questions in terms of four standard demographic characteristics: gender, age, educational attainment, and family income. For each East Asian country and the region as a whole, Table 3.6 reports the proportions adhering to each of the four cultural types within each demographic category.

Table 3.6 shows that men and women in East Asia are more alike than different in choosing their favorite and least favorite cultural types. In all five countries, both genders favor fatalism the least. In three countries – China, Korea, and Vietnam – the two genders also favor the same way of life most: egalitarianism in Korea, and hierarchism in China and Vietnam. Only in Japan and Taiwan is there a notable difference between the two genders. In Japan, males favor egalitarianism most, whereas females favor individualism most. In Taiwan, males favor egalitarianism most, in comparison to females who favor hierarchism most.

Although the two genders in most Confucian countries are more alike than not in choosing their favorite and least favorite way of life, they differ considerably in the extent to which they prefer each cultural type. For example, more females than males are attracted to the fatalistic

TABLE 3.6. Demographic Characteristics and Cultural Preferences (in percent)

Cultural Types	Gender		Age			Educational Attainment			Family Income		
	Male	Female	20–39	40–59	≥60	<High.sch	High sch.	College	Low	Middle	High
Individualism											
Japan	42.8	51.9	44.4	55.6	41.4	34.7	52.5	40.4	42.0	53.6	48.3
Korea	26.1	29.2	27.7	28.2	26.3	31.2	33.8	22.7	34.6	31.1	32.4
Taiwan	20.9	20.8	24.1	20.1	14.1	19.4	18.6	23.8	20.6	24.0	16.7
China	22.9	21.1	24.8	19.6	21.1	20.4	21.7	32.8	21.0	21.2	25.7
Vietnam	16.3	29.7	17.9	18.3	17.3	15.1	18.2	24.5	31.9	20.6	13.3
(Pooled)	23.5	26.1	24.9	25.0	24.2	20.1	26.2	26.0	27.8	26.0	20.9
Fatalism											
Japan	4.8	4.0	5.5	2.5	5.4	8.2	3.3	5.5	4.9	3.6	3.9
Korea	3.5	7.0	3.3	5.3	10.8	6.5	6.0	4.5	5.1	5.4	5.2
Taiwan	14.4	17.6	12.6	19.3	17.0	13.9	14.8	18.2	14.8	14.5	19.0
China	12.5	18.8	16.6	15.2	14.4	14.1	17.9	10.9	16.0	15.4	15.1
Vietnam	7.8	7.3	5.4	8.1	14.7	6.9	7.9	5.7	8.7	6.3	8.3
(Pooled)	9.2	11.7	8.9	11.3	12.4	11.4	10.4	9.5	11.3	9.3	9.9
Egalitarianism											
Japan	45.5	37.2	57.4	49.2	36.6	44.9	37.7	48.6	43.3	37.5	42.7
Korea	53.7	48.5	57.4	49.2	36.6	36.6	44.1	58.3	39.7	51.0	58.2
Taiwan	35.3	23.5	31.6	26.8	30.1	29.8	31.9	26.9	31.5	31.3	25.0
China	30.5	29.7	31.5	29.4	27.6	29.2	30.7	31.9	29.4	28.4	33.6
Vietnam	34.4	27.6	34.9	28.3	23.6	32.3	30.6	33.0	29.0	28.1	34.0
(Pooled)	38.7	32.7	39.0	33.2	32.5	31.2	33.9	43.4	33.9	35.2	38.4
Hierarchism											
Japan	6.8	6.9	6.0	5.4	9.4	12.2	6.5	5.5	9.8	5.4	5.2
Korea	16.7	15.3	11.5	17.3	26.3	25.8	16.1	14.5	20.6	12.5	17.3
Taiwan	29.4	38.2	31.8	33.8	38.8	36.9	34.7	31.2	33.1	30.3	39.4
China	34.0	30.4	21.7	35.8	36.8	36.4	29.7	24.4	33.5	35.0	25.7
Vietnam	41.5	45.4	41.8	45.3	44.5	45.7	43.4	36.8	30.4	45.0	44.1
(Pooled)	28.7	29.4	27.1	30.5	30.9	37.3	29.5	21.0	27.0	29.0	30.7

Source: 2005–8 World Values Surveys.

way of life, and more males than females are attracted to the egalitarian way of life. The most notable of these gender differences concerns the extent to which the two genders embrace egalitarianism as the preferred way of life. In every country, egalitarianism is more popular among males than among females. When all five countries are pooled together, male egalitarians outnumber female egalitarians by 6 percentage points (39% vs. 33%).

Much more than gender, age matters in cultural preferences. Only in two countries – Korea and Vietnam – do people in the three age groups favor the same cultural types most and least. In the three other countries – China, Japan, and Taiwan – the most and least favored types vary across the three age groups. In China, for example, fatalism is the least popular culture among all three age groups. Yet, young people in their 20s and 30s choose egalitarianism as their favorite type, whereas those older choose hierarchism. In Japan, where all three age groups are least attracted to the fatalistic way of life, the young and elderly are most attracted to egalitarianism, and the middle-aged are most attracted to individualism. In Taiwan, all three age groups are alike in favoring hierarchism most, but they disagree over which they favor least. Fatalism is least popular among the young and middle-aged, whereas individualism is least popular among the elderly. Thus in three of the five countries there exists considerable differences in either the most or least popular types of culture across the age groups.

In three countries – Japan, Korea, and Taiwan – however, egalitarians are most numerous among the youngest age group, and hierarchs are most numerous among the oldest age group. In these three countries, there is a clear cultural divide between the two extreme age groups: the young generation prefers to lead an egalitarian way of life, whereas the old generation remains attached to hierarchy. Of these three countries, the cultural divide between the young and old generations is most pronounced in Korea, where egalitarians constitute a majority (57%) of the young people and a minority (37%) of the elderly. This may be the reason why Korea has experienced more generational conflicts than any other country in Confucian Asia.

When all five countries are considered together, older age is associated positively with fatalism and hierarchism, but negatively with individualism and egalitarianism. In the entire region of Confucian Asia today, fatalists and hierarchs are most numerous among the age cohort of 60s and older, and individualists and egalitarians are most numerous among those in their 20s and 30s.

Educational attainment is associated with a division only for the most favored cultural type. In all five countries, fatalism is the least favored by all three educational groups: those with a primary education or less, those with a secondary education, and those with a college education. However, in only one country, Vietnam, do people regardless of educational level favor the same cultural type most: hierarchism. In the four other countries, there is considerable variation in the type of culture that each education group favors most. For example, the college educated in Japan, Korea, and Taiwan favor egalitarianism most, whereas their peers in China and Vietnam are most strongly in favor of individualism and hierarchism, respectively. In every country, nonetheless, the least educated are the most likely to favor hierarchical living, and the most educated are the least likely to do so. Undoubtedly, hierarchism is most popular among the least educated and least popular among the most educated. When all five countries are pooled together, more education is consistently associated with a lower proportion of hierarchs and a higher proportion of egalitarians.

Finally, I divided family income into three levels roughly equivalent in size – low, middle, and high – to examine whether and how income affects East Asians' most and least preferred types of culture. In every country, people in all income levels favor fatalism least. However, as with education, the most preferred way of life differs for different income levels within countries and also for the same income level across countries. Whereas individualism is most popular among high-income people in Japan, their peers in China and Korea choose egalitarianism, and their peers in Taiwan and Vietnam choose hierarchism. When all five countries are pooled together, however, more income, like more education, is associated with a larger proportion of egalitarians. Unlike education, however, it is associated with a smaller proportion of individualists and a larger proportion of hierarchs.

I now consider all four demographic variables together and attempt to identify the particular demographic characteristics of the people in Confucian Asia who are most and least likely to prefer each type of culture. The pooled analyses of these four variables, which are not reported in Table 3.6, indicate that individualism is least popular among high-income people with less than a high school education and most popular among low-income people with a high school education (15% vs. 32%). Fatalists or isolates are almost equally present in all population segments, yet they are least numerous among young people with a college education and

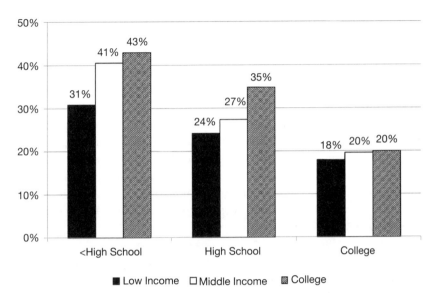

FIGURE 3.2. Demographic Characteristics of Adherents to Hierarchism: Education and Income. *Source:* 2005–8 World Values Surveys.

most numerous among the elderly with less than a high school education (7% vs. 12%).

Egalitarians, unlike isolates, vary considerably across all population segments, yet they are least and most prevalent, respectively, among elderly females with a high school education and elderly males with a college education (28% vs. 52%). Hierarchs vary across population segments to a greater extent than do adherents to any other cultural type. They are least and most popular, respectively, among young, low-income people with a college education and elderly, high-income people with little education (19% vs. 43%). Figure 3.2 shows that these adherents to the Confucian way of life are two and a half times more numerous among high-income people with little education than among low-income people with a college education (43% vs. 18%).

Summary and Conclusions

Confucianism has been identified with a wide variety of ethical principles and behaviors practiced for more than two millennia in China and five other East Asian countries. This inquiry into how Confucianism affects

East Asians' preferred way of life began with a conceptual investigation of Confucianism from historical and philosophical perspectives. I first defined it as a system of social and political ethics and explicated its underlying premises; I then compared those premises with those of the Western liberal ethical system. Unlike the Western ethical system created by thinkers of the Enlightenment, Confucianism is grounded in the philosophical premise that humans are inherently social beings with moral integrity. Only through the moral cultivation of the self and meaningful interactions with other people are people capable of creating *datong shehui*, a community of grand harmony. After a brief discussion of the key principles of Confucian social ethics, I examined how Confucianism as a hierarchical way of social life contrasts with three other distinct ways of life: individualism, fatalism, and egalitarianism.

Empirically, I first analyzed whether the contemporary publics of Confucian Asia still remain attached to the hierarchical way of life that Confucius and other early Confucians advocated. For this analysis, I examined the strength of attachment to family and friends and the level of compliance with the Confucian norms of benevolent behavior and behavioral propriety using WVS data. In none of the five countries surveyed do a majority still practice the Confucian hierarchical way of life; furthermore, this way of life is not even the most popular cultural type. Instead, more people have embraced the egalitarian or individualist way of life. In the region as a whole, egalitarians and individualists together constitute a majority. More notably, Confucian Asia as a whole is more individualistic than any of the four other non-Western cultural zones including Latin America.

Of the five countries analyzed, adherents to Confucian hierarchism are most numerous in Vietnam, the poorest nondemocracy, and they are least numerous in Japan, the most affluent and oldest democracy in the region. In contrast, individualists are least numerous in the poorest nondemocracy and most numerous in the richest democracy. Egalitarians are most numerous in Korea and least numerous in China and Taiwan. Despite these cross-country differences, all five countries are alike in that, of the four cultural types, fatalism is the least popular.

Of the various population segments defined by gender, age, education, and income, Confucian hierarchism is most popular among old people and people with little education, and least popular among young people, especially those with a college education. As the oldest generation passes from the scene and the number of young people receiving a college education increases, the popularity of Confucianism as a way of life is likely to diminish further in the years to come.

According to results of the multiple classification analysis (MCA) of the pooled five-country data, which are not reported in the text, however, neither age nor education affects hierarchical cultural preference most powerfully. Of the seven variables analyzed,[7] the type of resident regime – which is measured in terms of nondemocracy (China, Singapore, and Vietnam), third-wave democracy (Korea and Taiwan), and second-wave democracy (Japan) – is the most powerful influence. Far more powerfully than education, the experience of democratic rule drives people away from the hierarchical way of life. This seems to support the claim that democratization shapes cultural orientations as much as cultural orientations affect the process of democratization.

---

[7] These variables are gender (V235), age (V237), education (V238), income (V253), exposure to national and international news (V223 and V224), access to the Internet (V230), and the type of resident regime measured in terms of three categories: second-wave democracy (Japan), third-wave democracy (South Korea and Taiwan), and nondemocracy (China, Singapore, and Vietnam). The regime type, which indicates the length of democratic political experience, registers a *beta* coefficient of 0.18. This coefficient is at least two times larger than the ones for all other variables, including education (0.04) and Internet usage (0.07).

4

Confucianism as a Government of Paternalistic Meritocracy

Confucius lived during one of the most politically and socially turbulent periods in Chinese history, a time known as the Spring and Autumn period (722–481 B.C.). During this period, China, formerly united under the Zhou dynasty, was divided into small feudal states, which engaged in repeated cycles of civil wars and political turmoil. Mencius (3B:9) describes this period in this way: "After the death of Yao and Shun, the way of the Sages declined, and tyrants arose one after another.... When the world declined and the Way fell into obscurity, heresies and violence again arose. There were instances of regicides and parricide. Confucius was apprehensive and composed the *Spring and Autumn Annals*."

The people of Confucius's time desired to build a peaceful and harmonious community but struggled to restore social order and maintain political stability. Unlike medieval Europeans, however, their struggle did not center on how to "limit the power of established political authority, or secure a protected realm for individual conduct free from arbitrary coercion" (O'Dwyer 2003, 43). For Confucius and his followers, the goal was a government that promoted and secured a peaceful life for the people. Because limiting the power of established political authority was not necessarily the end sought, Confucius and his followers did not advocate the rule of law as an effective solution to the problem of incessant political strife and social disorder facing the warring states. Their main concern was how to establish and maintain a meritocratic government capable of creating *datong shehui*, or a community of grand harmony (Yao 2000, 275).

What constitutes and shapes government? A century after Confucius, Plato would approach this question from an idealistic perspective, but

Confucius was interested in exploring government from the practical or utilitarian perspective of making government work for each state's territory and citizens (M. Dawson 1942, 193; see also Ames and Rosemont 1998; L. Hsu 1975). He conceived of the state as having three essential components – government, territory, and citizens – and he saw government as an institution whose performance depended on the unique configurations of its territory, its citizens, and even their culture. He also viewed government as a dynamic phenomenon dealing with the constantly shifting relationships between the governor and the governed.

Unlike Plato, therefore, he was interested primarily in the practices of government and, more specifically, in condemning the practices of bad government while replacing them with those of good government (L. Hsu 1975). In distinguishing "bad" from "good," he based his judgments on the principles of meritocracy and paternalism. What Confucius and his followers condemned were exploitive practices of the military and purely legalistic forms of government, both of which were commonplace during his time (L. Hsu 1975).

Confucius and other early Confucians would have seen attempts to craft an ideal form of government suitable for all types of society as an exercise in futility. They noticed that the totality of natural resources and the influences of civil culture and virtue varied a great deal across state territories. Because one single form of government could not fit every divergent situation, they concluded that the development of a universally suitable form of government or a universally effective policy would be impractical (L. Hsu 1975, 83 and 140). Instead they were mainly concerned with the task of building within each state a government capable of maintaining a proper relationship between ordinary people and government officials. To develop such a relationship, early Confucians emphasized the importance of family life for inculcating both ordinary people and government officials in the virtues of proper behavior.

The Confucian Notion of Government

Confucius and his disciples placed great importance on family as the foundation of government. They believed that "to rightly govern the state, it is necessary first to regulate one's own family"; that "the filial piety with which the superior man serves his parents may be transferred as loyalty to the ruler"; and "[f]rom the love example of one family, love extends throughout the state; from its courtesy, courtesy extends throughout the state" (*The Great Learning* [9.1], quoted in M. Dawson

1942, 172). In other words, family life was seen as a training ground for children to learn not only how to be successful in their own lives but also how to become good subjects or good rulers.

All of the five great Confucian Classics,[1] which formed the program for educating the ruling classes, characterize family as "the first school of virtues" (Schwartz 1985, 100) and "the best institution for the training of individual character, virtue, and wisdom" (L. Hsu 1975, 68). Confucius, without reservation, identified family as the most powerful agent fostering moral development. Emphasizing the enduring influence that family has on the hearts and minds of people during their formative years, Confucius and his followers posited an early version of political socialization theory (Dawson and Prewitt 1969; Easton and Dennis 1969; Langdon 1969). This socialization theory – that early family life creates a repertoire of behavior that is carried into subsequent political life – is one notable characteristic of the Confucian model of government.

In this model, family life constitutes the cultural as well as structural foundation of government and becomes the centerpiece of political life. Confucius (*Analects* 2:21) summed up this view as follows: "Simply by being a good son and friendly to his brothers a man can exert an influence upon good government." The tight relationship between family and government leaves little to no room for an independent and intermediate public space (Hahm 2004, 98), space that is necessary for the emergence of civil society, as discussed in Chapters 5 and 6. This lack of civic life outside the realms of family and the state is an important characteristic of the Confucian model of government (Pye 1999).

For early Confucians, then, there was a powerful connection between how families functioned and how people behaved as citizens, but this cause-and-effect tie was not the only relationship drawn between family and government. The Confucian conception of government saw in the family a microcosm of the state. In *The Great Learning*, Confucius wrote,

To rightfully fulfill duties as a member in the family is to teach one how to rightfully fulfill the duties of citizenship. To know how to govern well a family is to govern a state. If the family is virtuous and benevolent, the whole state will become virtuous and benevolent.... Wishing to govern well their state, they first regulate their families. Their family being regulated, their states were rightly governed. The states being rightly governed, the whole kingdom was made tranquil and happy.

---

[1] These classics are *Shu Ching* (Classic of History), *Shih Ching* (Classic of Odes), *I Ching* (Classic of Changes), *Ch'un Ching* (Spring and Autumn Annals), and *Li Ching* (Classic of Rites).

For early Confucians, the characteristics of family life extended not only to the state but also to other social and natural phenomena, including community, country, and even the universe (Tu 1998a, 13). Ordinary people were taught to see and address the emperor as the son of Heaven and to treat the king as ruler-father and local magistrates as motherly or fatherly figures (*Mencius* 2A:5, 3A:3). For example, *The Book of Poetry* (16.1), which Confucius edited, proclaims that the "happy and gracious sovereign" is called "the father and mother of the people."

Thus, early Confucians not only stressed the importance of strong families for strong government but also advocated a patriarchal theory of government. They insisted that the state be governed exactly how the family is governed, and they used the family code as the basis of the government code (L. Hsu 1975, 35). As Confucius wrote in *The Great Learning* (14), "The filial piety with which the superior man serves his parents may be transferred as loyalty to the ruler; the fraternal duty with which he serves as his elder brother may be transferred as deference to elders; his regulation of his family may be transferred as good government in any official position." As in family relationships, therefore, the virtues of *ren* and *li* were accepted as the norms that should guide the relationship between the governor and the governed, and as in the parent-child relationship, the relationship between rulers and subjects followed the *hierarchical* and *paternalistic* principles of patriarchy, with authority on one side of the relationship and acquiescence on the other.

Under a patriarchal system of authority, the superior in command provides for the welfare of the subordinates in return for their loyalty and reverence. For this very reason, the Confucian classics often refer to rulers as the fathers and mothers of the people. These terms imply not only that the people are to be in submission to their leaders, but as Hsu (1975, 115) points out, also that rulers are duty-bound to love and care for the people as much as parents love their children. This form of paternalistic authoritarianism symbolizes a third notable characteristic of the Confucian model of government.

The Essentials of Good Government

Early Confucians addressed questions regarding the essentials of good government primarily from a utilitarian perspective, just as did Jeremy Bentham and other British utilitarian philosophers centuries later.[2] What

---

[2] Early Confucians except Mozi (470–391 B.C.) may not be considered utilitarians by the standard of strict impartiality that no one's interest is more important than another's.

is the ultimate end of good government? What enables that end to be realized? Who should rule? What should rulers do to promote good government? In *The Book of History*, one of the classics of Confucianism, Confucius is quoted as asserting that government is instituted to "secure for men the five blessings and secure them against the six calamities.... The five blessings are: ample means, long life, health, virtuous character, and an agreeable personal appearance; the six calamities, early death, sickness, misery, poverty, a repulsive appearance, and weakness" (quoted in M. Dawson 1942, 186).

In Confucianism, as in the Western utilitarianism of the nineteenth century, the ultimate object of good government is to maximize welfare and minimize suffering among people. For this very reason, Confucius proclaimed, "Good government obtains when those who are near are made happy, and those who are far attracted" (*Analects*, 13:16).

In the West, liberal thinkers have advocated minimal government in favor of private enterprise and competition. In striking contrast, early Confucians embraced government as "the most important" institution for human welfare (*Analects* 24:6) and emphasized the importance of its active role in building a nation of happiness. To these Confucians, government represented the only human-made institution that could encourage people to live harmoniously with one another, as well as productively with the natural environment in which they live (L. Hsu 1975). Therefore, they endorsed the active involvement of government in managing the economy and rejected the laissez-faire philosophy of minimal government. In this regard, they entrusted government institutions with a variety of public work projects, such as controlling flooding and minimizing the effects of other natural calamities. They also defended "the well-field system" of governmental control over the distribution and use of land as a legitimate tool to secure the basic welfare of the citizenry as a whole (*Mencius* 3A:3; see also Bell 2006, 238–43).

In a nutshell, early Confucians focused on the weaknesses of free markets in promoting the public welfare and proposed an earlier version of the fundamental Keynesian idea that a benevolent government must do what it can to avert economic trouble in areas where the free markets cannot. In addition to advocating governmental intervention in managing the economy and regulating the livelihoods of the people, they endorsed its active involvement in educating all people regardless of their class

---

However, by the standard that one is morally obligated to commit to improving the welfare of others or of society as a whole, they can be considered utilitarians.

standing. This notion of an active government can be considered an early version of the developmental state, which is now widely recognized as being primarily responsible for the socioeconomic modernization that has transformed East Asia over the past three decades (Johnson 1982; Woo-Cumings 1999).

Confucius also pondered what would be the most essential components of good government. When a student, Tsze-kung, once asked Confucius for his opinion on this matter,

The Master said, "The requisites of government are that there be sufficiency of food, sufficiency of military equipment, and the confidence of the people in their ruler." Tsze-kung said, "If it cannot be helped, and one of these must be dispensed with, which of the three should be foregone first?" The Master said, "The military equipment." Tsze-kung again asked, "If it cannot be helped, and one of the remaining two must be dispensed with, which of them should be foregone?" The Master answered: "Part with the food. From of old, death has been the lot of men; but if the people have no confidence in their rulers, there is no standing for the state" (*Analects* 12:7).

Of all the requisites of government, Confucius saw citizen trust as the one foundation without which the state and government could not survive and flourish. As Xinzhong Yao (1999, 38) notes, Confucius believed that trust (*xin*) is "the mutual commitment between the people and the government, without which the ruling is not justified and the social order cannot be maintained." When people no longer trust their government, therefore, it loses its legitimacy and becomes an oppressive enterprise. As Confucius said, "The superior man, having obtained their confidence, may impose tasks upon the people. If he has not gained their confidence, they will deem his acts oppressive" (*Analects* 19:10). When government is viewed as oppressive, people are not willing to cooperate with it; when they refuse to cooperate, the government eventually collapses (J. Chan 2007; L. Hsu 1975, 130; S. Hu 1997).

According to early Confucians, moreover, Heaven consents to the legitimacy of a government only when its people consent to it. Mencius put forth this view: "Heaven sees with the eyes of its people; Heaven hears with the ears of its people" (*Mencius* 5A:5). By directly linking popular support to the survival of the government, Confucians were positing a theory of political legitimacy that emphasizes popular support and trust as a foundation for regime survival and consolidation.[3] Two millennia

---

[3] According to Jiang Qing's analysis of "political Confucianism," as discussed in Daniel A. Bell (2008a, Appendix 2), there are two other types of political legitimacy: *Tian* (heaven)

later, contemporary political scientists have adopted this view, theorizing that new democracies become consolidated only when people embrace democracy as "the only game in town" (Linz and Stepan 1996).

Having identified public trust as the most essential component of government, the next step was to identify what the government can do to earn that trust. In early Confucian tradition, good government depends on the mutually beneficial relationship between rulers and the ruled. In The *Analects* (12:9), Confucius expressed this view: "If the people have plenty, their prince will not be left to want alone. If the people are in want, their prince will not be able to enjoy plenty alone." Mencius, too, supported this view, claiming, "If you will put benevolence in practice in your government, your people will love you in authority, and will be ready to die for them" (1B:12).

In view of this symbiotic relationship, Confucius urged leaders to engage in benevolent behavior and to avoid acts of cruelty, oppression, injury, and meanness (*Analects* 20: 2). "Do not do to others what you do not want done to yourself," he advised (*Analects* 12:2). Practicing this rule of *ren* (benevolence), the ruler can win the hearts of the people and gain their confidence. "By their generosity, they (rulers) win the heart of the people; by sincerity they cause the people to have confidence in them" (*Analects* 20:9). Or as Mencius (4A: 9) put it, "There is a way to win their hearts; amass what they want for them; do not impose what they dislike on them."

As a means of cultivating popular trust in government, Confucius and his disciples emphasized the importance of satisfying people's basic needs, including food, through the provision of public welfare (Bell 2006). Preventing starvation constituted the second core component of good government, after popular trust in government. In Confucian thought, the provision of economic welfare always takes priority over the provision of political and civil rights (Bell and Hahm 2003, 234).

According to Mencius (1A:3), governmental failure to prevent starvation is equivalent to murder, and the government should be held responsible for this failure. The government, which is morally responsible for the people's welfare, must make it a basic mission to provide help to those unable to help themselves and without family to help them. Concerning the question of who should receive governmental help, Mencius (1B:5)

---

and history. According to his view, a political system becomes legitimate only if all three elements including "human" are properly balanced.

said that "old men without wives, old women without husbands, old people without children, young children without fathers – these four types of people are the most destitute and have no one to turn to for help."

According to Leonard Hsu's (1975, 148–9) analysis of the Confucian principles of public relief work, early Confucians advocated providing regular allowances to the poor and the physically disabled so that they could be maintained sufficiently. In addition, they even advocated a program to distribute land and other wealth equally or equitably in the belief that "when the rich compete with the poor, nothing can prevent the strong from pressing on the weak" (quoted in M. Dawson, 1942, 193). In *The Analects* (16: 1), Confucius offered another rationale for this welfare program:

I have heard the rulers should not be concerned that they have not enough possessions and territories, but should be concerned that possessions are not equally distributed; they should not be concerned that they are poor, but should be concerned that the people are not contented. For with equal distribution, there will be no poverty; with mutual good will, there will be no want; and with contentment among the people, there can be no downfall and dissolution.

By advocating not only the equal distribution of land but also the provision of public welfare for the needy, early Confucians developed a structural foundation for the socialist welfare state and offered a moral justification for it. Nonetheless, it should be noted that "the Confucian emphasis on securing material welfare for the people does not imply a nanny state that takes care of every aspect of people's lives from the cradle to the grave" (J. Chan 2003, 237).

Virtuous Leadership

For Confucius and his students, as important as identifying the essentials of good government was determining who the rulers of such a government should be, because the quality of government depends exclusively on the quality of people in the government (Schwartz 1985, 97). Mencius said, "If the benevolent and the good and wise are not trusted, the state will only be a shell" (7B:12). Confucius said, "If good men were put in charge of governing for a hundred years, they would be able to overcome violence and dispense with killing altogether" (*Analects* 13:11). Accordingly, he advocated an open meritocracy (quoted in M. Dawson 2005, 222), saying, "Even among the sons of the emperor, the princes, and the great officials, if they were not qualified to rites and justices, they should be put down to the class of common people; even among the sons of the

common people, if they have good education and character and are qualified to rites and justice, they should be elevated to the class of ministers
and nobles."

For all early Confucians, people, not policies, make good governments;
thus they had little use for political institutions that distribute power and
for institutional reforms. Moreover, they opposed any type of hereditary
rule. In 6B:7, for example, Mencius admonished that even "Gentlemen
should not hold office by heredity." This notion of good government
served as a foundation for the development of meritocracy, which allowed
every citizen to take competitive examinations testing their virtues and
knowledge. This merit-based system enabled the most talented to rise to
the highest offices, replacing the rule by hereditary aristocracy in Confucian Asia long before such aristocracy was abandoned in the West (Collins
2008, 167).

To implement the meritocratic system, Confucius divided people into
classes according to the level of their intelligence and the quality of their
minds (*Analects* 7:3). He judged that only those with superior intelligence who were also virtuous and wise were qualified to become rulers.
Similarly, Mencius (3A:4) advocated the doctrine of the division of labor
by sorting people into the two categories of governors and the governed
based on their intelligence: "There are those who use their minds and
there are those who use their muscles. The former govern; the latter are
governed. Those who govern are supported by those who are governed."
According to Confucius, Mencius, and every other early Confucian, good
government can be achieved only when qualified leaders occupy governmental positions of responsibility. Therefore, they opposed the involvement of the masses in the political process and were not in favor of the
democratic notion of government by the people.

In defining what it takes to be a good leader, Confucius was specific;
throughout *The Analects*, he identified a variety of leadership qualities,
including sincerity and truthfulness in words and deeds, the ability to
maintain a sense of shame, the ability to learn quickly and eagerly, a
willingness to seek the advice of the governed, being respectful in manner, being reverent in the service of their lord, and being generous and
just in caring for the common people. Of all these qualities, Confucians
endorsed the possession of virtue – understanding of and commitment to
the common good – as the only proper basis for a claim to governmental
authority (Schwartz 1985, 76).

In a conversation with the ruler of Lu, Confucius advised, "The moral
character of the ruler is the wind; the moral character of those beneath

him is the grass. When the wind blows, the grass bends" (*Analects* 12:19). For Confucius, therefore, virtuous leaders were like "the north polar star, which keeps its place and all the stars turn towards it" (*Analects* 2:1). Mencius (2B:2) also emphasized the power of virtue as follows: "In the empire there are three things universally acknowledged to be honorable. Nobility is one of them; age is one of them. In courts, nobility holds first place; in village, age; and for usefulness to one's generation and controlling the people, neither is equal to virtue."

Why did Confucians emphasize virtue as the most important quality of governmental leadership? For them, the exercise of authority was an interactive or reciprocal process that always requires the cooperation of all those involved (Fox 1997, 546; Tamaki 2007, 296). In *The Great Learning*, virtue is called "the root," which enables the ruler to win the cooperation of the people. Consider these quotes from Confucius: "If a man is righteous, governance will follow without commandments. But if a man is not righteous, nobody will heed your orders" (*Analects* 13:6), and "If the rulers are honest, the people will naturally oblige" (*Analects* 14: 43). Also this one from Mencius: "Only the benevolent man is fit to be in high position. For a cruel man to be in high position is for him to disseminate his wickedness among the people" (*Mencius* 4A:1). Believing in all that virtue can achieve in politics, Confucians called for government by the extraordinarily virtuous and wise and not by ordinary people.

Principles of Good Government

Having identified the essentials of good government as well as the desired qualities for leaders, the next task was to discover the means that rulers should use to build and maintain a harmonious and prosperous community in which people can live in peace and happiness. Early Confucians advocated *minben* as the most important principle of governing. *Minben*, which originated from the pre-Confucian period, means treating "people" (*min*) as "roots" (*ben*). Mencius endorsed this view when he said, "The people are more important than the state and the state is more important than the king" (7B:14). Thus people, not the sovereign, form the foundation of the state. To govern according to this principle is to govern for the people (*min*) – for their economic prosperity and for their physical security – just as someone caring for a tree (*ben*) would need to tend its roots.

Minben also embodies the people's right to choose a new government even by rebellion. When rulers fail to put the interests of people before those of the rulers, such rulers lose the Mandate of Heaven (*pinyin*; *Mencius* 5A: 5). Mencius explained, "If the ruler made serious mistakes, they would remonstrate with him, but if repeated remonstration fell on deaf ears, they would depose him" (5B:9). By allowing ordinary citizens to remove malevolent dictators, this *minben* principle demands that rulers seek the people's prosperity and welfare as the ultimate end of good government (Nuyen 2000, 143).

To govern according to the principle of *minben* requires not only providing sufficient food and security but also disseminating virtue through education. Confucius explained the reasoning behind this view, saying, "When the man of high station is well instructed, he loves men; when the man of low station is well-instructed, he is easily ruled" (*Analects* 17:3). In the belief that education makes people virtuous, Confucius emphasized that people should be educated as soon as their livelihoods are secured:

When Confucius was traveling to Wei, Ran Yu drove him. Confucius observed, "What a dense population!" Ran Yu said, "The people having grown so numerous, what next should be done for them?" "Enrich them," Confucius replied. "And when one has enriched them, what next should be done?" Confucius said, "Educate them" (*Analects* 13:9).

Mencius (1A:7) similarly admonished that a government has to eliminate poverty first and then educate the people so that they can behave morally. Providing for the material well-being of the people comes first, and teaching moral well-being comes second. Classical Confucianism gives priority to the former because people can only be expected to behave morally only after they are relieved of poverty. As Benjamin Schwartz (1985, 105) points out, Mencius (3A:3) emphasized an economic livelihood as an indispensable precondition for moral education, as did Confucius earlier. In so doing, they posited a notion of a human needs hierarchy and advocated it as a policy tool for good governance more than two millennia before Abraham Maslow (1943) popularized the notion:

If they have a certain livelihood, they will have a fixed heart. If they have not a certain livelihood, they have not a fixed heart. And if they have not a fixed heart, there is nothing which they will not do in the way of self-abandonment, of moral deflection, of depravity, and of wild license (*Mencius* 3A:3).

To classical Confucians, moral education was essential to the building of a harmonious community because law and punishment were viewed as ineffective means for maintaining order. The important goal of social harmony could only be attained when people became virtuous and ful-filled their duties to others *voluntarily*. As a necessary means to build a virtuous nation, therefore, Confucius emphasized the importance of pro-viding education to all segments of the population by claiming that "there is no class distinction in education" (*Analects* 7:7).

Therefore Confucius should be recognized as the first advocate of mandatory universal education. Mencius echoed this sentiment, saying, "Men possess a moral nature; but if they are well fed, warmly clad, and comfortably lodged, without at the same time being instructed, they become like unto beasts" (*Mencius* 3A:4). Early Confucians were alike in believing that the state would be well governed only when people were universally educated and inculcated in virtues and when only the most virtuous were chosen to manage governmental institutions.

To obtain good government, early Confucians also advocated the use of moral persuasion rather than universally applicable penal laws, which they saw as working through coercion rather than voluntary consent (Fox 1997). As discussed in Chapter 3, they also believed that people are inherently good and capable of learning and achieving moral devel-opment; thus they can be persuaded to overcome their selfishness and to exercise moral discipline instead of being forced to do so by law. Thus, in Confucian thought, the most effective means for motivating people to fulfill their duties and remain loyal to the government is the rule of virtue or rule by morality, not the rule by law, which is the hallmark of democracy.[4]

Specifically, early Confucians opposed rule by law because they believed the threat of punishment forces people to submit to govern-ment and being forced leaves people feeling distrustful of authority. Early Confucians preferred instead to instruct people on the benefits of cooper-ation and then depend on their aversion to losing face and being shamed as an effective deterrent to crime:

Lead the people with administrative injunctions and keep them orderly with penal law and they will avoid punishments but will lack a sense of shame. Lead them with excellence and keep them orderly through observing ritual propriety and they will develop a sense of shame, and moreover will order themselves (*Analects* 2:3).

Thus, Confucius saw the rule of virtue as being not only more palatable to the people but also a more effective form of control.

---

4 Confucians were not against the use of law. Instead, they recognized it as the last resort after other means fail. For further detail, see Joseph Chan (2007).

The third Confucian principle of good government is known as *zhongyong* or the Doctrine of the Mean. This doctrine has rich and multifaceted meanings. Politically, it refers to a decision-making rule that leaders can use to achieve a state of harmony among those with different preferences and interests. The core idea of this rule is to find an optimal point that can maintain a balance between two opposing extremes and to take that balanced position (Cheung et al. 2006; Nuyen 2000).

To underline the importance of this decision-making principle, Confucius said, "Perfect is the virtue that is according to the Mean" (*Analects* 6:29), "to go beyond is as wrong as to fall short" (*Analects* 11:16), and "Holding on to the middle is closer to being right" (*Mencius* 7A:26). In *The Doctrine of the Mean*, Confucius praised Emperor Shun who "took hold of their two extremes, determined the Mean, and employed it in his government of the people" (quoted in Xu 2006, 142). As a political decision-making rule, therefore, the Confucian Doctrine of the Mean is often viewed as compatible with the democratic principle of majority rule, which also usually involves compromise. This Confucian rule of decision making predates the contemporary median voter theory, which holds that politicians should commit to a middle-of-the-road policy position preferred by the electorate to maximize the satisfaction of their preferences (Downs 1957).

Socially, the *zhongyong* doctrine represents the norm of being reasonable and moderate in dealing with other people and being open to many points of view. It also embodies "the disposition to view oneself as embedded in a social system and therefore to see things holistically and in social terms" (Cheung et al. 2006, 197). This social outlook distinguishes the doctrine from Aristotle's well-known doctrine of the mean, which refers merely to the preference for the midpoint between two extremes.

In conclusion, the Confucian model of good government differs from the liberal democratic model of good government in both its end and its means. In Confucianism, good government is equated exclusively with government for the people. Therefore, Confucius and his disciples emphasized the happiness and welfare of the people as the most important principle of good government, and they disregarded the modern democratic political ideals of the West such as liberty, equality, and fraternity (J. Chan 2007, 191; L. Hsu 1975, 114–15). To establish such a benevolent government, early Confucians called for government run by a virtuous and meritocratic leadership and not for a government by the people.

The Confucian model therefore contrasts sharply with the liberal democratic notion of government, with its emphasis on a government elected by the people, and operated according to the rule of law. As discussed in Chapter 2, these differences have led to the contemporary debate over whether China and other East Asian societies shaped by Confucianism can fully ascribe to liberal democracy as practiced in the West (Bai 2008; Collins 2008; Fukuyama 1995b; Hall and Ames 1987; Huntington 1991; Zakaria 2003).

Popular Attachment to Meritocracy

Confucius and his followers accepted the common people as the most important element in a state. Yet they rejected the democratic notion of government by the people because they believed that the common people are not cognitively capable of understanding the complexity of public affairs. What they advocated instead was government by a few virtuous leaders with talent. In *The Analects* (8.9), Confucius disapproved of government by the people for the reason that "the common people can be made to follow it, they cannot be made to understand it." For the same reason, Mencius (3A:4) advocated a division of labor between rulers and the ruled.

To what extent do the contemporary mass publics of Confucian Asia endorse the notion of moral meritocracy – government by moral elites – that Confucius and Mencius advocated for small-scale agrarian communities more than two thousand years ago? Would East Asians today be content to remain detached from the political process, as Confucius admonished in *The Analects* (8:14, 14:26): "Do not concern yourself with the matter of government unless they are the responsibility of your office?" Or are they actively seeking to take part in the process?

In this section, I address these general questions by analyzing the persistence and prevalence of moral meritocracy in Confucian Asia. For this analysis, I selected a pair of questions from the second wave of the Asian Barometer Surveys (ABS). One question in this pair deals with rule by moral leadership, and the other with the noninvolvement of the masses in politics. Table 4.1a reports affirmative responses to these questions asked in six countries in Confucian Asia: China, Japan, Korea, Taiwan, Singapore, and Vietnam. Because only one of the questions was asked in Korea, this country was excluded from most of the analyses reported here.

Early Confucians claimed that only those who have cultivated virtue and wisdom, no matter their station at birth, are qualified to participate in governmental affairs. What do people in Confucian Asia today think of government by moral leaders? To explore this question, the ABS asked

TABLE 4.1. *Attachment to the Principles of Paternalistic Meritocracy (in percent)*

A. Meritocracy

Country	Moral Leadership		Passive Citizenry		Levels of Attachment			
	Attached	Firmly Attached	Attached	Firmly Attached	Neither	One	Both	No Answer
Japan	32.9	(3.4)	49.9	(11.2)	27.8	39.3	18.2	14.7
Korea	62.3	(13.7)	–	–	–	–	–	–
Taiwan	32.8	(2.5)	81.3	(19.3)	11.7	54.0	28.0	6.3
China	33.0	(1.9)	56.0	(2.8)	12.1	33.0	21.9	33.1
Singapore	56.7	(7.8)	84.2	(30.3)	6.1	41.7	48.3	3.9
Vietnam	59.9	(20.5)	47.8	(19.9)	13.8	37.0	30.2	19.0
(Pooled)	46.0	(8.3)	63.8	(13.9)	14.3	41.0	29.3	15.4

B. Paternalism

Country	Parental Benevolence		Unconditional Deference		Levels of Attachment			
	Attached	Firmly Attached	Attached	Firmly Attached	Neither	One	Both	No Answer
Japan	34.6	(5.0)	23.9	(5.0)	41.6	33.4	10.4	14.6
Korea	56.1	(12.7)	36.4	(12.7)	26.7	41.7	23.6	8.0
Taiwan	75.0	(12.0)	25.6	(12.0)	18.1	53.9	22.0	6.0
China	79.1	(8.3)	69.6	(8.3)	3.4	13.9	61.9	20.8
Singapore	62.6	(13.5)	56.5	(13.5)	20.4	34.0	41.6	4.1
Vietnam	70.0	(40.2)	73.7	(40.2)	12.3	15.8	61.1	10.8
(Pooled)	62.9	(15.3)	47.6	(15.3)	20.4	32.1	36.8	10.7

Note: Parentheses are included to facilitate inter-item comparisons of percentages.
Source: 2005–8 Asian Barometer Surveys.

respondents to what extent they agreed or disagreed with this statement (Q139): "If we have political leaders who are morally upright, we can let them decide everything." In all six countries, minorities ranging from 2 percent in China to 21 percent in Vietnam remain firmly attached to meritocratic rule, expressing strong agreement with the statement. Only in two countries – Korea (14%) and Vietnam (21%) – are more than one in ten people unqualified supporters of nondemocratic rule by moral leaders.

When all six countries are considered together, these strong supporters form a small minority of less than one-tenth (8%) of the people in the entire region of Confucian Asia. This figure is, however, very close to those (9%) who are fully detached from the Confucian tradition of moral leadership in government. Not only are the extremes nearly evenly represented when the region is considered as a whole but so are the categories of somewhat more attached and somewhat more detached, resulting in an almost even split between attachment and detachment to the Confucian tradition (46% vs. 44%).

However, this even split does not hold within each of the region's countries. In three of the six Confucian countries – Korea (62%), Singapore (57%), and Vietnam (60%) – substantial majorities remain at least somewhat supportive of elitist or nondemocratic rule by moral leadership. In contrast, in the three other countries – China (33%), Japan (33%), and Taiwan (33%) – supporters of this rule constitute only about one-third of their respective populations. Thus in upholding the Confucian tradition of moral leadership the region's countries display a large divide.

Why are the people in China, Confucius's birthplace, less in favor of moral meritocracy than the people in authoritarian Vietnam or Singapore? Why are people in democratic Taiwan much less reluctant to endorse meritocracy than their peers in democratic Korea? Why do people in poor China and wealthy Japan equally disregard the importance of virtuous leadership in government? The level of socioeconomic modernization and political democratization provides few clues to these questions.

The Confucian notion of meritocracy does not allow ordinary people to participate in the political process. In a government led by moral leaders, people deemed neither virtuous nor cognitively competent are supposed to stay away from the process and follow the decisions made by their moral leaders, as long as the leaders treat them benevolently. Do people in Confucian Asia still prefer not to participate in the process as Confucius admonished more than two millennia ago: "When not in official position, do not be involved in its policies (*Analects* 8.14)?" To explore this question, the ABS asked respondents to what extent they agreed or disagreed with this statement (Q78): "If possible, I do not get involved in political matters." (Koreans were not asked this question.)

As in the case of moral meritocracy, those expressing either strong agreement or strong disagreement with the statement are in the minority (see Table 4.1a). However, those who expressed strong agreement outnumber those who expressed strong disagreement in four of the five countries in which the question was asked. In all five countries, more notably, those who remain at least somewhat attached to the Confucian tradition against mass participation in politics outnumber those who do not. In four countries, with the exception of Vietnam, half or more of the people are not interested in taking any role in the political process, putting them in line with Confucius's teaching.

When the five countries are considered together, nearly two-thirds (64%) are more unwilling than willing to participate in the political process. This figure is significantly larger than the one (46%) in favor of authoritarian rule by moral leadership. In Confucian Asia today, people remain more favorably oriented to this tradition of mass exclusion from politics than they do to the tradition of moral meritocracy.

However, views of mass exclusion also varied considerably across the five countries. In Singapore (84%) and Taiwan (81%), for example, more than four out of five people remain attached to it, in contrast to only 50 percent in Japan and 48 percent in Vietnam. Again, there seems to be no rhyme or reason for which countries have citizens who are more attached or detached from political participation; support for this particular principle, unlike that of moral leadership, seems to have little to do with the democratic or authoritarian type of regime or the level of socioeconomic development.

I now compare the different reactions that people in Confucian Asia have to each of the two principles of Confucian meritocracy. As pointed out earlier, in the region as a whole, more people are attached to the principle of politically passive citizenry than to that of moral leadership. Yet there is a great deal of difference across the five countries in the pattern of reactions to these two principles. In Singapore, majorities are attached to both principles. In Japan, in striking contrast, majorities are not attached to either of them. In China, Taiwan, and Vietnam, only one of the two principles attracts a majority. When Japan's pattern is compared with those of all of the other countries, it suggests that generations of democratic rule work to undermine Confucian political culture.

For each and all of the five countries except Korea, Table 4.1a reports the percentage of citizens at least somewhat attached to neither, one, and both of the two Confucian principles: moral meritocracy and a politically passive citizenry. When these five countries are considered together, the *partially attached* – that is those attached to one principle – are most numerous, constituting a plurality of nearly two-fifths (41%) of the population. The *fully attached*, those attached to both principles, constitute slightly less than one-third (29%). The *fully detached*, those attached to none of the principles, are least numerous and constitute a one-seventh minority (14%). When added together, the figures for the partially and fully attached indicate that a large majority of seven out of ten people (70%) in Confucian Asia remain attached to the Confucian legacy of moral meritocracy at least to some extent. More notable is that those *fully attached* to the legacy are more than twice as numerous as those unattached to it (29% vs. 14%).

Across the five Confucian countries, there is a great deal of variation in the extent to which people are attached to the Confucian legacy of meritocracy. In every country, neither the *unattached* nor the *fully attached* constitutes a majority. The relative size of these groups, however, varies a great deal. More than 20 percentage points separate the smallest and largest groups of *unattached* citizens (6% in Singapore and 28% in Japan). There is even a greater difference among the *fully attached*, which ranges from 18 percent in Japan to 48 percent in Singapore. In Japan, the oldest democracy in Confucian Asia, moreover, the *unattached* outnumber the *fully attached* by a large margin of 10 percentage points (28% vs. 18%). In all other countries, including newly democratized Taiwan, the *unattached* are outnumbered by the *fully attached* by large margins ranging from 10 percentage points in China to 42 percentage points in Taiwan.

It is not surprising that the *unattached* are most numerous in Japan, the oldest democracy in Asia; however, exposure to democracy does not necessarily result in strong detachment, because citizens in newly democratized Taiwan are more likely to express attachment than are those in the authoritarian countries of China and Vietnam. This finding suggests two things about the relationships between Confucian culture and democracy. First, the preponderance of a meritocratic orientation among the people does not pose a serious obstacle to democratic regime change. As shown in Taiwan, authoritarian rule has been transformed into a vigorous democracy even with a substantial level of full attachment to meritocratic rule. Second, the long experience of democratic rule, as in Japan, motivates people to dissociate themselves from the authoritarian Confucian culture. On balance, democracy seems to influence culture more than culture does democracy.

Popular Attachment to Paternalism

In Confucianism, good government must be paternalistic (*Mencius* 3A:5). Therefore "the relationship between the ruler and the masses is repeatedly cast as analogous to that of parents and their children" (Hall and Ames 1987, 143). As parents treat their children benevolently and care for their welfare, so should the rulers do for the masses. The masses, in return, should be deferential to the rulers as children are to their parents. Only when the rulers are benevolent to the ruled are the latter to remain deferential to the former, and so long as the rulers do their part, it is expected that the masses will have no reason to shirk theirs. When Duke Mu of Tsou asked what was the best thing he could do for his state, Mencius advised, "If you will put in practice a benevolent government, this people will love you and all above them, and will die for their officers" (*Mencius* 1B:12).

How do the contemporary publics of Confucian Asia understand their relationship with the government? Do they see it from the perspective of Confucian paternalism, which emphasizes parental benevolence? To address these questions, the ABS asked respondents to what extent they agree or disagree with this statement (Q64): "The relationship between the government and the people should be like that between parents and children."

In Table 4.1b, we see that a substantial majority of more than three-fifths (63%) of the people in the six Confucian countries endorsed the principle of benevolent government by agreeing with this statement. In five of these countries, moreover, majorities ranging from 56 percent in Korea to 79 percent in China endorsed it. Only in Japan, the region's oldest and richest democracy, did a relatively small minority of about one-third (35%) agree with it.

As with moral leadership, those *strongly attached* to the Confucian principle of paternalistic government constitute a minority in every country. Yet, the sizes of those minorities vary considerably across the six countries: Strong supporters of paternalistic government constitute a very small minority of less than one-tenth in Japan (5%) and in China (8%) but a plurality of two-fifths (40%) in Vietnam. Even in the two communist countries, there is a great deal of variation: Strong supporters are eight times more numerous in Vietnam than in China (40% vs. 5%). In all of the countries except Korea, however, supporters of benevolent government outnumber those of rule by moral leadership. In Confucian Asia as a whole, the idea of benevolent rule is more popular than that of moral leadership (63% vs. 46%).

The second principle of Confucian paternalism prescribes that ordinary people remain deferential to government officials as they do to their own parents.[5] Do people in Confucian Asia still prefer to remain deferential

---

[5] Nonetheless, it should be noted that the principle of graded love places parents above rulers when they are in conflict, as suggested in the following passage from *The Analects* (8:18): "In our village, those who are straight are quite different. Fathers cover up for their sons, and sons cover up for their fathers. Straightness is found in such behavior."

to those officials? Or have they become assertive and critical citizens? In this regard, the ABS asked whether they agree or disagree with this statement (Q134): "Government leaders are like the head of a family: we should all follow their decisions." Nearly half (48%) the people in six Confucian countries endorse the principle of authoritarian governance, which emphasizes the unconditional subordination of ordinary people to their political leaders.

A careful scrutiny of the data reported in Table 4.1b reveals that popular endorsement of this principle seems to depend greatly on whether respondents belong to a democratic or a nondemocratic regime. In the three nondemocratic countries – China (70%), Singapore (57%), and Vietnam (74%) – majorities remain attached to this principle of authoritarian rule. In communist Vietnam, nearly three-quarters are willing to comply with their leaders, as the Confucian principle prescribes. In striking contrast, in the three democracies of Japan (24%), Taiwan (26%), and Korea (36%), minorities of less than two-fifths remain attached to it. Obviously, the type – democratic or nondemocratic – of government in which people live affects the way they react to this principle of popular deference to the authorities. Evidently democratic regimes motivate their citizens to reject it, whereas nondemocratic regimes motivate them to hold onto it.

The patterns of popular support for Confucian paternalism take on more meaning when its two principles of benevolent leadership and deferent masses are considered together. In Japan, the oldest democracy, only minorities are attached to each of these two principles. In the two new democracies, Korea and Taiwan, minorities are attached to the principle of deferential masses, whereas majorities are attached to that of benevolent leadership. In all three nondemocracies – China, Singapore, and Vietnam – majorities are attached to both principles of paternalism. In Confucian Asia, people living in democracies are less supportive of paternalism than those living in nondemocracies. People in the oldest democracy are less supportive than are their peers in the new democracies. In Confucian Asia today, the longer people have lived in a democracy, the less supportive they are of paternalistic governance.

For each country and for Confucian Asia as a whole, Table 4.1b reports the proportions attached to neither, one, and both of the two principles of paternalism. One in five people (20%) in the region is not attached to either of the principles, and nearly two-fifths (37%) are attached to both of them. Nearly twice as many are fully attached to paternalism than are fully detached from it, and those fully attached to paternalism outnumber those fully attached to the two principles of meritocracy by 8 percentage points (37% vs. 29%). This suggests that the paternalistic tradition of Confucian political culture is more prevalent than the meritocratic tradition.

The prevalence of the paternalistic tradition, however, varies a great deal across the countries. Those fully attached to it constitute a very small minority of one-tenth in Japan (10%) and less than one-quarter in Taiwan (22%) and Korea (24%). Corresponding figures are 42 percent for Singapore, 61 percent for Vietnam, and 62 percent for China. Once again, the type of regime makes a significant difference: Support for paternalism is less prevalent in democratic than in nondemocratic countries, in new democracies than in old democracies, and in communist than in noncommunist authoritarian states. Citizens of communist states remain most strongly attached to paternalism, whereas those of the established democracy are least attached to it.

Overall Levels of Attachment to Confucian Political Culture

To what extent do East Asians remain adherent to the Confucian model of good government, which represents a mix of meritocracy and paternalism? To address this question, I measured the overall extent to which they are attached to all of the principles of meritocracy and paternalism. By counting the number of affirmative responses to the four questions measuring these principles, I constructed a 5-point scale estimating the extent of overall support for the Confucian model. On this scale, scores of 0 and 4 indicate, respectively, full detachment from and full attachment to the notion. I considered a score of either 3 or 4 as indicative of strong or high attachment. For each and for all of the five Confucian countries in which the four questions were asked, Table 4.2 reports their mean ratings on the scale and the percentages of their citizens who are highly attached.

On this 5-point scale, the five countries included for analysis averaged 2.3, a score higher than the scale midpoint of 2. This suggests that, on average, the people in Confucian Asia remain attached to more than half the four principles surveyed. The mean level of attachment is significantly higher in the three nondemocracies of China (2.9), Vietnam (2.7), and Singapore (2.7) than in the two democracies of Taiwan (2.2) and Japan (1.5). Those highly attached to the Confucian model are also

TABLE 4.2. *Overall Levels of Attachment to Paternalistic Meritocracy (on a 5-point scale)*

Countries	Scale Points					High Attachment (3 and 4)	Scale Mean
	0	1	2	3	4		
Japan	16.1%	25.8%	22.2%	11.2%	4.1%	15.3%	1.5
Taiwan	3.6	17.3	37.9	21.6	10.5	32.1	2.2
China	0.8	4.3	15.3	24.9	17.8	42.7	2.9
Singapore	1.9	13.9	24.4	27.1	26.5	53.6	2.7
Vietnam	2.8	9.0	16.2	28.4	21.4	49.8	2.7
(Pooled)	5.0	14.1	23.2	22.6	16.1	38.7	2.3

Source: 2005–8 Asian Barometer Surveys.

far more numerous in nondemocratic China (43%), Vietnam (50%), and Singapore (54%) than in democratic Taiwan (32%) and Japan (15%).[6] This finding of an inverse relationship between the level of a country's democratization and citizen support for the Confucian political tradition renders additional support for my claim that the democratization of political systems drives people away from political Confucianism.

Is popular affinity for the model of paternalistic meritocracy a phenomenon that exists only in Confucian Asia? Or is it also prevalent in non-Confucian Asia? To determine whether Confucian Asia is culturally distinctive, I compared the mean attachment level on the 5-point index and the proportion of the highly attached across two subregions of East Asia – Confucian and non-Confucian.

Figure 4.1 shows that, contrary to what one might expect, the highly attached are significantly more numerous in non-Confucian Asia, which includes Indonesia, Malaysia, Mongolia, the Philippines, and Thailand. In Confucian Asia, they constitute a minority of less than two-fifths (36%) versus a majority of 53 percent in non-Confucian Asia. Thus the Confucian legacy of paternalistic meritocracy is more prevalent in the non-Confucian region of East Asia.

On the 5-point scale tapping the level of overall attachment to this nondemocratic legacy, five Confucian countries – China, Japan, Singapore, Taiwan, and Vietnam – averaged 2.4, whereas five non-Confucian countries – Indonesia, Malaysia, Mongolia, the Philippines, and Thailand – averaged 2.7. Moreover, attachment levels are less variable in

---

[6] The highly attached are those who scored 3 or 4 on the 5-point scale.

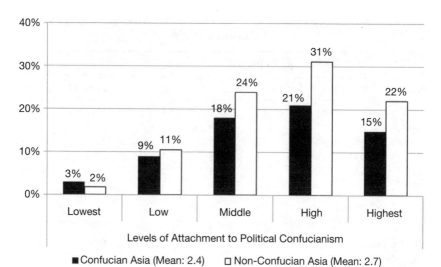

FIGURE 4.1. Levels of Attachment to Paternalistic Meritocracy in Confucian and Non-Confucian Asia. *Source:* 2005–8 Asian Barometer Surveys.

non-Confucian Asia than in Confucian Asia (.05 vs. 0.18 in standard deviation).

These findings of a higher mean and lesser variation suggest that the notion of paternalistic meritocracy is more uniformly popular among the mass publics of non-Confucian East Asia than among those of Confucian East Asia. Of the five countries in non-Confucian Asia, two – Mongolia (3.0) and Indonesia (2.6) – have been successfully transformed into democracies despite high levels of popular attachment to this notion. Evidently, paternalistic meritocracy is neither a unique cultural tradition of Confucian Asia nor a decisive obstacle to the democratization of authoritarian regimes in East Asia.

Demographic Analyses

What sorts of people in Confucian Asia remain highly adherent to the model of good government that Confucius and his followers advocated more than two millennia ago? To address this question, I first profiled those highly attached to most or all of its principles discussed earlier in terms of four demographic characteristics: gender, age, education, and family income. Table 4.3 uses these demographic variables to compare and contrast the proportions of Confucian adherents in each of the five countries where citizens were asked both pairs of questions.

TABLE 4.3. *Demographic Differences in Strong Attachment to Paternalistic Meritocracy (in percent)*

Countries	Gender		Age			Educational Attainment			Family Income		
	Male	Female	20–39	40–59	≥60	<High.sch	High.sch	College	Low	Middle	High
Japan	18.1	20.3	10.8	18.9	24.9	36.7	20.2	11.5	25.1	13.3	14.1
Taiwan	35.1	35.5	25.9	37.1	54.8	60.7	34.5	17.1	42.1	38.7	27.4
China	66.2	69.4	58.5	73.0	73.4	75.8	63.5	44.1	65.2	52.2	53.8
Singapore	53.9	60.6	55.8	55.3	65.1	71.9	55.7	43.5	63.5	65.2	46.4
Vietnam	63.5	64.8	63.0	65.8	63.8	76.7	64.3	37.5	73.7	62.9	62.1
(Pooled)	46.8	48.7	44.7	49.6	49.6	67.3	43.5	23.6	49.0	51.0	39.0

Source: 2005–8 Asian Barometer Surveys.

In every country, females are more supportive of the Confucian model than are their male counterparts. Only in Singapore, however, is the gender difference statistically significant (61% vs. 54%). Why is the gender difference most pronounced in the highly modernized nation of Singapore and less pronounced in poor Vietnam than rich Japan? The answers could be related to the extent to which the societies are patriarchal.

Age matters far more significantly than gender. In all of the countries except Vietnam, the proportions highly supportive of the Confucian political tradition vary considerably across the three age groups. In China, Japan, Taiwan, and Singapore, almost every step up in age brings an increase in the number of Confucian supporters. In Vietnam, however, age seems to have little impact, as the proportion of supporters hovers between 63 and 66 percent for all age groups. Yet Vietnam is like China and Singapore in that supporters constitute a majority in every age group. In Taiwan, they constitute a majority only in the oldest age group. In Japan, they constitute a minority in all three age groups. It is apparent that regime character affects the way in which age shapes popular reactions to the Confucian political legacy.

In all five countries, education matters significantly and consistently: The higher the level of education, the lower the level of support for Confucian moral meritocracy. In every country, the college educated are the least supportive, whereas the least educated (i.e., those without a high school education) are the most supportive of Confucian ideas of government. The least educated lead the former by large margins ranging from 25 percentage points in Japan to 44 percentage points in Taiwan. In every country, moreover, Confucian supporters among the college educated constitute a minority. From these findings, it is clear that more education, especially college education, orients people away from the Confucian tradition of good government.

Like education, income is, by and large, negatively associated with favorable orientations to the Confucian political tradition. In four of five countries – Japan, China, Taiwan, and Vietnam – low-income people are more supportive of the tradition than their wealthier peers in either the middle- or high-income groups. Yet in only two of these four countries, Taiwan and Vietnam, are high-income people the least supportive. In the two other countries, China and Japan, it is middle-income people who are the least supportive. In Singapore, they are the most supportive. When these findings are considered together, it is apparent that higher income, unlike more education, is not always instrumental in reducing popular support for Confucianism.

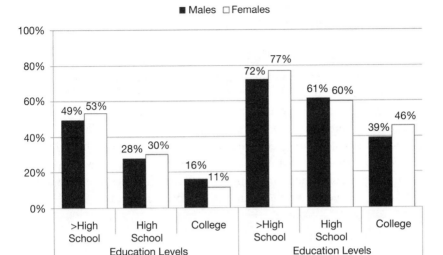

FIGURE 4.2. Regime Differences in the Effects of Gender and Education on Attachment to Paternalistic Meritocracy. *Source:* 2005–8 Asian Barometer Surveys.

Of the four demographic characteristics considered, gender and education have the most consistent effects on affinity for the Confucian tradition of paternalistic meritocracy: females are always more supportive of this tradition than are males, and those with less than a high school education are the most supportive, whereas those with a college education are the least supportive. In the analyses reported earlier, citizens of nondemocratic regimes are consistently more supportive of the Confucian political tradition than are those of democratic regimes. I now consider together these three variables – gender, education, and political regime – to identify those who are most and least adherent to the Confucian political tradition in the entire region of Confucian Asia.

Figure 4.2 reports proportions of Confucian adherents among males and females at three levels of education in democratic and nondemocratic countries. Regardless of the regime type in which they live, both males and females are always significantly less supportive of the Confucian tradition at a higher level of educational attainment. At every educational level, however, both males and females in nondemocratic countries favor Confucianism significantly more than their peers in democratic countries. In both democratic and nondemocratic countries, the gender that is more attached to the tradition varies according to the level of education.

As a result, the least educated in nondemocratic countries are the most likely to be supportive of the Confucian tradition, whereas the most educated in democratic countries are the least likely to be adherents. Among those least educated in nondemocratic countries, females are significantly more supportive of Confucianism than are their male counterparts (77% vs. 72%). Among those most educated in democratic countries, however, males are significantly more supportive than are females (16% vs. 11%). Accordingly, females with less than a high school education in nondemocracies and females with a college education in democratic countries are, respectively, the least and most likely to be supporters of the Confucian political tradition. Confucian supporters are seven times more numerous among the former than among the latter group (77% vs. 11%).

Cultural Preferences and Support for Confucian Tradition

In Chapter 3, we found that people in Confucian Asia, like those in other regions, differ considerably in the way they prefer to live with other people. Does this difference in their preferred way of life affect the way they react to the Confucian model of good government? Are upholders of hierarchical culture, which early Confucians advocated, more favorably oriented to the Confucian model than those who adhere to individualism or other cultural views?

To address these questions, I compare the proportions strongly supporting Confucian meritocratic paternalism across the four types of culture introduced in Chapter 3. For this analysis, I selected two pairs of questions asked in the second round of the Asian Barometer Surveys and identified upholders of four cultural types. For the group dimension of culture, I selected two questions tapping ties to family and nation (Q60 and Q76, respectively). For the grid dimension of social norms, I selected two questions tapping unconditional obedience to parents and teachers (Q56 and Q57, respectively). (Korea is excluded from this analysis because respondents there were not asked all of these four questions.)

For each and all of the five Confucian countries in which both pairs of questions were asked, Table 4.4 reports the proportions highly supportive of the Confucian model of paternalistic meritocracy among upholders of each cultural type. In all five countries, these proportions vary a great deal across the four cultural types. In Japan, for example, supporters of the Confucian model are four times more numerous among upholders of *hierarchism* than of *individualism* (34% vs. 8%). In all five countries, moreover, hierarchs are the most supportive of the Confucian political

TABLE 4.4. *Cultural Preferences and Support for Confucian Political Traditions (in percent)*

| Country | Preferred Cultural Type | | | | |
	Individualism	Fatalism	Egalitarianism	Hierarchism	(Entire)
Japan	8.0	13.5	18.8	33.7	15.2
Taiwan	24.0	32.0	37.3	52.9	32.1
China	18.3	33.7	48.4	57.6	42.7
Singapore	36.8	45.7	55.0	70.5	53.5
Vietnam	22.3	30.2	60.6	62.1	49.0
(Pooled)	20.0	28.4	45.2	57.9	38.7

Source: 2005–8 Asian Barometer Surveys.

tradition, and individualists are the least supportive of the same tradition. In all five countries, Confucian supporters among individualists are minorities, ranging from 8 percent in Japan to 37 percent in Singapore. Among hierarchs, they constitute a majority in four of these five countries, ranging from 53 percent in Taiwan to 71 percent in Singapore. When the five countries in Confucian Asia are considered together, those in favor of the Confucian paternalist meritocracy are most numerous among hierarchs (58%), who value group incorporation and elaborate role differentiation. They are followed by egalitarians (45%), isolates (28%), and individualists (20%), who value neither strong group incorporation nor elaborate social control. This clearly suggests a powerful relationship between cultural preferences and views of Confucian political tradition. It also suggests that hierarchical culture contributes to attachment to this tradition, whereas individualist culture detracts from it.

A careful analysis of these ratings reveals that supporters of Confucianism form a majority among hierarchs and egalitarians, whereas they form a minority among isolates and individualists. Attachment to Confucianism is significantly higher among hierarchs and egalitarians, who value strong group affiliations. This finding suggests that, of the two dimensions of cultural preferences surveyed, the group dimension matters far more significantly than the grid dimensions in shaping political preferences among the people in Confucian Asia.

Sources of Adherence to Confucian Good Government

Do many people in Confucian Asia still remain attached to the Confucian tradition of paternalistic meritocracy mainly because they desire to live in a hierarchical culture, which early Confucians advocated as a means of building a community of grand harmony? Or do they do so because of the type of regime in which they live? Can we account for the differences in Confucian political orientations by measuring exposure to such agents of change as democratization, modernization, and globalization?

To address these questions, I chose two types of culture, hierarchism and individualism, which are found, respectively, to be negative and positive influences on orientations toward Confucian political legacies. Then I analyzed these two cultural types as an influence on Confucian political orientations, as well as three other clusters of variables identified in previous research and literature as forces that shape political attitudes and beliefs. These three clusters of variables deal with the processes of socialization, modernization, and globalization, which people in historically Confucian Asia have been exposed to in varying degrees. In addition, I considered the type of regime, which reflects both the length of time of democratic political experience and the extent to which their regime is democratized. The three regime types I considered are nondemocracy (China, Singapore, and Vietnam), third-wave democracy (Korea and Taiwan), and second-wave democracy (Japan).

In Confucian society, males and females, as well as people of different ages, are supposed to play different roles in both private and public life. For this reason, I selected gender (SE002) and age (SE003) as two indicators of socialization. Modernization refers to the process of expanding socioeconomic resources that enables people to meet a variety of their needs and engage in an alternative to the traditional way of life. As education (SE005) and income (SE009) are key socioeconomic resources, I selected them as two indicators of modernization. Globalization refers to the process of gaining exposure to a variety of political ideas and practices not experienced in one's own country. Traveling overseas (Q68) and following developments in other countries (Q67) are considered indicators of globalization.

After pooling the samples of all five countries, I performed the multiple classification analysis (MCA) on the pooled data with a total of nine predictors. Table 4.5 reports *beta* coefficients for each predictor and multiple correlation coefficients for the entire sets of predictors. The *beta* coefficients allow us to determine the relative importance of each independent variable as an influence on the dependent variable. The multiple correlation coefficients allow us to assess how well the entire sets of independent variables predict the dependent variable.

TABLE 4.5. *Sources of Popular
Attachment to Confucian Political
Traditions (MCA estimates)*

Predictors	Beta
Socialization	
Gender	.02
Age	.01
Modernization	
Education	.17*
Income	.04
Globalization	
Foreign news	.01
Foreign travel	.05
Cultures	
Hierarchism	.12*
Individualism	.13*
Democratization	.27*
(R^2)	(.21)

* Significant at the .05 level.
Source: 2004–8 Asian Barometer Surveys.

Of the four clusters of theoretical variables considered, two clusters – socialization and globalization – have no significant direct effect on the extent to which people remain attached to the Confucian political legacy. The forces of socialization and globalization seem to affect their attachment indirectly through the type of culture in which they prefer to live. The two other clusters – modernization and culture – have a significant effect on attachment to Confucianism. Of the two indicators tapping modernization, however, only education is associated with significantly less support for Confucianism. In Confucian Asia, greater education, not more income, seems to motivate people to become significantly less supportive of Confucian government.

A more notable finding of Table 4.5 concerns the cultural cluster featuring preferences for hierarchism and individualism. Even when all other predictors are controlled for, both hierarchical and individualist cultural preferences significantly affect the dependent variable. According to MCA estimates, which are not reported in Table 4.5, hierarchical culture contributes significantly to affinity for the Confucian model of paternalistic meritocracy by 14 percentage points (56% vs. 42%), whereas individualist culture detracts significantly from it by 15 percentage points (35% vs.

50%). This contrasts with the finding that only one of the two indicators tapping modernization matters significantly.

The most notable feature of Table 4.5 concerns the extent to which the type of regime in which people have lived affects their attachment to Confucian political traditions: It is the most powerful of all the predictors entered in the analysis. Its *beta* coefficient (.27) is significantly larger than that of any other predictor, including those of education (.17), individualist culture (.13), and hierarchal culture (.12).

Finally, I examined how powerfully democratic regime experience affects attachment to the Confucian model of paternalistic meritocracy independent of all other influences considered. According to *adjusted* percentages resulting from the MCA analysis, which is reported in Table 4.5, a solid majority (53%) of the mass publics of nondemocracies remains attached to the Confucian legacies of paternalistic meritocracy even when the effects of all other variables are statistically removed. The corresponding figures for citizens of new and old democracies are 40% and 23%, respectively. Citizens of democracies are more motivated to dissociate themselves from those Confucian legacies than are those of nondemocracies, as are citizens of an old democracy than those of a new democracy. The longer citizens live in a democracy, the less likely they are to remain attached to those legacies.

In conclusion, the political environment in which people in Confucian Asia live matters significantly more than any of the eight personal attributes considered in this analysis. Consequently, many of the people in Confucian Asia are likely to remain attached to Confucian political traditions as long as they live in an authoritarian regime. This finding reinforces the importance of the earlier conclusion that democratization can take place even where large proportions of citizens are attached to Confucian ideas, because it shows that the first step in democratization is not changing people's attitudes toward their Confucian heritage; rather, people's attitudes toward their Confucian heritage will likely change when they experience democratization.

Summary and Conclusions

This chapter addressed four specific questions dealing with Confucianism as a system of government: one conceptual and the three other empirical. First I created a conceptual framework by defining the Confucian notion of good government in terms of its core constituents and principles, which I compared with those of liberal democracy. I then began the empirical analysis with an examination of the extent to which people in Confucian Asia support the two central ideas of meritocracy and paternalism. Then I identified the sorts of people who are most and least attached to those ideas and examined how people's preferred types of culture are associated with attachment to the Confucian political legacy. Finally I sought to determine why some people in Confucian Asia favor Confucianism as a system of government more than others.

In classical Confucianism, good government is equated exclusively with the government that works for the people by providing for their physical welfare and spiritual well-being. Substantively, however, it places greater priority on the economic welfare of individual citizens than on their political and civil rights. Procedurally, Confucian good government requires the rule by virtuous or moral leadership. Because government is managed exclusively by the morally superior class, it is fundamentally different from a democratic government elected by ordinary people and run by their representatives. In short, Confucian good government is neither democratic nor liberal: It is a paternalistic meritocracy.

Of the four specific principles underlying the Confucian government of paternalistic meritocracy, majorities of the mass publics in Confucian Asia as a whole still remain at least somewhat attached to two: the exclusion of ordinary people from the political process and benevolence by government officials. The principles of moral leadership and top-down hierarchical governance fail to win the support of a majority. Yet even these principles, which run directly counter to the core principle of democratic governance by the people, are endorsed by large minorities of more than two out of five people in Confucian Asia.

When all four Confucian political principles are considered together, a very small minority of 5 percent is detached from all of them, whereas more than three times as many (16%) remain fully attached to all of them. Although those fully attached do not constitute a majority in any Confucian country, the region still remains a great deal more attached to than detached from the model of paternalistic meritocracy, which Confucius and Mencius advocated for the building of a harmonious community called *datong shehui.*

All Confucian countries are alike in that large majorities of their adult populations remain attached to one or more of the principles of paternalistic meritocracy. Yet the breadth and depth of their attachment vary a great deal across the countries. For example, the Chinese are attached to nearly twice as many principles as are the Japanese (1.5 vs. 2.9 on a 5-point scale). People in nondemocracies remain far more deeply attached to these principles than in democracies. In the former, a majority or plurality of more than two-fifths is attached to most or all of the principles; in the latter, only a minority of less than one-third is equally attached to them.

Even within democratic countries there is significant variation in the proportion of the highly attached. It is significantly smaller in the older, second-wave democracy of Japan than in the younger, third-wave democracy of Taiwan (15% vs. 32%). Within the same region, people become less attached to these traditions when their regime is transformed into a democracy. They also become less attached to them the longer they experience democratic politics. This clearly suggests that democratic politics lessens popular attachment to Confucianism more strongly than the latter deters the former.

Surprisingly, popular attachment to this nondemocratic model of meritocratic government is more pervasive throughout the non-Confucian region than the Confucian region of Asia. In all the non-Confucian countries – Indonesia, Malaysia, Mongolia, the Philippines, and Thailand – majorities are either fully or mostly attached to those principles, a phenomenon that does not exist in four of five countries in the Confucian region. Evidently, popular affinity for the model of moral meritocracy that Confucius and his followers advocated is not confined to Confucian Asia.

When all five countries in Confucian Asia are considered together, the presence or absence of democratic rule in these countries emerges as the most powerful influence on the extent to which their people are attached to the political ideas of Confucianism. Even educational attainment, largely recognized as the strongest predictor of all political attitudes, is not as powerful as democratization in driving people away from Confucianism. In democratic countries in this region, therefore, the political ideas of Confucius will likely become less popular among the mass publics as their countries experience further consolidation and maturation of their democratic political systems.

In nondemocratic countries, the persistence of authoritarian rule is likely to encourage some citizens to remain attached to the Confucian meritocratic tradition primarily by inculcating them in the virtues of a hierarchical culture that emphasizes strong group affiliations and social control. The positive effect of this nondemocratic rule, however, may not be strong enough to offset the power of all other forces undermining the popularity of the Confucian tradition.

In response to the surging forces of socioeconomic modernization and globalization, for example, those citizens are more likely to be oriented away from the virtues of hierarchical culture and to those of individualist culture favoring democratic rule. Even without the democratization of their regime, an increasing number of ordinary people are likely to weaken in their adherence to Confucianism. In both democratic and nondemocratic Confucian Asia, therefore, Confucianism as a model of government is likely to lose its appeal. This process of democratizing Confucian political culture, however, will remain very slow.

PART III

ENGAGING IN CIVIC LIFE

5

Communitarianism and Civic Activism

In all human societies, there is a space in which people interact outside their families and apart from the state. This sphere in which people enter relationships and form associations of their own choosing is the realm of civil society (Alagappa 2004; Diamond 1999). Civil society has both a structural and a cultural dimension (Norris 2002; Putnam 1993). The informal groups and formal organizations that people enter into voluntarily represent the structural dimension of civil society, whereas the values and norms they share with other members of their formal and informal networks constitute civil society's cultural dimension. This chapter focuses on the structural dimension of civil society, exploring it in terms of interpersonal ties and associational activism. In the next chapter, I analyze civil society's cultural dimensions in terms of the shared norms of interpersonal trust and tolerance.

This chapter begins with a brief review of recent developments in the study of civil society. On the basis of this review, I explicate the Confucian notion of civic life and contrast it with the Western liberal model of civic life. I then examine whether the contemporary publics of Confucian Asia remain attached to the classical Confucian model or have embraced the Western liberal model. Next, I estimate the extent to which residents of Confucian Asia join in informal groups and participate in formal associations of various types. Finally, I determine how attachment to Confucian civic traditions affects formal and informal associations independently of other known influences on associational activism.

Recent Research on Civil Society and Democracy

For the past two decades, a great deal of theoretical and empirical research has been conducted on the role that civil society plays in the process of democratic transition and consolidation (Bermeo 2003; Burnell and Calvert 2004; Cohen and Arato 1992; Diamond 1994, 1999; Keane 1999; Paxton 2002; Putnam 1993, 2000; Warren 2000). It has found that, when citizens create a vigorous civil society by trusting each other and joining voluntary associations and groups, they are able to organize powerful opposition to a nondemocratic regime and replace it with a democratic one (Howard 2003; Karatnycky and Ackerman 2005; S. Kim 2000; Linz and Stepan 1996). Once democracies are established, the relational networks of civil society can contribute to good government (i.e., one that is accountable, effective, and limited) by preventing state agencies from abusing power and by making those agencies responsive to the people's preferences (Putnam 1993; Tavits 2006; Tusalem 2007). These voluntary associations also enable their members to learn the norms of democratic citizenship and participate in the political process (Boix and Posner 1998; Gibson 2001; Warren 2000).

Conceptually, the literature is in general agreement that civil society is a multidimensional phenomenon, encompassing physical and psychological connections among its members (Alagappa 2004; Chambers and Kymlicka 2001; Diamond 1994, 1999; Habermas 1989; Kumar 1993). There is also agreement that civil society's dimensions mutually reinforce each other (Newton 2001; Norris 2002): The structural dimension of social connections made through formal associations or informal groups motivates members to trust and tolerate other people, and the cultural dimension of interpersonal trust and tolerance motivates people to join those associations and groups. By reinforcing each other, these two dimensions of civic activism and norms produce a vigorous civil society that, in turn, leads to the improvement of democratic citizenship and governance (Newton 2001; Paxton 2002; Putnam 1993).

Theoretically, the constructive relationship between civil society and democracy is predicated on two principles of liberal democracy: liberal individualism and political pluralism (Galston 2002; Lomasky 2002; Talisse 2005). According to the principle of liberal individualism, government becomes more democratic and governs more judiciously when its powers are in check and its functions are limited in scope so that individuals are free to pursue their interests without impairment from the state. According to the principle of political pluralism, government becomes limited when civic associations are autonomous from the state and free to participate and compete with each other in the political process for the interest of their members.

Underlying these virtues of limited government and political contestation is the premise that the communal good – what is best for all members of society – is achieved through a negotiation process in which civic associations represent their members' interests. Consequently, civic associations become agents for democratic change only when they self-regulate and compete with each other to represent the interests of their respective members in the political process. Members of these associations become promoters of democracy only when they join with others to demand their share of benefits from the state. In this liberal notion of civil society, there is little room for the state and the civic associations to collaborate with one another for the benefit of the nation as a whole. There is also little room for the associations to collaborate with each other on interests of national concern. Nor is there much need for individual citizens to fulfill their duties to the community in which they live.

At an empirical level, much of the recent research on the structural dimension of civic activism has focused either on the extent to which people are involved in secondary and tertiary associations that are *formally* organized or on particular types of associations, whether bonding or bridging (Howard 2003; Norris 2002). As a result, little is known about the way in which people *informally* interact with each other in civil society on a person-to-person basis. Moreover, studies that have looked at informal social connections have focused only on the degree or density of such connections. Consequently, almost nothing is known about the quality of informal person-to-person relations, which remain the most common and important form of civic life in Confucian Asia (J. Chan 2004).

The Confucian and Liberal Models of Civil Society

Since the publication of Robert Putnam's *Making Democracy Work* (1993), the liberal model has become the dominant paradigm in studying the role of civil society in democratization. Scholars of the neo-Tocquevillean bent have all emphasized that civic organizations can perform their democratic functions successfully only when individual citizens are free to join them and the organizations are independent of the state so they can promote their members' shared interests. Therefore, the free and active participation of autonomous individual citizens in the political process is one important structural characteristic of liberal civil society, and another is the presence of competing groups and associations pursuing private interests independent of the state.

As discussed in earlier chapters, the Confucian conceptions of a good society and of a good government preclude individual citizens from pursuing their own interests independently of the interests of their families, communities, and states. As a form of benevolent paternalism, Confucian government does not encourage the masses to participate in the political process nor to interact with government officials, except for the act of remonstration when leaders fail to lead by moral example and run an oppressive government. Moreover, as a system of social ethics, Confucianism emphasizes the importance of creating a community of grand harmony called *datong shehui* in which people collaborate for the well-being of their community rather than compete for their own interests (W. Hu 2007; Madsen 2002, 2008; S. M. Kim 2010, 2011).

Unlike John Locke and other liberal thinkers, early Confucians believed that humans can live in peace and happiness only when they achieve harmony within themselves and with others (Li 2006, 2008b). To emphasize this viewpoint, Confucius said in *The Doctrine of the Mean*,

When there are no stirrings of pleasure, anger, sorrow, or joy, the mind may be said to be in a state of equilibrium. When those feelings are stirred and act in their due degree, there ensues what may be called a state of harmony. Equilibrium is the great root from which grow all acts of humanity; harmony is the universal path that guides them. Let the states of equilibrium and harmony exist in perfection, and a happy order will prevail throughout the heavens and earth, and all things will be nourished and flourish.

Accordingly, Confucius and his followers (*Mencius* 3B:1) endorsed harmony as the ultimate end of personal life as well as communal life; they characterized the building of a community of harmonious people as "the most important thing in human affairs." To build such a community, early Confucians emphasized the importance of mutual support between members of relational networks and the balancing of their divergent interests. Such a fiduciary community requires all members to shoulder responsibility and to maintain harmonious relationships with other people by acknowledging each individual's "oneness with all people" and with "humanity" (*Analects* 7:34, 8:13, 12:10, 19:3). As discussed in previous chapters, therefore, Confucianism is often viewed as incompatible with the liberal conceptions of citizenship and civil society that emphasize individual citizens' autonomy and independence (Nuyen 2002).

Indeed, in the Confucian community of grand harmony, there is no such thing as an "autonomous individual" (Fingarette 1972); humans are situated in a web of interpersonal relations, each of which requires the fulfillment of attendant responsibilities (Rosemont 2008, 51; Tu 1993, 143). Achieving moral perfection, indeed realizing full humanity, depends on an individual's carrying out his or her duties to others. Peaceful, prosperous communities exist only when individuals have attained this wholeness through mutual sharing.

In classical Confucianism, therefore, civil society constitutes much more than an aggregate of its individual components or parts: It represents an organic whole wherein individuals and their collectives are related to each other and depend on each other in a manner similar to the relationship between the individual cells of an organism (Tan 2003b, 53). The opening passage of *The Great Learning* (quoted in W. Chan 1963, 86), which Confucius wrote, presents this organic conception of social life by linking it with family and personal lives:

The ancients who wished to manifest their clear character to the world would first bring order to their states. Those who wished to bring order to their states would first regulate their families. Those who wished to regulate their families would first cultivate their personal lives. Those who wished to cultivate their personal lives would first rectify their minds.

This anthropocosmic or organic notion of society does not allow for conceiving the world in terms of unconnected parts that are free to pursue their own interests. Instead, just as when cells within an organism begin propagating for the sake of propagating – and not for the sake of the organism – the result is cancer, so, in the Confucian tradition, do individuals and groups that begin pushing their own interests apart from those of their communities and states become a threat.

In this Confucian communitarian perspective, the family is the only social group with which the state is supposed to interact. Because no other intermediate associations are supposed to exist as independent entities, their presence poses "a challenge to its organic, family-like view of the ideal society" (Nosco 2008, 29; see also Fox 1997). Within this society, people and their social groups (their families) are inseparable parts of their communities. Mutually cooperative and harmonious relationships, not competitive and adversarial relationships, are the most distinguishing characteristic of Confucian civic life.

Moreover, as discussed in Chapter 4, the Confucian doctrine of paternalistic governance does not allow voluntary associations to play an independent role in the political process; their intervention in the process is considered destructive to its ideal of the paternalist state (Nosco 2008, 27). In such a state, where virtuous leaders work for the welfare of their people, rulers are not just umpires overseeing the provision of fair opportunities to subjects pursuing their own interests but parents entrusted with the fundamental responsibility of educating individuals and families to overcome selfishness and contribute to the welfare of the entire community.

In this Confucian tradition of paternalistic rule, therefore, social groups and the state should form a mutually interdependent and complementary communion rather than a confronting polarity (Rozman 2003). In principle, civic associations are not allowed to remain adversarial and antagonistic to the state. In this regard, Richard Madsen (2008, 6) notes that in a Confucian state, "People-based groups cannot properly exist without the general permission, guidance, and supervision of the government."

In addition, the Confucian doctrine called "Doctrine of the Mean" deters individuals and groups from acting solely for their own benefit. This doctrine prohibits the imposition of one's personal views on others, but instead calls for maintaining a balance or equilibrium between divergent views. As a means of achieving such a balance, it emphasizes the importance of avoiding direct competition among individual citizens and their groups and adopting a nonassertive approach to the resolution of conflicts.

In classical Confucianism, nonetheless, people are entrusted with a responsibility to remonstrate with government officials who fail to fulfill their moral responsibilities (Nosco 2008, 37; see also de Bary 1998; de Bary and Tu 1998). This suggests that a Confucian civil society can work against and independently of the state; however, even in this situation, the ultimate goal of citizen protest against the state is to create *datong shehui*, a community of grand harmony, by restoring government for the people, but not by the people. The responsibility of remonstration therefore cannot be deemed compatible with an adversarial and competitive model of civil society. As Sor-hoon Tan (2003b) notes, the model that is suitable for societies with a strong Confucian heritage is likely to be a *complementary and cooperative model* that recognizes interdependence between civil society and the state.

Thus, the Confucian communitarian model of civil society and the Western liberal model contrast sharply because they are predicated on diametrically opposing conceptions of human nature and development (Fan 2004, 92; see also S. M. Kim 2010, 2011). Of the two models, which one do contemporary publics in Confucian Asia prefer? To address this question, I first examine Confucian Asians' adherence to the Confucian principles of interpersonal and intergroup relationships using the Asian Barometer Surveys (ABS). I then explore the extent to which people in Confucian Asia associate with other people informally and formally. Finally, I examine how Confucian civic orientations shape their informal and formal associations.

The Preferred Model of Civil Society

Interpersonal Life

How do people in Confucian Asia perceive themselves vis-à-vis their fellow citizens? Do they perceive themselves as free, autonomous individuals as in the Western liberal conception of civil society? Or do they perceive themselves as interdependent and mutually supporting relational beings, as prescribed in the Confucian notion of the self? These are two contrasting conceptions of interpersonal relations and the roles that individual citizens should play as the building blocks of a civil society (Tao and Brennan 2003; Tu 1985).

To ascertain the views that people in Confucian Asia have of interpersonal relationships, I selected a pair of questions from the second round of the ABS. The first question (Q30) asked respondents how strongly they agreed or disagreed with the following statement: "By helping people in trouble today, someone else will help me when I am in trouble someday." This item was intended to tap adherence to the norm of *shu* (reciprocity), which both Confucius (*Analects* 15:24) and Mencius (7A:4) called "the most comprehensive principle of conduct for all life." The second question (Q58) asked respondents how strongly they agreed or disagreed with this statement: "When one has a conflict with a neighbor, the best way to deal with it is to accommodate the other person." This item was intended to tap adherence to the norm of harmonious relations with other people (*Analects* 1:12).

Together these two questions are intended to tap attachment to the Confucian model of *mutually supportive relations* among individual human beings. Affirmative responses to both questions indicate full endorsement of this model. In contrast, negative responses indicate full endorsement of the liberal model of *autonomous and competitive* interpersonal relationships. An affirmative response to one question and a negative response to the other points to adherence to a mix of these two

TABLE 5.1. *Levels of Attachment to the Confucian Norms of Civic Life*
(in percent)

A. Norms of Interpersonal Life

| | Principles of Interpersonal Relations | | | | | | |
| | Reciprocity | | Mutual Accommodation | | Levels of Attachment | | | |
Country	Firmly Attached	Attached	Firmly Attached	Attached	Neither	One	Both	No Answer
Japan	75.6	(27.6)	72.3	(9.6)	5.2	27.6	56.4	10.8
Korea	62.5	(9.6)	59.9	(7.8)	13.1	40.0	39.2	7.7
Taiwan	76.7	(53.8)	27.9	(1.8)	3.7	52.7	22.4	14.8
China	77.4	(56.4)	60.5	(2.5)	10.1	31.3	47.7	17.2
Singapore	86.6	(46.4)	74.5	(10.8)	2.5	31.1	64.4	2.0
Vietnam	96.2	(82.9)	83.9	(35.6)	0.5	13.9	81.2	4.4
(Pooled)	79.2	(46.1)	63.2	(11.4)	5.9	32.8	51.9	9.5

B. Norms of Communal Life

| | Principles of Communal Life | | | | | | |
| | Priority of Community | | Intergroup Harmony | | Levels of Attachment | | | |
Country	Firmly Attached	Attached	Firmly Attached	Attached	Neither	One	Both	No Answer
Japan	42.8%	(6.2%)	40.8%	(4.3%)	23.3%	37.5%	19.2%	20.0%
Korea	39.9	(4.0)	35.5	(3.1)	32.4	35.3	17.8	14.4
Taiwan	51.5	(4.5)	57.4	(5.0)	17.0	40.6	31.2	11.2
China	75.6	(8.7)	56.6	(3.7)	2.0	20.1	47.9	30.0
Singapore	72.7	(11.5)	49.3	(7.5)	13.8	41.9	38.9	5.3
Vietnam	88.3	(47.9)	39.5	(14.3)	3.9	40.7	37.0	18.4
(Pooled)	61.8	(13.8)	46.5	(8.3)	15.4	36.0	32.0	16.6

Note: Parentheses are intended to facilitate inter-item comparisons of percentages.
Source: 2005–8 Asian Barometer Surveys.

models and suggests a shift from the Confucian model to the liberal model
of interpersonal relationships.

For six East Asian countries, Table 5.1a reports the proportions affirming each of the two Confucian principles, as well as none or both of them.
In all six countries, substantial or large majorities – ranging from 63 percent in Korea to 96 percent in Vietnam – endorse the view that people
are mutually dependent on each other. In all six countries considered
together, nearly eight out of ten people (79%) endorse this Confucian

principle of reciprocity at least somewhat. This confirms that people in Confucian Asia tend to uphold the Confucian conception of humans as relational beings rather than the liberal notion of humans as autonomous selves.

Nonetheless, it should be noted that those whose support of the principle of reciprocity is unqualified form less than half (46%) of the population of Confucian Asia. Equally noteworthy is that there is a great deal of variation among the proportions of unqualified upholders across the countries in the region, ranging from 10 percent in Korea to 83 percent in Vietnam. Only in three countries – China (56%), Taiwan (54%), and Vietnam (83%) – do unqualified supporters constitute majorities, and in Singapore, they constitute a near majority (46%). In contrast, in Japan (28%) and Korea (10%), they constitute small minorities. Throughout the region, popular attachment to the Confucian notion of interpersonal reciprocity varies a great deal more in depth than in breadth.

When asked about how to deal with conflict with a neighbor, in all six countries except Taiwan (28%), majorities, ranging from 60 percent in Korea to 84 percent in Vietnam, opt for an accommodating approach. However, only minorities ranging from 2 percent in Taiwan to 36 percent in Vietnam express unqualified endorsement of this approach. In every country, moreover, significantly fewer people express support for this approach than for the principle of interpersonal reciprocity. Nearly one out of seven (16%) supporters of the reciprocity principle chooses not to give in to their neighbors. Such unwillingness to put the principle of harmonious relations into practice is most pronounced in Taiwan, where nearly as many as two out of three (64%) supporters of the Confucian principle of reciprocity refuse to accommodate their neighbors. I see nothing in the data to explain why more than three times as many people in Taiwan as in the other Confucian Asian countries are unwilling to accommodate their neighbors.

To analyze affirmative responses to both questions I constructed a 3-point index to register the overall endorsement levels of the Confucian communitarian and Western liberal models of interpersonal relationships. A score of 0 on this index indicates no endorsement of the Confucian model and full endorsement of the Western model. A score of 2 indicates the reverse, and a score of 1 indicates partial endorsement for each of the two models. For each and all six countries in Confucian Asia, Table 5.1a reports percentages of each level of endorsement.

Vietnam stands out from the five other countries with 81 percent of its population fully endorsing the Confucian model; it is ahead of the next most Confucian country in this matter (Singapore, 64%) by almost

20 percentage points. In Japan (56%) a smaller majority is fully supportive of the Confucian model that emphasizes the importance of interdependent and cooperative interpersonal relationships. In China (48%), Korea (39%), and Taiwan (22%), full supporters constitute minorities. Among the three nondemocracies – China, Vietnam, and Singapore – supporters of Confucian interpersonal relations are most numerous in the socioeconomically least developed country of Vietnam. In contrast, among the three democracies – Japan, Korea, and Taiwan – they are most numerous in the oldest democracy of Japan.

Despite these national differences in full adherence to the Confucian model, it should be noted that, in all six countries, those who completely reject this model in favor of the liberal model featuring independent and competitive interpersonal relationships form the smallest group. Only in Korea (13%) and Taiwan (10%) do more than one in ten embrace the liberal model by rejecting the principle of reciprocity and favoring an adversarial relationship over a cooperative relationship with a neighbor. When all six countries are considered together, supporters of the Confucian model are eight times as numerous as those of the liberal model (52% vs. 6%). In Confucian Asia today, the principles of Confucianism, not Western liberalism, still guide interpersonal relationships.

Communal Life

Confucianism, unlike liberal individualism, does not endorse the primacy of individuals and their inalienable rights; instead, it emphasizes the community "more than the individual's life itself" (Fingarette 1972, 17). In Confucianism, each individual can become truly human only through experiencing harmonious interactions with others (*Analects* 18:2). Therefore, followers of Confucianism place the interests of their communities ahead of their own interests and their communal duties to others ahead of their individual rights by "cultivating oneself to bring comfort to the people" (*Analects* 14:42). The desire of Confucian followers to build a community of grand harmony where they can live in peace and happiness motivates them to value cooperation and consensus among all members of the community.

Therefore do people in Confucian Asia prefer, in principle, the Confucian model of the complementary public-regarding civic life to the liberal model of the competitive self-regarding civic life? To address this question, I selected another pair of questions from the ABS. The first question (Q76) asked respondents how strongly they agreed or disagreed with this statement: "For the sake of the national community/society, the individual should be prepared to sacrifice." The second question (Q136) asked respondents how strongly they agreed or disagreed with this statement: "Harmony of the community will be disrupted if people organize lots of groups." These two questions are intended to tap attachment to the two central Confucian principles of communal life: the priority of the community over its components and harmonious relationships among those components. Affirmative responses to both questions confirm full support for the Confucian model, whereas negative responses confirm full support for the liberal competitive model. In contrast, one affirmative and one negative response indicate partial support for each model and suggest a transition from the former to the latter.

For the six Confucian countries, Table 5.1b reports the proportions affirming each of the two Confucian principles – one emphasizing communal interests and the other emphasizing cooperative or noncompetitive relations among formal associations or groups of citizens. Based on the responses to these two questions, the table reports the proportions endorsing the Confucian model fully, the liberal model fully, and a mix of the two. Of the two principles, there is more variance across nations in the endorsement of the first, communitarian principle, which stresses the priority of communal interests over individual interests. In four countries – China (76%), Taiwan (52%), Singapore (73%), and Vietnam (88%) – majorities endorse this principle at least somewhat. In two countries, Japan (43%) and Korea (40%), about four in ten endorse it to the same extent.

Unqualified or strong supporters of the principle of prioritizing communal interests fail to form a majority in any country. Vietnam is the only country in which the strongly supportive form a near majority (48%). In the five other countries, about 10 percent or less expressed unqualified support for it. When all six countries are pooled together, strong supporters of the Confucian communal principle form a small minority of 14 percent of the population in historically Confucian Asia. When these supporters are compared across regime types, it is evident that the three nondemocracies of China (76%), Singapore (73%), and Vietnam (88%) register significantly higher levels of support for the principle of prioritizing communal interests than do the three democracies of Japan (43%), Korea (40%), and Taiwan (52%). Authoritarian regimes seem to be more successful than democratic regimes in motivating people to value the community in which they live and to be less self-centered.

Concerning the Confucian principle of achieving a harmonious community by preventing the formation of competing groups, the residents of all six countries are rather divided. Less than half (47%) chose the Confucian principle of harmonious cooperation over the liberal principle of adversarial competition. Only in China (57%), Taiwan (57%), and Singapore (49%) does a majority or near majority endorse this Confucian principle at least to some extent. In the three other countries, only minorities – ranging from 36 percent in Korea to 41 percent in Japan – endorse harmonious or cooperative intergroup relationships. In Japan, Korea, Singapore, and Vietnam, where a majority of their respective populations endorse the Confucian principle of cooperative interpersonal relationships, a minority endorse the same principle for intergroup relationships.

These findings indicate that the Confucian model is preferred to its liberal alternative to a greater extent in the informal interpersonal sphere of civic life than in the formal communal sphere. A comparison of Tables 5.1a and 5.1b shows that, in the six Confucian countries as a whole, those fully supportive of Confucianism in the interpersonal sphere outnumber those equally supportive of it in the communal sphere by a large margin of 20 percentage points (52% vs. 32%). Of the four countries in which full supporters constitute a majority or a near majority, moreover, the full supporters of Confucian interpersonal principles lead full supporters of Confucian communal principles in three, including Japan, Singapore, and Vietnam. These differences suggest that people in Confucian Asia tend to differentiate civic life into two spheres: informal interpersonal and formal communal. Their adherence to Confucianism remains stronger in their informal relationships than in their formal associations.

There is, nonetheless, a notable exception to this conclusion. For example, in Taiwan, a small minority (22%) endorses the Confucian principle of cooperation in interpersonal association over the liberal principle of competition, in contrast to a significantly larger minority (31%) for the same Confucian principle in intergroup associations (compare tables 5.1a and 5.1b). Only in Taiwan are people more supportive of the Confucian principle of cooperation in intergroup associations than in interpersonal associations. Apparently, people in Confucian Asia have become less Confucian and more liberal in the formal communal sphere of civil society than in its informal interpersonal sphere (32% vs. 52%).

To show more precisely how much more strongly people in Confucian Asia remain attached to Confucian interpersonal life than Confucian communal life, Table 5.2 reports those who support cooperation in only one of these two spheres (i.e., the informal sphere but not in the formal sphere, or the formal sphere but not in the informal sphere). When all six countries are pooled together, there are twice as many supporters of Confucianism in the informal interpersonal sphere than in the formal

TABLE 5.2. *Four Patterns of Cooperative Orientations*
(in percent)

Countries	Life Spheres of Cooperation			
	None	Interpersonal	Intergroup	Both
Japan	9.7	42.0	10.4	30.4
Korea	21.9	36.2	11.8	23.7
Taiwan	28.7	9.6	39.2	18.2
China	6.6	22.8	18.9	37.7
Singapore	12.4	36.1	10.9	38.4
Vietnam	5.8	49.5	5.2	34.3
(Pooled)	14.2	32.7	16.1	30.4

Source: 2005–8 Asian Barometer Surveys.

spheres (33% vs. 16%). In four countries – Japan, Korea, Singapore, and Vietnam – the former are more than three times as numerous than the latter. As pointed out earlier, people in Confucian Asia differentiate civil society into two separate spheres, interpersonal and communal. In the interpersonal sphere that involves face-to-face contact, they prefer to develop cooperative and harmonious associations. In the communal sphere of organized associations, many (15%) want their groups to compete rather than cooperate with each other.

To what extent do people in Confucian Asia remain attached to the Confucian value of cooperation? To address this question, Table 5.2 shows the percentages that affirmed cooperation for both interpersonal relations and intergroup associations and for neither of them. The unwillingness to support cooperation in either setting indicates the rejection of the Confucian value of cooperation in favor of the liberal value of competition. In contrast, the willingness to support cooperation in both settings, interpersonal and intergroup, indicates full support for the Confucian value of cooperation.

When all six countries are considered together, those who support cooperation in just one setting are most numerous (49%), followed by those who support cooperation for both interpersonal relations and intergroup associations (30%); 14 percent did not value cooperation at all. Thus more than twice as many people are fully adherent to the Confucian value of cooperation than are fully adherent to its liberal alternative of competition. The figures also make it clear that full supporters of the Confucian value of cooperation constitute a relatively small minority of less than one-third (30%) of the Confucian Asian population. China and

TABLE 5.3. *Overall Levels of Attachment to the Confucian Model of Civic Life*

Country	Attachment Levels					(Mean)
	Lowest	Low	Middle	High	Highest	
Japan	1.3%	11.4%	23.1%	27.5%	11.9%	(2.5)
Korea	5.6	18.4	26.2	22.7	8.7	(2.1)
Taiwan	2.3	15.1	27.6	24.0	8.8	(2.3)
China	0.1	1.9	10.8	22.9	27.2	(3.2)
Singapore	0.5	6.4	21.6	37.5	27.1	(2.9)
Vietnam	0.2	1.0	8.1	39.2	31.8	(3.3)
(Pooled)	1.7	9.0	19.6	29.0	19.3	(2.7)

Source: 2005–8 Asian Barometer Surveys.

Singapore are the only two countries with a plurality (38%) fully adherent to the value. Korea (24%) and Taiwan (18%) are the only two countries with less than one-quarter fully adherent.

Communitarian Civic Life

In the Confucian model of communitarian civic life, individuals and the state supplement each other instead of opposing each other, although higher priority is placed on the interests and values of the latter than of the former (Bell 2010; de Bary 1998). Civic associations also cooperate rather than compete with each other for mutual benefits. To what extent do people in Confucian Asia still remain attached to this communitarian model? To what extent do they endorse its liberal alternative?

To explore the overall level of affinity for the Confucian and liberal models of civic life, I considered together the extent to which respondents indicate a preference for Confucian interpersonal values and Confucian intergroup values. After summing pro-Confucian responses to the two pairs of questions – the first pair dealing with interpersonal relations and the second with communal life – I constructed an index of Confucian civic orientations with scores ranging from a low of 0 to a high of 4. On this index, the lowest score of 0 indicates full detachment from the Confucian communitarian model of civil society and full attachment to the Western liberal model of civil society; the highest score of 4 indicates full attachment to the former and unqualified antipathy for the latter.

Table 5.3 shows that on this index the six countries had an average score of 2.7, which is above the midpoint of 2, indicating greater attachment to the Confucian model than the Western one. With a score of 3.3, Vietnam, the least modernized country both socioeconomically and politically, registers the highest level of popular attachment to the principles of Confucian civic life. This communist country is followed by China (3.2), Singapore (2.9), Japan (2.5), Taiwan (2.3), and Korea (2.1). Interestingly, popular attachment to the Confucian communitarian model of civic life is higher in the three nondemocratic countries of China, Singapore, and Vietnam than in the three democracies of Japan, Korea, and Taiwan. This raises the question of whether support for Confucianism is a cause of or consequence of authoritarian rule. In China, Vietnam, and Singapore, these two factors are most likely to reinforce one another, with Confucianism discouraging popular demand for democratic regime change and authoritarian rule discouraging detachment from Confucianism.

Another notable feature of Table 5.3 is that in every country, only minorities, ranging from 9 percent in Korea and Taiwan to 32 percent in Vietnam, remain fully attached to the Confucian communitarian model. This indicates that in every Confucian country, majorities have begun to shift their preferred model of civic life away from the Confucian model toward the liberal model in the wake of the powerful wave of political democratization and economic liberalization over the past three decades. Yet those who have shifted fully to the liberal model constitute a very small minority of 6 percent or less in every country. Moreover, in every country, the fully liberal are outnumbered by those who remain fully attached to the Confucian model, confirming its prevalence over the liberal model.

However, of the two subregions of Confucian Asia – democratic and nondemocratic – the legacies of Confucian civic life are far more pronounced in the nondemocratic countries of China, Singapore, and Vietnam. In these countries nearly 30 percent remain fully attached to Confucian civic life, in contrast to much smaller minorities of about 10 percent or less in the democratic subregion. Thus, the fully attached to Confucian civic life are nearly three times more numerous in Confucian Asia's nondemocracies than in its democracies (29% vs. 10 %).

When all six countries are considered together, a relatively small minority of 19 percent remains fully attached to the Confucian communitarian model and a larger minority of 29 percent is mostly attached to it. When these two figures are combined together, a near majority (48%) of people in Confucian Asia still remain more attached to than detached from the traditions of Confucian civic life. More notably, in Confucian Asia today, those attached to the Confucian model are four and a half times more numerous than those attached to the Western liberal model (48% vs. 11%; see Table 5.3). This can be considered another piece of evidence that Confucianism still remains a formidable cultural tradition in Confucian Asia. Nonetheless, the region is no longer deeply embedded in the traditions of communitarian civic life that Confucius and his disciples advocated, but it is in great flux from the communitarian to the liberal model of civic life.

In Asia, is the Confucian model of communitarian civic life prevalent only in the Confucian region? If not, is it more prevalent in Confucian Asia than in non-Confucian Asia? To address these questions, I compared the percentages of Confucian supporters across the two regions. In three out of six countries in Confucian Asia, supporters of the model constitute majorities – ranging from 50 percent in China to 71 percent in Vietnam. In contrast, in all five non-Confucian countries in which the two pairs of questions discussed earlier were asked, supporters of the Confucian model form majorities: Mongolia (60%), Indonesia (69%), the Philippines (57%), Thailand (57%), and Malaysia (53%). Supporters of the Confucian model averaged 48 percent in the six Confucian countries, in contrast to 61 percent in the five non-Confucian countries. On the 5-point index tapping the overall level of attachment to the Confucian model, the Confucian countries averaged 2.7, in contrast to 2.9 for the non-Confucian countries. It is thus apparent that the Confucian civic model is less popular in historically Confucian East Asia, which has experienced socioeconomic modernization to a greater extent, than in non-Confucian East Asia.

Demographic Analyses

In Confucian Asia, which segments of the population remain the most and least supportive of the Confucian communitarian model? In Table 5.4, I explore this question in terms of four standard demographic characteristics: gender, age, education, and income. For this analysis, I define "supporters of the Confucian model" as those who are favorably disposed to all or most of its four principles, scoring above the midpoint (2.0) of the 5-point index tapping Confucian civic orientations. I then compare the proportions of supporters across each demographic variable and identify the demographic characteristics that are most and least often associated with support.

Throughout Confucian Asia, gender matters little. Only in Korea do the two genders differ significantly in support of the Confucian communitarian model: Korean males are significantly more attached to the

TABLE 5.4. *Demographic Differences in Attachment to the Confucian Civic Model* (in percent)

	Gender		Age			Educational Attainment			Family Income		
	Male	Female	20–39	40–59	≥60	<high.sch	high.sch	College	Low	Middle	High
Upholders											
Japan	52.8	51.8	48.1	46.0	61.0	66.4	53.0	47.0	59.5	51.0	50.0
Korea	40.7	36.1	33.2	38.5	53.8	43.8	41.2	33.3	52.7	37.5	37.1
Taiwan	42.4	42.0	30.8	45.4	65.1	62.8	42.8	25.9	48.1	42.6	32.7
China	79.4	79.6	74.0	81.7	85.1	83.4	77.6	65.6	78.6	72.4	71.0
Singapore	69.3	69.5	69.0	66.4	78.3	79.2	68.0	62.1	72.1	72.5	62.7
Vietnam	88.2	88.8	87.8	89.1	89.0	93.9	87.6	84.6	88.6	87.9	88.9
(Pooled)	62.5	60.2	52.7	61.3	70.0	75.8	63.0	45.3	60.5	60.3	58.5
No Close Ties											
Japan	8.0	9.8	6.6	6.8	11.9	12.2	11.2	3.7	16.4	6.6	6.1
Korea	26.0	33.3	26.4	26.5	45.5	52.2	30.7	21.3	47.4	29.7	23.9
Taiwan	11.1	15.3	8.3	10.7	28.9	24.3	20.8	8.3	19.0	11.2	7.2
China	6.2	6.3	3.8	6.3	10.0	7.4	5.3	2.5	15.0	7.0	7.0
Singapore	26.4	29.7	17.0	27.8	52.2	53.8	23.6	9.9	46.1	25.8	14.5
Vietnam	44.8	48.7	50.7	42.2	59.9	55.0	44.6	39.5	46.7	48.7	44.9
(Pooled)	20.7	23.6	21.6	19.8	27.1	30.0	22.4	13.2	34.3	24.2	22.2
Close Ties											
Japan	76.9	70.1	79.6	80.4	64.3	59.8	72.5	82.1	55.5	76.1	81.0
Korea	56.6	48.0	57.7	52.3	37.5	30.1	50.1	62.1	31.0	51.0	60.2
Taiwan	65.2	58.9	69.4	63.5	43.5	44.2	65.5	71.4	49.6	67.1	73.9
China	61.4	56.8	64.2	59.3	50.7	56.6	61.8	65.0	40.0	55.8	60.5
Singapore	58.1	55.4	69.5	59.5	29.2	30.2	60.2	78.5	34.4	59.5	75.1
Vietnam	29.0	25.1	24.5	33.1	34.7	20.4	31.3	34.2	24.7	26.4	31.7
(Pooled)	57.6	53.4	57.6	57.8	47.9	42.5	55.7	69.7	39.8	56.2	60.2
Nonjoiners											
Japan	26.9	30.4	35.8	26.1	27.4	35.8	27.7	25.8	33.3	28.1	21.4
Korea	69.9	82.8	82.7	68.4	77.7	85.0	75.1	75.7	81.8	75.0	72.8
Taiwan	70.0	71.3	83.4	63.9	58.1	66.2	70.9	74.5	70.9	70.5	70.5
Singapore	89.7	90.6	90.4	90.4	88.6	93.5	90.2	85.6	91.2	89.7	88.3
Vietnam	37.4	45.9	46.5	37.2	35.1	49.3	39.5	33.9	51.6	44.6	34.6
(Pooled)	65.6	69.6	73.8	66.8	58.5	74.6	66.8	60.4	69.2	66.0	52.5
Multiple Joiners											
Japan	43.8	44.5	32.8	51.6	43.8	29.9	45.6	50.4	35.5	42.3	55.0
Korea	16.3	5.3	6.1	17.7	7.8	1.4	11.3	12.8	5.8	10.9	14.1
Taiwan	10.9	8.6	3.7	13.9	14.0	9.9	10.5	8.0	9.0	10.5	11.4
Singapore	2.5	1.0	1.7	1.7	1.8	0.4	1.5	4.3	1.1	1.2	3.4
Vietnam	27.1	20.6	21.7	25.9	27.0	18.5	25.1	30.7	20.9	19.4	29.5
(Pooled)	16.6	13.8	10.2	16.9	20.5	9.1	15.3	22.2	12.3	14.3	25.7

Source: 2005–8 Asian Barometer Surveys.

Confucian civic model than are their female counterparts (41% vs. 36%). However, age does matter significantly in all the countries except Vietnam. In the five countries where age matters significantly, supporters of the Confucian model are most numerous among those in their 60s and older. In three of these countries – Korea, China, and Taiwan –higher age is always associated with a greater proportion of Confucian supporters. When the six countries are pooled together, the same pattern of consistently positive relationship holds: The young are the least favorably oriented and the old the most favorably oriented to the principles of Confucian communitarian civic life.

Unlike age, education and income are both negatively associated with Confucian civic orientations. Of these two socioeconomic variables, however, education's effect is far more consistent and stronger. In every country, increases in educational attainment are always accompanied by significant decreases in support for Confucian communitarianism. As a result, there is a large gap of 31 percentage points in support levels between the least and most educated population segments in Confucian Asia: Among those with less than a high school education, supporters of Confucianism constitute a large majority of 76 percent, whereas among the college educated, supporters form a minority of 45 percent. Between the two extreme income groups, Table 5.4 shows a much smaller gap of 2 percentage points (61% vs. 59%). Although higher income groups are less supportive of Confucianism, supporters of Confucian civic life constitute majorities in all income groups.

When all six countries are pooled together, age and education emerge as the two demographic variables that are most strongly associated with the dependent variable. Table 5.4 shows that, in the entire region of Confucian Asia, older age contributes to popular support for the Confucian model of communitarian civic life, whereas higher education detracts from it. Figure 5.1 shows the interaction of these two demographic variables to identify the most and least supportive of the Confucian civic model. Among each of the three age groups, higher education always accompanies a significantly lower level of attachment to the Confucian model. However, higher age is not always associated with a higher level of such attachment, as suggested by a pooled analysis of the two variables. Among the college educated, higher age always brings greater support, with the oldest cohort being most supportive of the Confucian model. Among the least educated, young people support Confucianism significantly more than their older counterparts. Consequently, in Confucian Asia today, young people with less than a high school education and those with college education are, respectively, the most and least ardent supporters of the Confucian civic model. The former are nearly two times more likely to endorse this model than their cohorts with a college education (84% vs. 43%). Among the least educated segment of the Confucian

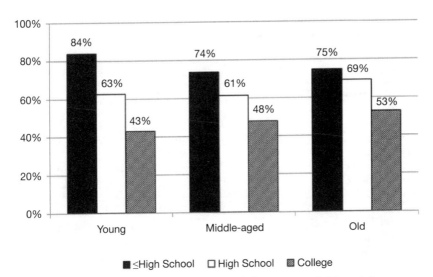

FIGURE 5.1. Demographic Characteristics of the Least and Most Adherent to the Confucian Model of Civic Life: Age and Education. *Source:* 2005–8 Asian Barometer Surveys.

Asian population, why are young people more favorably oriented to Confucianism than their older peers (84% vs. 75%)? The current data do not offer an explanation.

Informal Association

Confucianism teaches that humans are social beings who become fully human only through association and cooperation with other people, as discussed in Chapter 3 in great detail. To what extent are people in Confucian Asia closely connected with other people, as Confucius and his followers admonished them to be "close to one another by nature" (*Analects* 17: 2).

Breadth

To estimate the breadth of East Asians' informal interpersonal associations, the ABS asked the question, "On average, about how many people do you have contact with in a typical week?" Respondents were asked to choose one of five categories: (1) 0–4 people; (2) 5–9 people; (3) 10–19 people; (4) 20–49 people; and (5) 50 or more people. For each and all of the six Confucian countries, Table 5.5 shows their populations' distributions across these five categories.

TABLE 5.5. *Informal and Formal Associations* (in percent)

Associations	Countries						
	Japan	Korea	Taiwan	China	Singapore	Vietnam	Pooled
Informal Association							
Breadth							
<5 people	33.2	16.1	18.7	32.3	16.4	29.7	24.4
5–9 people	30.6	30.1	28.9	26.1	25.1	41.3	30.5
10–19 people	22.4	27.7	29.0	20.1	28.8	18.3	24.5
20–49 people	9.6	17.2	15.5	12.0	18.1	8.0	13.4
50 or more	4.0	8.2	7.1	9.5	16.1	2.7	7.1
Depth							
Being Asked for Help							
Never	16.6	39.2	33.0	36.9	34.2	56.5	36.1
Seldom	27.2	33.7	30.3	27.2	35.3	20.6	29.0
Occasionally	45.8	22.2	27.9	22.4	23.5	14.6	26.1
Often	8.1	1.7	8.0	7.3	5.0	3.8	5.6
Asking for Help							
No, nobody	18.3	36.1	18.1	7.9	35.8	56.3	28.7
Yes, few	48.5	37.0	30.8	27.0	45.5	30.3	36.5
Yes, some	27.6	22.4	41.3	45.1	14.3	8.3	26.5
Yes, many	3.1	1.7	7.2	17.2	3.1	2.3	5.8
Closeness							
Low	8.9	29.7	13.3	6.2	28.0	46.5	22.1
Middle	17.7	18.1	24.6	34.7	15.2	24.4	22.4
High	73.4	52.2	62.1	59.1	56.8	29.1	55.5
Formal Association							
Level							
None	28.8	76.5	70.6	–	90.1	41.1	61.9
One	27.1	12.8	19.6	–	8.1	34.6	20.6
Two	22.7	6.2	7.2	–	1.1	16.2	10.5
Three	21.5	4.5	2.6	–	0.7	7.8	7.0
Types							
Bridging	17.2	5.2	17.4	–	3.1	30.4	15.1
Bonding	17.7	8.1	1.4	–	2.3	12.8	8.0
Mixed	36.6	9.8	9.6	–	4.3	10.2	13.5

Source: 2005–8 Asian Barometer Surveys.

Of the five categories, the people of Confucian Asia as a whole chose the categories of "5–9 people" and "50 or more people" most and least often, respectively. In every country, those contacting 50 or more people a week constitute the smallest minority, and yet the percentages choosing this level vary considerably from 3 percent in Vietnam to 16 percent in Singapore. The modal or most popular response categories also vary considerably across the countries. In two countries – Korea and

Vietnam – pluralities, ranging from 30 to 41 percent, chose the "5–9 people" category. In Japan and China, the most frequently chosen item was the bottom category of "fewer than 5 people," at about 33 percent. In Taiwan and Singapore the middle category of "10–19 people" was the most popular choice, at 29 percent.

Across the countries, the proportions choosing the lowest two of the five categories also vary considerably. In China (58%), Japan (64%), and Vietnam (71%), substantial majorities reported contacting fewer than ten people a week, whereas in Korea (53%), Taiwan (52%), and Singapore (63%), majorities reported that they contacted ten or more people a week. In three of the six countries – Japan (33%), China (32%), and Vietnam (30%), which include the richest and poorest in Confucian Asia – as much as one-third of the population contacted fewer than five people in a week. Singapore is the only country with more than one-third (34%) of its population contacting twenty or more people a week. For reasons that cannot be specified here, informal interpersonal contacts are most extensive in Singapore and most limited in Japan and Vietnam.

Depth

Do more extensive interpersonal contacts entail close or meaningful relationships between those in contact? To address the closeness or depth of interpersonal relationships, I chose a pair of questions asked in the second wave of the ABS. The first question (Q28) asked, "How often are you asked to help influence important decisions in other people's favor?" Respondents could choose one of four categories: (1) "never," (2) "seldom," (3) "occasionally," and (4) "often." The second question (Q29) asked, "Are there people you ask to help influence important decisions in your favor?" Once again respondents could choose one of four categories: (1) "nobody," (2) "a few," (3) "some," and (4) "a lot." Affirmative answers to the first question, – not choosing the "never" category, indicate that other people have established ties close enough to the respondent to trust his or her advice. Affirmative answers to the second question, – not choosing the "nobody" category – on the other hand, indicate that the respondent is close enough to others to trust their advice.

When asked how often they had been asked to help others, a small minority of 17 percent in Japan to a solid majority of 57 percent in Vietnam replied "never" (see Table 5.5). Similarly, when asked about the number of people they could ask for help, a small minority of 8 percent in China to a solid majority of 56 percent in Vietnam replied "nobody." Vietnam is the only country where majorities answered both of these questions negatively. Japan is the only country where relatively small minorities of less than 20 percent answered both questions negatively.

When all six Confucian countries are analyzed together, 36 percent of the entire population in Confucian Asia reported "never" being asked for help, and 29 percent reported having "nobody" to ask for help. A comparison of these two figures suggests that in Confucian Asia these days, there are more people asking for help than people giving help (69% vs. 61%). These figures, each of which refers to a different aspect of close interpersonal relations, suggest that more people in Confucian Asia are disposed to receive help from others than to give help to others. They also suggest that a solid majority has established at least a partially close tie to others in their informal networks. In Vietnam where a majority replied negatively to both of the two questions, however, only a small minority can be expected to be closely connected with other people.

I then summed up affirmative responses to both questions and constructed a 3-point index measuring the closeness or depth of interpersonal relationships or ties. On this index, a score of 0 means that a person lives an isolated life with no close ties to others; scores of 1 and 2 mean the establishment of one-sided and close reciprocal interpersonal relationships, respectively. Table 5.5 reports that 22 percent of the entire population in historically Confucian Asia live an isolated life (i.e., a life with no close tie to anyone) and another 22 percent have a close one-sided relationship with others. A bare majority (56%) experiences close reciprocal ties in interpersonal life, which involve not only helping others but also being helped by others.

Table 5.5 shows a great deal of variation across the six Confucian countries in the extent to which people are closely connected with one another. Of the six countries, poorest Vietnam is the only country in which a near majority (47%) of the people lives an isolated life. It is also the only country in which people without any close ties to others outnumber those with close reciprocal relationships (47% vs. 29%). In the five other countries, those who experience close reciprocal interpersonal ties constitute majorities and outnumber those who live an isolated life by large margins of more than 20 percentage points. Of these five, Korea (30%) and Singapore (28%) are the only two countries where more than one-quarter of the population have not established a close tie with other people. For some unknown reasons, such loners are more than two times more numerous in these two countries than in China (6%), Japan (9%), and Taiwan (13%).

TABLE 5.6. *Experiencing a Fully Close Interpersonal Life by Levels of Interpersonal Contacts*

Countries	Number of People in Contact a Week					*(eta)*
	<5	5–9	10–19	20–40	50 or more	
Japan	54.5%	75.5%	91.0%	80.8%	93.0%	(.33)
Korea	43.0	49.2	58.3	54.7	56.6	(.11)
Taiwan	44.1	61.1	68.8	69.3	73.4	(.20)
China	50.1	62.1	63.1	64.0	72.6	(.15)
Singapore	39.7	52.5	59.7	69.5	64.2	(.19)
Vietnam	15.9	30.9	37.8	45.2	58.1	(.23)
(Pooled)	41.5	53.7	64.0	64.6	68.6	(.18)

Source: 2005–8 Asian Barometer Surveys.

Of all the countries in Confucian Asia, Japan is the only country with a large majority – 73 percent of its population – living a well-connected life. As discussed earlier, Japan, along with Vietnam, has the lowest level of interpersonal contact on a weekly basis. Although Singapore has the highest level of such contact, Japan leads Singapore in the proportion experiencing close reciprocal ties by 16 percentage points (73% vs. 57%). Across the countries, there appears to be little relationship between the levels of interpersonal contact and the closeness of interpersonal life.

On the individual level, however, there is a positive relationship between the two variables. In every country, the more people whom individual citizens meet with weekly, the more likely they are to live an interpersonal life with close reciprocal ties to these people. Even in Japan and Vietnam, where there is the lowest level of interpersonal contact, interacting with a greater number of people is associated with increasingly closer or fuller ties to others (see Table 5.6). In Vietnam, for example, those who meet fifty or more people a week are more than three times more likely to experience close reciprocal relationships than those who meet less than five people a week (58% vs. 16%). Understandably, a person may need to know many other people to find those with whom he or she can develop close ties.

In Confucian Asia, who are the people living an isolated life, and who have close reciprocal ties with others? Table 5.4 shows that, in all six Confucian countries, more females than males report living an isolated life with no close ties to others; conversely fewer females than males report experiencing close reciprocal ties to others. Surprisingly, females are thus less well connected with other people than their male

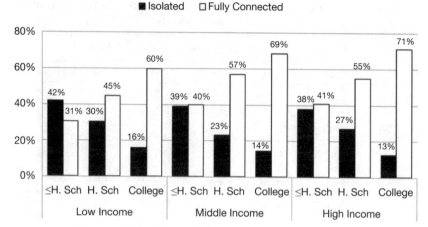

FIGURE 5.2. Demographic Characteristics of the Most and Least Connected to Other People: Income and Education. *Source:* 2005–8 Asian Barometer Surveys.

counterparts. Increasing age is more often associated with no close ties and with the lack of close reciprocal ties. Only in Vietnam is there a positive relationship between age and close interpersonal ties. In all six countries including Vietnam, however, more education and income are always or nearly always associated with decreases in the proportion of isolated people and increases in the proportion of well-connected people. In Japan, Taiwan, and Singapore, for example, college-educated people are more than three times less likely to live an isolated life than those without a high school education.

Of the four demographic variables, education and income are the two that are most often associated with the lowest and highest levels of interpersonal ties. In Figure 5.2, these two variables identify the least and most connected population segments of Confucian Asia. At each income level, more education is always associated with a smaller proportion of isolated people and a larger proportion of well-connected people. At two of the three education levels, low and high, more income, like higher education, is also always associated negatively with being isolated and positively with being well connected. Therefore the isolated are most prevalent among low-income people with less than a high school education (42%) and are least prevalent among high-income people with a college education (13%). In striking contrast, the well connected are least numerous among low-income people with less than a high school education (31%) and most numerous among high-income people with a college education

(71%). The contrasting patterns of interpersonal life of these two segments of the Confucian population suggest that socioeconomic resources are the key to transforming an isolated life into a well-connected life in historically Confucian Asia.

Formal Association

In addition to informal networks of social life, people associate with others through formal organizations or groups. These groups vary from being open to every segment of the population to being limited to a particular segment. To measure participation in formal networks, the ABS asked a battery of three open-ended questions (Q20–Q22), each of which asked respondents to identify their membership in organizations or formal groups. Unlike in the World Values Survey, the ABS respondents were not provided with a list of specific organizations or groups, nor were they asked whether they were an active or inactive member. They were simply asked to name up to three of the most important formal organizations and groups with which they were formally affiliated. Because the Chinese survey failed to ask any of the three questions to most of its respondents, China was excluded from our analysis of associational membership.

What types of formal organizations or groups are the most and least popular in Confucian countries? Table 5.7 reports the distribution of formal associational memberships across the twenty organizations most frequently named by respondents to the ABS. The pooled data from the five countries show that each type of organization has managed to recruit only small minorities, ranging from less than 1 percent to 14 percent. The residential association (14%) is the only type whose membership exceeds the 10 percent mark. Only two other types – sports and recreation clubs (6.6%) and agricultural associations (5.1%) – draw members from more than 5 percent of the people.

The associations' popularity varies a great deal across the five countries considered, although no category is uniformly popular among a substantial proportion in any Confucian country. Only the agricultural association and political party types are popular in Vietnam, a one-party state that has been neither democratized nor industrialized; 17 percent of Vietnam's population belongs to an agricultural association, whereas 14 percent claim membership in the ruling Communist Party. Sports and recreation clubs are a top association type only in affluent Japan (19%). In contrast, residential associations are popular in three countries: Japan (46%), Korea (20%), and Vietnam (22%). Alumni associations are

TABLE 5.7. *Distribution of Formal Associational Memberships across Twenty Associations* (in percent)

Associations & Groups	Countries					
	Japan	Korea	Taiwan	Singapore	Vietnam	Pooled
Political parties	2.0	1.2	1.6	0.3	14.4	3.9
Residential associations	45.5	19.9	3.5	2.4	21.7	14.0
Religious groups	4.2	5.4	7.4	3.6	1.4	4.6
Sports/recreation clubs	19.0	4.0	7.1	1.1	2.4	6.6
Culture organizations	1.4	0.5	4.0	0.4	1.7	1.8
Charities	1.2	0.4	4.5	0.6	3.2	2.2
Public interest groups	1.8	2.1	2.3	0.4	2.1	1.8
Labor unions	6.7	0.5	0.6	0.9	2.8	2.1
Agricultural associations	7.2	0.4	1.1	0.1	17.2	5.1
Professional organizations	3.3	0.6	3.0	0.3	2.2	2.0
Business associations	0.7	0.2	0.7	0.1	0.9	0.6
Parent-teacher associations	6.3	0.4	0.7	0.3	2.7	1.9
Producer cooperative	2.2	0.1	0.3		0.6	0.6
Consumer cooperative	6.4	0.1			0.3	1.2
Alumni associations	13.7	10.3	0.5	1.0	0.5	4.9
Candidate support organizations	1.7	0.1	0.1	0.1	0.6	0.5
Other occupational organizations	2.4	1.6	0.3	0.2	2.4	1.3
Other volunteer organizations	7.6	1.9	2.5	0.6	11.8	4.8
Hometown associations		3.5				0.7
Clan associations		2.1				0.4

Source: 2005–8 Asian Barometer Surveys.

popular in Japan and Korea, where 14 percent and 10 percent of the populations belong to these associations, respectively. In Taiwan and Singapore none of the twenty associations or groups recruited more than 10 percent of their respective populations as members.

Membership Density

How actively are people in historically Confucian Asia involved in formal associations or groups? To address this question concerning the density of associational membership, I first counted the total number of those associations or groups that they joined. Then I distinguished joiners from nonjoiners and divided joiners into single and multiple joiners by their number of organizational and group affiliations.

Table 5.5 reports that more than three out of five people (62%) in the five Confucian countries surveyed are not a member of any formal organization or group. Across the countries, however, the proportions of nonjoiners vary considerably. In Singapore, an overwhelming majority (90%) are nonjoiners. Nonjoiners also constitute substantial majorities in Korea (77%) and Taiwan (71%). In contrast, nonjoiners are a minority in Japan (29%) and Vietnam (41%), which is in striking contrast with the findings about interpersonal contact: Although Japan and Vietnam have the lowest levels of interpersonal contact, they are also the only two countries in which joiners of formal associations outnumber nonjoiners. In fact, there are more joiners in poor, authoritarian Vietnam than in rich Singapore and in democratic Korea and Taiwan. In Confucian Asia, it is evident that neither democratization nor socioeconomic modernization is instrumental in promoting formal associations. It is also evident that a high level of informal association does not necessarily lead to a high level of formal association.

How many people in Confucian Asia are joiners of multiple formal associations? Table 5.5 shows that, in the region as a whole, those who join more than one association constitute a small minority of 18 percent, and joiners of multiple associations are less prevalent than joiners of single associations (18% vs. 21%). Across the five countries, once again, there is a great deal of variation in the proportions of each category of joiner. In Japan, joiners of multiple associations constitute 44 percent of the population. In Vietnam, these joiners form a smaller minority of 24 percent; they constitute much smaller minorities in Korea (11%) and Taiwan (10%), and in Singapore, they form a very small minority of less than 2 percent (1.8%). In all countries except Japan, members of multiple associations are outnumbered by members of single associations. In Japan, however, the former outnumber the latter by a large margin of 17 percentage points (44% vs. 27%). Participation in multiple associations, not just one single association, seems to result from both an extended period of democratic rule and a high level of socioeconomic modernization.

Membership Type

People in Confucian Asia, like their peers in other regions, differ in whether they prefer "bonding" or "bridging" types of associations (Norris 2002). The bonding type connects "people who are like one another in important respects," whereas the bridging type links "people who are unlike one another" (Putnam and Goss 2002, 11). Of the twenty associations listed in Table 5.7, five belong to the bonding type that

reinforces closely knit networks among people sharing similar backgrounds or beliefs; these five are residential associations, religious groups,
alumni associations, hometown associations, and clan associations. The
fifteen other associations are examples of the bridging type of social networks that bring together people of different backgrounds. After determining whether joiners have memberships in only one or both types, I
grouped then into three types: bonding, bridging, and mixed.

For each country and for each type, Table 5.5 shows the relative size
of each type of associational membership. Taken as a whole, East Asians
are almost twice as likely to belong only to bridging organizations than
only to bonding organizations (15% vs. 8%) and are slightly more likely
to belong only to bridging organizations than to a mix of both (15%
vs. 14%). However, in Japan and Korea, bridging organizations are less
popular. Consequently, no single type of association can be considered
the most popular throughout the entire region of Confucian Asia.

Characteristics of Joiners and Nonjoiners

Who are the least likely to join formal associations, and who are the
most likely to join multiple associations? Table 5.4 explores these questions. All five countries are alike in that nonjoiners are more numerous
among females than males, but the association of gender with multiple joiners differs among them. In Japan, for example, multiple joiners are more numerous among females; in contrast, in the other four
countries, multiple joiners are more numerous among males. In all five
countries, nonjoiners are most numerous among the young in their 20s
and 30s, whereas multiple joiners are most numerous among the middle-
aged in their 40s and 50s in two countries: Japan and Korea. In two
other countries, Taiwan and Vietnam, multiple joiners are most numerous among the elderly in their 60s and older. In Singapore, age makes
little difference in the likelihood of being either a nonjoiner, a single-
association joiner, or a multiple-association joiner. When the five countries are considered together, however, nonjoiners are significantly more
numerous among younger people, and multiple joiners are significantly
more numerous among older people.

Across the five countries there are also considerable differences in the
levels of education and income most often associated with nonjoiners
and multiple joiners. In four countries – Japan, Korea, Singapore, and
Vietnam – nonjoiners are most numerous among the least educated and
the poor, whereas multiple joiners are most numerous among the college

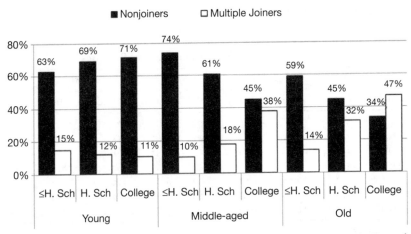

FIGURE 5.3. Demographic Characteristics of the Least and Most Active in Formal Associations: Age and Education. *Source:* 2005–8 Asian Barometer Surveys.

educated and the most affluent. In Taiwan, however, nonjoiners are most numerous among the college educated but are equally numerous across the three income categories; multiple joiners are equally distributed across the three categories of education and of income. When the five countries are considered together, however, more education and income are always accompanied by a smaller proportion of nonjoiners and a larger proportion of multiple joiners.

Age and education have a greater impact on the proportions of non-joiners and multiple joiners than do gender and income. In Figure 5.3, I pooled data from the five countries to profile the least and most active in formal associations in terms of age and education. Of the nine population segments defined by these two variables, middle-aged people with less than a high school education are the least likely to join any formal association and the least likely to become a member of multiple associations. Old people with a college education are the most likely to join an association and to become a member of multiple associations. The former, as compared to the latter, are more than two times more likely to be a nonjoiner (74% vs. 34%) and nearly five times less likely to become a multiple joiner (10% vs. 47%). More notably, among old college-educated people, multiple joiners outnumber nonjoiners. Apparently, old age and college education together are capable of transforming nonjoiners into multiple joiners.

TABLE 5.8. *Breadth and Depth of Interpersonal Contact by Levels of Attachment to the Confucian Norms of Interpersonal Life*

	Dimensions of Interpersonal Relations							
	Breadth				Depth			
Country	Low	Middle	High	(eta)	Low	Middle	High	(eta)
Japan	15.7%	15.3%	13.7%	(.02)	69.2%	70.5%	78.3%	(.08)*
Korea	22.3	25.7	24.3	(.02)	43.7	55.2	54.6	(.05)
Taiwan	22.8	23.9	22.1	(.02)	61.2	66.5	56.2	(.05)
China	25.7	20.5	22.8	(.03)	52.9	63.7	58.3	(.02)
Singapore	36.0	29.0	30.2	(.02)	64.0	60.3	54.7	(.08)*
Vietnam	20.0	11.5	10.3	(.04)	66.0	37.6	28.0	(.08)*
(pooled)	23.0	22.4	19.4	(.03)	55.2	61.4	52.8	(.06)*

*Statistically significant at the 0.05 level.
Source: 2005–8 Asian Barometer Surveys.

Confucianism and Civic Activism

When people in Confucian Asia embrace the Confucian principles of reciprocal and accommodative interpersonal relationships, do they associate with other people differently? Do those who are attached to these principles associate with others more frequently and more closely than those who are not? To explore these questions, I first compared the percentages of the broadly connected (i.e., those contacting twenty or more people a week) at each of the three levels of attachment to the Confucian principles (see Table 5.8).

Contrary to what would be expected, greater attachment to the principles of reciprocity and mutual accommodation is more often associated with a smaller number of people in contact. More surprisingly, in two countries, Japan and Vietnam, the number of people in contact is consistently smaller at each higher level of attachment. When all six countries are considered together, the relationships between the two variables are *negative* in direction, although not statistically significant. Apparently, stronger attachment to the Confucian principles of interpersonal reciprocity and accommodation does not correspond to the expansion of interpersonal networks.

Are those attached to these principles more closely connected with other people than are the unattached? A careful scrutiny of the data in Table 5.8 also reveals no consistent pattern of relationship between attachment to Confucian norms and the depth of interpersonal ties. In

TABLE 5.9. *Joiners of Voluntary Associations by the Levels of Attachment to the Confucian Norms of Communal Life*

Countries	Joiners of All Associations				Joiners of Bonding Associations			
	Low	Middle	High	(eta)	Low	Middle	High	(eta)
Japan	74.2%	70.7%	72.9%	(.03)	50.6%	51.7%	58.0%	(.05)
Korea	19.7	23.5	29.8	(.08)*	15.4	18.4	20.8	(.05)
Taiwan	24.1	26.6	35.6	(.10)*	8.2	9.8	12.5	(.05)
Singapore	8.0	9.8	10.5	(.02)	5.1	7.2	5.9	(.03)
Vietnam	70.0	66.0	57.4	(.09)*	20.5	24.6	24.6	(.02)
(Pooled)	34.2	35.6	29.5	(.05)	21.4	19.9	15.8	(.06)*

*Statistically significant at the 0.05 level.
Source: 2005–8 Asian Barometer Surveys.

Japan, for example, stronger attachment to Confucian norms is always accompanied by a higher proportion experiencing close reciprocal ties in interpersonal life. In Singapore and Vietnam, however, stronger attachment to Confucian norms of interpersonal relations is always accompanied by a decrease in the proportion experiencing close reciprocal ties. In the three other countries, there is no consistent relationship between the two variables. It is impossible with the data at hand to explain why attachment to the same Confucian notion of interpersonal life contributes to the experience of close reciprocal ties in Japan, while failing to do so in all other countries.

Does attachment to the Confucian notion of harmonious communal life have any correspondence with the likelihood of Confucian Asians' participating in formal associations and groups? Are Confucian Asians who are attached to Confucian norms more or less active in formal associations than those unattached? To address these questions, I compared the proportions of joiners across three levels of attachment to norms underscoring the primacy of community and community harmony. Table 5.9 reveals a statistically significant relationship between the two variables in three of the five countries. In two of these countries, Korea and Taiwan, the relationship is consistently *positive* (i.e., the higher the level of attachment to Confucianism, the higher the level of associational activism). In Vietnam, however, the pattern is reversed with those least and most attached to Confucianism being, respectively, the most and least likely to join at least one formal association. On balance, there is no clear pattern of relationship between levels of attachment to Confucian group life and associational activism.

However, there is a clear *positive* relationship between attachment to the norms of Confucian communal life and the bonding type of activism. In all five countries, those unattached to Confucian communal norms are the least likely to join bonding associations. In all except for Vietnam, moreover, a higher level of attachment to the norms is always accompanied by a greater prevalence of participation in bonding associations. Although not statistically significant, this positive relationship suggests that Confucian communal life encourages people to join those associations seeking to strengthen existing ties among their members.

Sources of Informal and Formal Associations

How do Confucian civic orientations affect the way in which people associate with others informally and formally? Do these orientations affect their involvement in informal and formal associations more or less powerfully than other known influences on civic life? To explore these questions, I performed on a set of four dichotomous dependent variables an MCA analysis of seven independent variables: overall attachment to the Confucian principles of interpersonal and communal life, gender (SE02), age (SE003), education (SE005), income (SE009), trust in the people in contact (Q26), and the type of resident regime (the last variable was discussed in Chapter 3).

As discussed in earlier chapters, gender and age together reflect different patterns of socialization, whereas education and income tap exposure to the structural forces of modernization. The level of trust that people place in others with whom they are interacting is widely known as an important component of social capital (Norris 2002; Paxton 2007). Each of the three regime types – nondemocracy, third-wave democracy, and second-wave democracy – in which people have lived indicates the length of their democratic political experience.

For five countries except China, in which the formal associational membership and family income questions were not asked, Table 5.10 reports MCA estimates of *beta* together with multiple correlation coefficients. *Betas* are standardized regression coefficients estimating the relative predictive power of each independent variable on each of four measures of association – two informal (breadth and depth) and two formal (joiners in all formal associations and joiners in the bonding type of associations) – after the effects of all other independent variables on the dependent variables are statistically removed.

TABLE 5.10. *Sources of Informal and Formal Civic Engagement* (MCA estimates)

Predictors	Informal Association		Formal Association	
	Breadth	Depth	All	Bonding
	Beta	*Beta*	*Beta*	*Beta*
Gender	.04	.02	.05	.01
Age	.08*	.05	.11*	.13*
Education	.07*	.15*	.06*	.05
Income	.05	.08*	.12*	.08*
Confucianism	.02	.06*	.08*	.06*
Trust	.10*	.09*	.07*	.02
Regime Type	.07*	.20*	.33*	.33*
(R^2)	(.03)	(.11)	(.16)	(.11)

*Significant at the .05 level.

Source: 2005–8 Asian Barometer Surveys.

According to the *betas* reported in this table, when all the countries are pooled, Confucian civic orientations, like family income, have no significant effect on the breadth of respondents' interpersonal lives, as measured by the number of people contacted in a typical week. Instead, this breadth is significantly shaped by four variables: age, education, trust in other people, and regime type. Of these four variables, trust and age are the two most powerful influences on the breadth dimension of informal associational life. As much as growing age reduces interpersonal contact, greater interpersonal trust increases it. From these findings, it is evident that the breadth of interpersonal contact in Confucian Asia is largely shaped by the forces of psychological motivation and physical strength, not by Confucian civic orientations.

In contrast, Table 5.10 shows that Confucianism matters significantly in fostering the closeness of relationships between those in informal networks. As do all other variables except gender, attachment to Confucian civic norms contributes significantly to closer ties between the people in contact. Yet, it does not foster it most powerfully, nor does it do so consistently. Regime type and education are the two most powerful influences promoting closer interpersonal relationships monotonically. As people in historically Confucian Asia live in a more democratic regime, they tend to experience a more mutually rewarding interpersonal life. Compared to less than half (49%) of the people in nondemocracies and less than three-fifths (57%) in third-wave democracies, nearly three-quarters

(74%) in the oldest second-wave democracy experience close reciprocal ties in interpersonal life, even after the positive effects of all other variables have been statistically removed.[1]

Attachment to the Confucian model of communitarian civic life also significantly affects the level of participation in formal associations or groups, especially in the bonding type: A high level of such attachment is always accompanied by a higher percentage of joiners in those associations or groups. According to MCA estimates, those fully attached to such ideals are one-and-a-half times more likely to become joiners than their unattached peers (43% vs. 28%) even after the effects of all other variables have been statistically removed. Those fully attached are also more likely to become joiners in the bonding type of associations than their unattached peers (24% vs. 18%). The embrace of Confucian civic norms, however, is not the most powerful influence on formal associational membership. The most powerful one is the type of regime in which people live. Even after the effects of all other variables have been statistically removed, associational members are more than two times more numerous in Japan, the oldest democracy, than in nondemocracies and third-wave democracies (72% vs. 31%).

In summary, Confucianism as a model of communitarian civic life significantly affects the way people in Confucian Asia interact with others in person and in groups, but it does not affect their interpersonal and intergroup relationships either powerfully or pervasively. Those connections are largely shaped by the forces of democratization and modernization.

Summary and Conclusions

This chapter began with a conceptual investigation of the Confucian notion of civil society, the sphere in which people interact with others on a voluntary basis. In explicating this notion, I set forth the Confucian tradition's understanding of what civil society is and is not; this understanding provides a foundation for further empirical analysis of civil society in the region. In Confucian thought, society is not merely an aggregate of free and autonomous individuals seeking to maximize their own interests. Nor is it a collective of interest groups competing against each other to maximize their own members' interests. Instead, it is a fiduciary community in which individual citizens and their groups complement each

---

[1] These percentages came from results of the MCA analysis of the depth of informal association, which is reported in Table 5.10.

other by fulfilling their mutually interdependent responsibilities. It is also an organic communion, wherein individuals and their groups are related to each other in an orderly fashion. Confucian civil society represents a complementary and cooperative model of civic engagements with the state. It contrasts sharply with the Western liberal model that emphasizes the importance of the individual over the community and that values competitive and antagonistic relationships between a civil society and the state.

In the informal sphere of civil society, which involves face-to-face personal contact, people in Confucian Asia tend to prefer the Confucian model of interdependent and cooperative relationships to the liberal model of independent and competitive relationships. Of the six Confucian countries surveyed, Taiwan is the only country where only a small minority supports the Confucian model. However, in the formal sphere of civil society – the sphere of organizational and group memberships – those fully supporting the Confucian communitarian model form small minorities in all six countries. In every country, moreover, more people support the liberal model in the formal sphere than in the informal sphere. This indicates that people in Confucian countries are far more liberalized in formal intergroup relations than in informal interpersonal relationships.

When the preferred models of informal and formal associations are considered together, only small minorities in all six countries are shown to be attached exclusively to either of the two contrasting models. Yet those exclusively attached to the Confucian communitarian model outnumber those attached to the Western liberal model. Supporters of the former are most numerous among the least educated, whereas supporters of the latter are most numerous among the college educated.

When considered together, these findings suggest three things. First, Confucian Asia today is no longer a region deeply embedded in the Confucian traditions of interdependent and cooperative civic life. Second, the Confucian civic traditions still remain more popular than the Western liberal traditions. Third, these traditions will become less prevalent with increases in college education. It should also be noted that the communitarian traditions, which Confucius and other early Confucians emphasized for harmonious civic life, are not unique to Confucian Asia; those traditions are valued as much in non-Confucian Asia as in Confucian Asia.

Regardless of Confucian Asians' attachment to those Confucian civic traditions, a majority in the region has established a close reciprocal tie with other people in their informal networks. Yet a much larger majority has failed to establish a relationship with unknown fellow citizens through the formal networks of voluntary associations or groups. Fewer than two out of five people (38%) in Confucian Asia as a whole are formally connected with other people through memberships in multiple associations. This minority of the connected is concentrated among high-income people with a college education. The isolated, informally or formally, are concentrated among low-income people with less than a high school education.

Within Confucian Asia, there is considerable variation in the extent and pattern of popular attachment to Confucian civic traditions. There is also notable national variation in the extent and patterns of social connections and in the way people associate with others. Of the six countries, Korea's people are least supportive of the Confucian civic traditions. Taiwan is the only country in which people value the Confucian civic traditions less in the informal sphere than in the formal sphere of civic life. China is the only country with a majority of the population endorsing the principle of harmony or accommodation in both interpersonal and communal life spheres. China is also the only nation with less than 10 percent of its population living isolated from other people. Japan is the nation of well-connected informal networks, whereas Vietnam is the most isolated nation with the greatest lack of such networks. Singapore stands out from the rest of Confucian Asia as the nation with the largest majority of nonjoiners in formal groups or associations.

Do Confucian civic traditions affect the way people in Confucian Asia associate with other people informally and formally? Bivariate analyses of the ABS data reveal no pattern of consistently significant relationship between these variables. Multivariate analyses of the pooled data, however, reveal that attachment to those traditions contributes significantly to closer ties between those in informal networks, although not to ties in larger interpersonal networks. It also contributes to joining formal associations, especially those bonding the similar backgrounds and interests that people hold. Confucian civic traditions, therefore, cannot be blamed for the underdevelopment of associational activism in Confucian Asia, which is known to be essential for democratic transition and consolidation.

6

Familism and Civic Orientations

Since the publication of Robert Putnam's (1993) seminal study of civic traditions in Italy, the norms and networks of civic life have been a subject of extensive research from a variety of disciplinary perspectives (Hooghe and Stolle 2003; Mishler and Rose 2001, 2005; Newton 2001; Putnam 1993, 2000; van Deth 2007; Warren 1999; Zmerli and Newton 2008). From this research a general consensus has emerged that interpersonal trust and tolerance constitute the key civic norms shaping the quality of public life and the performance of both political and social institutions. Among the scholars who have followed Alexis de Tocqueville's lead in the study of American civic norms and associational activism, there is a growing recognition that no society or polity can survive and thrive for an extended period of time without a trusting and tolerating public (Sander and Putnam 2010, 9; Sharma 2008).

Specifically, trust generalized to strangers has been found to promote the quality of communal life by leading people to cooperate and compromise, to play an active role in their community, and to behave morally (Putnam 1993). It has also been found to facilitate economic development by reducing "transaction costs" in markets (Fukuyama 1995a). Meanwhile, interpersonal tolerance has been understood to improve the quality of democratic government by allowing for a variety of policy alternatives and admitting their criticism (Badescu and Uslaner 2003; Uslaner 2002). In short, interpersonal trust and tolerance are widely recognized in the extant literature on civil society and political culture as the two essential civic norms promoting social cooperation and democratic governance (Jackman and Miller 1998; Theiss-Morse and Hibbing 2005).

In Confucianism, mutual trust (*xin*) is a cardinal virtue governing both interpersonal and political life (Lu 2001). The ultimate goal of Confucius's teachings was to build a harmonious community called *datong shehui*, made possible through citizens engaging in mutually beneficial interactions. To reach this goal, early Confucians emphasized the importance of developing a strong sense of mutual trust among ordinary citizens. Further, they advocated trust as the most fundamental principle of governance. As discussed in Chapter 4, Confucius taught the idea of government based on the trust of people and prioritized the cultivation of such trust ahead of the development of the economy and the military (*Analects* 12:7; see also *Mencius* 7B: 12). He also admonished the ruler to initiate a fully *xin* relationship with the people so that they would engage in such a relationship in response to his initiative (*Analects* 13:4). Thus Confucius and his followers recognized mutual trust as a prerequisite of building a harmonious community and good governance more than two millennia before contemporary scholars of the neo-Tocquevillean bent did.

In Confucianism, the family constitutes the foundation of all interpersonal relationships, including those between the ruled and the ruler. Yet by espousing a family-centered civic and political life, Confucianism is generally believed to have the paradoxical effect of discouraging rather than encouraging people to trust those outside their immediate family circles (Hahm and Bell 2004). Because Confucianism emphasizes the principle of graded love, its family-style ethics has been considered incompatible with the egalitarian principles of modern civic and political life that require interactions between citizens who do not know one another (J. Chan 2004). To date, however, very little empirical research has been done to examine how broadly and deeply people in East Asia remain attached to Confucian familism (Lee and Hsiao 2010). Even less research has been conducted to determine whether attachment to this traditional value encourages or discourages people from embracing the civic norms of interpersonal trust and tolerance.

To what extent do people in Confucian Asia trust each other? To what extent are they willing to tolerate those who hold views different from them? Why are some people in the region more trusting and tolerant than others? Does the Confucian way of family life motivate them to trust and tolerate other fellow citizens? Or does it discourage them from doing so? This chapter addresses these questions by exploring the *cultural dimension* of civil society in the region. I first explicate the notion of Confucian familism by examining the place the family occupies in civic life and its potential impact on interpersonal trust and tolerance. This conceptual explanation is followed by empirical analyses both of the extent to which people in Confucian countries remain attached to familism's central tenets and of the extent to which they trust other people, known and unknown, and tolerate those with conflicting interests and divergent goals. Finally, I examine the relative importance of Confucian familism as an influence on the civic norms of trust and tolerance.

The Notion of Confucian Familism

Throughout history, few teachers have emphasized the importance of the family to the well-being of individual citizens and of their communities as much as have Confucius, Mencius, and other early Confucians (Slote and De Vos 1998). For classical Confucians, the family is not merely a natural and biological unit; it constitutes the most fundamental and pervasive unit of social life. Three of the five cardinal human relationships – father and son, husband and wife, and elder and younger brothers – are encompassed in the family unit, and it serves as the environment in which human beings begin to learn how to behave as moral persons. Being the most powerful and enduring influence on the proper development of future social relationships, the family is the bedrock of all other interpersonal relationships.

In Confucian tradition, virtues directing family life are considered the foundation for all other virtues, including loyalty to the ruler. We see this, for example, when Confucius emphasizes filial piety (*hsiao*) as the highest virtue of all, as in the following passage:

The Duke of Sheh informed Confucius, saying, "Among us here there are those who may be styled upright in their conduct. If their fathers have stolen a sheep, they will bear witness to the fact." Confucius said, "Among us, in our part of the country, those who are upright are different from this. The father conceals the misconduct of the son, and the son conceals the misconduct of the father. Uprightness is to be found in this" (*Analects* 13:18).

In the West, there is no equivalent to the Confucian concept of filial piety. In a narrow sense, it refers to the duty of children to look after their parents. In a broad sense, it refers to the devotion of children to their parents and the parents' unfailing love for their children, which make filial piety an obligation of both children and parents. Only when children respect their parents and parents love their children does a family achieve harmony and serve as a model for the rest of society. In short, the family is an institution of ethical mutuality in which all members complement each other.

For this reason, *The Book of Documents*, one of the five classics compiled and edited by Confucius, identifies several categories of people who violate family virtues and characterizes them as criminals who are worse than murderers. Included in these categories are sons who, instead of serving their fathers respectfully, greatly wound their fathers' hearts; fathers who, being unable to cherish their sons, hate them; younger brothers who, not bearing in mind the evident intention of Heaven, do not respect their elder brothers; and elder brothers who, forgetting the tender regard in which they should hold their younger brother, are unfriendly to them (quoted in Ebrey 1991, 54).

In short, Confucian familism emphasizes the importance of strong bonds and ties among members of the family, and it sets forth specific modes of thinking and behavior. To think according to Confucian familism, one must have a family-centered ideology or mindset (Rappa and Tan 2003, 89). According to Mencius, "The content of benevolence is the serving of one's parents; the content of dutifulness is obedience to one's elder brothers; the content of wisdom is to understand these two and to hold fast to them" (4A:27).

Unlike the ideology of individualism that stresses the independence and self-reliance of the individual, Confucian familism endorses the prevalence of the family group and its well-being over the interests and needs of its individual members. To implement familism, Confucianism upholds the practice of shared decision making. Confucian individuals are not supposed to make decisions alone, even on personal matters; they must consult with all of their family members and share the decision with them (Fan 2004, 82).

Confucian familism also affects life outside the family; it represents a way of life in which a person divides others into groups and subgroups that are then treated in accordance with their importance to the person's family. The more important or closer people are to the person's family, the more favorably they are treated, as Mencius (7A:46) admonishes, "As for a *ren* person, there is no one that he does not love, but he takes attention to his kin and others who are worthy to be the most pressing task."

Favoring the intimate, Confucian familism is an ideology of *graded or differentiated love*, which requires individuals first to love their own family members and then extend this love to others according to the closeness of their relationship (S. Cheng 1990, 512; Hwang 2001, 189).

As Ruiping Fan (2004, 83) points out, "For any human individual, there are close relatives, general relatives, remote relatives, far remote relatives. . . . Confucian *ren* requires differentiated love, not equal love. It is love with distinction, and care with gradation."

Advocating graded love or treatment based on the closeness of the relationship, Confucian familism is often viewed as running counter to the liberal principle of treating people equally and impartially (Pye 1968). Moreover, its promotion of family bonds above all other sorts of social ties has been accused of encouraging *amoral familism* in which moral obligations are confined to the nuclear family alone so that its members feel no sense of responsibility to larger groups, such as the community and the nation (Banfield 1958; N. Kang 2004). Familism is also linked to a low-trust society in which people do not trust those outside the immediate family circle (Fukuyama 1995a; Realo, Allik, and Greenfield 2008).

According to recent research on trust in Confucian societies, people who adhere to strong familism prefer to work with members of their own family (Bell and Hahm 2003; Tan and Chee 2005). Once outside the family, they prefer to deal with those in their networks of family-like affective relationships established through kinship, schooling, work, or the region of their birthplace. As a result, those who remain attached to the tradition of familism are considered unlikely to trust those outside these networks of personal ties, even if outsiders can be known to be trustworthy.

In Confucian societies with an emphasis on such *affective* interpersonal relationships, previous research has assumed that people trust only those with whom they have built strong emotional ties through close interpersonal relationships while being suspicious of "outsiders" (Tan and Chee 2005). In Japan, for example, Toshio Yamagishi and Toko Kiyonari (2000) found that people trust members of their networks but not those outside those networks. As a result, a large gap exists between the levels of *particularized trust*, given to those within the interpersonal network, and *generalized trust*, given to those outside the network.

In the East Asian societies influenced by the principles of Confucian familism, *affective ties* are known to serve as the foundation for the development of interpersonal trust. People in these societies seem likely to work with others according to *affective-based trust*, which depends on the frequency and intimacy of interpersonal interactions, rather than *cognitive-based trust*, which depends on a trustee's credentials and qualifications. Among those who view the world with the mindset of familism, therefore, affective-based trust is likely to outweigh cognitive-based trust.

To see whether these assumptions hold true in Confucian Asia, the first question one must ask is, "To what extent do people of Confucian Asia still uphold familism?" Having answered that and divided Confucian Asians into those who remain family centered and those who do not, one can then ask, "Are the family centered less likely to trust strangers than those who are not family centered?" and "Are the family centered more likely to operate with affective-based trust than with cognitive-based trust?" In the sections that follow, I explore these questions using data from the first and second waves of the Asian Barometer Surveys (ABS).

Adherence to Confucian Familism

To measure the extent of popular adherence to the Confucian tradition of familism, I selected a pair of questions from the second round of the ABS. The first question (Q56) asked respondents how strongly they agreed or disagreed with this statement: "Even if parents' demands are unreasonable, children should do what they ask." The second question (Q60) asked how strongly they agreed or disagreed with this statement: "For the sake of the family, the individual should put his or her own personal interests second." The first question was used to determine the extent to which East Asians endorse the norm of filial piety. The second question was used to determine the extent to which they are family- or self-centered in prioritizing and pursuing the sometimes conflicting goals of personal and family life.

Table 6.1 reports the proportions who agreed at least somewhat and strongly with each and both of these two questions. In three countries – China (51%), Singapore (48%), and Japan (46%) – a majority or a near majority is willing to obey their parents even when they felt their parents were making unreasonable demands. In the three other countries, larger majorities, ranging from 57 percent in Vietnam to 73 percent in Taiwan, are not always willing to obey their parents. Equally notable is that those strongly willing to obey their parents constitute very small minorities: from 3 percent in China and Taiwan to 15 percent in Vietnam.

When all six countries are considered together, only one out of sixteen people (6%) is strongly disposed toward the Confucian norm of filial piety. More notably, a larger minority (11%) is strongly detached from than strongly attached to the norm. These findings suggest that the Confucian virtue of filial piety is no longer faithfully observed throughout Confucian Asia. Of the six countries, Taiwan stands out from the rest as a country with a large majority of more than two-thirds (70%) unattached

TABLE 6.1. *Attachment to Familism*

Country	Obey Parents		Sacrifice for the Family		Levels of Attachment			
	Attached	Firmly Attached	Attached	Firmly Attached	Neither	One	Both	No Answer
Japan	45.9%	(6.6%)	79.2%	(16.1%)	9.9%	46.9%	37.6%	5.6%
Korea	39.9	(4.2)	78.3	(15.3)	14.0	48.0	34.2	3.8%
Taiwan	27.0	(2.6)	85.0	(12.6)	8.5	62.5	23.5	5.5%
China	50.5	(3.3)	84.9	(13.5)	2.8	40.7	44.1	12.4%
Singapore	48.0	(6.2)	91.5	(33.3)	3.1	52.4	43.1	1.4%
Vietnam	43.2	(15.3)	89.9	(49.5)	4.8	50.5	40.6	4.1%
(Pooled)	42.4	(6.4)	84.8	(23.4)	7.2	50.2	37.2	5.4%

Note: Parentheses are included to facilitate inter-item comparisons of percentages.
Source: 2005–8 Asian Barometer Surveys.

to the norm. Why are the Taiwanese significantly less obedient to their parents than their peers in other Confucian countries? The data do not allow a satisfactory answer to this question.

When asked about whether they would sacrifice personal interests for the sake of the family, large majorities ranging from 78 percent in Korea to 92 percent in Singapore express a willingness to do so. In four countries – China (14%), Japan (16%), Korea (15%), and Taiwan (13%) – small minorities of between 13 and 16 percent are *strongly willing* to put the family ahead of the self. In Singapore those *strongly willing* to do so account for more than one-third of the population (33%). In Vietnam, they even constitute a near majority (49.5%).

When all six countries are considered together, more than eight out of ten people (85%) in Confucian Asia are more willing than unwilling to put the welfare of their family ahead of their own. More notably, nearly one out of four people (23%) is strongly willing to do so. These two percentages are from two to three times as high as the percentages of those who express a willingness to obey their parents at least somewhat (42%) or strongly (6%). Evidently, many East Asians are willing to sacrifice their own interests for their families' even when they are unwilling to give unconditional obedience to their parents.

More noteworthy is the finding that more than twice as many people in nondemocracies (China, Singapore, and Vietnam) as in democracies (Japan, Korea, and Taiwan) remain *strongly attached* to the Confucian tradition of putting the family's interests above one's own (32% vs. 15%).

Evidently, democratic rule encourages people to pursue their own interests independent of their family, as the grid-group cultural theory of democratic politics suggests.

To what extent do people in Confucian Asia still remain fully attached to Confucian familism? To address this question, we need to consider responses to both questions, each of which deals with different components of familism. For each country, Table 6.1 reports the percentages fully and partially attached to familism and the percentages unattached to it. In every country, those partially attached outnumber the unattached, with the partially attached ranging from 41 percent in China to 63 percent in Taiwan. In contrast, those fully attached range from a low of 24 percent in Taiwan to a high of 44 percent in China, and it is only in the three nondemocracies – China, Singapore, and Vietnam – that more than 40 percent of the population remain fully attached to familism. In every Confucian East Asian country, however, those fully attached to familism outnumber those unattached by a large margin that ranges from 15 percent in Taiwan to 41 percent in China. On the basis of this finding, it is fair to conclude that East Asia still remains a family-centered region.

Are people in historically Confucian East Asia more family centered than those in non-Confucian East Asia, which consists of Mongolia, the Philippines, Thailand, Cambodia, and Malaysia? There is virtually little difference in the extent to which these two groups of Asian countries are generally attached to familism. Among the people in Confucian East Asia, 37 percent are fully attached to familism and 7 percent are unattached to it, in contrast to 35 and 8 percent in non-Confucian East Asia, respectively. Thus Confucian East Asia is no more family centered than non-Confucian East Asia.

In Confucian Asia today, which segments of the people remain fully or strongly attached to the Confucian notion of familism? Table 6.2 explores this question in terms of gender, age, education, and family income. There is little difference between males and females in the level of full attachment to familism. Only in Japan do males outnumber females by a large margin of 10 percentage points (45% vs. 35%).

Unlike gender, age matters significantly in all countries except Singapore. In the five countries of China, Japan, Korea, Taiwan, and Vietnam, the older people are, the more strongly they are attached to familism. As a result, the two extreme age groups – the young in their 20s and 30s, and the elderly in their 60s and older – are, respectively, the least and most strongly attached to familism in these countries. In Singapore, however, there is virtually no difference across the three age groups: Young

TABLE 6.2. *Demographic Differences in Familism and Civic Orientations (in percent)*

Shared Norms	Gender		Age			Educational Attainment			Family Income		
	Male	Female	20–39	40–59	≥60	<High.sch	High sch.	College	Low	Middle	High
Familism											
Japan	45.0	35.0	31.4	39.5	44.6	54.1	36.0	37.8	38.7	40.7	38.2
Korea	38.1	33.0	30.9	37.5	44.3	50.0	37.0	28.8	44.5	36.0	33.2
Taiwan	44.7	42.6	21.3	22.5	33.7	37.6	21.9	20.2	27.8	23.4	23.3
China	25.5	24.3	21.4	22.6	37.8	37.5	21.8	20.1	55.0	44.2	41.5
Singapore	44.7	42.6	44.2	43.2	43.8	41.5	43.9	45.9	36.9	42.9	50.3
Vietnam	41.3	43.4	38.3	43.6	50.0	53.0	40.4	32.2	45.4	39.9	43.0
(Pooled)	40.7	37.9	34.6	40.2	46.0	49.2	37.6	32.8	37.0	36.6	38.3
Social Trust											
Japan	30.7	30.1	30.2	32.9	28.4	20.2	29.4	36.6	18.5	30.5	38.1
Korea	33.8	28.3	29.7	33.0	30.6	25.7	31.0	32.6	27.4	32.4	31.3
Taiwan	37.3	30.3	35.1	34.1	30.5	25.2	32.8	34.7	26.2	33.6	42.4
China	50.8	49.3	48.2	49.8	53.8	48.3	50.5	59.0	52.4	55.0	57.1
Singapore	33.2	26.8	29.4	28.7	33.1	22.1	30.4	36.3	19.2	27.6	42.3
Vietnam	58.8	59.3	56.3	61.2	62.6	64.9	59.0	45.5	54.6	60.1	60.0
(Pooled)	40.6	37.0	38.9	39.4	37.6	37.8	39.4	38.2	29.7	36.3	44.5
Political Trust											
Japan	42.5	40.0	41.2	35.5	46.3	47.7	40.4	39.7	37.0	42.1	42.2
Korea	20.8	22.7	20.3	23.4	21.9	23.4	22.2	20.6	31.2	23.3	19.6
Taiwan	26.8	19.7	18.3	21.3	39.4	34.1	23.7	13.8	29.9	22.3	17.0
China	59.0	64.1	51.9	62.6	74.4	70.3	54.7	37.5	68.4	51.2	51.2
Singapore	82.5	87.3	87.8	80.9	90.6	86.8	83.8	87.4	80.6	86.3	87.0
Vietnam	94.6	94.4	94.0	95.1	94.7	93.6	95.7	89.1	92.2	94.8	95.1
(Pooled)	54.9	54.2	53.1	54.1	57.9	65.0	56.0	40.0	58.6	52.8	54.9

(continued)

TABLE 6.2 (continued)

Shared Norms	Gender		Age			Educational Attainment			Family Income		
	Male	Female	20–39	40–59	≥60	<High.sch	High sch.	College	Low	Middle	High
Affective Trust											
Japan	33.4	35.0	26.0	34.2	42.6	54.0	31.8	27.8	44.3	31.9	34.2
Korea	27.0	25.7	22.1	27.9	36.7	37.3	25.4	24.2	27.8	27.5	20.5
China	33.9	37.4	32.5	39.9	33.3	50.0	29.7	12.7	42.6	45.5	31.9
Taiwan	24.5	27.1	32.5	39.3	33.3	45.1	23.5	14.1	34.0	23.9	12.8
(Pooled)	30.6	32.3	26.1	34.3	38.4	48.4	27.9	20.7	36.0	31.2	30.1
Tolerance											
Japan	69.4	75.4	67.4	72.5	75.5	75.8	73.5	70.7	75.4	73.5	74.2
Taiwan	61.3	58.8	52.7	62.6	72.3	73.9	61.0	46.0	66.1	60.4	49.1
China	56.4	57.7	51.3	58.7	63.2	60.8	54.0	40.0	52.6	48.8	46.3
Singapore	79.8	77.2	74.3	78.5	87.8	83.1	77.3	77.2	82.7	77.8	76.4
Vietnam	66.4	68.9	74.3	69.6	67.7	64.1	69.4	63.8	65.8	72.7	63.9
(Pooled)	66.9	68.1	62.3	68.9	73.8	70.2	67.5	63.7	72.6	70.3	66.0
Twin Norms											
Japan	21.9	24.8	18.9	26.2	23.1	17.1	23.0	27.1	14.8	22.1	29.2
Taiwan	23.3	17.2	18.3	21.7	22.2	19.6	20.6	20.8	18.2	19.8	21.7
China	28.1	28.1	24.6	28.5	32.6	29.2	26.6	23.7	27.8	24.3	30.0
Singapore	26.4	22.7	21.7	24.4	31.8	20.1	25.0	28.5	17.6	21.4	36.8
Vietnam	42.4	43.5	40.8	44.2	46.5	42.4	45.0	30.5	37.8	45.9	42.4
(Pooled)	28.7	27.1	26.4	28.6	29.4	26.6	26.1	29.1	22.1	26.5	34.3

Source: 2005–8 Asian Barometer Surveys.

Singaporeans value family life as much as their older counterparts (44% vs. 44%), and they also value it more than their peers in any other Confucian country.

In terms of education and family income, Singapore stands out, once again, from the rest of the Confucian Asian countries. In China, Japan, Korea, Taiwan, and Vietnam, a higher level of education is always accompanied by a significantly smaller percentage of people fully attached to familism. In Singapore, in striking contrast, education makes relatively little difference. In fact, a higher level of education is accompanied by a slightly larger percentage of strongly attached respondents: they constitute 42 percent of those with less than a high school education, 44 percent of the high school educated, and 46 percent of the college educated.

Singapore stands out yet again in the analysis of family income. In China, Japan, Korea, Taiwan, and Vietnam, income has either an inconsistent or negative effect on adherence to familism. In China, for example, the percentage of the fully attached to family life decreases sharply as income increases, from 55 percent among low-income people to 42 percent among high-income people. In Singapore, however, the percentage increases as dramatically, from 37 to 50 percent. More income, like higher education, encourages Singaporeans to value family life to a greater extent. Only in this affluent nondemocracy does greater exposure to socioeconomic modernization contribute to familism; in all other Confucian countries it has the opposite effect.

Which segments of the population in the entire region of Confucian Asia are the most and least fully attached to the tradition of Confucian familism? Of the four demographic characteristics, education and age matter more significantly than gender and income. In Table 6.2, we see that, for the six Confucian countries as a whole, the levels of full attachment to familism are lowest for those with a college education (33%) and young people in their 20s and 30s (35%); they are highest for those with less than a high school education (49%) and the elderly in their 60s and older (46%). To identify the most and least fully attached to the Confucian family tradition, I consider in Figure 6.1 only these two demographic characteristics together, solely for the reason of parsimonious analysis.

When all six countries in the region are considered together, the more people are educated, the less they are attached to familism, regardless of their age. However, older age does not always result in more attachment. Only among those with a high school education or less are the oldest cohorts the most fully attached to familism. Only among those with a high school or college education are the youngest cohorts the least

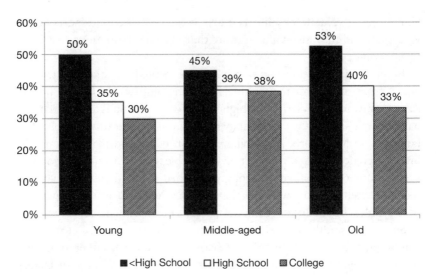

FIGURE 6.1. The Demographic Characteristics of the Least and Most Attached to Familism: Age and Education. *Source*: 2005–8 Asian Barometer Surveys.

fully attached to it. Therefore the college educated, especially among young people, and those with little formal education, especially among the elderly, are the least (30%) and most fully attached (53%) to the tradition, respectively. It should be noted, however, that Singaporeans do not fit into this characterization.

Interpersonal Trust

Cooperation among people requires them to trust one another (Putnam 1993; Uslaner 2002). In no society, however, do all citizens trust one another either equally or fully: Individual citizens trust some of their fellow citizens a lot, others a little, and still others, not at all. Consequently there is considerable variation in the form and radius of interpersonal trust among individual citizens and across the country in which they live (Fukuyama 1995a).

Further, not only the targets of trust but also the reasons for trust vary considerably. In one form – specific or *particularized trust* – trust develops through frequent interactions with the person to be trusted. In another form, *generalized trust*, trust develops in a way that allows it to be conferred on strangers. Interpersonal trust can also be differentiated into two other forms, *cognition-based* and *affect-based*, classifications that distinguish between two ways of deeming a person trustworthy:

cognition-based trust involves careful rational thinking, whereas affect-based trust involves intuitive positive feeling (Lewis and Weigert 1985). Depending on the targets of trust, interpersonal trust can be differentiated into political and social trust: Political trust involves government officials, wheareas social trust deals with known and unknown people who are not government officials.

Previous research on the effects of Confucianism on interpersonal trust has posited that people in Confucian Asia who adhere to familism express a low level of generalized trust but a high level of particularized trust (Tan and Chee 2005; see also Bell and Hahm 2003; J. Chan 2004). The research also suggests that they express a low level of generalized trust when they participate in the "bonding" type of associations but a high level of generalized trust when they participate in the "bridging" type of associations.

In this section, I measure and compare across six countries the levels and patterns of trust in terms of particularized trust versus generalized trust, political trust versus social trust, and affect-based trust versus cognition-based trust. I also identify the demographic characteristics of those who are most and least willing to trust their relatives, as well as a variety of "strangers." In addition, I examine whether trust in strangers spills over into trust in government officials.

Particularized vs. Generalized Trust

To measure the extent of particularized interpersonal trust, I selected an item (Q24) from the ABS surveys. On a 4-point verbal scale ranging from "a great deal of trust" to "none at all," this item asked respondents to express the extent to which they trust their relatives. Figure 6.2 reports the percentages expressing at least some degree of trust in them. In five of six countries, very large majorities, ranging from 77 percent in China to 91 percent in Singapore, express at least some degree of trust in their relatives. Only in Vietnam, however, an overwhelming majority (97%) does not express trust in them.[1] Equally surprising is that virtually none of the Vietnamese does express a great deal of trust in their relatives; in the other countries, the substantial minorities expressing unqualified trust range from 23 percent in Taiwan to 40 percent in Japan. When the

---

[1] The third wave of the Asian Barometer Survey conducted in Vietnam during the months of September and October 2010 also reveals a similar pattern of no trust in relatives. While 7 percent expressed some degree of trust in them, a vast majority of 89 percent did not express trust in them (Asian Barometer 2011, 9).

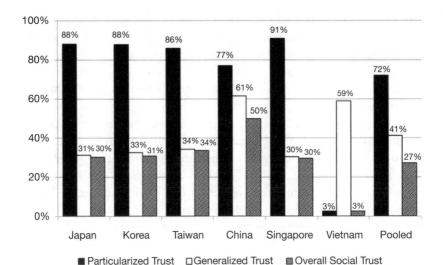

FIGURE 6.2. Levels of Interpersonal Trust. *Source:* 2005–8 Asian Barometer Surveys.

six countries are considered together, about three-quarters (72%) express some degree of trust in their relatives, but just one-quarter (25%) express a great deal of trust.

To what extent do East Asians trust strangers, fellow citizens with whom they are not acquainted? To estimate the level of *generalized interpersonal trust*, I selected another item (Q23) from the ABS that was designed to tap respondents' assessments of the trustworthiness of most people. It asked respondents whether they agreed more with the view that "most people can be trusted" or the view that "you must be very careful in dealing with them." Figure 6.2 shows that in four of the six Confucian countries – Japan, Korea, Taiwan, and Singapore – small minorities of about one-third state that most people in their country were trustworthy. Only in the two communist countries – China (61%) and Vietnam (59%) – does a substantial majority of about 60 percent express trust in fellow citizens with whom they were unacquainted.

Are Confucian countries all low-trust societies, as claimed in the literature (Fukuyama 1995a)? To address this question, I developed a fourfold typology of societal trust by considering the levels of particularized and generalized trust. The first step was to determine whether the levels of particularized and generalized trust in each country were either low (less than 50% of the citizens exhibiting the given trust) or high (50% or more of the citizens exhibiting the given trust). This division offered the potential of four types of societies.

The most negative of the four types is the society in which the levels of particularized and generalized trust are both low; as Figure 6.2 indicates, none of the countries falls into this type. The most positive type is the society in which the levels of both types of trust are high: China fits this type. The two other types are those in which the level of one kind of trust is high but the level for the other kind is low. Four countries – Japan, Korea, Taiwan, and Singapore – fall into the type in which particularized trust is high but generalized trust is low, whereas Vietnam falls into the type in which particularized trust is low but the generalized trust is high. According to these results, five of the six Confucian societies are lower in generalized trust and one country is lower in particularized trust. Of the 13 countries surveyed in the second round of the ABS, Vietnam is the only country with greater trust in strangers than in relatives and neighbors. Why the Vietnamese trust their relatives less than neighbors and they trust their neighbors less than strangers is a real mystery. Evidently, the more the Vietnamese know about other people, the less they trust in them.

In historically Confucian Asia as a whole, how large is the population segment that expresses both particularized trust in relatives and generalized trust in strangers? Figure 6.2 shows that those trusting of relatives and other people constitute a bare majority in China (50.1%). In the five other countries, they constitute relatively small minorities ranging from less than 1 percent in Vietnam (0.6%) to 34 percent in Taiwan. When all six countries are considered together, a minority of just under 30 percent (27%) trusts their relatives and, in general, their fellow citizens (see Figure 6.2). These findings support the earlier characterization of Confucian Asia as a region of low-trust societies, although China does not fit this characterization.

Are trust levels in historically Confucian Asia lower than in non-Confucian East Asia? In the six Confucian East Asian countries considered as a whole, nearly three out of four people (72%) express particularized trust, whereas two out of five people (41%) express generalized trust. In the six non-Confucian Asian countries considered as a whole, the corresponding figures are 82 percent for particularized trust and 14 percent for generalized trust. There is a wide gap between the two regions in the proportions of those who express both particularized and generalized trust: over two times as many people in historically Confucian East Asia as in non-Confucian Asia express full trust in other people

(27% vs. 12%). These findings, when considered together, suggest that Confucianism may not be a negative influence on interpersonal trust, as claimed in the literature (Fukuyama 1995a).

In Confucian Asia today, what kind of people are most likely to trust others, both those known and unknown to them? Table 6.2 shows the demographic characteristics of the most trusting population in terms of gender, age, education, and income. In terms of trust, there is no statistically significant difference between males and females in three countries: Japan, China, and Vietnam. In contrast, in Korea, Taiwan, and Singapore, the percentages of males who trust other people are either 6 or 7 points higher than the percentages of trusting females. In terms of age also, there is no regionwide pattern of differences. Only in China, Taiwan, and Vietnam does age matter significantly in levels of trust. In the two communist countries of China and Vietnam, older age is associated with greater social trust. In democratic Taiwan, however, older age is connected to a lower level of interpersonal trust. I have been unable thus far to ascertain why aging has different impacts under different regimes.

Education, like age, does not affect interpersonal trust uniformly across all six countries, but its effect is more consistent. In all of the countries but Vietnam, more formal education is accompanied by a significantly higher level of trust in other people; as a result, the least educated are the least trusting, whereas the most educated are the most trusting. In Vietnam, the pattern is reversed, with college-educated people being the least trusting, whereas those without a high school education are the most trusting. Family income, like education, correlates with significantly greater social trust in five countries: In Japan, China, Taiwan, Singapore, and Vietnam, low-income and high-income people are, respectively, the least and most trusting of other people. In Korea, however, middle-income people, not high-income people, are the most trusting.

When all six countries are considered together, gender and income are the two demographic variables that have the most significant impacts on Confucian Asians' levels of trust. In Figure 6.3, I use these two variables to identify the most and least trusting segments of the population in Confucian Asia. The figure shows that, among females and males, higher income is always accompanied by a higher level of social trust. It also shows that, at each income level, males are more trusting than their female counterparts. As a result, low-income females (29%) and high-income males (46%) are the least and most trusting segments of the entire population in Confucian Asia.

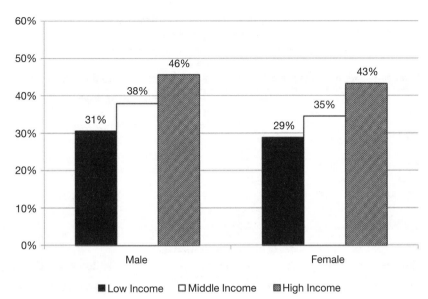

FIGURE 6.3. Demographic Characteristics of the Least and Most Trusting People: Gender and Income. *Source:* 2005–8 Asian Barometer Surveys.

Political Trust

To what extent do people in Confucian East Asia trust those who run their governments? Do those with high levels of trust in their families and fellow citizens trust government officials more than those with low levels of trust in their families and fellow citizens? Does social trust have any positive spillover effect on political trust in Confucian Asia, as is the case in some other regions (Mishler and Rose 2005)? To explore these questions, I selected an item (Q130) from the second wave of the ABS that asked respondents in all six countries to what extent they agreed or disagreed with this statement: "You can generally trust the people who run our government to do what is right." I classified those who agreed with this statement either strongly or somewhat as expressing at least some degree of trust in government officials. For each and all of the six countries, Table 6.3 shows the percentages expressing such degrees of trust in government officials.

The most striking feature of the data reported in this table is the contrasting way in which people of democratic and nondemocratic countries rate their government officials. In the three democratic countries, minorities ranging from 20 percent in Korea to 39 percent in Japan rate government officials as at least somewhat trustworthy. In contrast, in the three

TABLE 6.3. *Levels of Trust in Government Officials in Confucian and Non-Confucian Asia*

A. Confucian Asia
"You can generally trust the people who run our government to do what is right"

Country	Strongly Agree	Somewhat Agree	Somewhat Disagree	Strongly Disagree	No Answer
Japan	2.4%	36.7%	40.9%	15.0%	5.0%
Korea	0.7	19.5	52.5	20.3	7.0
Taiwan	0.8	21.0	62.8	8.8	6.6
China	3.0	49.2	31.2	1.5	15.1
Singapore	15.1	67.4	12.3	2.5	2.7
Vietnam	44.7	43.0	4.4	0.7	7.2
(Pooled)	11.1	39.5	34.0	8.1	7.3

B. Non-Confucian Asia
"You can generally trust the people who run our government to do what is right"

Country	Strongly Agree	Somewhat Agree	Somewhat Disagree	Strongly Disagree	No Answer
Mongolia	49.6%	37.8%	9.0%	2.3%	1.3%
Philippines	14.8	31.7	32.7	18.8	16.8
Thailand	15.7	52.5	20.6	3.6	7.6
Indonesia	5.4	69.8	19.8	1.0	4.0
Malaysia	12.3	58.8	20.6	4.1	4.2
(Pooled)	19.5	50.1	20.5	6.0	3.9

Source: 2005–8 Asian Barometer Surveys.

nondemocracies, majorities ranging from 52 percent in China to 88 percent in Vietnam rate them positively. In none of the democratic countries, moreover, do more than 5 percent express a great deal of trust in government officials, whereas in the nondemocracies of Singapore and Vietnam those expressing high levels of trust are 15 and 45 percent, respectively. Among the six Confucian countries, the general level of political trust is highest in the three nondemocracies and lowest in the two new third-wave democracies. Japan, the region's oldest democracy, falls in between these two groups of countries.

Why are government officials in autocratic regimes trusted more by their citizenry than their counterparts in democratic regimes? According to the literature on this subject (Dalton and Shin 2006; Norris 1999), democracy, unlike its alternatives, allows citizens to become critical of their government officials when those officials fail to meet their preferences. Because they can criticize those officials, citizens of democracies are

TABLE 6.4. *The Relationship between Social Trust and Political Trust*

Country	Levels of Social Trust			(eta)
	Low	Middle	High	
Japan	22.1%	42.3%	45.5%	(.13)*
Korea	8.8	21.6	26.4	(.14)*
Taiwan	18.8	24.0	22.9	(.09)*
China	51.8	59.1	65.4	(.12)*
Singapore	70.0	87.0	85.2	(.04)
Vietnam	80.0	93.7	95.4	(.05)
(Pooled)	33.3	53.9	61.9	(.15)*

* Significant at the 0.01 level.

Source: 2005–8 Asian Barometer Surveys.

not likely to report unconditional trust in leaders of their government. In contrast, citizens of authoritarian regimes are not allowed to access critical information about the misconduct of their government officials; nor are they allowed to criticize misbehaving officials. Consequently, they are expected to remain more trusting than critical of their governmental leaders.

In the Asian context, however, this theory does not offer a satisfactory account of political trust. In non-Confucian Asia, Table 6.3 shows that people of two new democracies, Indonesia (75%) and Mongolia (87%), rate their government officials far more positively than negatively. In fact, they express more trust in their officials than do citizens of two nondemocracies: Malaysia (71%) and Thailand (68%). Thus in non-Confucian Asia, democracy is not linked with a low level of political trust. Only in Confucian Asia is there this linkage. Obviously, not all democracies produce critical citizens, nor do all democracies perform equally well. I have not been able to ascertain why it is that only democracies in Confucian Asia produce critical citizens.

In historically Confucian Asia, does trust in other fellow citizens spill over to trust in politicians? Table 6.4 shows that, in all six Confucian countries, the level of political trust is lowest among those with the lowest level of interpersonal trust. Moreover, in four of the six countries – China, Japan, Korea, and Vietnam – a higher level of social trust is always accompanied by a higher level of political trust. When all six countries are considered together, the percentage expressing political trust increases significantly at each higher level of social trust: from 33 percent at its low level to 62 percent at its high level. Thus in historically Confucian Asia, there is a positive relationship between social and political trust. Although the magnitude of this relationship is weak (*eta* = .15), it can be considered a piece of evidence supporting the "spillover" hypothesis.

What sorts of people trust government officials? Do the types of people exhibiting this trust vary across Confucian Asia? Table 6.2 shows little difference between the two genders in four of the six countries. Only in China and Taiwan do they differ significantly: In the former, females are more trusting of government officials than are their male counterparts (64% vs. 59%), and in Taiwan, males are more trusting than females (27% vs. 20%). Age matters little in two countries, Korea and Vietnam. In the four other countries – China, Japan, Taiwan, and Singapore – old people are the most trusting of government officials. In China, Japan, and Taiwan, young people are the least trusting of them.

Education, like age, does not matter significantly throughout the region. In Singapore, and Vietnam, for example, there is no consistently positive or negative pattern of relationship between the two variables. In the four other countries – the three democracies of Japan, Korea, and Taiwan, as well as communist China – education is consistently negatively associated with political trust. In these countries, therefore, the least and most educated are, respectively, the most and least trusting of government officials. Such a negative relationship is most pronounced in China, where those who trust government officials are nearly twice as numerous among those with less than a high school education than among the college educated (70% vs. 38%).

Family income, like education, exhibits no regionwide pattern of relationship with political trust. In China, Korea, and Taiwan, people with lower incomes are more trusting of their governmental officials than are those with higher incomes. In contrast, in Japan, Singapore, and Vietnam, the higher the income level, the higher the level of trust in those officials.

When the magnitude of income and education differences is compared for each country, three patterns emerge: in Japan, Singapore, and Vietnam, those variables make no significant difference. In Korea, income matters significantly more than education. In China and Taiwan, the reverse is true. Why these two variables of socioeconomic resources found to promote social trust affect both the direction and magnitude of political trust so differently across the countries within Confucian Asia cannot be addressed with the data at hand.

Finally I pooled the six countries together and compared the extent to which each of the four demographic variables affects political trust. Table 6.2 shows that two of the four variables, education and income,

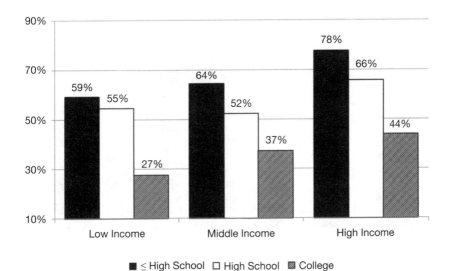

FIGURE 6.4. Demographic Characteristics of the Least and Most Politically Trusting: Income and Education. *Source:* 2005–8 Asian Barometer Surveys.

are more significantly associated with political trust than the other two variables. Figure 6.4 considers these two variables together to identify the least and most politically trusting segments of people in Confucian Asia. At every income level, more education is consistently associated with a lower level of political trust. More income is consistently associated with a higher level of political trust, except among the high school educated, in which those with a middle income are actually a little less likely to exhibit trust than those with a low income. Overall, low-income people with a college education and high-income people with less than a high school education are, respectively, the least and most trusting of governmental officials. The politically trusting constitute less than a third (27%) of those with a high level of education but little income, in contrast to a large majority of more than three-quarters (78%) of those with little education but a high income.

Affect-Based Trust vs. Cognition-Based Trust

How do people of Confucian Asia judge other people's trustworthiness? Do they base their judgments on affective or emotional ties to the target of their trust, or do they carefully weigh such qualities of the target as professional or technical competence? To determine whether interpersonal trust among Asians is primarily affect- or cognition-based, I selected a

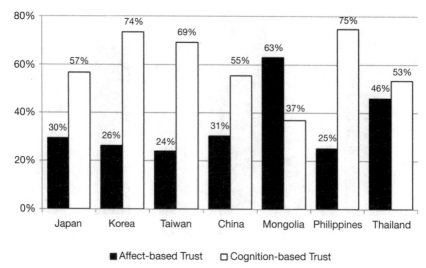

FIGURE 6.5. Levels of Affect-Based and Cognition-Based Trust in Confucian and Non-Confucian Asia. *Source:* 2001–3 East Asia Barometer Surveys.

question (Q65) from the first wave of the ABS conducted in four of the six Confucian East Asian countries: China, Japan, Korea, and Taiwan. The question asked respondents to what extent they agreed or disagreed with this statement: "When hiring someone, even if a stranger is more qualified, the opportunity should still be given to relatives." Affirmative and negative responses to this question indicate opting for affect-based and cognition-based trust, respectively.

In all four countries surveyed, those who gave negative responses outnumber those who gave positive responses (see Figure 6.5). When these four countries are considered together, more than twice as many people are willing to hire new employees on the basis of professional competence than on the basis of affective ties (62% vs. 28%). Evidently, throughout Confucian Asia, affect-based trust is much less common than cognition-based trust.

This finding runs counter to what is expected from the Confucian notion of familism, which stresses the importance of personal ties and graded love in social life. In Confucian Asian countries these days, as in other modernized societies, the presence of affective ties (or the lack of them) no longer serves as a dominant criterion for judging the trustworthiness of strangers. Also worth noting is the finding that *affect-based trust* is actually significantly less common in Confucian countries than in non-Confucian countries (28% vs. 46%).

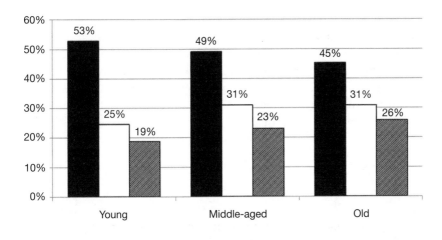

FIGURE 6.6. Demographic Characteristics of the Affectively Least and Most Trusting People: Age and Education. *Source*: 2001–3 East Asia Barometer Surveys.

What kinds of people value affective ties more than professional or technical competence? Table 6.2 explores this question, once again, in terms of the four demographic characteristics. Gender makes no significant difference in any of the four surveyed countries. In three of the countries, however, age has a significant impact on the relationship between the presence of affective ties and the judgment of trustworthiness. In Japan and Korea, affective trust is significantly more common among the elderly in their 60s and older than it is among their younger peers. In Taiwan and China, however, such trust is most common among the middle-aged. Among the three levels of education and income, those in the low and high levels are the most and least likely to base trust on affective ties, respectively.

When all four surveyed countries are considered together, age and education are the two variables with the greatest impact on levels of affect-based trust. In Figure 6.6, I consider these two variables together to identify the characteristics of those least and most likely to base their trust on affective ties in Confucian Asia. The figure shows that, in all three age groups, a higher level of education is always associated with a lower level of affect-based trust. Yet older age is not always accompanied by a higher level of such trust in all three levels of education. Among the college educated, the trust level increases with older age. Among the least educated, however, it decreases with older age. As a result, it is young people with less than a high school education, not their old peers, who are the most likely to base their trust on affective ties. Young people with a college education are the least likely to do so. Those who value affective ties in judging trustworthiness are nearly three times more numerous among the former than among the latter (53% vs. 19%).

Tolerance

In addition to interpersonal trust, tolerance is an essential norm of civilized civic life. Without tolerance for people from different backgrounds or with unpopular ideas, there cannot be a civil community in which people can fully exercise their political rights and civil liberties and live in peace (UNESCO 2003). In democracy, tolerance makes it possible to give everyone equal voice, thereby extending those rights and liberties to unpopular and disliked groups. As Paul Sniderman et al. (1989, 25) assert, "The more tolerant citizens are of the rights of others, the more secure are the rights of all, their own included." Hence, political tolerance has long been viewed as essential for a stable and effective democratic system (Gibson 2006; see Sullivan, Pierson, and Marcus 1982; Sullivan and Transue 1999).

To what extent are the people of Confucian Asia willing to put up with those who hold interests or goals that are different from their own? To explore this question, I selected an item (Q59) from the second wave of the ABS, which was asked in only five countries; Korea was not included. The item asked respondents to what extent they would agree or disagree with this statement: "A person should not insist on his opinion if his coworkers disagree with him."

Table 6.5 shows that, in all five countries surveyed, a near majority or a majority, ranging from 48 percent in China to 77 percent in Singapore, agree with the statement to some extent, thereby expressing a willingness to tolerate those who do not agree with their views. When all five countries are pooled together, 62 percent of Confucian Asians are at least somewhat willing to tolerate other people with whom they do not agree. Yet, those strongly willing to do so constitute a small minority of less than 10 percent of the people in four of the surveyed countries; in Vietnam 19 percent of the people express an unqualified willingness to tolerate others who disagree with them.

TABLE 6.5. *Levels of the Willingness to Tolerate People with a Different Viewpoint*

	"A person should not insist on his opinion if his co-workers disagree."				
Country	Strongly Agree	Somewhat Agree	Somewhat Disagree	Strongly Disagree	No Answer
Japan	7.2%	58.6%	22.5%	2.4%	9.3%
Taiwan	2.8	52.3	35.2	1.4	8.3
China	1.0	46.9	34.9	1.2	16.0
Singapore	9.2	68.0	16.4	4.6	1.8
Vietnam	18.5	44.6	24.1	6.2	6.7
(Pooled)	7.7	54.1	26.6	3.2	8.4

Source: 2005–8 Asian Barometer Surveys.

Are people in historically Confucian Asia more or less tolerant than their peers outside their region? In terms of the overall size of the tolerant population, there is virtually no difference between Confucian and non-Confucian Asia (67% vs. 65%). Nonetheless, there is a great deal of difference between the two Asian subregions in terms of the size of the strongly tolerant population. There are more than three times as many strongly tolerant people in non-Confucian Asia than in Confucian Asia (26% vs. 8%). In five of six non-Confucian Asian countries, the strongly tolerant constitute substantial minorities ranging from 21 percent in Thailand and Indonesia to 48 percent in Mongolia. In contrast, in none of the five Confucian countries do the strongly tolerant form a minority of more than 20 percent. Evidently, historically Confucian Asia is a region that does not produce strong tolerance among its citizens.

What kinds of people are the most and least tolerant of others in Confucian Asia? In terms of gender, there is little difference in four of the surveyed countries (see Table 6.2); only in Japan, where females are significantly more tolerant than males (75% vs. 69%), is there a notable difference. Unlike gender, age matters significantly in every country except Vietnam. In Japan, China, Taiwan, and Singapore, older people are significantly more tolerant than their younger peers. Education and income, unlike age, are negatively associated with interpersonal tolerance in most countries. In Japan, China, Taiwan, and Singapore, a higher level of education is associated with a significantly lower level of interpersonal tolerance. In China, Taiwan, and Singapore, higher income is also associated with a significantly lower level of such tolerance. The higher the level

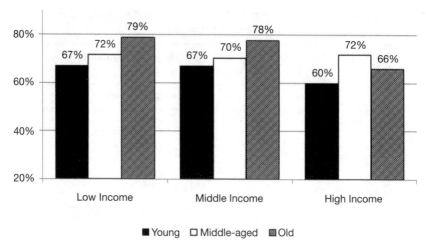

FIGURE 6.7. Demographic Characteristics of the Most and Least Tolerant: Age and Income. *Source:* 2005–8 Asian Barometer Surveys.

of socioeconomic resources Confucian Asians command, the less willing they are to listen to the views different from their own. This finding runs counter to what is generally known in the literature (Bobo and Licari 1989; Gibson and Gouws 2005). It is, therefore, the most distinctive and discouraging feature of civic life in Confucian Asia.

Analyzing all five countries together reveals the demographic characteristics of the most and least tolerant population in Confucian Asia. Of the four demographic variables considered, age and income matter most. In Figure 6.7, I use these two variables to identify the least and most tolerant populations in Confucian Asia. The figure shows that older age is always associated with a higher level of tolerance among low and middle-income people, whereas higher income is always associated with a lower level of tolerance among old people. Young people with high incomes (60%) and old people with low incomes (79%) are, respectively, the least and most tolerant population segments of Confucian Asia.

Civic-Mindedness: Endorsing the Norms of Trust and Tolerance

A civil society becomes fully civilized only when its citizens uphold both norms of interpersonal tolerance and trust. If they adhere only to one of these norms, they cannot form a truly communal union for an extended period of time (Diamond 1997). In Confucian Asia today, how many

TABLE 6.6. *Levels of Attachment to Civic Norms*

Country	Trust	Tolerance	Neither	One	Both
Japan	30.4%	72.5%	20.0%	56.6%	23.4%
Taiwan	33.8	60.1	26.7	53.0	20.4
China	50.1	57.0	21.3	50.6	28.2
Singapore	29.7	78.6	16.3	59.1	24.6
Vietnam	58.5	67.6	16.3	40.9	42.8
(Pooled)	40.4	67.5	20.0	52.1	27.9

Source: 2005–8 Asian Barometer Surveys.

people are willing to uphold both of these twin norms of civilized civic life? Which Confucian nations uphold these two norms the least and the most? To address these questions, I calculated and compared across countries the percentages of those who expressed the willingness to tolerate people with different views and to trust other people unknown to them.

Five countries are used in this analysis; Korea is excluded because of the lack of data on the norm of tolerance. In two of the five countries, China and Vietnam, majorities adhere to both of these two civic norms (see Table 6.6). In the three other countries – Japan, Taiwan, and Singapore – majorities are willing to tolerate other people with different views and to trust their own relatives, but they are unwilling to trust those unknown to them. In the region as a whole, more than one-quarter (28%) of those who are tolerant are not generally trusting of strangers. Obviously, embracing one civic norm does not motivate people in Confucian Asia to embrace the other civic norm.

Even in China and Vietnam, where a majority is, in general, willing to trust strangers, those who show high levels of both tolerance and trust constitute a minority, as in the three other countries (see Table 6.6). Only in these two communist countries and Singapore, however, is a quarter or more of the population fully civic-minded, embracing both civic norms. When all five countries are considered together, the partially civic-minded – those who embrace only one civic norm – constitute a majority (52%) of the population, and the fully civic-minded form a relatively small minority (28%). Although those unattached to any civic norm are least numerous (20%), a lack of adherence to civic norms is ubiquitous throughout Confucian Asia, and it seems to be much more acute in the democratic part of the region than in the nondemocratic part.

How does Confucian Asia compare with non-Confucian Asia in terms of the proportions upholding none, one, and both of the two civic norms?

In none of the five Confucian countries do the fully unattached constitute minorities larger than 30 percent, nor do the fully attached form minorities smaller than 15 percent. However, in three of the six non-Confucian countries – the Philippines, Malaysia, and Cambodia – more than 30 percent are fully unattached. In five of these six countries, with the exception of Thailand, less than 10 percent are attached to both norms.

When all of the countries in each subregion are considered, Confucian Asia has a notably smaller proportion of residents who are fully unattached than does non-Confucian Asia (20% vs. 31%). In the proportion of the fully attached, moreover, Confucian Asia leads non-Confucian Asia by an even larger margin of 19 percentage points (28% vs. 9%). These findings indicate that adherence to civic norms is more likely in Confucian Asia than in non-Confucian Asia. This can be considered another piece of evidence suggesting that Confucianism may not discourage people from endorsing the civic norms vital to democratization.

Which segments of the Confucian Asian populace are most civic-minded, endorsing the twin norms of interpersonal trust and tolerance that are known to be essential to democratic politics? Between the two genders there is no significant difference in four countries (Table 6.2); Taiwan is the exception, with significantly more fully civic-minded males than females (23% vs. 17%). Unlike gender, age matters significantly in all five countries but not in the same direction. All five are alike in that young people are the least civic-minded, and in four countries, the elderly are the most so; however, in Japan, the most civic-minded are the middle-aged.

Education also matters significantly in four countries, but again not uniformly. In Japan, and Singapore, the fully civic-minded are most numerous among the college educated and least numerous among those with less than a high school education; in China, however, the relationship is exactly the opposite. Income, like education, is positively associated with civic-mindedness in Japan, Taiwan, and Singapore, so that each step up in education comes with an increase in civic-mindedness. In China, too, high-income people are the most civic-minded, but the least civic-minded are middle-income people; in Vietnam, the civic-minded are least numerous among low-income people, making it like Japan, Taiwan, and Singapore, but they are most numerous among middle-income people.

Let us now consider all five countries to determine the demographic characteristics of the most and least civic-minded in Confucian Asia.

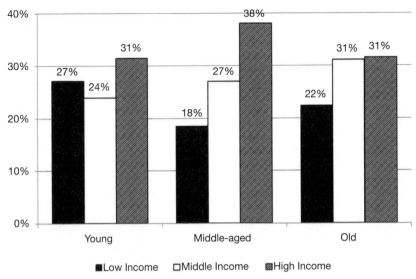

FIGURE 6.8. Demographic Characteristics of the Fully Civic-Minded: Age and Income. *Source:* 2005–8 Asian Barometer Surveys.

Of the four demographic variables, income and age are the two most strongly and consistently associated with the dependent variable of civic-mindedness. I used these two variables to identify the demographic characteristics of the least and most civic-minded in Confucian Asia. Contrary to what is expected from the positive relationships that income and age have with the dependent variable, low-income people in their 20s and 30s are not the least civic-minded; nor are the most civic-minded the high-income people in the 60s and older. Instead the least and most civic-minded of the population in Confucian Asia are, respectively, low- and high-income people who are middle-aged (see Figure 6.8). The fully civic-minded are more than twice as numerous among the latter than the former (38% vs. 18%).

Familism and Civic Norms

Do Confucian countries remain low-trust societies because of the legacies of familism as Fukuyama (1995a) and others have suggested? To test this hypothesis, I examined whether there was any significant negative relationship between the levels of attachment to familism and the percentages

TABLE 6.7. *Attachment to Civic Norms by Levels of Familism*

A. Particularized and Generalized Trust

Country	Particularized Trust				Generalized Trust			
	Low	Middle	High	(*Eta*)	Low	Middle	High	(*Eta*)
Japan	87.9%	88.7%	88.3%	(.00)	30.6%	32.9%	30.6%	(.01)
Korea	84.2	87.7	89.7	(.05)	32.6	33.3	32.2	(.02)
Taiwan	81.7	86.6	86.9	(.04)	32.1	35.6	31.7	(.30)*
China	55.6	74.8	80.5	(.11)*	55.6	63.7	61.4	(.04)
Singapore	86.2	89.0	93.2	(.08)*	9.7	25.0	37.9	(.16)*
Vietnam	–	–	–		42.9	59.8	62.3	(.09)*
(Pooled)	82.5	87.8	87.7	(.04)	32.8	40.5	44.5	(.06)*

B. Political Trust and Affect-Based Trust

Country	Political Trust				Affect-Based Trust			
	Low	Middle	High	(*Eta*)	Low	Middle	High	(*Eta*)
Japan	31.6	38.1	48.1	(.11)*	19.9	30.4	48.7	(.23)*
Korea	16.2	23.3	22.7	(.06)	21.4	19.5	33.7	(.19)*
Taiwan	19.3	22.2	29.4	(.08)*	18.9	23.9	38.0	(.14)*
China	48.1	51.5	69.6	(.19)*	36.5	40.0	47.5	(.16)*
Singapore	62.1	85.4	86.3	(.11)*	–	–	–	–
Vietnam	93.5	94.1	95.4	(.03)	–	–	–	–
(Pooled)	34.4	51.9	62.5	(.16)*	23.9	26.8	43.8	(.17)*

C. Tolerance and Civic-Mindedness

Country	Tolerance				Civic-Mindedness			
	Low	Middle	High	(*Eta*)	Low	Middle	High	(*Eta*)
Japan	48.9	71.1	80.8	(.20)*	13.2	26.0	23.2	(.09)*
Taiwan	40.5	59.6	68.8	(.15)*	10.8	20.3	23.4	(.08)*
China	55.6	48.4	74.7	(.16)*	16.0	24.3	32.9	(.11)*
Singapore	48.4	77.2	82.8	(.15)*	6.9	19.0	32.5	(.17)*
Vietnam	60.0	65.4	75.7	(.07)*	28.9	42.1	46.3	(.08)*
(Pooled)	48.9	64.9	74.0	(.14)*	14.9	26.0	32.7	(.09)*

* Significant at the 0.05 level.
Source: 2005–8 Asian Barometer Surveys.

expressing particularized and generalized trust. For each of the three levels of attachment to Confucian familism, Table 6.7 shows the percentages of citizens willing to trust their own relatives, strangers, and government officials. It also shows the percentages of those willing to tolerate other people with different views and of the fully civic-minded, who both trust and tolerate others.

As expected from the Confucian tradition of graded love, people in Confucian Asia who are attached to familism are more likely to trust their relatives than are those who are not attached to this Confucian tradition. Table 6.7 shows positive relationships between familism and trust in four of six Confucian countries, including Korea, Taiwan, China, and Singapore. When these four countries and Japan are considered together (Vietnam was excluded from this analysis because an overwhelming majority of 97 percent expressed no trust in relatives), moreover, there emerges a clear pattern of a consistently positive relationship between the two variables. Because of this relationship, those unattached to familism are the least trusting of relatives (83%), whereas those fully attached to this tradition are the most trusting of them (88%).

In contrast, Table 6.7 does not exhibit the same pattern of a consistently positive relationship between levels of familism and generalized trust in most of the Confucian countries. Only in Singapore and Vietnam is a higher level of attachment to familism always accompanied by a significantly higher level of trust in strangers. In the four other countries, the proportions expressing such generalized trust vary relatively little or inconsistently across the three different levels of attachment to familism. When all six countries are considered together, however, a clear pattern of a consistently positive relationship emerges between the two variables.

As with the case of particularized trust, those expressing trust in strangers are the least numerous among the unattached and the most numerous among the fully attached to Confucian familism. More notably, in the entire region of Confucian Asia, the fully attached are nearly one-and-a-half times more likely to trust strangers than are the unattached (33% vs. 45%). These findings run counter to the argument that the Confucian legacy of familism is responsible for creating low-trust societies in Confucian Asia (Fukuyama 1995a).

Does familism also create greater trust in government officials as it does with particularized and generalized trust? Table 6.7 confirms this positive relationship. In all countries but Korea a higher level of familism is always accompanied by a higher level of political trust. Even in Korea, the level of political trust is lowest among the least attached to familism and significantly higher among the fully attached than among the unattached (23% vs. 16%). When all six countries are pooled together, those fully attached to familism lead the unattached in trusting government officials by a large margin of 29 percentage points (63% vs. 34%). Together, these figures strongly suggest that familism is more conducive than detrimental to popular trust in governmental officials.

In Table 6.7 we also see that familism is, by and large, positively related with affect-based trust. In four countries – China, Japan, Korea, and Taiwan – those weighing personal ties more importantly than professional or technical competence in hiring a new employee are most numerous among those fully attached to familism, and except for Korea, those expressing such affect-based trust are consistently more numerous at each higher level of familism. When all four countries are considered together, the proportion expressing affect-based trust is lowest (24%) at the lowest level of familism and highest (44%) at attachment to familism's highest level. In Confucian Asia, those fully attached to familism are nearly twice as likely to value affective ties as are those unattached to it. As in the case of other types of trust, familism seems to contribute to affect-based trust.

Table 6.7 also shows a positive relationship between Confucian familism and interpersonal tolerance. In four of the five countries – Japan, Taiwan, Singapore, and Vietnam – a higher level of attachment to familism is always accompanied by a larger percentage of those who are tolerant. As a result, there is a large gap in tolerance between the low and high levels of attachment to familism in these four countries. In Japan and Singapore, for example, less than 50 percent of those unattached to familism are tolerant of others who disagree with them, in contrast to more than 80 percent of those highly attached to familism. When all five countries are pooled together, the proportion of the tolerant is 25 percentage points higher among the fully attached than among the unattached (74% vs. 49%). The more strongly that people in Confucian Asia adhere to familism, the more willing they are to tolerate other people with different views.

Most notable is the finding that in three of the five countries – China, Taiwan, and Singapore – the fully civic-minded, those who endorse both norms of trust and tolerance, are more than two times more numerous among those who are fully attached to familism than among those detached from it. In Singapore, these fully civic-minded citizens are more than four times more numerous among the attached to familism than the unattached (33% vs. 7%). When all five countries are considered together, those who are fully civic-minded are more than twice as numerous among the attached than the unattached (33% vs. 15%). Throughout the region, Confucian familism seems to contribute to rather than detract from the building of a civilized civic community by encouraging people to embrace the twin norms of trust and tolerance. In this respect, it is different from amoral familism, which is known to be detrimental to democratization.

Sources of Shared Civic Norms

The analyses presented in this chapter make it clear that in Confucian Asia today more people are unwilling than are willing to trust and tolerate their fellow citizens. What motivates some people to embrace these twin civic norms of interpersonal trust and tolerance and others to shun these norms? Does activism in associational life encourage them to internalize these norms, as Robert Putnam (1993) and other neo-Tocquevilleans have suggested? Or does familism, independently of other forces, discourage them from becoming civic-minded, as Francis Fukuyama (1995a) has observed? How do the Confucian traditions of familism and communitarianism compare with the forces of modernization and socialization as an influence on the civic norms?

In this section, I consider four sets of variables and the type of resident regime as sources of popular attachment to the civic norms of trust and tolerance, and I compare their relative influence on adherence to both norms. As in previous chapters, I include two pairs of variables tapping socialization (gender and age) and modernization (education and income) along with associational activism, both formal (Q20–22) and informal (Q27), and adherence to Confucian familism and communitarianism.[2] Associational activism is measured in terms of the number of people in informal interactions and the membership of formal associations. Communitarianism is measured in terms of reciprocity, harmony, the priority of communal interests, and cooperation among formal associations or groups, as discussed in Chapter 5. There are three categories of regime type: nondemocracy, third-wave democracy, and second-wave democracy. In the multivariate analysis, the willingness to tolerate and trust other people is the dependent variable, which is measured on a 3-point scale (see Table 6.8).

Of the six Confucian countries, only four – Japan, Taiwan, Singapore, and Vietnam – asked all of the sets of questions tapping the dependent and independent variables. For each and all of these four countries, Table 6.8 reports the MCA estimates of the extent to which each independent

---

[2] Chapter 5 describes in detail a 5-point index tapping attachment to the Confucian communitarian model of civic life.

TABLE 6.8. *Sources of Civic-Mindedness* (MCA estimates)

Predictors	Beta
Socialization	
Gender	.01
Age	.03
Modernization	
Education	.04
Income	.08*
Social Capital	
Persons in Contact	.00
Associational Membership	.06
Bridging Associations	.03
Confucianism	
Familism	.12*
Communitarianism	.11*
Regime Type	.03
(R^2)	(.07)

* Statistically significant at the 0.05 level.
Source: 2005–8 Asian Barometer Surveys.

variable affects the dependent variable independently of all other independent variables. The most notable finding of the table is that the Confucian traditions of familism and communitarianism are the two most powerful of seven significant influences on civic-mindedness. According to the magnitude of their *beta* coefficients, the contribution of these two legacies of Confucian social ethics to civic-mindedness is significantly greater than that of any of the other five significant variables, including age, income, and associational membership.

Of the two Confucian legacies, familism outweighs communitarianism as a promoter of civic-minded citizenship. Contrary to the findings in the literature, familism contributes to rather than detracts from embracing the civic norms. Evidently, the more closely that people in Confucian East Asia are attached to their own families, the more closely they are attached to those outside their families as well. This is the most credible evidence disputing the widely held claim that Confucianism poses a serious obstacle to the development of civic community in Confucian Asia (Fukuyama 1995a; Pye 1999).

Another notable finding of the table concerns formal and informal associations. As known in the literature on social capital, joiners of formal associations are significantly more civic-minded than nonjoiners, but the particular type of associations they join matters little, as does the number of people whom a person contacts regularly. All in all, people in Confucian Asia are not motivated to become broadly civic-minded when they experience close reciprocal relationships with a large number of other known people. This poses a direct challenge to the Confucian notion of human nature that people become virtuous through constant interactions with others, which was discussed in Chapter 3.

Equally surprising is that education, unlike family income, does not contribute to the development of a civic-minded citizenry. The inability of education to produce civic-minded citizens in Confucian Asia is surprising in view of the positive role it is known to play in other parts of the world (Bobo and Licari 1989; Orces 2008; Peffley and Rohrschneider 2003). Equally surprising is that democratic rule detracts from rather than contributes to trusting and tolerating fellow citizens. As compared to 29 percent in nondemocracies, 28 percent of people in third-wave democracies and 26 percent in a second-wave democracy are fully civic-minded.[3] The longer that people live in a democracy, the less they become civic-minded.

How much do the devotees of the five levels of familism differ in embracing the twin norms of interpersonal trust and tolerance? To address this question, Figure 6.9 reports two separate percentages derived from the MCA analysis, one *unadjusted* and the other *adjusted* for the nine other variables listed in Table 6.8. The *unadjusted* percentages in Figure 6.9 show the differences in the average level of full civic-mindedness reported by those in the five levels of familism. The *adjusted* figures show these differences after the effects of the other independent variables on such civic-mindedness have been statistically removed.

A careful comparison of these percentages reveals that the legacies of Confucian familism are a powerful force contributing to the building of civic-minded nations in East Asia. According to the *unadjusted* percentages, the fully civic-minded are more than three times more numerous among those attached to all those legacies considered in this analysis than those unattached to any of them (44% vs. 14%). With the *adjusted* percentages, the fully civic-minded are 2.5 times more numerous among those fully attached than among those fully unattached (40% vs. 16%). As expected, the magnitude of their difference falls considerably after the other influences have been statistically removed. Nonetheless, the

---

[3] All these percentages came from results of the MCA analysis of fully civic-mindedness, which is reported in Table 6.8.

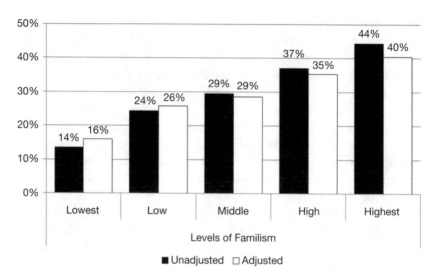

FIGURE 6.9. Unadjusted and Adjusted Percentages of the Fully Civic-Minded by Levels of Familism. *Source:* 2005–8 Asian Barometer Surveys.

differences remain not only substantial but also consistent after the adjustment of those variables.

Equally notable is that the adjusted percentages of the fully civic-minded increase *steadily* as attachment to familism increases from the lowest to the highest level: 16 percent for the lowest level, 26 percent for the low level, 29 percent for the middle level, 35 percent for the high level, and 40 percent for the highest level. The more devoted East Asians are to the legacies of Confucian family life, the more likely they are to become fully civic-minded. This finding is another piece of evidence supporting our claim that Confucianism is fundamentally different from what is known in the West as amoral familism. It also dispels the widely held belief that Confucian familism deters people from trusting and tolerating other people outside their immediate family circle.

Summary and Conclusions

This chapter examined the cultural dimension of civil society in Confucian countries from a number of comparative perspectives. Of the various norms required for civilized civic life, it focused on interpersonal trust and tolerance, the two norms widely known to shape the process of democratic regime change as well as governance. For citizens to participate and compete in the democratic political process, they should be allowed to express their views regardless of how popular or unpopular those views are, and for these citizens and their parties to reach an agreement on policy making, they need to trust each other. Only when fellow citizens trust and tolerate each other can they join in associations and work together for their communities. For these reasons, interpersonal trust and tolerance are also known as the twin norms of civilized and democratic civic life (Gibson and Gouws 2005; Sullivan and Transue 1999; Uslaner 2002).

To what extent do people in Confucian Asia trust and tolerate others? Does a low level of trust exist in all of the societies in this region, as the existing literature on civil society and social capital suggests? Does the Confucian tradition of familism remain an ideology of graded love, or has it been transformed into a basis for an amoral life that discourages Confucian East Asians from embracing the norms of trust and tolerance? To address these questions, I first explicated the original notion of Confucian familism and then discussed its potential danger for inhibiting trust of strangers and thus for producing a low-trust society. Analyses of the public opinion surveys recently conducted in six Confucian countries revealed that majorities of their adult populations remain partially attached to Confucian familism. The same analyses also revealed that five of the six countries are, indeed, low-trust societies, mainly due to low levels of trust in strangers, as opposed to family members.

More notably, in every Confucian country, those who trust both family members and strangers constitute a minority. Those who are willing to tolerate people with whom they do not agree, however, constitute a majority in every country. Accordingly, there is a large gap between the willingness to tolerate and to trust throughout the entire region of Confucian Asia. This regionwide pattern of failing to uphold civic norms fully is not exclusive to Confucian Asia: The same pattern is also found in non-Confucian Asia.

Even more notable is the finding that attachment to Confucian familism contributes to East Asians' embrace of the two civic norms; this runs counter to previous studies, which have suggested that such attachment discourages the development of trust and tolerance (Alesina and Giuliano 2011; Banfield 1958; Fukuyama 1995a; Lee and Hsiao 2010). Even when associational activism and other known influences on the norms are statistically controlled for, attachment to the family promotes a willingness to tolerate and trust other people in all five Confucian societies, which include two democracies and three nondemocracies. These findings suggest that Confucian familism is not responsible for the low levels of social capital in the region's societies. They also suggest that Confucian familism is not an amoral familism that favors the family at the expense of all other associations; the tradition seems instead to foster positive feelings toward all people.

Between Confucian and non-Confucian Asia there is little difference in the extent to which people are attached to the two principles of Confucian familism. The two Asian regions are also more similar than different in their people's willingness to tolerate people who express different views. Where the two regions part ways is over interpersonal trust. In levels of particularized and generalized trust, Confucian Asian countries lead non-Confucian countries; however, with respect to the levels of political trust and affect-based trust, Confucian Asian countries fall behind. In short, levels of trust differ significantly in the two regions despite their similarity in popular attachment to Confucian familism. This finding also indicates that familism may not be a powerful deterrent to interpersonal trust in Confucian Asia.

Within Confucian Asia there is also a notable difference in the extent to which people trust their government officials. In all three democracies, only a minority trusts these officials. In striking contrast, large majorities trust their officials in the two nondemocracies of Singapore and Vietnam. This pattern of regime-based differences in political trust is not observable in non-Confucian countries: In non-Confucian Asia, majorities of both democratic and nondemocratic countries express trust in their government officials. I was unable to determine with the data at hand why only democracies in Confucian Asia motivate the mass publics to become critical citizens.

Of the six Confucian countries, China is the only high-trust country where a majority is fully willing to endorse each of those norms. Vietnam is also the only country where more education is associated with less interpersonal trust. Singapore is the only country where the college educated are the most attached to Confucian familism, whereas the least educated are the least attached to it. Taiwan is the only country where the fully attached to Confucian familism form a small minority of less than one-third. Japan is the only country where levels of political trust are the highest among the socioeconomically worst-off. Korea is the only nation in which males weigh affective ties more heavily than females in judging the trustworthiness of other people.

Despite these national differences, countries in Confucian Asia share a number of important characteristics. They no longer remain fully family-centered nations of graded love. Nor do they remain nations of affective trust. Like their counterparts in the democratized West, they have become nations of cognitive or knowledge-based trust. There is little doubt that the forces of democratization, modernization, and globalization have contributed to these transformations. These forces, however, are not all facilitating the building of civic nations in Confucian Asia. With more education, for example, people in the region become less tolerant of others, contrary to what has been noted elsewhere. This negative impact of education on tolerance is the most disturbing aspect of civil society development in Confucian Asia today.

PART IV

EMBRACING DEMOCRACY

7

Conceptions of Democracy

Democracy is government by the people. As such, it requires citizens who are informed and active in the political process. In principle, therefore, a democratic government cannot be foisted on citizens who are unwilling to embrace and support it as the preferred alternative to all forms of nondemocratic government. Nor can it, in practice, survive and flourish for an extended period of time unless citizens can recognize its virtues and distinguish democratic practices from undemocratic ones (Griffith et al.1956, 129).

Thus, to survive and develop over time, new democracies – or those that have been democracies for awhile but do not yet function as full democracies – must transform their citizens (Dahl 1997; Dalton 2008; Diamond 1997; Putnam 1993; Shin 2007). The first step in this transformation is education: Citizens must understand what constitutes democracy and be able to differentiate it from its alternatives. The next step is internalization: Citizens must develop a conviction of the virtues of democratic rule, and this conviction must in turn lead to an acceptance of democracy as "the only game in town" (Linz and Stepan 1996). Only with informed and continuing support from the mass citizenry can limited democracies grow into fully functioning democracies (Rose and Shin 2001). Those citizens who express such support can be called democrats with a small "d" – functioning citizens of a democratic state.

Both in principle and practice, therefore, all democracies need democrats. However, newly democratizing countries, as compared to older, more consolidated democracies, have a greater need for an increasing number of democrats for the expansion and consolidation of limited democratic rule (Mishler and Rose 1996). In countries with a long tradition of authoritarian rule, citizens must undergo both steps of the transformation, education and internalization, so they will no longer confuse nondemocracy with democratic rule or support nondemocratic methods of governance for problems needing quick solutions.

Popular understanding of democratic politics and the preference for it constitute the two fundamental domains of the political dimension of democratic citizenship, as discussed in the Introduction. In this chapter, I examine the *cognitive* domain of democratic understanding, and in the next, I analyze the *affective* domain of democratic support. When considered together, these two domains allow us to determine and compare the levels and patterns of popular commitment to democracy across Confucian countries.

The Notion of Democratic Citizenship

For decades, political scientists and social psychologists have conducted a great deal of theoretical and empirical research on democratic citizenship (Borgida et al. 2009; van Deth 2007). To date, much of this theoretical research has focused on the complex issue of how individuals balance the interests of their communities with their personal and family interests. In an attempt to resolve the never ending conflicts between communal and individual interests, many democratic theorists have advanced a variety of approaches, including liberal democratic, social democratic, communitarian, and republican theories (Barber 1984; MacIntyre 1984; Rawls 1993; Rosenberg 2007). Each of these theoretical approaches offers a different image of a "good citizen" of a democratic state and presents a different mix of the specific norms and roles that individual citizens must observe and play to become such citizens.

In theoretical research, individual citizens are, more often than not, assumed to be capable of judging their own interests and those of their communities. They are also assumed to be the best judges of their own interests and can become better judges of communal interests by deliberating public issues with other citizens involved (Fishkin 2009; D. Thompson 1970). Consequently, citizens' rationality in evaluating their own interests and their reasonableness in dealing with other people have served as the two basic premises underlying much of the theoretical research on democratic citizenship (Rawls 1993; Rosenberg 2007). As Borgida et al. (2009, 2) note, these two premises have often led to an overly optimistic view that ordinary people should be able to cultivate all the requisite qualities of democratic citizenship "under the right set of institutional circumstance." Included in these qualities are political knowledge and information, understanding and internalization of democratic norms and values, and political interest and involvement.

In contrast to theoretical research on democratic citizenship, empirical research has examined the images citizens themselves have of a "good citizen" and how those images differ from the ones prescribed by democratic theorists. It has also studied ordinary citizens' inclinations to observe the norms required for becoming fully functioning democrats and their capacity to play the various roles associated with good citizenship. To date, empirical research has been conducted primarily in the United States and other consolidated democracies of the West.

Because citizens of these regions have a great deal of experience with democratic politics, there has been no need either to examine whether they understand democracy in principle or to assess how capable they are of distinguishing democracy from nondemocracy in practice. Accordingly, researchers have focused on the other important aspects of democratic citizenship prescribed in the theoretical literature, including cognitive enlightenment, political involvement, civic-mindedness, and solidarity (Dalton 2007; Nie, Junn, and Stehlik-Barry 1996). The resulting studies based on public opinion surveys have revealed a wide gulf between the qualities of democratic citizenship prescribed in the theoretical literature and those attained by many citizens of consolidated Western democracies (Converse 1964; Delli Carpini 2009).

In all dimensions of democratic citizenship, ordinary people are found considerably lacking concerning the requisite qualities for collective self-rule. Many have little factual information about government and politics. Moreover, their attitudes are neither stable over time nor coherent ideologically. These negative findings directly challenge the optimistic theoretical assumption that ordinary people have all the capacities and inclinations necessary to become good citizens of a democratic state (Borgida et al. 2009). More notably, the same findings raise serious questions about the potential and motivations of citizens of newly democratizing and authoritarian countries with little or no experience with democratic politics to become democrats capable of expressing informed and coherent support for democracy.

Nonetheless, the empirical evidence available from the established democracies of the West confirms that democratic citizenship is a multidimensional phenomenon encompassing not only what people think and feel about democratic politics but also how they work out its application. Of all the various dimensions of citizen orientations and behaviors, cognitive enlightenment has been found to be the most fundamental component. Political knowledge, for example, has been found to shape many beliefs, attitudes, and behaviors supportive of democratic politics (Delli Carpini 2009, 24–6; Diamond 1997). Consequently, people become politically more tolerant and active when they are informed about the various aspects of democratic political life. This finding suggests that the growth of democratic knowledge among mass publics is crucial to building democratic political culture and nations of democrats. For this reason, this chapter is devoted to an in-depth analysis of the contours of democratic conceptions among Confucian Asian people.

Recent Research on Democratic Conceptions

Over the past two decades, many public opinion surveys have been conducted to explore conceptions of democracy held by ordinary citizens (Baviskar and Malone 2004; Camp 2001; Canache 2006; Fuchs 1999; Miller, Hesli, and Reisinger 1997; Moreno 2001; Ottemoeller 1998; Schedler and Sarsfield 2007). These national and cross-national public opinion surveys have asked both open- and closed-ended questions to ascertain popular conceptions of democracy. Regional barometers, including the Afrobarometer, the Asian Barometer, and the Latinobarometer, have asked open-ended questions and encouraged respondents to talk about the meaning of democracy in their own terms (www.globalbarometer.net). Some of these barometers and other national and multinational surveys have asked closed-ended questions and requested respondents to choose from a list of one or more characteristics that correspond most closely to their conceptions of democracy (McIntosh and Abele 1993; Shin 1999). Still other surveys have asked both open- and closed-ended questions and compared responses to the two types of questions (Fuchs and Roller 2006; Simon 1998).

The open-ended approach is intended to address two specific questions: Do ordinary citizens have the capacity to articulate the concept of democracy? If they do, in what specific terms do they define or understand it? The closed-ended approach is also intended to address two specific questions: Do ordinary people have the capacity to weigh the various properties of democracy? If they do, which properties do they consider the most and least essential? Both types of questions are occasionally asked together to determine the overall cognitive capacity of ordinary citizens to define the concept of democracy and to prioritize its properties for effective democratic governance.

The best examples of the closed-ended approach are the United States Information Service-commissioned surveys conducted in Hungary, Poland, Romania, and Bulgaria between early 1991 and early 1993 (McIntosh and Abele 1993). In these surveys, respondents were asked to weigh six values – three political and three economic – and to choose the one they considered most important to their country's democratic development. Their responses to this closed-ended question were compared to popular opinion in three old democracies in Europe: Britain, France, and West Germany. Whereas the mass publics of the consolidated democracies in Western Europe emphasized the political values of political freedom, party competition, and a fair justice system, those of the new Eastern European democracies gave more weight to the economic values of prosperity, equality, and security. This pattern of conceptual differences was also confirmed in the 1993 Korea Democracy Barometer survey in which two-thirds of the respondents chose economic rights over political rights (Shin 1999, 60).

Over the past two decades, more multinational public opinion surveys have begun using the open-ended approach. The 1998 Hewlett survey directed by Roderic Ai Camp, for example, asked a pair of open-ended questions to compare popular conceptions of democracy in three Latin and Central American countries: Costa Rica, Mexico, and Chile. Since then, three regional barometers – the Afrobarometer, the Asian Barometer, and the Latinobarometer – have asked an open-ended question to address the same issue. These multinational surveys all asked respondents to define democracy in their own words, but they were not all based on the same notion of democracy. For example, the Hewlett survey treated democracy as a single-dimensional concept and thus allowed respondents to identify only one property. In contrast, the three regional surveys treated democracy as a complex concept and allowed respondents to name up to three of its properties.

The 1992 and 1995 surveys conducted in Russia and the Ukraine allowed their samples of average citizens and elites to identify all of the values and practices, political and otherwise, that they associated with democracy (Miller et al. 1997). The number of their responses was counted to determine their levels of cognitive development concerning democracy. This analysis was based on the premise that "citizens who have more to say about the meaning of democracy has [sic] more fully developed cognitions of democracy than those who say little or [have] nothing to say about it" (Miller et al. 1997, 164). In addition, the types of values and practices the two samples associated most frequently with democracy were compared to determine whether the leaders and masses of these postcommunist countries shared a common democratic political culture.

The Post-Communist Citizen Project directed by Samuel Barnes and Janos Simon (1998) asked both closed and open-ended questions. Their surveys, conducted in eleven Central and Eastern European countries, first asked closed-ended questions to determine whether decades of communist rule succeeded in "homogenizing" mass political attitudes. Specifically, respondents were asked to rate on a 4-point scale the relevance of eleven political and other values to democracy. In addition, the surveys asked one open-ended question: "What does democracy mean for [sic] you?" Responses to the closed-ended questions were analyzed to identify the most and least important categories of democratic components and to compare the patterns of their distribution across eleven formerly communist countries. Responses to the open-ended question were analyzed to assess the ability of the mass publics to define democracy, as well as to identify the most and least popular images of democracy among the masses of each society.

When considered together, the results of all these national and multinational surveys clearly indicate that, in most countries, majorities have been exposed to the concept of democracy and are cognitively capable of defining it in their own words. They are also capable of assessing the most and least essential of its components. Undoubtedly, these and other survey findings have contributed to broadening our knowledge about the cognitive dimension of democratic citizenship by enabling us to *estimate* and *describe* the extent to which mass publics can impute meaning to the concept of democracy.

Nonetheless, these surveys do not allow us to *evaluate* citizens' cognitive capacity to conceptualize or define democracy in depth. Specifically, they do not allow us to determine whether those citizens capable of defining democracy are also capable of distinguishing it from its alternatives. As a result, the extant literature offers little information about how accurately or inaccurately the mass publics are informed about democracy. Using the latest, fifth round of the World Values Surveys (WVS) and the second wave of the Asian Barometer Surveys (ABS), this chapter aims to describe and then evaluate the cognitive capacity of citizens in six historically Confucian nations – China, Japan, Korea, Singapore, Taiwan, and Vietnam – to understand democracy.

Democratic Values and Norms

As government by the people and for the people, democracy involves a multitude of rights and responsibilities for individual citizens, as well as for the institutions representing their interests. As a concept, democracy therefore refers to a variety of things and is a concept difficult for ordinary people to grasp or define fully (Dalton, Shin, and Jou 2007; Schedler and Sarsfield 2007; see also Collier and Levitsky 1997; Dahl 1989, 1997). As Philippe Schmitter and Terry Karl (1991, 76) suggest, however, "the various patterns must be habitually known, practiced, and accepted by most, if not all, actors."

How well do ordinary people in Confucian East Asia understand democracy? How capable are they of distinguishing it from its non-democratic alternatives? Why are some Confucian Asian people savvier about democracy than others? To determine how accurately and fully the Confucian Asian publics understand democracy, I analyzed individual citizens' opinions about four tenets of democratic systems: free and fair elections, civil liberties, civilian control of the military, and the separation of church and state (Collier and Levitsky 1997; Huber, Rueschemeyer, and Stephens 1997).

Throughout the entire history of democratic development, there is no consensus on the meaning of democracy. Yet scholars have most often identified these tenets as the four most definitive characteristics of a democratic regime and its alternatives (Dahl 1998; Sartori 1995). The surveys measured the first two positively; that is, respondents were asked to assess the essentiality of popular elections and civil liberties to democracy. In contrast, the last two were measured negatively; that is, respondents were asked to rate the essentiality of military intervention and intervention from religious authorities, the opposite of what should be found in a democracy.

Free and fair elections are an integral part of democratic rule. Elections legitimize the government and provide a mechanism for political dialogue between rulers and citizens. Moreover, they allow citizens to choose from alternative political platforms and side with divergent parties, and they facilitate political activism and mobilization. As Elizabeth Spiro Clark (2000) notes, "Without regular genuinely competitive elections, essential democratic elements of accountability and equality (one person-one vote) are missing." For this reason, in *Polyarchy*, Robert Dahl (1971) identifies participation, especially in the process of electing political leaders, as an underlying dimension of a fully democratic society. Informed democrats are thus expected to understand and endorse popular elections in a political system.

Although elections are an important ingredient of democracy, elections by themselves do not make a democracy; in other words, while the absence of free and fair elections necessarily makes a country undemocratic, the holding of such elections does not necessarily make the country democratic (Karl 2000). In the world of new democracies, elections are not always accompanied by the protection of individual freedom and self-expression within the political arena. In many countries, democratically elected leaders rule by decree, impose restrictions on speech and assembly, and tolerate abuse of human rights (Carothers 2002; Zakaria 2003). Only when citizens are fully protected from such restrictions and abuses can they participate freely in the electoral process and exercise their right to vote in free and fair elections. The protection of civil rights and liberties, therefore, is also essential to democracy.

In addition, a fully democratic system requires that a popularly elected government remain autonomous from other societal groups and organizations. This autonomy depends on citizens recognizing the authority of their elected regime. It also requires that representatives be held accountable to the people's preferences. If other groups and individuals, such as the military or religious authorities, undermine the authority of an elected government, then its democratic legitimacy is at risk (Schmitter and Karl 1991). Among Robert Dahl's minimal *procedural* conditions for a modern democracy, for example, is the stipulation that "control over government decisions about policy is constitutionally vested in elected officials" (Dahl 1982, 11). For that to be so, the control cannot belong to religious authorities; neither can it belong to those who would take it through military might.

As Schmitter and Karl (1991, 81) explain, "Democracy is in jeopardy if military officers, entrenched civil servants, or state managers retain the capacity to act independently of elected civilians or even veto decisions made by the people's representatives." To determine whether global citizenries acknowledge the legitimacy of their elected government, we need to measure their aversion to military intervention and religious involvement in matters of state. Citizens with an accurate conception of democracy are expected to reject both a military takeover and interference by religious figures; to do otherwise would be to mistake authoritarian practices for democratic ones.

Although I do not presume that these four tenets constitute an exhaustive list of those found in democratic regimes, I am confident that they exist as core values in all consolidated democracies. Two of the four values, free elections and the protection of liberties, tap political contestation and inclusiveness as conceptualized by Dahl and empirically verified by Coppedge et al. (2008) and others. The two other values, civilian control of the military and the separation of church and state, address the legitimacy and autonomy of democratic governance.

The Method of Analysis

To determine the astuteness of Confucian Asian citizens' democratic conceptions, I analyzed a set of four questions (V153, V154, V156, and V157) from the WVS conducted between 2005 and 2007. The WVS asked these questions in five Confucian countries – China, Japan, South Korea, Taiwan, and Vietnam – and forty-two other countries, including three non-Confucian countries in East Asia: Indonesia, Malaysia, and Thailand; responses were weighted by country to account for variations in the sample sizes.

The questions asked respondents to assess the essentiality of (1) free and fair elections, (2) protection of liberties, (3) military intervention, and (4) intervention of religious authorities; whereas the first two are straightforward measures of democratic tenets, the last two are more roundabout in asking respondents to assess conditions that are antithetical to the democratic tenets of citizen control of the military and separation of church and state. Respondents evaluated each question on a 10-point scale, with 1 signifying "not at all an essential characteristic of democracy" and 10 signifying "an essential characteristic of democracy."

The initial analysis focused on whether citizens felt able to assess the essentiality of each of the four dimensions. I calculated the percentage of respondents offering no assessment of each of the four dimensions and labeled these respondents as *unsure* about democracy. Next, I assessed whether citizens were capable of evaluating each dimension correctly. I calculated the percentage of those who, by choosing scores below the scales' midpoint of 5.5, incorrectly identified either free elections or protection of liberties as an *unessential* property of democracy and/or the intervention of either religious or military authorities as one of its *essential* properties. These respondents we labeled as *misinformed* about democracy.

With these two categories of responses, *unsure* and *misinformed*, I constructed four types of democratic understanding: *the uninformed, the partially informed, the ill informed,* and *the well informed* (see Table 7.1).

TABLE 7.1. *Four Types of Citizen Capacity to Understand Democracy*

		Evaluated Properties	
		Not All	All
Misinformed	None	Partially Informed	Well informed
Properties	Yes	Uninformed	Ill informed

The uninformed are those whose responses include either all nonresponses or some mix of nonresponses, incorrect responses, and correct responses. *The partially informed* are those who fail to assess at least one property but who have correct views of all those they do assess. *The ill informed* are those who assess all four dimensions but misunderstand the essentiality of at least one to democracy. The *well informed* are those who accurately assess all four dimensions of democracy. At times, to simplify the analysis, I combined *the uninformed, the partially informed*, and *the ill informed* into a broader group labeled the *poorly informed*.

The Capacity to Recognize and Evaluate Democracy

The people of Confucian Asia are widely known to prefer democracy as much as do people in other regions (Chu et al. 2008; Shin 2008), but are they aware of what is essential or unessential in a democracy? For each of the five Confucian countries,[1] Table 7.2 reports the percentages of those unable to determine whether each of the four regime characteristics is essential to democracy, as evidenced by a nonresponse. It also presents the percentages of those unable to evaluate at least one of the four dimensions correctly and those unable to evaluate all of them correctly. I labeled these respondents as *unsure* about democracy.

Table 7.2 shows that the proportions of the *unsure* about each of the four regime characteristics vary a great deal across the five Confucian countries. Of the five countries, the *unsure* are most numerous in China and least numerous in Korea and Taiwan. In China, more than 20 percent are *unsure* about each of the four characteristics. More than 40 percent of the Chinese feel unable to judge the relevance of the role of religious leaders and the military to the democratic political process. Nearly

---

[1] Singapore, one of the six historically Confucian countries chosen for this study, was not included in the fifth wave of the WVS.

TABLE 7.2. *Inability to Assess Essentiality of Regime Characteristics:*
Nonresponse

Country	Popular Elections	Protecting Liberty	Military Takeover	Religious Interpretation	At Least One	All Four
Japan	9.9%	19.5%	12.7%	19.6%	31.1%	6.0%
Korea	0.0	0.1	0.1	0.0	0.1	0.0
Taiwan	0.6	0.8	1.5	1.5	2.0	0.5
China	21.6	29.5	42.6	49.9	58.9	16.6
Vietnam	4.1	4.2	14.6	13.0	21.1	2.5
(Pooled)	7.0	11.0	14.0	17.0	22.6	5.1

Source: 2005–8 World Values Surveys.

two-fifths (59%) of the Chinese are *unsure* about at least one characteristic. This figure is nearly three times as high as for Vietnam (21%),
another communist country in the same region. It is indeed difficult to
explain why, of these two communist nations, the Chinese, who are
socioeconomically far better off, are far more *unsure* about democracy
than the Vietnamese.

Among the Koreans and the Taiwanese, in striking contrast, less than
2 percent are *unsure* about the essential or unessential nature of each
regime characteristic as a property of democracy. Those who are unsure
about at least one of the four characteristics, moreover, constitute a very
small minority of 2 percent or less. Whereas a solid majority (59%) of
the Chinese population still remains *unsure* about the basic constituents
of democracy, overwhelming majorities of Koreans (99%) and the
Taiwanese (98%) feel capable of assessing the essentiality of all four
components. Thus across the region known for a popular affinity for
democracy, there is a great deal of variation in the extent to which people
feel capable of assessing the basic properties of democracy.

Another notable feature of Table 7.2 concerns the willingness of the
Japanese to assess those properties. Although they are citizens of the oldest democratic and most educated nation in Asia, nearly one in three
Japanese adults (31%) is *unsure* whether at least one of the four regime
properties surveyed is essential or unessential to democracy. This figure is 30 percentage points higher than for the Korean and Taiwanese
people, who have much less experience with democratic rule. More surprisingly, the Japanese figure is 10 percentage points higher than for the
Vietnamese (21%), who have no experience with democratic politics at
all. Why is it that so many Japanese are *unsure* about the characteristics
of the democratic regime in which they have lived all or most of their

lives? The public opinion surveys do not allow us to answer this puzzling question adequately. As with the notions of *tatemae* and *honne* discussed in Chapter 1, however, I surmise that Japanese culture, which is known to discourage people from revealing their personal views, especially to a stranger, may hold the key to answering this question (Bachnik 2007).

Careful scrutiny of Table 7.2 reveals that, in Korea and Taiwan, the proportions of the *unsure* vary little across the four regime characteristics considered. In contrast, in Japan, China, and Vietnam, the proportions vary considerably: more than twice as many people are *unsure* about the role of religious leaders than about free elections. Whereas citizens in all five countries are least *unsure* about the essentiality of free elections, the *unsure* about this dimension of democracy are more than two times more numerous among the Japanese than among the Vietnamese, who have no democratic experience at all (10% vs. 4%). Why do so many Japanese remain unsure about the role that free elections play in the democratic political process, even after six decades of participating in those elections? Is it because they believe those elections have contributed more to the persistence of corrupt governance than a well-functioning democracy in their country (Pharr 2000)? Or again, might it just be a matter of culture interfering with measurement?

When these countries are pooled together, people in Confucian Asia as a whole are most *unsure* about the proper role of religious leaders (17%), and then the intervention of the military (14%), protecting civil liberties (11%), and holding free elections (7%). Evidently, the Confucian Asian people are more ambivalent about the two characteristics of authoritarian rule showing up in a democracy than about the absence of key democratic characteristics. Altogether, nearly one-quarter (23%) of the Confucian population is *unsure* about at least one of the four regime characteristics being queried. A much smaller minority of 5 percent is *fully unsure* or feels unable to assess any of those characteristics. China is the only country with more than 10 percent *fully unsure* (17%).

How accurately or inaccurately are the mass publics of Confucian Asia informed about democracy? Do they have a correct interpretation of what a successful democracy requires? To address this question, I calculated the percentages of those who *incorrectly* assessed the essentiality of each regime characteristic to democracy. I labeled these respondents as *misinformed* about democracy.

Table 7.3 reports the percentage of the *misinformed* for each country and the Confucian region as a whole. The five countries differ considerably in the specific regime characteristics about which their citizens are

TABLE 7.3. *The Misinformed about Four Regime Characteristics: Incorrect Reponses*

Country	Popular Elections	Protecting Liberty	Military Takeover	Religious Interpretation	None	At Least One	All Four
Japan	8.7%	13.2%	6.1%	11.1%	63.8%	30.2%	0.6%
Korea	11.8	22.9	17.3	15.1	52.0	47.9	0.2
Taiwan	7.4	6.2	20.5	15.7	59.9	39.6	0.2
China	6.8	5.1	35.5	14.9	37.4	46.1	0.0
Vietnam	3.7	2.4	52.1	72.4	14.2	83.3	0.2
(Pooled)	8.0	10.0	26.0	26.0	45.5	49.0	0.0

Source: 2005–8 World Values Surveys.

most and least *misinformed*. For example, protecting civil liberties is the one most likely to receive an incorrect assessment in Japan (13%) and Korea (23%). In China (5%), Taiwan (6%), and Vietnam (2%), however, this is the least misunderstood characteristic of the four. Whereas in Taiwan (21%), the role of the military is the most misunderstood, it is the characteristic least likely to be misunderstood in Japan (6%).

A further comparison of these ratings across the countries shows that Koreans are the most *misinformed* citizens about popular elections (12%) and civil liberties (23%), whereas the Vietnamese are the least *misinformed* about these two democratic regime characteristics (8% and 10%, respectively). China (37% vs. 46%) and Vietnam (14% vs. 83%) are the two countries in which the misinformed outnumber the informed. Vietnam is the only country with a majority deeming religious leaders (52%) and the military (72%) as essential players in democracy. Japan is the only country with less than 10 percent (6%) misinformed about the role of the military. Most notably, Korea is the only country in which more than 10 percent are misinformed about each of all four characteristics. Why does the set of the most and least *misinformed* characteristics vary from one country to another in the same Confucian cultural region? Regime type and socioeconomic modernization do not seem to hold the answer.

When all five countries are pooled together for an overview of the Confucian region, the roles of the military and religious leaders are the two regime characteristics that are most misunderstood. One out of four people (26%) in the region misunderstands each of these two authoritarian political practices, considering each as conducive to democracy. In striking contrast, one in ten people (10%) misunderstands the practice of protecting civil liberty, considering it to be unessential to democracy. A smaller minority (8%) mistakenly believes that holding free elections has little to do with democracy. A comparison of these domain ratings reveals that people in Confucian Asia are more misinformed about the age-old practices of authoritarian rule than those of democracy.

When we pool together all four characteristics, nearly one-half (49%) of the people in Confucian Asia are *misinformed* about at least one of them. A smaller minority (46%) correctly assesses all of the four characteristics.[2] Of the five countries surveyed, those offering no incorrect assessments are most numerous in Japan (64%), followed by Taiwan (60%), Korea (52%), China (37%), and Vietnam (14%). In the three democracies of Japan, Korea, and Taiwan, majorities are not at all *misinformed* about democracy. In the two communist countries of China (37%) and Vietnam (14%), in striking contrast, less than two-fifths of the people are *fully informed*, and they are also outnumbered by the *misinformed*. This indicates that people in Confucian Asia become less *misinformed* about democracy as they personally experience it. These findings seem to support the theory of democratic learning that emphasizes the importance of democratic experience for the development of a democratic political culture (Mishler and Rose 2002; Rohrschneider 1999). Yet, it should be noted that *the misinformed* are more numerous in democratic Korea than in authoritarian China (48% vs. 46%).

Across each of the five Confucian countries, let us now compare the percentages of those *misinformed* and those *unsure* about at least one of the four regime characteristics, which are reported in Tables 7.2 and 7.3. In two countries, Japan and China, the *unsure* outnumber the *misinformed*. In the three other countries, Korea, Taiwan, and Vietnam, the latter outnumber the former. From this finding, one speculates whether there are two subcultures of verbal communication in Confucian Asia. In China and Japan, it seems that people prefer to remain silent unless they feel confident in their answer. In contrast, their counterparts in Korea, Taiwan, and Vietnam are more likely to voice an opinion than to remain silent, regardless of how confident they feel in their response. These two types of communication cultures, one reticent and the other assertive, can affect the process of democratization as they can encourage or discourage political competition and compromise among the mass citizenry.

All in all, how well do people in Confucian Asia understand democracy as a system of government? I addressed this question in terms of the four types of citizens discussed earlier: *the uninformed, the partially informed,*

---

[2] The remaining 5% are the *fully unsure*, who feel unable to rate any of the four regime characteristics.

TABLE 7.4. *Types of Understanding Democracy*

| Country | Types of Democratic Understanding | | | |
	Well Informed	Ill Informed	Partially Informed	Uninformed
Japan	43.7%	25.2%	26.1%	5.0%
Korea	52.1	47.8	0.0	0.1
Taiwan	58.7	39.3	1.7	0.3
China	11.4	29.7	42.5	16.4
Vietnam	6.0	72.9	10.8	10.3
(Pooled)	34.4	43.0	16.2	6.4

Source: 2005–8 World Values Surveys.

the ill informed, and *the well informed.* Table 7.4 reports how the mass citizenries of historically Confucian Asia are distributed across the four types of democratic understanding. In the region as a whole, those in *the ill-informed* group are the most numerous, with a near majority of 43 percent. They are followed by *the well informed* at 34 percent, *the partially informed* at 16 percent, and *the uninformed* at 6 percent. When *the uninformed, the partially informed,* and *the ill informed* are grouped together as the *poorly informed,* they constitute a substantial majority (65%). Within Confucian Asia today, the *fully informed* about democracy (i.e., those who are fully capable of evaluating democracy's essential and unessential properties) constitute a minority of about one-third (34%).

Across the five countries in the region, however, there is a great deal of variation in the sizes of the *fully informed* and the *poorly informed* groups. *The fully informed* constitute majorities in Taiwan (59%) and Korea (52%) and a plurality in Japan (44%), but small minorities in China (11%) and Vietnam (6%). The citizens of the three democracies are four times more likely to be fully informed about democracy than are their peers in the two nondemocracies.

Of the three types that fall in the category of *poorly informed,* being *uninformed* is the least prevalent in all five countries. Yet the most prevalent type of poorly informed democratic conceptions varies within the democratic and nondemocratic subregions of Confucian Asia. In Japan and China, being *partially informed,* which again refers to those who did not evaluate all four properties but who were correct in what evaluations they did offer, is more prevalent than being *ill informed,* which refers to those who evaluated all four properties but got at least one assessment wrong. In Korea, Taiwan, and Vietnam, the pattern is reversed with *the ill informed* being the most prevalent.

TABLE 7.5. *Regional Differences in the Cognitive Capacity to Understand Democracy*

| Country | Types of Democratic Understanding | | | |
	Well Informed	Ill Informed	Partially Informed	Uninformed
Confucian Asia	34.4%	43.0%	16.2%	6.4%
West	59.4	34.2	4.7	1.8
Eastern Europe	40.3	40.0	14.9	4.8
South Asia	14.7	78.9	3.8	2.6
Middle East	19.0	65.3	9.8	5.8
Latin America	33.2	53.7	8.7	4.4
Africa	20.8	65.3	8.2	5.8
(Pooled)	38.5	48.2	9.2	4.1

Source: 2005–8 World Values Surveys.

How does Confucian Asia compare with other regions, including Southeast Asia, in terms of being fully and poorly informed about democracy? Table 7.5 reports the distribution of the four types of democratic understanding for the seven regions defined by the types of culture, as discussed in Chapter 3. Only in the democratized West are *fully informed* citizens a majority (59%) of the population and the *poorly informed* a minority (41%). In all other regions *fully informed* citizens constitute minorities, ranging from 15 percent in South Asia to 40 percent in Central and Eastern Europe. In the percentage of *fully informed* citizens, Confucian Asia ranks third, ahead of four other regions, including Latin America, the region with the second longest period of democratic political experience, where only one-third (33%) of its citizens are fully and accurately informed about democracy.

As in every other region except for the West, Confucian Asia has more ill informed citizens than well-informed citizens. It is also similar to all other regions, including the democratized West, in that it has far more *ill informed* citizens than ones who are either *partially informed* or *uninformed*. Yet, this region stands out from all other regions as having the highest percentage of citizens *partially informed* (16%) or *uninformed* (6%) about democracy (see Table 7.5).

Divergent Conceptions of Democracy

Up to now, the analysis has focused on a systematic examination of how well or poorly people in Confucian Asia understand democracy. In this

TABLE 7.6. *Types of Democratic Conceptions*

| Country | Types of Conceptions | | | |
	Authoritarian	Authentic	Hybrid	Others*
Japan	1.7%	74.2%	13.5%	10.6%
Korea	1.9	69.1	24.9	4.1
Taiwan	0.8	65.8	31.1	2.3
China	1.6	41.2	38.3	18.9
Vietnam	0.4	15.5	80.3	3.8
(Pooled)	1.3	53.2	37.6	7.9

* Others include those who fail to rate all four regime characteristics and
who rate none of those characteristics as essential to democracy.
Source: 2005–8 World Values Surveys.

section, I focus on the specific terms in which they understand democracy. Do Confucian Asian people tend to define democracy in different terms? If they do, what are the most and least popular democratic conceptions? Do these conceptions vary across the countries within the region?

To address these questions, I identified three types of democratic conceptions. The first type conceives of democracy solely in terms of its own characteristics: free elections and civil liberties. The second type conceives of democracy solely in terms of authoritarian regime characteristics: military and theocratic intervention. The third type conceptualizes democracy in terms of both democratic and authoritarian regime characteristics. These three types are, respectively, called *authentic, authoritarian,* and *hybrid.* Whereas *authentic* conceivers include *the well informed* and *partially informed,* who are accurately informed about all four or fewer regime characteristics, *authoritarian* and *hybrid* conceivers include those with either *pro-authoritarian* or *mixed* misconceptions of democracy. Table 7.6 reports for each country the percentages of its citizens of each type.

In all five countries, *authoritarian* conceivers, who define democracy exclusively in terms of religious and military intervention in politics, are least numerous and constitute a negligent minority of less than 2 percent. This reveals that in every Confucian country, only a very few citizens completely mistake authoritarian rule for democracy. However, unlike *authoritarian* conceivers, the relative sizes of *authentic* and *hybrid* conceivers vary a great deal across the countries. In the three democracies – Japan (74%), Korea (69%), and Taiwan (66%) – *authentic* conceivers constitute majorities of 65 percent or more. In contrast, in China, they form a plurality of 41 percent, and in Vietnam, they make up a small minority of 16 percent.

Thus, among Confucian Asian people, *authentic* conceptions of democracy are more common among citizens of democracies than among those of nondemocracies. Among citizens of democracies, such conceptions are more common in the old democracy of Japan than in the new democracies of Korea and Taiwan. Of the two nondemocracies, China and Vietnam, *authentic* conceivers are more common in the more modernized and globalized China. When these national differences are taken into account, it is evident that democratization, modernization, and globalization seem to promote an *authentic* understanding of democracy, and this effect is most powerful in combination with each other.

Of the three democratic conceptions, *hybrid* conceptions, which include both democratic and authoritarian regime properties as essential to democracy, vary to the greatest extent across the countries – from a low of 14 percent in Japan to a high of 80 percent in Vietnam. This distribution pattern reverses that of *authentic* conceptions, which vary from a low of 16 percent in Vietnam to a high of 74 percent in Japan. A careful comparison of how the type of regime under which citizens live influences their democratic conceptions, however, suggests that the forces of democratization and modernization do not have identical effects. It seems that democratization is more instrumental in discouraging *hybrid* conceptions, whereas modernization is more instrumental in encouraging *authentic* conceptions of democracy.

When all five countries are considered together, *authentic* conceivers form a bare majority (53%) of the Confucian Asian population. They are followed by *hybrid* conceivers (38%) and *authoritarian* conceivers (1%). Nearly two-fifths of people in the region understand democracy as a regime with the mixed characteristics of democratic and authoritarian rules.

How does Confucian Asia compare with other regions, including Southeast Asia, in terms of mistaking a *hybrid* regime for democracy? For the seven cultural zones discussed earlier, Table 7.7 reports the percentages holding each type of democratic conception. The democratized West and the formerly communist West have larger majorities of *authentic* conceivers and smaller minorities of *hybrid* conceivers than Confucian Asia. This pattern of democratic conception contrasts sharply with that evident in South Asia, the Muslim zone, and Africa, where *hybrid* conceivers form majorities and *authentic* conceivers form minorities. Compared to all non-Western regions, including Latin America, people in

TABLE 7.7. *Regional Differences in Understanding Democracy*

| Country | Types of Conceptions | | | |
	Authoritarian	Authentic	Hybrid	Others*
Confucian Asia	1.3%	53.2%	37.6%	7.9%
West	1.8	70.6	22.6	5.0
Eastern Europe	1.6	56.6	33.6	8.2
South Asia	4.2	27.8	60.2	7.8
Middle East	2.8	28.4	59.4	9.6
Latin America	2.1	48.7	42.5	6.7
Africa	2.9	36.3	53.6	7.2
(Pooled)	2.1	52.6	38.3	7.0

* Others include those who fail to rate all four regime characteristics and who fail to define democracy in terms of any of those characteristics.
Source: 2005–8 World Values Surveys.

Confucian Asia have a more authentic and less mixed-up conception of democracy.

On the basis of these findings, we can make four points about popular conceptions of democracy in Confucian Asia. First, throughout the entire region of Confucian Asia, very few are totally incapable of distinguishing democracy from its alternatives or mistake authoritarian rule for democracy. Second, in every country, many citizens have yet to acquire complete and correct conceptions of democracy and thus remain inclined to mistake a *hybrid* regime for a democracy. Third, people in democracies are cognitively more capable of understanding democracy than those in nondemocracies, and those in an old democracy are more capable than those in new democracies; this positive relationship between democratic experience and *authentic* democratic conception seems to support the theory of democratic learning. Finally, the higher percentage of Confucian Asians with *authentic* conceptions compared to those held in all other non-Western regions suggests that a heritage of Confucianism may not be a major deterrent to developing the cognitive capacity of democratic citizenship.

The Most Essential Property

Democracy is a phenomenon with multiple properties, and each of these properties is not considered equally essential to its development (Bratton et al. 2005; Dalton et al. 2007). Which properties of democracy do Confucian East Asians consider the most essential? To address this question,

TABLE 7.8. *Ratings of Four Regime Properties as the Most Essential to Democracy in Confucian Asia*

Country	Popular Elections	Protecting Liberty	Economic Equality	Economic Security	No Answer
Japan	34.7%	11.9%	17.4%	27.3%	8.7%
Korea	35.4	14.5	35.7	10.1	4.3
Taiwan	26.9	4.2	18.5	45.2	5.2
China	22.2	3.6	24.1	30.8	19.3
Singapore	27.9	20.3	17.7	28.0	6.2
Vietnam	37.2	5.8	24.9	19.6	12.5
(Pooled)	30.7	10.0	23.0	26.8	9.4

Source: 2005–8 Asian Barometer Surveys.

I analyzed the second wave of the Asian Barometer Surveys (ABS). This survey asked a closed-ended question (Q92) in six Confucian countries including Singapore. It asked respondents to consider four well-known properties of democracy – (1) opportunities to change the government through elections, (2) the freedom to criticize those in power, (3) reducing the gap between the rich and the poor, and (4) guaranteeing basic necessities – and to choose the one property they considered the most essential.

Table 7.8 shows that nearly one out of ten people (9%) in six Confucian countries did not answer this closed-ended question. Among those who did answer it, 31 percent endorse popular elections as the most essential property. This property is followed in popularity by economic security (27%), economic equality (23%), and freedom (10%). It is worth noting that not one of the properties attracted the endorsement of even a bare majority and that at least 10 percent of citizens chose each one. This is a clear indication that Confucian Asians are more divided than united in their prioritization of what should be done to build a democracy in their countries.

Equally notable is that of the four properties considered, political freedom ranks as the least important criterion for a democracy. Only a small minority of Confucian Asians, one in ten people (10%), considers freedom to be the most important property. This figure is less than one-half the proportion who opted for economic equality (23%) or security (27%). Evidently, for Confucian Asians, economic security and equality count far more heavily than political freedom. This conception accords, by and large, with the Confucian notion of good government (discussed

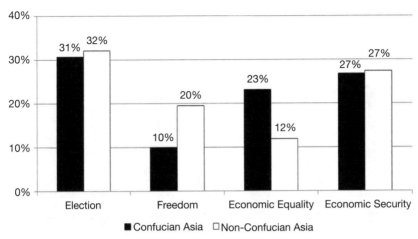

FIGURE 7.1. The Perceived Priority of Four Democratic Regime Properties in Confucian and Non-Confucian Asia. *Source:* 2005–8 Asian Barometer Surveys.

in Chapter 4), which emphasizes the welfare of people over their freedom to participate in the political process.

Table 7.8 shows national differences in the percentages choosing each of the four democratic components as the most essential. Of the four properties, elections are most popular in two countries, Japan (35%) and Vietnam (37%), with the endorsement of more than one-third of their respective populaces, and are least popular in none of the six countries. Political freedom is most popular in none of these countries and least popular in four: Japan (12%), Taiwan (4%), China (4%), and Vietnam (6%). Economic equality is most popular in one country, Korea (36%), and least popular in one country, Singapore (18%). Economic security is most popular in three countries – Taiwan (45%), China (31%), and Singapore (28%) – and least popular in one country, Korea (10%).

When these rankings are compared across the four properties, economic security and political freedom stand out as the most and least popular of the four democratic properties, respectively. In all Confucian countries except Korea, more than one-quarter of the populace endorses economic security. Political freedom is the only property with the endorsement of less than one-quarter in any country and less than one-tenth of the populace in half of the countries surveyed.

This low prioritization of political freedom in Confucian Asia contrasts sharply with what is found in the non-Confucian region of Asia. Figure 7.1 shows that non-Confucian Asians do not discount this

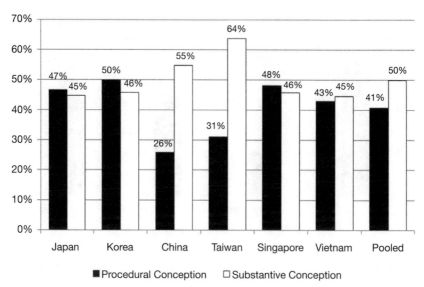

FIGURE 7.2. Procedural and Substantive Conceivers of Democracy. *Source:* 2005–8 Asian Barometer Surveys

property; in fact, they weigh it far more heavily than economic inequality (20% vs. 12%). The proportion of citizens seeing the expansion of political freedom as the most essential task of democratization is twice as great in non-Confucian Asian as in Confucian Asia (20% vs. 10%). This disparity is even more notable considering how similarly citizens of the two Asian regions prioritize elections (31% vs. 32%) and economic security (27% vs. 27%). Confucian culture seems to matter more in weighing the relative importance of democratic properties, particularly in the importance assigned to freedom and economic equality, than in describing and evaluating those properties.

Do Confucian Asians tend to view democracy less procedurally than substantively, as suggested in the Confucian conception of good governance? I addressed this question by collapsing the aforementioned four properties into two categories: *political-procedural* (changing the government through elections and criticizing government leaders freely) and *economic-substantive* (reducing the income gap and providing for basic necessities). For the sake of brevity, I shortened the category names to *procedural* and *substantive* democratic conceptions, respectively. Figure 7.2 reports the percentages falling into these two broad categories for each country.

Figure 7.2 shows that the six Confucian countries are divided into two camps: In the first camp, *procedural* and *substantive* conceivers are evenly or nearly evenly balanced: Japan, Korea, Singapore, and Vietnam belong to this camp. In the second camp, *substantive* conceivers outnumber *procedural* conceivers by a large margin of about 30 percentage points: China and Taiwan belong to this camp. Why do some Confucian countries see a balance between *procedural* and *substantive* conceivers, and others tip the scale in favor of a *substantive* concept? This cannot be answered in terms of the political and socioeconomic variables we have been analyzing.

When all six countries in Confucian Asia are considered, there are more *substantive* conceivers than *procedural* conceivers in the region. *Substantive* conceivers outnumber *procedural* conceivers by a substantial margin of 9 percentage points (50% vs. 41%). In striking contrast, the latter outnumber the former in non-Confucian Asia by a larger margin of 13 percentage points (52% vs. 39%). These findings reinforce the earlier claim that, in governments with Confucian heritages, the outcomes of political decisions matter far more than the process of making those decisions.

Demographic Analyses

The analyses presented here identify different types of recognizing and understanding democracy. Because these types are too many to analyze and relate to demographic characteristics across the countries in Confucian Asia, I chose three for theoretically relevant reasons. I chose the *fully informed* type because democracy as government by the people requires a fully informed citizenry. I chose *hybrid conceivers* rather than the two other types, *authentic* and *authoritarian*, in view of the well-known fact that they often misperceive their existing regime as a democracy and oppose democratization. Of *procedural* and *substantive* conceivers, I chose the former because they are known to be more committed to democratic rule once it is established (Bratton et al. 2005).

The Fully Informed
In Confucian Asia today, which population segment has the highest proportion of members fully and accurately informed about democracy? Which segment has the lowest? Table 7.9 identifies these population segments in terms of four demographic variables – gender, age, education,

TABLE 7.9. *Demographic Differences in Understanding Democracy* (in percent)

	Gender		Age			Educational Attainment			Family Income		
	Male	Female	20–39	40–59	≥60	<High.sch	High.sch	College	Low	Middle	High
Informed Conceivers											
Japan	50.1	38.6	43.5	44.5	43.0	35.0	40.1	55.7	40.8	40.1	50.7
Korea	54.8	49.4	54.6	49.9	49.4	42.3	51.8	53.7	49.8	50.0	56.3
Taiwan	61.3	56.0	60.5	56.9	56.9	52.4	54.1	69.8	54.3	60.3	60.9
China	14.2	9.2	14.2	10.0	9.8	7.2	14.9	23.8	11.6	14.5	14.4
Vietnam	7.0	4.7	5.2	6.4	8.1	5.0	5.6	11.8	4.4	6.1	6.4
(Pooled)	37.4	31.5	35.5	32.8	34.9	19.2	31.6	54.1	34.7	36.2	36.0
Hybrid Conceivers											
Japan	15.0	12.3	16.8	11.8	12.2	13.6	14.5	11.4	14.8	15.6	12.9
Korea	23.2	26.5	22.9	25.5	29.8	32.1	24.1	24.3	25.2	25.7	23.5
Taiwan	30.2	32.1	29.2	32.7	33.3	34.4	33.6	25.1	31.8	28.9	34.4
China	41.5	35.6	41.6	37.4	33.7	31.4	46.1	45.2	36.6	44.7	49.7
Vietnam	83.8	76.6	82.6	79.0	74.5	74.5	83.0	77.9	70.2	78.9	84.4
(Pooled)	39.5	35.9	41.0	36.1	33.0	40.7	42.1	26.1	30.3	39.8	44.7
Procedural Conceivers											
Japan	55.0	39.1	48.6	48.3	44.2	35.1	42.9	57.7	33.3	47.7	55.8
Korea	54.2	45.8	48.5	51.2	50.3	43.5	47.2	55.7	40.4	49.4	55.7
Taiwan	36.5	25.5	35.9	29.7	24.0	16.6	30.1	48.5	23.9	31.8	41.6
China	30.2	21.4	30.3	25.7	20.0	20.3	31.8	38.1	27.3	31.1	29.5
Singapore	51.7	44.2	57.4	47.4	30.3	24.7	49.3	73.0	28.3	47.8	67.8
Vietnam	46.9	38.7	43.9	41.4	43.1	39.2	43.8	47.5	30.3	37.6	53.7
(Pooled)	45.6	35.9	44.0	40.3	36.1	27.5	41.2	56.2	27.4	42.6	54.1

Sources: 2005–8 World Values Surveys and 2005–8 Asian Barometer Surveys.

and income – as done in previous chapters. For this analysis, I returned to respondents' assessments of the essentiality of four foundational characteristics of democratic systems: free and fair elections, civil liberties, civilian control of the military, and the separation of church and state.

Of the four demographic variables, gender and education matter consistently in all five countries. More males than females are fully informed about democracy in every country. However, the level of difference varies considerably across the countries from a low of 2 percentage points in Vietnam to a high of 11 percentage points in Japan. It is indeed a mystery why gender differences are most pronounced in the region's most educated and democratized nation, Japan, and the least pronounced in the region's least modernized and democratized nation, Vietnam. When all five countries are pooled together, Confucian Asian males are significantly, although not drastically, more informed about democracy than their female counterparts (37% vs. 32%).

Unlike gender, age does not matter uniformly throughout the region. In Japan and Vietnam, there is little difference across the three age groups. In the three other countries of Korea, Taiwan, and China, young people are significantly more likely to be fully informed about democracy than either of the two older groups. When all five countries are pooled together, the three age groups are not significantly different from one another in how accurately and fully they understand democracy. About one-third of each group is well informed about all four regime characteristics considered for this analysis. The finding that people from the oldest age cohort, who have much more experience with authoritarian rule, are about as informed about democracy as their younger peers runs counter to what is expected from socialization theory.

In every country, higher education is always associated with a higher percentage of citizens who are well informed about democracy. As a result, those with a college education and those with a primary education or less are the most and least well informed, respectively. The differences between these two groups range from a low of 7 percentage points in Vietnam to a high of 21 percentage points in Japan. Once again, education differences, like gender differences, are most and least pronounced in these two most and least modernized countries.

A much clearer pattern of education differences emerges when the five countries are considered together. Whereas a majority (54%) of the college educated in Confucian Asia as a whole understands democracy fully and accurately, a small minority (32%) of those with a high school education understands it equally well. Among those with less than a high school education, a much smaller minority (19%) is equally well informed about democracy. The fully informed about democracy are nearly three times more numerous among the college-educated than those without a high school education. As expected in modernization theory, the more educated people in Confucian Asia are, the better informed they are about democracy.

Another notable finding on education concerns national differences in the extent to which the college educated are well informed. In the two communist countries, China (24%) and Vietnam (12%), the well informed constitute small minorities of less than one-quarter, even among the college educated. In the other three democratic countries, Japan (56%), Korea (54%), and Taiwan (70%), they form majorities running up to 70 percent. College-educated citizens in these democracies are from two to six times more likely to be informed about democracy than their peers in nondemocracies.

In addition, Table 7.9 shows that educational differences between these two types of regimes are much greater than the educational differences found within each type of regime and within each country in each regime type. Those without even a high school education in the three democratic countries understand democracy better than those who are college educated in the two nondemocracies. From these findings, it is evident that Confucian East Asians do most of their learning about democracy outside the classroom. It is also evident that a democratic regime promotes democratic knowledge more powerfully than does a college education.

Table 7.9 also shows that, in all three democracies, sizable proportions of the population with a college education are not fully informed about what constitutes democracy; the proportion of less than fully informed college-educated citizens ranges from 30 percent in Taiwan to 46 percent in Korea. This finding suggests that there is much room for improvement in the quality of political science education in these democratic countries' colleges. Of all five countries, Taiwan is the only one in which majorities of all three education groups, including the least educated, are fully informed. Vietnam stands out as having the least fully informed populace at every education level.

Income, unlike education, has no regionwide pattern of a consistent or significant positive relationship with the dependent variable. In all three democratic countries, however, there is a significant difference between the two groups at either end of the income spectrum: low-income people are significantly less informed than high-income people, probably because the latter are more educated. In the two communist countries, there is no

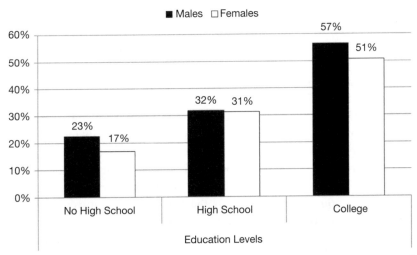

FIGURE 7.3. The Demographic Characteristics of Fully Informed Conceivers of Democracy: Gender and Education. *Source:* 2005–8 World Values Surveys.

such income difference. Why do economic resources fail to contribute to democratic understanding among citizens of nondemocratic countries? An answer to this question may be that, within these countries, people, even those with economic resources, are not free to access materials offering nonofficial versions of democracy.

Of the four demographic variables, pooled analyses reveal that gender and education are the only two variables consistently and significantly associated with the dependent variable in all or most of the five countries. Figure 7.3 uses these two demographic variables together to identify those who are most and least fully informed about democracy among the Confucian Asian population. The figure shows that the more people are educated, the more fully and accurately they are informed about democracy, regardless of their gender. At each educational level, the well informed are more numerous among males than females. As a result, males with a college education and females with a primary education or less are the most and least well informed about democracy in Confucian Asia today, respectively (57% vs. 17%).

Hybrid Conceivers

Earlier I reported that nearly 40 percent of people in Confucian Asia (37%) misconceive of democracy as a *hybrid* regime, which combines the institutional characteristics of democracy with those of authoritarian regimes. Which segments of the Confucian Asian population are the most and least likely to uphold this particular misconception of democracy? I explored this question in terms of the four standard demographic characteristics of gender, age, education, and income and selected out the two variables that are most consistently and strongly associated with *hybrid* conceivers for further analysis.

Table 7.9 reveals no regionwide consistent and significant pattern of gender differences. In three countries – Japan, China, and Vietnam – more males than females have a *hybrid* misconception. In the two new democracies, Korea and Taiwan, the pattern is reversed: females, not males, are more likely to mix democratic and authoritarian characteristics in their conception of democracy. Of the five countries, however, China and Vietnam are the only two countries with gender differences of statistical significance. In these two communist countries, males lead females in having a *hybrid* conception by a substantial margin of 6 or 7 percentage points. In the entire region of Confucian Asia, as in these two communist countries, *hybrid* conceivers of democracy are more numerous among males than females (40% vs. 36%).

As with gender, there is no regionwide pattern of a consistent or significant relationship between age and *hybrid* conceptions. In the two new democracies, Korea and Taiwan, *hybrid* conceivers are more numerous among each higher age group. In the two nondemocracies, China and Vietnam, the pattern is reversed, with the youngest and oldest groups having the most and least *hybrid* conceivers, respectively. In Japan, as in the two nondemocracies, *hybrid* conceivers are most numerous among the youngest set, although they are not least numerous among the oldest. These contrasting patterns of national differences have little to do with either regime type or modernization level. In the entire region of Confucian Asia today, younger age is associated with a greater chance for having a *hybrid* view of democracy. It is, indeed, difficult to understand why in three Confucian countries, including Japan, young people, who are the most exposed to the powerful forces of democratization, modernization, and globalization, are the most likely to equate democracy with a *hybrid* system.

Contrary to what can be expected from the theories of modernization linking education with democratic learning, there is no regionwide pattern of a consistently negative relationship between higher levels of education and *hybrid* misconceptions. In Korea and Taiwan, for example, *hybrid* conceivers are most numerous among the least educated, that is, those without a high school education. In Japan, China, and Vietnam, however, they are most numerous among the high school educated. When these five countries are considered together, the high school educated and the college educated of the Confucian Asian population are the most and least likely to be *hybrid* conceivers, respectively. As with age, neither regime type nor socioeconomic modernization explains the patterns of differences associated with education that are observed throughout the region.

Income, like education, has no regionwide pattern of a positive or negative relationship with the dependent variable. Only in the two communist countries, China and Vietnam, is a higher level of income always accompanied by a higher percentage of *hybrid* misconceivers. In Taiwan also, misconceivers are most numerous among the economically well off. In two other countries, Japan and Korea, there is little difference across the three income groups. When all five countries are considered together, however, there emerges a consistent positive relationship between the two variables. In Confucian Asia, low- and high-income people are the least and most likely to misunderstand democracy as a *hybrid* regime: The more affluent people are, the more likely they are to misunderstand democracy as a *hybrid* regime. Why do rich people in the region subscribe to the *hybrid* notion of democracy to a greater proportion than do their poor peers? Do they do so because they are major beneficiaries of economic development under the current or past authoritarian regime?

Of the four demographic variables examined, which ones affect *hybrid* conceptions most? According to the pooled analyses reported in Table 7.9, the two most powerful variables affecting the dependent variable of *hybrid* conceptions are education and income. In Figure 7.4, I consider these two variables together to develop a demographic profile of the most and least likely *hybrid* misconceivers in the region as a whole. The figure shows that, at each of the three education levels, more people from a higher income group are likely to equate democracy with a *hybrid* regime. It also shows that, at each income level, fewer people from a higher education group are likely to do so. As a result, high-income people with less than a high school education and low-income people with a college education are the most and least likely to subscribe to the misconception of democracy as a *hybrid* regime, respectively. Among the Confucian Asian population, *hybrid* misconceivers are two-and-a-half times more numerous among undereducated wealthy people than among poor people with a college education (64% vs. 26%).

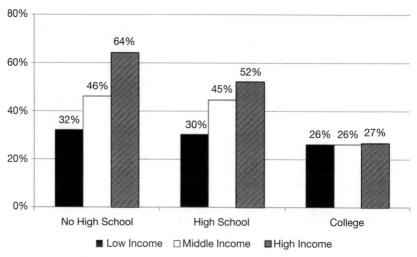

FIGURE 7.4. The Demographic Characteristics of Hybrid Conceivers of Democracy: Education and Income. *Source:* 2005–8 World Values Surveys.

Another notable feature of Figure 7.4 concerns the relative importance of education and income as an influence on *hybrid* misconceptions. Among the college educated, there is virtually no difference across the three income levels. Regardless of their income level, about one-quarter of the college-educated population mistakes a *hybrid* regime for democracy. At every income level, however, a higher level of education is associated with a steady and significant decline in such misconceptions. The magnitude of such a decline is significantly larger than that of any increase associated with income. Undoubtedly, education is a more powerful influence on *hybrid* misconceptions than income.

Procedural Conceivers

Finally, I identify the demographic characteristics of those who are most and least likely to choose either free elections of government officials or the freedom to criticize those officials as the most essential property of democracy. This analysis takes us back to the ABS question asking respondents to choose from among four properties the one most essential to democracy: (1) popular elections, (2) freedom to criticize those in power (protecting liberty), (3) economic equality, and (4) economic security. As before, I considered those respondents choosing either popular elections or the freedom to criticize officials as having a *procedural* conception of democracy, the conception that scholars and policy makers see as the most conducive to democratization (Dahl 1971; Huntington 1991). As I did with *hybrid* conceptions of democracy, I identified upholders of the *procedural* conception in terms of gender, age, education, and income.

Table 7.9 shows that, in every country, those who conceive of democracy in *procedural* terms are significantly more numerous among males than females. The gender difference ranges from a low of 8 percentage points in Singapore and Vietnam to a high of 16 percentage points in Japan. The table also shows that in three countries – Japan, Korea, and Singapore – *procedural* conceivers constitute a majority of males. In none of the six countries, however, are a majority of females procedural democrats. Clearly, throughout Confucian Asia, people's gender affects whether their view of democracy is primarily *procedural*. When all six countries are pooled together, males in the region lead females by a large margin of 10 percentage points (46% vs. 36%). Japanese males (55%) are most attached to *procedural* democracy, whereas Chinese women (21%) are the least so.

Unlike gender, age does not matter significantly in all six countries. Only in three countries – Taiwan, China, and Singapore – does it matter significantly, and the effect is consistently negative: Older age is always accompanied by a significantly smaller percentage committed to *procedural* democracy. In Japan, Korea, and Vietnam, there is neither a significant nor a consistent pattern of relationship between the two variables. Of the six countries, age differences are most pronounced in Singapore, where 27 percentage points separate the youngest and oldest cohorts, and least pronounced in Vietnam, where there is no difference. When all six countries are pooled together, however, there emerges a consistent negative relationship across the three age groups. In Confucian Asia today, the youngest and oldest sets of people are the most and least strongly attached to *procedural* democracy. The youngest Singaporeans (57%) are the most attached, whereas the oldest Chinese (20%) are the least attached.

More than any other demographic variable considered, education matters both significantly and consistently in all six countries. In every country, a higher level of education always accompanies a significantly higher percentage of *procedural* conceivers. Regardless of the type of regime in which respondents live, people with a college education endorse *procedural* democracy to the greatest extent, whereas those with less than a high school education do so to the least extent. Educational differences, however, vary considerably across the countries. The differences are largest in Singapore, where 48 percentage points separate the least and most educated groups; Singapore is followed by Taiwan (32%), Japan (23%), China (18%), Korea (12%), and Vietnam (9%).

Even among people with the same level of education, moreover, there are considerable differences across the countries. Among the college educated, for example, Singaporeans endorse *procedural* democracy nearly two times more than do their Chinese counterparts and 1.5 times more than do their peers in Taiwan. These differences have little to do with either regime type or national levels of socioeconomic modernization. When all six countries are considered together, people in Confucian Asia become steadily more attached to a *procedural* conception of democracy as they become more educated. *Procedural* conceivers constitute a solid majority (56%) of the college-educated Confucian population, whereas they form a small minority (28%) of those without a high school education.

Like education, income contributes significantly to attachment to *procedural* democracy. In all countries except China, *procedural* conceivers are the least and most numerous among the two extreme income groups. Only in China are they the most numerous among middle-income people and the least numerous among low-income people. As with all other demographic variables, income has a considerably varied impact across the countries. The difference between low- and high-income groups, once again, is largest in Singapore, with a 40-percentage-point spread. This spread is 17 percentage points higher than for Japan, an equally wealthy country in Asia, and ten times higher than for China, the most populous nondemocracy in the world. Evidently, regime type and national levels of socioeconomic modernization have little to do with how income affects *procedural* conceptions of democracy. When all six countries are pooled together, higher income always accompanies more attachment to *procedural* democracy. Of the three income groups, the high-income bracket is the only one with a majority (54%) in favor of *procedural* democracy, and the low-income bracket is the only one with less than one-third in favor of it.

Of the four demographic variables, education and income are the two most powerful influences on support for *procedural* democracy. In Figure 7.5, I identify the most and least attached to this view of democracy in the region in terms of these two socioeconomic variables. To estimate their joint effect I constructed a 5-point index of socioeconomic resources combining these values. The figure reports the percentage of *procedural*

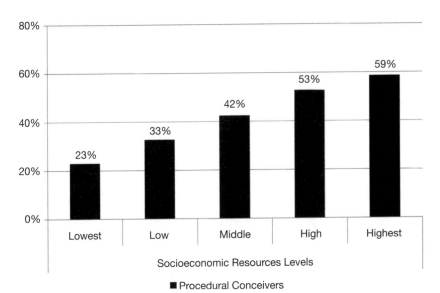

FIGURE 7.5. Liberal-Procedural Conceivers of Democracy by Levels of Socioeconomic Resources. *Source:* 2005–8 Asian Barometer Surveys.

conceivers falling into each of the five resource levels. It shows that these percentages rise steadily with socioeconomic resources, from a low of 23 percent among the most socioeconomically disadvantaged to a high of 59 percent among the most advantaged. This indicates great potential for further socioeconomic modernization in Confucian Asia to enable more people to leave behind a *substantive* view of democracy in favor of a *procedural* conception.

These demographic analyses show that *fully informed* citizens, citizens who think of democracy in *procedural* terms, and *hybrid* conceivers who mix authoritarian and democratic principles are not heavily concentrated into the same segments of the Confucian population; instead, they are dispersed across the different population segments. *The fully informed* are most numerous among males with a college education. *Procedural* conceivers are most numerous among high-income people with a college education. *Hybrid* conceivers are most numerous among high-income people who fall into the least educated group. In Confucian Asia today, it seems to be the level of education that determines whether high-income people become supporters of a *hybrid* regime or a *procedural* democracy.

TABLE 7.10. *Cultural Differences in Well-Informed and Hybrid Conceptions of Democracy*

	Individualism	Fatalism	Egalitarianism	Hierarchism
A. Well-informed Conceptions				
Japan	46.4%	61.5%	51.3%	32.5%
Korea	51.8	53.8	53.4	47.5
Taiwan	62.4	69.1	52.6	58.5
China	19.0	13.8	12.4	13.8
Vietnam	10.3	10.0	5.9	4.3
Pooled	41.2	41.5	38.7	28.6
B. Hybrid Conceptions				
Japan	13.6%	7.7%	15.8%	22.5%
Korea	22.4	30.2	23.9	31.4
Taiwan	22.8	24.3	37.5	33.7
China	42.5	43.6	47.4	48.7
Vietnam	71.5	78.3	82.9	89.3
(Pooled)	30.6	38.4	39.3	55.0

Source: 2005–8 World Values Surveys.

Confucianism and Democratic Conceptions

Do Confucian legacies affect the way people in Confucian Asia understand or misunderstand democracy? Do the legacies also inspire them to prioritize its essential characteristics differently? To address these questions, I first analyzed the fifth wave of the WVS and estimated the proportion of well-informed conceivers and hybrid conceivers of democracy for each of the four types of cultural preferences discussed in Chapter 3. Then I analyzed the second wave of the ABS and estimated the proportion of procedural conceivers of democracy for each of the five levels of political Confucianism discussed in Chapter 4.

For the five countries in which were asked the entire set of questions tapping democratic conceptions and cultural preferences, Table 7.10 reports the percentages of the well informed and hybrid conceivers among upholders of each type of cultural preference: individualists, fatalists, egalitarians, and hierarchs. In three countries – Japan, Korea, and Vietnam – upholders of Confucian hierarchical culture are the least well informed about democracy. Among those hierarchs, moreover, hybrid conceivers are most numerous in four countries – Japan, Korea, China, and Vietnam.

TABLE 7.11. *Procedural Conceptions of Democracy by Levels of Attachment to Paternalistic Meritocracy*

Country	Lowest	Low	Middle	High	Highest	(Eta)
Japan	55.3%	53.1%	50.5%	48.2%	34.1%	.08*
Taiwan	47.2	40.2	29.8	31.5	25.7	.10*
China	37.5	39.5	38.2	32.9	27.7	.07*
Singapore	73.7	60.4	57.4	45.0	36.6	.11*
Vietnam	50.0	53.3	49.4	46.4	50.0	.09*
(Pooled)	55.7	52.7	45.5	42.9	39.2	.10*

* Significant at the .05 level.
Source: 2005–8 Asian Barometer Surveys.

When all five countries are pooled together for a regionwide analysis, a clearer pattern of a relationship between culture and democratic conceptions emerges. Individualists (41%) and fatalists (42%) understand democracy most fully and accurately, followed by egalitarians (39%), and hierarchs (29%). Of those who misunderstand democracy as a hybrid regime, however, hierarchs (55%) rank first, followed by egalitarians (39%), fatalists (38%), and individualists (31%). Well-informed conceivers are most numerous among individualists and fatalists, and least numerous among hierarchs. In contrast, hybrid conceivers are least numerous among individualists and most numerous among hierarchs. Evidently, cultural preferences affect conceptions of democracy.

Let us now examine whether Confucian political legacies matter in procedural conceptions of democracy. Of these five countries in which the Asian Barometer Surveys asked the entire set of questions tapping procedural conceptions and attachment to political Confucianism, four countries – Japan, Taiwan, China, and Singapore – exhibit a *negative* relationship between the two variables (see Table 7.11). Only in Vietnam is there relatively little variation in the proportion of procedural conceivers across five levels of adherence to Confucianism.

When all these countries are considered, however, a higher level of Confucian adherence is always accompanied by a smaller proportion of procedural democratic conceivers (starting from 56 and 53 percent at the two lowest levels through 45 percent at the middle level to 43 and 39 at the two highest level of Confucian attachment). In this monotonic negative relationship, the fully attached to Confucianism are 1.5 times less likely to define democracy procedurally than the fully detached from it. The embrace of Confucian political traditions, featuring paternalism and meritocracy, seems to discourage East Asians from conceiving democracy in procedural terms as their peers in the West do.

Influences on Democratic Conceptions

Why are some citizens fully capable of understanding democracy while others are not? And why do those who have a good grasp on the basic components of democracy not agree on which properties are the most important? To date, these questions have been addressed primarily from the perspectives of three theories: modernization, learning, and socialization theories.

Modernization theory has long argued that socioeconomic development, especially in terms of educational attainment and economic welfare, increases citizen awareness and knowledge of democracy (Diamond 1999; Inglehart 1997; Inglehart and Welzel 2005; Lipset 1959). Much previous research has supported this theory, finding education and income to be powerful forces contributing to citizen capacity to define democracy. In Uganda, for example, Ottemoeller (1998, 105) found a significant educational difference in familiarity with the concept of democracy, and this difference was most pronounced between those who were and were not exposed to secondary education. In Latin American countries, differences in education and information have also been associated with divergent conceptions of democracy (Moreno 2001).

Learning theory, unlike modernization theory, emphasizes citizens' different regime experiences as the most powerful influence shaping conceptions of democracy (Mattes and Bratton 2007; Rose, Mishler, and Haerpfer 1998). According to Dieter Fuchs (1999, 125), East Germans lived all or most of their lives under communist rule and thus think of democracy in both *procedural* and *substantive* terms. In contrast, West Germans, who were not exposed to the egalitarian principle of communism, see democracy in minimalist, *procedural* terms. Likewise, Hispanic immigrants in the United States become significantly more liberal in conceptualizing democracy than their compatriots at home even after a relatively short period of five years (42% vs. 32%); ten years after arriving in the States, Hispanic immigrants become closer to non-Hispanic Americans in holding the liberal democratic conception (54% vs. 68%; Camp 2001, 19). Because of national differences in regime experience and exposure to modernization, democratic conceptions are also found in all multinational public opinion surveys to vary considerably across countries even within the same region.

Socialization theory, like learning theory, recognizes different life experiences as a powerful force shaping cognitive and other political attitudes among the mass citizenry. Unlike learning theory, which focuses on experiences throughout the lifespan. socialization theory focuses on early life experiences (i.e., what people experienced during their childhood and youth). According to the 1998 Hewlett survey conducted in Chile, Mexico, and Costa Rica, for example, young people, as compared to their older counterparts, were more likely to emphasize freedom and the protection of minorities and were more liberal in their democratic conceptions (Moreno 2001, 44–5).

In light of these three theories, I chose a set of six variables as influences on democratic conceptions: the four demographic variables – gender, age, education, and income – plus attachment to Confucian legacies and the type of political system in which respondents live. Those who prefer to live in the Confucian culture of hierarchical collectivism are expected to mistake a *hybrid* regime for democracy more often than upholders of competitive individualism and other cultural types.[3] They are also expected to be more unsure and misinformed about democracy than their cultural rivals. Those who remain attached to Confucianism as a model of good governance[4] are expected to understand democracy in *procedural* terms less often than those who do not.

Fully Informed Conceptions

Why is it that some people in Confucian Asia are fully capable of assessing the essentiality of free and fair elections, civil liberties, civilian control of the military, and the separation of church and state to democracy, whereas many others are not? To address this question, I focused on those who evaluated all four characteristics accurately, who were previously labeled as the *well informed*. I estimated the effects of the six independent variables described earlier on this categorical dependent variable of being *well informed* by using multiple classification analysis (MCA). As discussed in earlier chapters, MCA is capable of handling both independent and

---

[3] Chapter 3 describes in detail how the four types of culture and three types of regime are measured.
[4] Chapter 4 describes a 5-point index tapping attachment to the political legacies of paternalistic meritocracy.

TABLE 7.12. *MCA Analysis of Influences on Democratic Conceptions*

Predictors	Democratic Conceptions		
	Informed	Hybrid	Procedural
Socialization			
Gender	.04	.00	.07*
Age	.01	.01	.01
Modernization			
Education	.08*	.08*	.10*
Income	.00	.08*	.12*
Regime Type	.42*	.40*	.15*
Confucianism	.06*	.10*	.05*
(R^2)	(.21)	(.21)	(.07)

Note: Entries are *beta* coefficients.
* Significant at the .05 level.

dependent variables measured on a nominal scale. Table 7.12 reports the results of this analysis.

According to the *beta* coefficients reported in the table, three of the six independent variables exert significant influence on respondents' capability to understand fully what constitutes democracy. These three variables are education (0.08), regime type (0.42), and cultural preference (0.06). Of these three variables, the regime type under which respondents live has the greatest power to determine whether they are well informed about the basic tenets of democracy. Regime type is nearly four times as powerful as either education or preference for the Confucian way of life.

Results concerning the effects of modernization are split because education is found to contribute significantly to democratic cognitive capacity but income is not. Income is more likely to affect this capacity indirectly through education. Of the four types of cultural preferences considered, the *well informed* or the cognitively capable are the least numerous among upholders of hierarchical collectivism and egalitarianism, and the most numerous among fatalists (see Figure 7.6). Contrary to what socialization theory predicts, neither gender nor age significantly affects the dependent variable of being *well informed*. When all these findings are considered together, the personal experience of democratic politics and income emerge as the most and least potent contributor to the development of fully informed democratic citizenries.

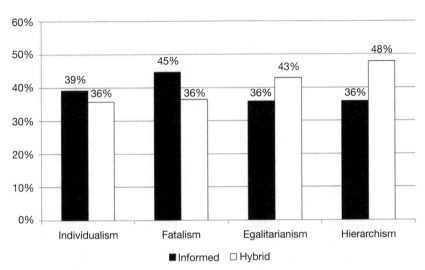

FIGURE 7.6. Fully Informed and Hybrid Conceptions of Democracy by Four Culture Types (adjusted percentages). *Source:* 2005–8 World Values Surveys.

Hybrid Conceptions

Why does a plurality of Confucian Asian people mistake a *hybrid* regime for democracy? Table 7.12 shows that four of the six independent variables considered have a significant independent effect on the dependent variable of *hybrid* conceptions. Of these four, the type of regime (.40) in which respondents live is, once again, the most powerful influence on respondents' likelihood to make this mistake. It is followed by culture type (.10), education (.08), and income (.08). The independent effect of regime type, as estimated by its *beta*, is four times or more powerful than the effect of any of the five other independent variables. Furthermore, the magnitude of its effect on *hybrid* conceptions is less than its effect on being fully informed about democracy (0.40 vs. 0.42). This suggests that democratic political experience is more instrumental in promoting fully accurate conceptions of democracy than in reducing hybrid conceptions.

Additional results of the MCA, which are not reported in Table 7.12, reveal that with regime shifts from nondemocracy through new democracy to old democracy, the proportions of *hybrid* conceivers decrease sharply even after the effects of all other independent variables have been statistically removed. After this statistical adjustment, *hybrid* conceivers form a large majority of 67 percent of the adult population in the two communist countries of China and Vietnam. In the two new democracies, they constitute a minority of 29 percent. In the oldest democracy of Japan, they form a much smaller minority of 18 percent. This pattern of a strong inverse relationship between the length of democratic experience and *hybrid* conceptions renders strong support for democratic learning theory.

After the resident regime type, the preferred type of culture ranks as the second strongest influence on the dependent variable. Of the four culture types, *hybrid* misconceivers are most numerous among upholders of hierarchical collectivism (48%) and least numerous among those attached to competitive individualism and to fatalism (36%; see Figure 7.6), even after the effects of all other variables have been statistically removed by the MCA. More than any other preferred type of culture, the Confucian cultural legacies of hierarchism and collectivism motivate people to conceive of democracy as a mixed regime.

Education and income, like regime and culture types, have significant effects on the dependent variable (see Table 7.12). As modernization theory predicts, higher education significantly improves Confucian Asians' chances of having correct conceptions of democracy. Contrary to what is expected from the theory, however, more income has the opposite, negative effect. The wealthy, who were or have been the main beneficiaries of economic development under authoritarian rule, still seem to think of some authoritarian practices as an essential component of democratic governance. Once again, gender and age have no significant independent effect on *hybrid* misconceptions.

Procedural Conceptions

As discussed earlier in this chapter, previous research has revealed that exposure to socioeconomic modernization and the experience of democratic politics encourage people to conceive of democracy in *procedural* terms. Results of the MCA, which are reported in Table 7.12, confirm that the attainment of more education and income contributes significantly to *procedural* democratic conceptions. When the effects of all independent variables are statistically removed, each of these two variables tapping socioeconomic modernization increases, separately, the proportion of *procedural* conceivers by as much as 15 percentage points or higher: Education effects an increase from 39 to 54 percent, and income from 37 to 54 percent.[5] According to their *betas* reported in Table 7.12

---

[5] All these percentage figures came from results of the MCA analysis of procedural democratic conceptions, which is reported in Table 7.12.

(0.12 for income and 0.10 for education), economic wealth motivates Confucian Asian people to embrace *procedural* conceptions of democracy to a greater extent than does education.

The MCA analyses reveal that regime type is, once again, the most powerful influence on the dependent variable of *procedural* conceptions. However, there is no consistent pattern of relationship between the two variables. Contrary to what is expected from previous research, citizens of democratic states are significantly less likely to understand democracy in liberal-*procedural* terms than those of nondemocratic countries (39% vs. 51%); however, citizens of Japan are much more likely to do so than those of Korea and Taiwan (48% vs. 33%). These conflicting findings indicate that the experience of democratic politics does not always orient Confucian Asians toward *procedural* democratic conceptions and away from *substantive* conceptions. Nor does longer democratic experience necessarily produce a larger family of *procedural* democrats.

As expected, given the Confucian notion of good governance, which was discussed in Chapter 4, stronger attachment to its principles of meritocracy and paternalism discourages people in Confucian countries from becoming *procedural* democratic conceivers. The MCA analysis, which is not fully reported in Table 7.12, reveals that, as attachment to those principles rises, the percentage of *procedural* conceivers declines steadily from a high of 50 percent (among those least committed to Confucianism) to a low of 43 percent (among those most committed to Confucianism). However, the net effect of attachment to Confucianism is much less pronounced than that of either of the variables tapping modernization or democratic experience. The magnitude of *beta* coefficients for the latter is from two to three times larger than the former (see Table 7.12).

Summary of Influences

Gender and age, which tap into the practices of socialization during the early period of life, are the only two variables with no significant effect on the dependent variables. This clearly suggests that childhood or adolescent life experience, unlike current political life experiences, matters little in the conception of democracy.

Of the six independent variables considered as potential influences on democratic conceptions, five affect those conceptions significantly. Of these five variables, three – regime type, education, and attachment to Confucianism – significantly affect all three different types of democratic conceptions considered: being *well informed*, *procedural* conceptions, and *hybrid* conceptions. Confucian cultural or political orientations are indeed one of three pervasive influences on the cognitive dimension of democratic citizenship. Unlike democratic regime experience and education, however, such Confucian orientations detract from, rather than contribute to, the process of enhancing the cognitive capacity of ordinary citizens to understand democracy accurately.

Summary and Conclusions

As government by the people, democracy depends on the participation of ordinary citizens in the political process. To be effective "democrats," these ordinary people must become well informed about how democracy works differently from its alternatives, and they must learn to prefer in all cases the ways of democracy. Thus, there are both a *cognitive* and an *affective* dimension to transforming ordinary citizens into democrats. Of these two dimensions this chapter has focused on the first, the *cognitive* dimension, and analyzed it in terms of the extent to which people in Confucian Asia are capable of understanding democracy, as well as the specific terms in which they conceive of it. In addition to identifying the patterns of democratic conceptions and the demographic characteristics of upholders of the various conceptions, the chapter has sought to examine the sources of the various conceptions and their consequences.

In terms of their overall capacity to understand democracy as a political system in practice, the mass publics of Confucian countries are, by and large, far from being fully and accurately informed about democracy's essential and unique properties. Only about one-third (34%) of these publics are fully and accurately informed about the practices of democratic politics and their differences from those of military and theocratic rule. A majority remains either *ill informed, partially informed*, or *uninformed*. In all five Confucian countries surveyed in the fifth round of the WVS, moreover, the *ill informed* constitute substantial minorities of more than one-quarter. In the proportions of the *well informed* and the *ill informed*, Confucian Asia does compare favorably with other regions, except for the two Western cultural zones, one fully democratized and the other newly democratizing. However, in the proportions of the *partially informed* and the *uninformed*, the region compares unfavorably with all other regions. It is the only region in which nearly one-quarter of its citizens (23%) are either *partially informed* or *uninformed* about democracy.

People in Confucian Asia seem to be more in agreement on the specific terms in which they understand democracy than on the extent to which they accurately recognize those terms. Of three typical patterns of defining democracy, a bare majority (53%) fit into the *authentic* pattern, defining democracy exclusively in terms of both characteristics of democracy: free elections and civil rights. The next most popular pattern is the *hybrid* pattern, which includes those who define democracy in both democratic and authoritarian terms. Nearly 40 percent of people (38%) in Confucian Asia mistake a *hybrid* regime for democracy.

The least popular pattern is the *authoritarian* pattern, in which respondents define democracy exclusively in terms of one or both authoritarian regime characteristics: religious leaders interpreting the laws and military intervention in politics. They form a very small minority (1%). A larger minority of 8 percent is unable to assess the essentiality of any of the four basic democratic tenets. Compared to six other world regions, including the West, Confucian Asia is least *authoritarian* in defining democracy. Of all other regions outside the West, it is most *authentic* and least *mixed* in its assessment.

In Confucian Asia, *well-informed* and *authentic* conceivers of democracy are heavily concentrated in the three democratic countries of Japan, Korea, and Taiwan. In each of these three countries, *authentic* conceivers constitute a substantial majority of two-thirds or more. In communist China and Vietnam, they form minorities and are outnumbered by the cognitively *uninformed* and *hybrid* conceivers who mix democratic and authoritarian principles in their conceptions of democracy. The prevalence of *well-informed* and *authentic* conceivers in the subregion of democratic countries and of *hybrid* conceivers in the subregion of nondemocratic countries clearly indicates that personal experience of democratic politics promotes not only the overall cognitive capacity to understand democracy but also shapes the particular mode of thinking about democracy. In Confucian Asia, democratic politics promotes the growth of democratic knowledge and thereby enlarges the family of democrats.

Of the three democracies in the region, Japan has the greatest population of *authentic* conceivers; however, even in that country, hybrid conceivers constitute a substantial minority of more than 10 percent. The *ill informed* are most numerous in Korea, but the *uninformed* are least numerous. *Hybrid* conceivers are most numerous in Taiwan, although the *authoritarian conceivers* are least numerous. Between the two nondemocracies, considerable differences exist. Whereas *authentic* conceivers are two times more numerous in China than in Vietnam, *hybrid* conceivers are two times more numerous in Vietnam than in China. Between the democratic and nondemocratic subregions of Confucian Asia and within each subregion, there is a great deal of variation in the way people think about democracy.

Of these five democratic and nondemocratic countries in Confucian Asia, Japan is the only country in which less than one-third are *misinformed* about at least one of the four regime characteristics queried. It is also the only country in which less than 20 percent mistake a *hybrid* regime for democracy. China is the only country with a majority that fails to recognize at least one of the four regime characteristics. It is also the only country in which more than 10 percent fail to recognize all of them. Korea is the only country with more than 20 percent *misinformed* about the essentiality of political freedom to democracy and with more than 10 percent *misinformed* about each of the four characteristics. Taiwan is the only country with a solid majority accurately informed about each characteristic and the only one where twice as many citizens subscribe to the *substantive* rather than *procedural* notion of democracy. Singapore is the only country whose citizens weigh political freedom more heavily than economic equality as the most essential property of democracy; it is also the only country with a majority of young people endorsing the *procedural* notion of democracy. Vietnam is the only country in which majorities not only are *misinformed* about at least one of the four regime characteristics but also mistake a *hybrid* regime for democracy.

Confucian Asian people also differ a great deal over the properties they consider least and most essential to the building of a democracy in their country. When asked to name the most essential of four *procedural* and *substantive* democratic regime characteristics, no one characteristic attracted a majority, and no characteristic failed to draw less than 10 percent of the vote. Across most of the countries, however, economic security and political freedom are mentioned most and least often, respectively. When political freedom is considered together with popular elections, political-*procedural* conceivers of democracy are less numerous than economic-*substantive* conceivers, who prioritize economic outcomes over political processes. In the minds of the Confucian Asian people, democracy means government for the people more than it means government by the people.

Despite such subregional and national differences, there are some notable commonalities throughout Confucian Asia. In all five countries, very few are either completely *unsure* of or completely *misinformed* about the fundamental characteristics of democratic rule. Very small minorities of less than 2 percent understand democracy exclusively in terms of authoritarian regime characteristics. In every country, moreover, those who mistake authoritarian regime characteristics for democratic ones outnumber those who mistake democratic characteristics for authoritarian ones. This suggests that regardless of whether or not they live in a democracy, people in Confucian Asia are experiencing more difficulty with dissociating themselves from the legacies of authoritarian rule than in embracing those of democracy.

Throughout Confucian Asia, gender matters uniformly in being fully and accurately informed about democracy and defining it in *procedural* terms. In every country, the fully cognitively capable and *procedural* democratic conceivers are more numerous among males than females. They are also more numerous among those with higher education and larger incomes. When gender differences are considered together with those of socioeconomic resources, females in Confucian Asian countries seem to be less well informed in understanding democracy and less *procedural* in thinking about it because they are more socioeconomically disadvantaged.

What factors significantly affect the extent to which Confucian Asian people understand democracy and the way they think about democracy? Of the six variables chosen to represent four different theoretical perspectives, the type of regimes in which respondents live turns out to be the most powerful influence on their capacities to understand democracy fully and accurately. The longer Confucian Asian people have lived in a democracy, the more likely they are to become *well informed* about it. As a result, they are less likely to misconceive of it as a *hybrid* regime, while becoming more likely to appreciate the importance of its processes rather than its substantive outcomes. In promoting the cognitive quality of democratic citizenship, democratic learning matters a great deal more than any other factor considered.

Exposure to socioeconomic modernization and attachment to Confucianism affect all three dependent variables significantly. Higher education increases Confucian Asians' chances of being *well informed* about democracy and being *procedural* democratic conceivers, while reducing their likelihoods to be *hybrid* conceivers. Unlike education, however, a larger income increases Confucian Asians' chances of being *hybrid* conceivers, while reducing their likelihood of being *procedural* conceivers. Evidently, these two key factors of modernization have a divergent effect on misconceptions of democracy as a *hybrid* regime. The positive effect of income on such misconceptions may be attributable to the unique history in the region in which authoritarian rule has contributed to economic development.

Attachment to Confucianism, unlike education, detracts significantly from the informed understanding of democracy and *procedural* conceptions of democracy. Specifically, attachment to the Confucian culture of hierarchical collectivism keeps Confucian Asian people from reorienting themselves from *hybrid* to authentic conceptions of democracy. In contrast, adherence to the Confucian political principles of paternalism and meritocracy motivates them to remain attached to *substantive* notions of democracy. These findings linking Confucianism to both *hybrid* and *substantive* conceptions of democracy render unambiguous support for the convergence thesis that a Confucian heritage is intrinsically incompatible with the Western type of liberal-*procedural* democracy, but it can be reformulated to develop different types of nonliberal democracy (Bai 2008; Bell 2006; Kim 2008; Tan 2003a).

8

Support for Democracy

Residents of authoritarian and democratizing countries do not necessarily become fully democratic citizens on gaining an accurate understanding of what is democracy, even when that understanding includes how democracy differs from its alternatives. They must also embrace democracy as the most preferred regime type and democratic practices as the most preferred means of governance. Thus the belief that democracy is preferable to all of its alternatives is widely regarded as the most fundamental of democratic political orientations (Diamond 2008a; Linz and Stepan 1996; Shin and Wells 2005).

The extent to which citizens hold this belief has a direct connection to the pace and possibilities for democratic development (Fails and Pierce 2010; Norris 2010; Qi and Shin 2011; Welzel 2007); because democracy is government by the people and for the people, changes in a democratizing country's laws, institutions, and other formal rules will matter little in the real world of politics if the citizens do not support their country's democratization. For this reason, there is a growing consensus in the literature on third-wave democracies that democratization is incomplete unless support of democracy is unqualified and unconditional among an overwhelming majority of the mass citizenry (Booth and Seligson 2009; Bratton, Mattes, and Gyimah-Boadi 2005; Norris 1999, 2011; Rose, Mishler, and Haerpfer 1998; Shin 2007, 2011).

This chapter focuses on the notion of democratic support and seeks to identify its patterns among the Confucian Asian population and to determine its sources. In the following section, I critically review public opinion research on citizen orientations to democracy-in-principle and

267

democracy-in-practice. Based on this review, the second section explicates the notion of democratic support and identifies its patterns. The third section introduces six major theoretical perspectives on the genesis of democratic support and discusses strategies for testing each of them. The next two sections analyze how Confucian East Asians react to democracy and its alternatives as a regime structure and as a process of governance.

Based on these analyses, the sixth section ascertains four types of political orientations and compares their distributions across countries in Confucian Asia. The seventh section profiles upholders of each political orientation in terms of gender, age, education, and income. The eighth section examines whether the Confucian legacies of paternalism and meritocracy matter significantly to popular acceptance of liberal and nonliberal democracy in the six countries constituting historically Confucian Asia. The ninth section tests all six theories of democratic support and discusses its most powerful influences. The final section highlights key findings and discusses their direct implications for the ongoing debate on the compatibility of Confucianism and democracy.

Recent Research on Citizen Support for Democracy

Since the fall of the Berlin Wall in 1989, numerous scholars and research institutes have conducted public opinion surveys to unravel the contours, sources, and consequences of democratic orientations among the mass publics in Africa, Asia, Europe, and Latin America (Diamond 2001; Heath, Fisher, and Smith 2005; Mattes 2007). Studies based on these surveys have offered a number of valuable insights into how mass political orientations affect the process of democratization.

First, of the many measures of citizens' democratic political orientations, such as their views of its efficacy and their levels of tolerance and trust, support for democracy is recognized as the most fundamental (Bratton et al. 2005; Rose et al. 1998). Second, democratic support among the masses, especially in new democracies, is a highly complex phenomenon with multiple layers (Dalton 1999; Klingemann 1999; Shin 2007). Third, democratic support is also a highly dynamic phenomenon with multiple dimensions (Lagos 2001; Rose and Mishler 1994; Shin 1999).

Although these are important findings, these studies have suffered from a conceptual flaw in failing to consider that democracy-in-practice is *not a one-size-fits-all phenomenon* but one that varies *in kind*. Accordingly, citizen support for democracy varies across its different manifestations, which also vary a great deal from one country to another and from one population group to another even within the same country.

Over the past two decades, numerous attempts have been made to differentiate newly emerging democracies from old established democracies and even to distinguish differences among the newly emerging democracies (Collier and Levitsky 1997; Croissant 2004; Karl 2005; Lijphart 1999; O'Donnell 1994; O'Donnell et al. 1986; Rose and Shin 2001). Yet survey-based studies to date have focused exclusively on the question of whether people prefer democracy in general to its alternatives, and they have failed to examine how support for democracy varies according to its types. To test the Incompatibility Thesis that holds that liberal democracy is not suitable for Confucian Asia, as discussed in Chapter 2, it is necessary to identify supporters of democracy first and then differentiate them into liberal and nonliberal categories.

With few exceptions (McDonough et al. 1998; Shin and Wells 2005; see also Chu and Huang 2010), earlier studies have looked exclusively at the *level* or *quantity* of pro-democratic and anti-authoritarian regime orientations. One popular mode of analysis has computed the percentages of citizens supportive of democracy and unsupportive of its alternatives and then compared those percentages on a separate basis. Another equally popular method has been to construct a composite index of either democratic support or authoritarian opposition and to compare its mean scores across time and space. With these percentages and means alone, however, we are not able to ascertain the *qualitatively different patterns* in which democracy and authoritarianism interact with one another in the minds of ordinary citizens with little experience and knowledge of democratic governance.

To overcome these deficiencies in the literature, I conceptualized democratic support as a multilevel and multidimensional phenomenon and analyzed four distinct patterns in which orientations to democracy and its alternatives interact with each other. I conducted this analysis at the regime level and the process level. Of these four patterns, I focused on the two patterns of liberal and nonliberal democratic support to test the Incompatibility Thesis that claims that Confucianism is incompatible with liberal democracy, but may be supportive of nonliberal democracy or soft authoritarianism (J. Chan 2007; Neher 1994; Zakaria 1994, 1997). In a full-fledged test of this thesis, I considered Confucianism and five other clusters of variables theorized to affect citizen support for democracy.

The Conceptualization of Democratic Support

What constitutes support for democracy? The literature on democratic political culture claims that popular support for democracy, especially in new democracies, is a highly complex and dynamic phenomenon with multiple dimensions and layers. Democratic support constitutes a multi-layered or multilevel phenomenon because citizens comprehend democracy in different ways, ranging from thinking of democracy in abstract terms, or democracy-in-principle, to thinking of it as a kind of regime with specific processes for formulating and implementing policies, or democracy-in-practice. Democratic support is a multidimensional phenomenon because it involves more than the acceptance of democratic institutions and processes; it also involves the rejection of democracy's alternatives in principle and dissociation from them in practice.

To ordinary citizens who have lived most of their lives under authoritarian rule, democracy at one level represents a political system that can allow them to participate and compete in the political process freely. At another level, democracy refers to the process in which its institutions actually work to govern their daily lives (Dahl 1971; Mueller 2001; Rose et al. 1998). Therefore popular support for democracy-in-practice needs to be differentiated into two levels: regime and process. The regime level is concerned with the constitutional structures that specify the mode of selecting leaders and that define leaders' powers together with the rights and duties of the citizenry. The process level is concerned with the various aspects of formulating and implementing policies that affect citizen's lives.

More often than not, people react more differently than similarly to democracy at these two levels (Klingemann 1999; Mishler and Rose 1996; Norris 1999). It is therefore imperative to consider support at both the regime and process levels. However, it is essential to recognize support at the regime level as more fundamental than support at the process level because regime structure shapes political processes and not vice versa.

As mentioned earlier, democratic support, especially among citizens of new democracies, involves more than favorable orientations to democratic ideals and practices. Citizens with little experience and limited sophistication about democratic politics may be uncertain whether democracy or dictatorship offers fully satisfying solutions to the many problems facing their societies. Consequently, democratic novices often embrace both democratic and authoritarian political propensities simultaneously (Rose and Mishler 1994; Shin 1999, 2008). This means their acceptance of democracy does not necessarily result in their rejection of authoritarianism. To determine the authenticity of support for democracy, it is therefore necessary to determine whether democracy is preferred to its alternatives at both the regime and process levels.

To identify support for democracy and discern its distinct types, I analyzed democratic and nondemocratic orientations at both of these levels. I began with the regime level because, as discussed earlier, support at this level is more fundamental than support at the level of democratic processes. I compared the magnitude of democratic and nondemocratic orientations at the regime level and determined citizens' relative preferences, identifying two basic types of political regime orientations: democratic regime support and nondemocratic regime support.

For those who expressed democratic regime support, I compared the magnitude of democratic and nondemocratic orientations at the process level, differentiating two subcategories based on their support for democracy: liberal and nonliberal. Those who preferred democracy at both the regime and process levels were considered supporters of liberal democracy. Supporters of nonliberal democracy, which is often associated with Asian-style democracy, preferred nondemocracy at the process level, while preferring democracy at the regime level. In addition to these three types of political orientations – *nondemocrat, liberal democrat,* and *nonliberal democrat,* I added another category for those who, for unknown reasons, abstained from judging between democratic and nondemocratic structures and processes: I called this type the *politically indifferent.* To measure these four types of political orientations, I analyzed four pairs of questions from the second round of the Asian Barometer Surveys (ABS).

Theories of Citizen Support for Democracy

Why do citizens react differently to democracy and authoritarianism? Why do some citizens refuse to support democracy, whereas others embrace it? What motivates citizens to support liberal democracy rather than nonliberal democracy? To date, most scholarly attempts to analyze citizen reactions to democratic change have focused primarily on how and why people react differently to democracy and its alternatives at the regime level. As a result, relatively little is known about how and why they react as they do to democratic and authoritarian processes. Much less is known about the ways in which their democratic and nondemocratic reactions interact with each other. Even so the literature provides several complementary theoretical perspectives on the potential sources of those patterns.

Socialization and Cultural Values

Why do so many citizens of third-wave democracies remain attached to the political values and practices of the authoritarian past even after a substantial period of democratic rule? One theory emphasizes the cumulative effect of decades of *socialization to nondemocratic values*, including the values of communism, Confucianism, and Islam that emphasize collectivism, , and hierarchism (Dahrendorf 1990; Eckstein et al. 1998; Hahn 1991; Jowitt 1992; Sztompka 1991). Attachment to such nondemocratic values makes it especially difficult for citizens to reorient themselves toward the values of liberalism and pluralism that figure significantly in the new democratic political order. The more that people adhere to the collectivistic or hierarchical values of the pre-democratic period, such as those of Confucianism, the more cautious they are about embracing democracy as the preferred form of government.

Democratic Political Learning

This theory, often called the *political learning and resocialization model*, attributes upward shifts in democratic support to longer or positive experiences with the functioning of democratic institutions (Converse 1969; Dahl 1989; Fuchs 1999; Fuchs, Guidorossi, and Svensson 1995; Weil 1994). Through repeated involvement in the new political process over time, people become familiar with and integrated into the political system in which they live (McClosky and Zaller 1984). Familiarity with the new democratic process breeds contentment or satisfaction with it and encourages people to endorse the view that democracy is superior to its alternatives.

Modernization and Cognitive Competence

Modernization or *neo-modernization theory* emphasizes the role of socioeconomic development in generating democratic political orientations. According to Ronald Inglehart and Christian Welzel (2005), economic development enables an increasing number of people to satisfy their basic needs and consequently acquire new knowledge and skills through formal education. Through this process of socioeconomic development, they become exposed to the new values of postmaterialism and the virtues of democracy. They also become cognitively capable of dealing with the complexity of political life and thereafter influencing its process.

Regime Performance

This theory emphasizes the *performance* of the democratic regime under which citizens currently live (Evans and Whitefield 1995; Hofferbert and Klingemann 1999; Rose et al. 1998; Shin and McDonough 1999). It contends that citizens shift their support for democratic regime change based on their assessments of how such change serves their interests (Gastil 1992; see also Schwartz 1985). If they feel that democratization promotes their priorities, citizens become more supportive of the process; if they feel that it hinders them, they become less supportive. Although the two models are broadly similar, the performance model differs from the learning model in stressing a range of socioeconomic influences on democratic commitment, whereas the latter focuses on citizen understanding of democracy and experience with its practice. In the empirical literature, however, there is a general agreement that subjective evaluations of political performance matter more than those of economic performance.

Social Capital

Followers of Alexis de Tocqueville have long argued that a viable democracy requires a vibrant and robust civil society. Neo-Tocquevilleans emphasize the importance of citizen involvement in social networks of associations and groups in fostering norms of reciprocity and trust among the mass public (Diamond 1999; Edwards et al. 2001; Norris 2002). According to Robert Putnam (1993), for example, citizens active in civic affairs and trusting of other fellow citizens embrace the virtues of democracy in general and also support the current democratic system. In the literature on civil society, associational activism and interpersonal trust are generally viewed as contributing to the allegiance of citizens to democracy-in-practice and their commitment to democracy-in-principle (Mishler and Rose 2001, 2005; Newton 2006; Putnam 2000; Zmerli and Newton 2008).

Summary of Models

These five theoretical models, as well as cognitive competence, offer alternative explanations of why citizens of new democracies become and remain attached to democratic rule or detached from nondemocratic rule. Taking all of these models together, therefore, we can arrive at a comprehensive account of the reasons citizens react differently to democratic regime change. None of the previous studies to date has explained different types of democratic and nondemocratic support in terms of all these major theoretical models. Consequently, we know a lot about why people become more or less strongly attached to democracy or detached from authoritarianism at the regime level, but we know very little about why their reactions to institutional democratization take on different patterns when the regime and process levels are analyzed together.

Orientations to Democratic and Authoritarian Regimes

Has democracy become for a majority of the Confucian Asian population the only political game worth playing? To address this question more accurately than what has been done in the literature (Bratton et al. 2005; Chu et al. 2008; Linz and Stepan 1996; Rose et al. 1998), it is necessary to measure the extent to which this region's citizens not only accept democracy as a system of government and as a set of practices but also reject authoritarianism as a system of government and a set of practices. As discussed earlier, I accomplished this task by examining responses to four sets of questions asked in the six Confucian countries by the ABS project. I recoded and recombined these responses in a variety of ways, as described later, to identify democratic and authoritarian orientations and to ascertain four distinct types of political orientations, including support for liberal and nonliberal democracy.

Attachment to Democracy as a Regime
I began the examination of regime preferences among the citizenries of the six Confucian countries by selecting a pair of questions from the ABS that would enable an estimate of the general level of support for a democratic regime. These questions assess the desirability and the suitability of democracy-in-principle and of democracy-in-practice. I considered positive or pro-democratic responses to the questions individually and collectively to measure the mean level of democratic attachment at the regime level.

The first question (Q97) asked respondents to indicate on a 10-point scale the sort of regime they found most desirable. A score of 1 indicates a desire for a "complete dictatorship," whereas a score of 10 indicates preference for a "complete democracy." The results in Table 8.1a indicate that an absolute majority of the people in each of the six Confucian countries expressed a desire for democracy. The percentages of those with a score of 6 or higher on this 10-point scale ranged from 65 percent in China to 94 percent in Korea. When all six countries are pooled together, 86 percent preferred democracy to dictatorship, whereas just 5 percent preferred dictatorship to democracy and 9 percent did not respond. Thus

TABLE 8.1. *Orientations to Democracy and Its Alternatives as a Regime*

A. Orientations to Democracy as a Regime

Country	Domain		Overall Attachment			
	Desire	Suitability	None	Partial	Full	No Answer
Japan	88.8%	75.5%	3.2%	12.4%	73.7%	10.7%
Korea	94.1	79.2	2.6	14.6	76.5	6.3
Taiwan	83.1	67.1	5.1	19.7	63.4	11.8
China	64.9	69.6	0.3	3.0	58.5	38.2
Singapore	90.7	86.3	5.1	11.1	82.7	1.1
Vietnam	92.9	90.4	0.2	1.8	89.9	8.1
(Pooled)	85.8	78.0	2.7	10.4	74.1	12.7

B. Orientations to Authoritarianism as a Regime

Country	Civilian Dictatorship	Military Dictatorship	Overall Attachment			
			None	Partial	Full	No Answer
Japan	15.0%	4.3%	75.9%	14.6%	1.9%	7.6%
Korea	12.0	4.7	79.5	10.1	3.1	7.3
Taiwan	16.8	6.2	73.0	14.6	3.5	8.9
China	9.4	13.8	52.8	7.6	6.3	33.3
Singapore	9.5	4.2	83.5	9.0	2.2	5.3
Vietnam	11.7	24.0	56.5	19.9	6.3	17.3
(Pooled)	12.4	9.5	70.2	12.6	3.9	13.3

C. Relative Preferences for a Democratic or Nondemocratic Regime

Country	Regime Types			No Answer	Mean on 5-Point scale
	Authoritarian	Mixed	Democratic		
Japan	2.2%	4.4%	78.3%	15.1%	1.4
Korea	1.8	5.7	80.1	12.4	1.4
Taiwan	2.8	7.2	74.2	15.8	1.2
China	0.5	4.2	46.4	49.0	0.9
Singapore	1.3	5.6	87.2	5.9	1.6
Vietnam	0.1	6.0	73.9	20.0	1.3
(Pooled)	1.4	5.5	73.3	19.7	1.3

Source: 2005–8 Asian Barometer Surveys.

regardless of where they live and how much they know about democracy, most East Asians prefer, at least in principle, to live in a democratic regime.

Citizens' perceptions of democracy's suitability are somewhat lower than their desire for democracy. The second ABS question (Q98) asked respondents to rate the suitability of democracy on a similar 10-point scale. A score of 1 on this scale indicates "completely unsuitable," whereas a score of 10 indicates "completely suitable." A majority but a much smaller one, in every East Asian country but China, indicated that they consider democracy suitable by choosing a rating of 6 or higher on this scale. In Japan, Korea, and Taiwan, more than 10 percentage points separate those who found democracy suitable from those who found it desirable. The smallest gap between desirability and suitability is in Singapore and Vietnam, both of which have a difference of less than 5 percentage points. Only in China does a larger majority consider democracy suitable than desirable (70% vs. 65%). When all six countries are analyzed together, 8 percent of the Confucian Asia population desiring to live in a democracy judge it to be unsuitable for their country. Evidently, the less abstract the notion of democracy becomes, the less popular support there is for it.

In addition to evaluating the two items of desirability and suitability individually, I combined affirmative responses to these questions into a 3-point index to measure the overall level of support for democracy as a regime. On this index, a score of 0 means no support, a score of 1 indicates partial support, and a score of 2 means full support. The last three columns of Table 8.1a report the proportions expressing no, partial, and full support for democracy at the regime level.

Those expressing no support for democracy constitute very small minorities in all East Asian countries, and their proportions vary relatively little, from less than 1 percent in China and Vietnam to 5 percent in Taiwan and Singapore. Those expressing full support for democracy as a political system, however, vary a great deal more – from 59 percent in China to 90 percent in Vietnam. Vietnam, a communist one-party state, is the only country in which almost everyone who responded fully supported democracy as a political system. In four other countries – Japan (74%), Korea (77%), Taiwan (63%), and Singapore (83%) – full supporters form smaller but still impressive majorities. Interestingly, full supporters of a democratic regime are significantly more numerous in the two non-democracies of Vietnam and Singapore than in democratic Japan, Korea, and Taiwan. This finding seems to run counter to the learning model that holds that people become supportive of democracy through participating in its process.

Table 8.1a also reveals a great deal of national variation in the proportions of the fully indifferent or the uninformed, those who failed to answer both questions tapping orientations to democracy as a regime. The rates of such indifference vary from 1 percent in Singapore to 38 percent in China. China's figure is nearly five times higher than Vietnam's (8%), its neighboring poorer communist state, and more than three times higher than the next highest rate of indifference (Taiwan, 12%). Japan's indifference rate (11%) is significantly higher than Korea's (6%) and Singapore's (1%). Evidently, there is little relationship between a country's levels of political democratization and socioeconomic modernization and the inability or unwillingness of its citizens to judge the virtues of democracy. With the ABS data alone, I was unable to determine why significantly larger proportions of people from China, Taiwan, and Japan had no opinion to express about democracy.

Attachment to Nondemocratic Regimes

To what extent do East Asians still remain attached to nondemocratic regimes? To address this question, the ABS asked respondents whether they would favor a return to an authoritarian regime: to a one-ruler civilian dictatorship (Q124) or a military dictatorship (Q126). Table 8.1b shows that in all six countries, those favoring a return to each of these types of dictatorship constitute small minorities of less than one-quarter. Only in Vietnam does nearly one-quarter (24%) favor a return to military dictatorship. Vietnam is also the only country in which more than 10 percent of the population favor a return to each of the two types of dictatorship. Vietnam and China are the only two countries where more people favor a military dictatorship than a civilian dictatorship. When all six countries are considered together, Confucian Asians are slightly more favorably oriented to a civilian than military dictatorship (12% vs. 10%).

To estimate the overall levels of attachment to authoritarianism at the regime level, I combined responses that expressed affinity for nondemocracy into a 3-point index scale. As with the index of democratic regime support, scores of 0 and 2 mean, respectively, no and full attachment, whereas a score of 1 indicates partial attachment. In all six Confucian Asian countries, less than 10 percent express a full attachment to authoritarianism: this percentage is lowest in Japan (2%) and Singapore (2%) and highest in China (6%) and Vietnam (6%). However, the difference between the attachment levels of these two groups of countries is relatively small.

Those who express full detachment from authoritarian regimes form a majority in all six countries. As with those fully attached to democracy, the proportions of the fully detached from authoritarianism vary a great deal from a bare majority of 53 percent in China to a large majority of 84 percent in Singapore. These proportions are significantly lower in the poorest countries of China and Vietnam than in the four more affluent countries. When these two groups of countries are compared, it is evident that full detachment from authoritarianism, unlike full attachment to democracy, increases with levels of socioeconomic development but not with years of experience with democratic rule.

As with democracy, more than 10 percent of the people (13%) in historically Confucian Asia failed to answer both questions tapping orientations to nondemocracy. This proportion varies considerably from a low of 5 percent in Singapore to a high of 33 percent in China. China and Vietnam are the only two countries where more than 10 percent of the people offered no judgment, either favorable or unfavorable, on nondemocratic regimes. More notably, people in China, Japan, and Taiwan are more indifferent about democracy than nondemocracy. In contrast, people in Vietnam, Korea, and Singapore are more indifferent about nondemocracy than democracy. National differences in such patterns of political indifference have no obvious ties to levels of democratization or modernization.

Net Regime Preferences

Having considered democracy and authoritarianism as distinct dimensions, we can now ask whether citizens prefer democracy, authoritarianism, or some mixed type of regime. If they do prefer democracy, to what extent do they prefer it to the alternatives? To address these questions, I subtracted citizens' scores on the 3-point authoritarian regime preferences index from those on the democratic regime preferences index to create a 5-point index revealing the relative prevalence of democratic or authoritarian regime preferences.

On this 5-point net regime preference index, the two negative scores (-2 and -1) indicate an overall preference for an authoritarian regime, whereas the two positive scores ($+1$ and $+2$) indicate an overall democratic regime preference. The two extreme scores of -2 and $+2$ indicate complete support for authoritarian and democratic regimes, respectively. A score of 0 indicates a balance between the two kinds of regime preferences or a preference for a mixed or hybrid regime. To summarize and highlight cross-national differences, I collapsed the negative and positive scores into two categories: authoritarian and democratic.

Table 8.1c reports for each country the percentage of citizens who express a preference for an *authoritarian, democratic,* and *mixed* regime. It also reports the percentage failing to express any regime preference, as well as each country's mean score on the 5-point summary index (with higher positive scores indicating a stronger preference for democracy).

The mean scores reported in the table are all positive, which indicates that citizens in all six East Asian countries prefer democracy to other types of regimes. However, the magnitude of these net democratic regime preferences varies considerably across the countries. Singapore is the only country averaging higher than 1.5 on the −2 to +2 index, whereas China is the only country averaging less than 1.0. All six countries, when considered together, averaged 1.3, a score above the midpoint of the scale's positive spectrum.

Table 8.1c shows that, in every country, less than 5 percent prefer an authoritarian regime to a democratic regime, and less than 10 percent prefer a mixed regime. Considering authoritarian and mixed regime preferences together shows that support for nondemocratic regimes varies relatively little from 5 percent in China to 10 percent in Taiwan. The proportions abstaining from expressing a regime preference, however, vary a great deal more, from less than 10 percent in Singapore to almost half the population (49%) in China. In the four other countries, the indifferent average 20 percent or less. As discussed earlier, it is difficult to determine why China stands out from the other countries in its high level of indifference. However, in all six countries, China included, more people express a preference for a mixed regime than an authoritarian regime.

Another notable feature of Table 8.1c is that large majorities of more than 70 percent embrace democracy as the most preferred regime in all of the Confucian countries, except for China where a near majority (49%) fails to express any regime preference. Even in China, where just 46 percent of the population favors democracy, nearly ten times as many people prefer democracy to its alternatives than prefer nondemocracy to democracy (46% vs. 5%). In all of the other countries, those who prefer democracy outnumber those who prefer nondemocracy by large margins, ranging from 8:1 in Taiwan to 12:1 in Singapore and Vietnam.

When all six countries are pooled together, democracy becomes the most preferred type of regime among nearly three-fourths (73%) of the population in Confucian Asia. More notably, a solid majority (57%) is *unqualified* in its commitment to democracy by accepting democracy fully and rejecting its alternatives fully (see Figure 8.1). From these findings, one may be tempted to conclude that democracy has already become "the only game in town" in Confucian Asia (Linz and Stepan 1996).

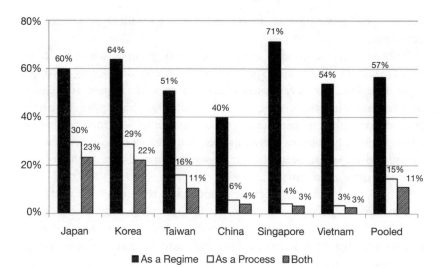

FIGURE 8.1. A Variety of Unqualified Commitment to Democracy. *Source:* 2005–8 Asian Barometer Surveys.

Orientations to Democratic and Authoritarian Processes of Governance

Democratic political systems, especially in newly democratized countries, do not always follow the procedures and rules proclaimed in their constitutions. Political leaders and institutions in new democracies often resort to a variety of authoritarian methods of governance, including the illegal arrest of opposing political leaders and the censorship of the news media. As a result, their regimes are often called a delegative democracy, flawed democracy, or nonliberal democracy (Croissant 2004; Economist Intelligence Unit 2010; O'Donnell 1994; Zakaria 1997, 2003). It is therefore necessary to determine whether citizens of new democracies or authoritarian states, who embrace democracy as the most preferred regime, also prefer the methods of democratic governance to those of authoritarian governance.

Orientations to the Process of Democratic Governance

Now that we have examined citizens' evaluations of democracy and authoritarianism at the regime level and found that citizens generally prefer democracy, we can begin exploring views of democracy as a political process and ask to what extent democracy has become the most preferred method of governing in Confucian Asia. Do large majorities of people prefer to resolve political issues and manage governmental functions democratically? To address these questions, I selected two pairs of ABS items, one focusing on procedural norms of democratic governance and the other on authoritarian practices of governance.

Democratic political systems operate according to a variety of procedural norms that outline acceptable leadership practices. Unlike their authoritarian counterparts, democratically elected leaders have to follow constitutionally established rules and procedures, based on the rule of law and the separation of powers. To measure citizens' support for these principles, I considered, both individually and collectively, pro-democratic responses to a pair of ABS questions.

The first survey item (Q141) asked respondents how strongly they agreed or disagreed with this statement: "When the country is facing a difficult situation, it is okay for the government to disregard the law in order to deal with the situation." In four countries – Japan (64%), Korea (74%), China (55%), and Taiwan (68%) – majorities endorse the rule of law by disagreeing with the statement. In the two other countries, Singapore (36%) and Vietnam (43%), minorities endorse this democratic norm (see Table 8.2). Adherents to this democratic principle of constitutionalism are significantly more numerous among citizens of the three democratic states than those of the three nondemocratic states, a confirmation of the democratic learning theory. When all six countries are considered, a small majority (57%) of the entire Confucian Asian population endorses the rule of law.

To what extent do people in Confucian Asia support the principle of checks and balances between the executive and legislative branches? The ABS survey asked respondents how strongly they would agree or disagree with this statement (Q138): "If the government is constantly checked by the legislature, it cannot possibly accomplish great things." In only three countries – Japan (54%), Korea (57%), and Vietnam (52%) – do a majority endorse the principle of checks and balances by disagreeing with the statement. In the three other countries, minorities ranging from 21 percent in China to 46 percent in Singapore uphold the democratic principle. In the case of democratic Taiwan, supporters of this norm constitute a small minority of one-third (34%), a figure that is significantly lower than those of nondemocratic Singapore and Vietnam. When all six countries are pooled together, a minority of 44 percent endorses this democratic principle of legislative oversight. When this percentage is compared with that supporting the rule of law, it is evident that the Confucian Asian

TABLE 8.2. *Orientations to Democracy and Its Alternatives as a Process of Governance*

| | | | A. Orientations to Democracy as a Process of Governance | | | |
| Country | Rule of Law | Legislative Oversight | Overall Attachment | | | |
			None	Partial	Full	No Answer
Japan	64.1%	53.5%	11.4%	29.1%	41.2%	18.3%
Korea	74.3	56.6	11.8	31.4	47.2	9.6
Taiwan	67.9	34.3	15.6	44.5	26.6	13.4
China	55.4	20.5	10.7	24.5	16.8	47.9
Singapore	36.2	46.0	27.5	42.7	17.7	12.2
Vietnam	42.7	52.1	16.0	28.2	29.4	26.4
(Pooled)	56.8	43.8	15.5	33.4	29.8	21.3

| | | | B. Orientations to Authoritarianism as a Process of Governance | | | |
| Country | Judicial Dependency | Media Censorship | Overall Attachment | | | |
			None	Partial	Full	No Answer
Japan	25.2%	17.1%	50.8%	21.6%	9.3%	18.3%
Korea	21.0	35.5	47.3	30.3	11.8	10.6
Taiwan	33.0	21.2	46.8	29.5	11.0	12.7
China	39.6	49.2	12.2	23.5	25.2	39.2
Singapore	45.7	70.9	15.5	41.2	36.1	7.2
Vietnam	50.6	72.9	5.5	16.7	45.2	32.7
(Pooled)	35.8	44.5	29.7	27.1	23.1	20.1

| | | | C. Relative Preferences for the Democratic or Nondemocratic Method of Governance | | |
| Country | Process Types | | | Nonresponses | Mean on 5-Point Scale |
	Authoritarian	Mixed	Democratic		
Japan	9.7%	15.3%	51.4%	23.6%	0.68
Korea	12.2	20.1	53.8	13.9	0.68
Taiwan	13.2	23.1	45.8	18.0	0.45
China	18.0	13.1	16.1	52.8	−0.03
Singapore	39.3	26.8	19.4	14.5	−0.30
Vietnam	27.7	23.3	11.8	37.2	−0.23
(Pooled)	20.0	20.3	33.1	26.7	0.21

Source: 2005–8 Asian Barometer Surveys.

population is far more reluctant to embrace the principle of checks and balances than the rule of law (44% vs. 57%).

A careful comparison of percentages in Table 8.2a reveals three different patterns of embracing democratic principles. The most positive pattern is evident in Japan and Korea in which a majority endorses both principles. The most negative pattern is evident in Singapore where a majority rejects them both. China, Taiwan, and Vietnam fall into a third, middle-of-the-road pattern in which a majority supports one principle and a minority supports the other. These three divergent patterns of democratic procedural support contrast sharply with the single pattern of democratic regime support seen in every country, in which a majority fully supports democracy at the regime level. This finding clearly indicates that people in Confucian Asia are much less supportive of democracy as a political process than as a political regime. It also indicates that support for the democratic process varies across the countries to a greater extent than does support for a democratic regime.

To measure the overall level of support for democracy as a political process, I summed pro-democratic responses to the two questions into a 3-point index. As discussed earlier, scores of 0 and 2 indicate, respectively, no attachment and full attachment to the democratic processes; scores of 1 indicate partial attachment. For each country, Table 8.2a reports the percentages of the unattached, partially attached, and fully attached. The most striking result in the table is that, in each country, only a minority expresses full attachment to the democratic process. These minorities of the fully attached, however, vary considerably across the six countries. In Japan and Korea, more than 40 percent of the population fully support democratic political processes, whereas less than 20 percent in China and Singapore are fully supportive of democracy at the process level. In Taiwan, about one-quarter (27%) is equally supportive of it.

When all six countries are analyzed together, just 30 percent of Confucian Asia's population emerge as fully supportive of democracy as a method of governance. This percentage is less than half that of full supporters of democracy as a regime (74%). This large disparity between those fully supportive of democracy as a regime and as a method of governance appears in every country. To many people in the region, democracy as a political system must mean one thing, whereas democracy as a political process means another.

Many people found it more difficult to judge democracy as a political process than as a regime structure. Table 8.2a reports that more than one-fifth (21%) of the Confucian Asian population failed to answer both questions tapping orientations to democracy as a process. This figure is more than 1.5 times higher than the proportion of those who failed to respond to questions tapping democratic regime orientations (21% vs. 13%). In every country, moreover, those who failed to answer the two questions on democratic process orientations were significantly more numerous than the ones who did not answer the questions on democratic regime orientations. In the case of Singapore, the former were more than ten times more numerous than the latter (12% vs. 1%). Apparently, the less abstract constituents of democracy are, the more difficult it is to judge their preferability.

Orientations to the Process of Authoritarian Governance

Given these relatively low levels of support for democracy as a process, we may wonder to what extent the contemporary publics of Confucian East Asia remain attached to the procedures of authoritarian governance. To address this question, I again considered responses to a pair of ABS items, with each item dealing with a different practice of authoritarian rule. Pro-authoritarian responses to the questions reveal the levels of affinity for authoritarianism at the process level, where policies are formulated and implemented on a daily basis.

One common practice of authoritarian governance is the subservience of the judicial branch to the executive. To measure citizens' acceptance of this practice known as judicial dependence, the first ABS question asked respondents how strongly they agreed or disagreed with this statement (Q137): "When judges decide important cases, they should accept the view of the executive branch." The percentage of authoritarian responses (those in agreement with this statement) varies considerably from a little more than 20 percent (21%) in Korea to a bare majority (51%) in Vietnam.

A comparison of these responses across the six countries reveals two patterns (see Table 8.2b). In each of the three democratic countries – Japan (25%), Korea (21%), and Taiwan (33%) – less than one-third of the population remains attached to this method of authoritarian governance. In the three authoritarian countries – China (40%), Singapore (46%), and Vietnam (51%) – much larger minorities of 40 percent or more are attached to it. As the socialization theory holds, citizens of authoritarian countries, who are more accustomed to this practice of authoritarian rule, remain more supportive of it than their counterparts in democratic countries. When the six countries are considered together, a little more than one-third (36%) of the Confucian Asian population approves the age-old authoritarian practice of the executive commanding the judiciary.

The second question concerns the government censorship of the news media, another common practice of authoritarian governance. The ABS asked respondents how strongly they agreed or disagreed with this statement (Q135): "The government should decide whether certain ideas should be allowed to be discussed in society." Agreement with the statement is considered acceptance of government censorship. In Confucian Asia as a whole, this practice of authoritarian governance is more popular than that of the subservient judiciary (45% vs. 36%). Support for censorship is also more strongly correlated with the country's type of political system than is the dependent judiciary. In democratic Japan (17%), Korea (36%), and Taiwan (21%), minorities of less than 40 percent support the practice of censoring certain ideas, including those critical of the government. In Singapore (71%), and Vietnam (73%), supporters of censorship constitute a large majority of more than 70 percent. China falls in the middle, with nearly half its population (49%) supporting this authoritarian practice.

As is the case with endorsing democratic procedural principles, there are three patterns of supporting authoritarian procedural principles. In the most authoritarian pattern a majority endorses both authoritarian principles: Vietnam fits this pattern. The least authoritarian pattern is the one in which minorities support each principle: Japan, Korea, Taiwan, and China fit this pattern. In a third, middle-of-the-road pattern, a minority supports one principle and a majority supports the other: Singapore fits this pattern. The most surprising of these results is that authoritarian China, together with the three democratic countries, falls into the least authoritarian pattern.

As with democratic process orientations, a substantial minority of 20 percent failed to answer the two questions tapping the methods of authoritarian governance. In every country, more people failed to answer these questions than those tapping the structure of an authoritarian regime. In Japan, for example, more than twice as many people failed to answer the former questions than the latter ones (18% vs. 8%). Specific methods of governance, either democratic or authoritarian, are more difficult to judge than the general structure of the political regime.

Net Process Preferences

Having examined views of democratic and authoritarian practices individually, we can consider these two procedural dimensions together to determine the particular set of political processes East Asians most prefer. Do they prefer the democratic process to the authoritarian one for formulating and implementing public policies? If they do, to what extent do they prefer the former to the latter? To address these questions, I again constructed a 5-point index by subtracting the 3-point index measuring authoritarian process preferences from the index measuring democratic process preferences. The two extreme scores of -2 and $+2$ indicate, respectively, complete attachment to authoritarian and democratic processes. To ease cross-national comparisons, I grouped the two negative scores (−2 and −1) into one category of having an overall authoritarian preference and the two positive scores (+1 and +2) into one category of having an overall democratic preference. A score of 0 indicates a balance between the two preferences or a preference for a hybrid mode of governance.

The mean scores reported in Table 8.2c are positive for all three democratic countries and negative for all three nondemocratic countries. This indicates that people in democracies prefer the democratic method to the authoritarian method of governance, whereas people in nondemocracies prefer the latter to the former. This supports the theory of democratic learning, which contends that democratic regime experience drives people toward the democratic method of governance and nondemocratic regime experience drives them toward nondemocratic methods of governance. In historically Confucian Asia today, the method of governance people prefer seems to have a lot to do with the particular type of regime in which they live.

Table 8.2c also shows that, in all three democratic countries, supporters of the democratic method of governance outnumber the combined total of supporters of the authoritarian and mixed methods of governance by a margin of 10 percentage points. In all three nondemocratic countries, however, supporters of a nondemocratic method outnumber those of the democratic method by a larger margin of 15 percentage points or more. This reinforces the earlier point that the experience of democratic rule encourages East Asians to embrace the democratic process, whereas the experience of authoritarian rule encourages them to remain attached to the nondemocratic process. These two distinct patterns of process preferences contrast sharply with the single pattern of regime preferences in which people in all six countries prefer democracy to authoritarian and mixed regimes.

There is another notable difference in the way Confucian Asians react to democratization at the regime and process levels. They are much more indifferent about the latter than the former, as is seen when contrasting the findings in Tables 8.1c and 8.2c. In every country, more people offered no judgment on the processes than on the structures of authoritarian and democratic rules. Even in Japan, the most educated nation in Asia, 15 percent failed to answer all four items tapping regime orientations, in contrast to 24 percent who failed to respond to all four questions dealing with democratic and nondemocratic processes. When all six countries are pooled together, more than one-quarter (27%) of respondents did not choose a preferred method of governance; this figure is 7 percentage points higher than the one (20%) relating to regime orientations.

Most notable is that only a small minority of 15 percent of the entire Confucian Asian population is *unconditionally* attached to the democratic process; that is, they are fully attached to the democratic process and fully detached from the nondemocratic process (see Figure 8.1). This percentage is about one-fourth of those *unconditionally* attached to democracy as a regime (57%). This finding reinforces the notion that, for a majority of the Confucian Asian population, democracy evokes one reaction at the regime level and a very different reaction at the process level. It is also evident that democracy is far from becoming the only political game in town.

The *unconditionally* attached to the democratic process constitute a minority in each of the six countries (see Figure 8.1), yet the percentages vary a great deal – from 5 percent or less in China, Singapore, and Vietnam to 30 percent in Japan. The differences in these percentages are most pronounced between the two groups of democratic and nondemocratic countries. In the former, consisting of Japan (30%), Korea (29%), and Taiwan (16%), 26 percent are unconditionally attached to the democratic process; in the nondemocratic countries, which include China (6%), Singapore (4%), and Vietnam (3%), only 5 percent are equally attached. Evidently, the particular type of regime in which people in historically Confucian Asia live has a powerful impact on their judgments on the merits and demerits of authoritarian and democratic processes.

Patterns of Mass Political Orientations

Thus far, I have analyzed how ordinary people in six Confucian countries react to democracy and authoritarianism not only at the regime level but also at the process level. These analyses reveal that, although majorities in all of the Confucian East Asian countries prefer democracy to nondemocracy at the regime level, only in half the countries do majorities prefer democracy to nondemocracy at the process level. Overall, a large majority of 73 percent of East Asians prefer to live in a democratic regime, but just 33 percent favor democratic processes over nondemocratic ones.

On the basis of these survey findings, we can confidently state that, at the regime level, democracy has already won the support of the majority

TABLE 8.3. *Types of Political Orientations*

Country	Nondemocrat	Nonliberal Democrat	Liberal Democrat	Indifferent
Japan	6.6%	20.4%	46.5%	26.5%
Korea	7.5	25.4	47.2	19.9
Taiwan	10.1	28.0	39.3	22.6
China	4.6	20.2	11.8	63.4
Singapore	6.9	59.3	18.3	15.5
Vietnam	6.1	44.1	11.1	38.7
(Pooled)	7.0	32.9	29.0	31.1

Source: 2005–8 Asian Barometer Surveys.

of the Confucian Asian population. However, at the process level of formulating and implementing policies, nondemocracy is more popular than democracy. Throughout Confucian Asia, therefore, democracy seems to be far from secure or in a favored position.

What proportion of the Confucian Asian population is fully supportive of democracy on both the regime and process levels? What proportion is partially supportive, favoring democracy on only one of these levels? Do the fully supportive outnumber the partially supportive? I addressed these questions using a fourfold classification of regime and process orientations.

As discussed earlier, supporters of democracy as a regime are divided into two groups: *nonliberal* and *liberal*. Liberal democrats support democracy both as a political system and a political process, whereas nonliberal democrats support democracy only at the regime level. A third group includes *nondemocrats*, who refuse to support democracy at the regime level and are therefore considered nondemocratic regardless of their preferences at the process level. A fourth group includes *the politically indifferent*, who did not indicate a preference at any of the two levels. In this framework, democratic support at the regime level is considered more essential than support at the process level for solidifying democratic citizenship.

For each country and for East Asia as a whole, Table 8.3 reports the percentages falling into each of these four groups. One notable finding concerns the relative proportions of liberal and nonliberal democrats in the region as a whole, as well as in each country. In none of the six countries, including the oldest democracy in the region, Japan, do liberal democrats constitute a majority. They account for a near majority in only two countries, Japan (47%) and Korea (47%), and a plurality of

39 percent in Taiwan. In the three nondemocratic countries, they form much smaller minorities, ranging from 11 percent in Vietnam to 18 percent in Singapore. In these countries, moreover, they are outnumbered by nonliberal democrats. This preponderance of nonliberal democrats over liberal democrats in nondemocratic Confucian Asia contrasts sharply with that of liberal democrats over nonliberal democrats in democratic Confucian Asia.

When all democratic and nondemocratic countries are pooled together, liberal democrats constitute a minority of less than one-third (29%). In fact, they are less prevalent than nonliberal democrats (33%) and the indifferent (31%). Most notably, unqualified supporters of liberal democracy constitute a very small minority of the Confucian Asian population. Only one in every ten people (11%) is exclusively in favor of democracy as a regime and a political process (see Figure 8.1).[1] Even in Japan (23%) and Korea (22%), the two most democratic countries in the region,[2] only about one in five voters is a liberal democrat (see Figure 8.1). This analysis shows that Confucian Asia is far from being a region of liberal democrats. This may be one reason why democratization in the region has been slow in liberalizing authoritarian values despite its success in achieving socioeconomic modernization.

How does Confucian Asia compare with non-Confucian Asia in embracing liberal democracy? For each of these two regions, Figure 8.2 reports the percentages of liberal and nonliberal democrats together with those of nondemocrats and the indifferent. Both regions are alike in that liberal democrats form a relatively small minority and are less numerous than nonliberal democrats. However, nonliberal democrats are more numerous in non-Confucian Asia (39% vs. 33%), whereas liberal democrats are more numerous in Confucian Asia (29% vs. 19%). Liberal democrats, who constitute a near majority or a plurality in three of the six Confucian countries, form a plurality in only one of the six non-Confucian countries, Indonesia. Evidently, liberal democrats are not only more numerous but also more prevalent in Confucian Asia than non-Confucian Asia. This suggests that Confucianism may not be fully responsible for the slow pace of building liberal democracy in Confucian Asia.

---

[1] These supporters of liberal democracy are unqualified in supporting democracy by opposing all of its alternatives at the levels of both regime and process.
[2] The Economist Intelligence Unit (2010) rates only these two countries as full democracies.

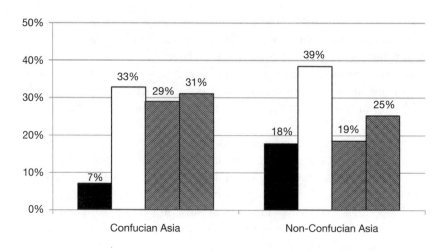

FIGURE 8.2. The Most and Least Prevalent Types of Political Orientations in Confucian and Non-Confucian Asia. *Source:* 2005–8 Asian Barometer Surveys.

Demographic Analyses

In Confucian Asia today, which segments of the population are the most and least supportive of nonliberal and liberal democracy? Which segments are the most and least supportive of nondemocratic rule? Which segments remain the most and least politically indifferent? Continuing with the method of earlier chapters, I examined respondents' demographic characteristics in terms of gender, age, education, and family income. This analysis reveals that support for *nondemocracy* and *nonliberal democracy* is neither significantly nor consistently associated with any of these demographic variables in all or most of the six countries (see Table 8.4). As a result, there is no regionwide pattern of demographic differences in endorsing either nondemocracy or nonliberal democracy.

In striking contrast, all four demographic variables do have a significant and consistent effect throughout the region on support for both liberal democracy and indifference. In all six countries, males are more likely than females to become liberal democrats and much less likely to remain politically indifferent citizens. The magnitude of gender difference in support for liberal democracy, however, varies considerably, from less than 5 percentage points in China and Vietnam to more than 20 percentage points in Japan. Gender difference in political indifference also varies considerably, from a low of 7 percentage points in Singapore to a

TABLE 8.4. *Demographic Characteristics and Types of Political Orientations*
(in percent)

	Gender		Age			Educational Attainment			Family Income		
	Male	Female	20–39	40–59	≥60	<high.sch	high.sch	College	Low	Middle	High
Nondemocrat											
Japan	6.6	6.6	10.1	4.9	6.2	7.3	8.0	4.2	4.6	4.9	6.5
Korea	9.2	6.1	5.7	8.3	10.6	9.5	9.7	4.1	7.0	9.5	6.3
Taiwan	6.6	6.6	8.1	12.3	9.9	13.6	10.3	6.1	13.1	10.3	5.1
China	4.7	4.5	4.3	5.0	3.9	5.1	4.3	2.4	4.5	2.3	2.3
Singapore	9.2	11.0	4.9	8.4	7.3	10.1	7.0	3.2	7.8	8.8	1.7
Vietnam	5.3	6.9	6.5	6.0	5.0	6.0	6.3	5.0	9.0	4.9	6.2
(Pooled)	7.0	6.9	6.3	7.5	6.9	8.1	7.5	4.4	8.8	7.9	5.4
Nonliberal Democrat											
Japan	20.5	20.5	26.3	19.8	18.0	15.7	24.1	18.9	16.2	24.7	20.5
Korea	24.0	26.7	25.3	24.7	27.1	32.2	24.6	24.5	24.0	24.8	28.7
Taiwan	29.0	27.1	33.5	27.6	18.2	19.1	33.0	25.8	23.1	32.5	29.4
China	23.9	16.3	22.7	20.7	15.7	13.9	26.9	29.3	31.8	22.7	31.8
Singapore	59.2	59.4	62.2	55.1	66.1	59.9	60.1	55.9	58.9	63.4	51.4
Vietnam	52.1	35.3	41.4	47.3	45.6	30.8	48.4	49.5	29.8	47.0	47.9
(Pooled)	35.2	30.6	35.7	33.2	27.8	26.5	37.6	29.9	33.5	38.9	35.3
Liberal Democrat											
Japan	57.3	36.8	50.9	51.9	39.9	23.0	43.6	63.5	34.1	48.2	60.2
Korea	51.3	43.2	50.3	49.9	32.9	27.0	44.0	58.0	36.0	46.2	49.4
Taiwan	46.8	31.7	48.4	39.1	21.3	14.9	41.3	60.3	29.5	42.8	53.7
China	13.9	9.5	17.9	10.0	6.9	6.7	15.7	33.3	9.1	22.2	25.0
Singapore	21.7	14.7	20.9	19.2	10.3	9.2	17.7	31.4	15.9	13.1	35.0
Vietnam	13.4	8.6	11.5	11.2	9.4	8.8	10.9	17.8	5.9	11.5	13.2
(Pooled)	33.5	24.5	32.2	29.1	23.5	12.5	27.8	52.1	21.9	31.8	39.5
Politically Indifferent											
Japan	15.9	36.1	12.9	23.5	35.9	53.9	24.3	13.4	45.7	22.1	12.8
Korea	15.7	24.0	18.8	17.2	29.4	31.3	21.9	13.6	33.0	19.5	15.9
Taiwan	15.1	30.1	9.9	21.0	50.7	52.5	15.5	7.9	34.1	14.3	11.3
China	57.4	69.8	55.0	64.3	73.5	74.1	53.1	34.1	52.2	51.1	40.9
Singapore	12.0	19.2	12.0	17.5	17.0	20.7	15.3	9.7	17.5	14.4	11.9
Vietnam	29.1	49.4	40.7	35.4	39.6	54.8	34.4	27.7	55.6	36.9	32.6
(Pooled)	24.3	37.9	25.7	30.1	41.8	52.9	27.1	13.6	35.8	21.2	19.8

Source: 2005–8 Asian Barometer Surveys.

high of 20 percentage points in Japan. Of the six countries, the impact
of gender is most pronounced in Japan, in which the percentage of male
liberal democrats is more than 1.5 times greater than the percentage of
female liberal democrats (57% vs. 37%) and the indifferent are more
than twice as numerous among females (36% vs. 16%). Indeed it is a
mystery why the region's oldest democracy and most modernized nation
remains a bastion of gender disparity in political life.

Like gender, age is consistently and negatively associated throughout the Confucian region with support for liberal democracy. In all six

Confucian countries, liberal democrats are least numerous among the oldest of three age cohorts, and in five of the countries – Korea, Taiwan, China, Singapore, and Vietnam – liberal democrats are most numerous among the youngest set. Thus, there is a clear regionwide pattern of an inverse relationship between age and the percentage of liberal democrats. However, this pattern does not hold with age and indifference. Only in three countries – Japan, China, and Taiwan – are advances in age always associated with a higher prevalence of indifference. In the three other countries, there is no consistent relationship, negative or positive, between the two variables.

Of the six Confucian countries, age differences in support for liberal democracy are most pronounced in democratic Taiwan and least pronounced in communist Vietnam. In Taiwan, for example, people in the youngest cohort are more than twice as likely as people in the oldest group to be liberal democrats (48% vs. 21%), whereas people in the oldest cohort are five times as likely as people in the youngest to be politically indifferent (9% vs. 51%). In Vietnam, there is little or virtually no significant difference across the three age cohorts either in embracing liberal democracy or in remaining politically indifferent. Separating the Confucian Asia countries into two groups, democratic and nondemocratic, reveals that age affects people's chances for being liberal democrats and politically indifferent to a greater extent in the three democratic countries than in the three nondemocratic ones.

Unlike age, education has, in all six countries, a consistent positive association with the percentage of liberal democrats and a consistent negative association with the prevalence of political indifference. In every country, a higher level of education is always accompanied by a higher percentage of liberal democrats and a lower percentage of the indifferent. As a result, those without a high school education are the least likely to be liberal democrats and the most likely to be indifferent. In contrast, those with a college education are the most likely to be liberal democrats and the least likely to be indifferent. When all six countries are considered together, the college educated, as compared to their peers without a high school education, are four times more likely to support liberal democracy (52% vs. 13%) and four times less likely to be indifferent (14% vs. 53%).

Although the direction of the association between education and support for liberal democracy is positive in all six countries, its strength varies considerably. In China and Taiwan, for example, the college educated are four times more likely to support liberal democracy than those without a high school education, whereas in Korea and Vietnam, the most educated are only about two times more supportive of liberal democracy than the least educated. In terms of political indifference as well, the impact of education differs considerably: The weakest impact is in China and Singapore, where the least educated are twice as likely as the most educated to be indifferent, whereas the strongest impact is in Japan and Taiwan, where the least educated are five times as likely as the most educated to be indifferent. When the six countries are compared, such educational differences, like age differences, are most pronounced in democratic Taiwan and least pronounced in nondemocratic Vietnam.

Another point worth noting is that even among the college educated, the percentages of liberal democrats vary a great deal – from a small minority of 18 percent in Vietnam to a substantial majority of 64 percent in Japan. In all three democratic countries – Japan (64%), Korea (58%), and Taiwan (60%) – a solid majority of 58 percent or higher of the highest education group endorses liberal democracy. However, in all three nondemocracies – China (33%), Singapore (31%), and Vietnam (18%) – only a minority of 33 percent or less does the same. This suggests that college education alone will not be the panacea for creating liberal democrats in these three countries. It also suggests that a college education in democracies is far more instrumental in promoting support for liberal democracy than a similar level of education in nondemocracies.

Throughout the region, the politically indifferent constitute a uniformly small minority of one-third or less among those with a high school or college education. Among those without a high school education, however, the percentages of the politically indifferent vary considerably from a low of 21 percent in Singapore to a high of 74 percent in China. In four of the six countries, including democratic Japan and Taiwan, a majority of the least educated citizens remain politically indifferent. Only in Korea and Singapore does a majority express political preferences at both the regime and process levels. This finding suggests that the quality of civic education varies considerably across the countries in Confucian Asia. It also suggests that democratic countries are not necessarily doing a better job of educating their children about democratic politics than nondemocratic countries.

Income, like education, is positively associated with the percentage of liberal democrats but negatively associated with the percentage of the politically indifferent. In every country, liberal democrats are least numerous among low-income people and most numerous among high-income people. In contrast, the politically indifferent are most numerous among the former and least numerous among the latter. When all

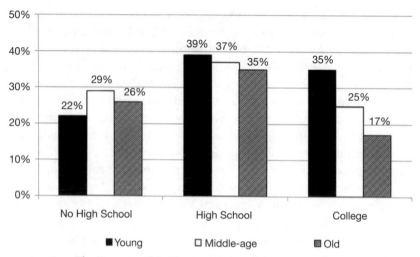

FIGURE 8.3. The Demographic Characteristics of the Most and Least Supportive of Nonliberal Democracy: Age and Education. *Source:* 2005–8 Asian Barometer Surveys.

countries are considered together, high-income people, as compared to their low-income counterparts, are nearly two times more supportive of liberal democracy (40% vs. 22%) and nearly two times less likely to be politically indifferent (20% vs. 36%). When these income differences are compared with those associated with education, it is evident that income matters much less than education in shaping how Confucian East Asians react to democratic change.

Up to now, we have examined the individual relationships between each type of political orientation and each demographic variable. The pooled analyses reported in Table 8.4 reveal that supporters of non-democracy vary relatively little across the categories of any demographic variable. Supporters of nonliberal democracy vary across the categories of age and education to a greater extent than those of gender and income. In addition, supporters of liberal democracy and the politically indifferent vary across the categories of education and income more consistently and significantly than across those of gender and age. On the basis of these results, I selected age and education to identify the most and least likely to belong to nonliberal democrats, and education and income to identify the most and least likely to belong to liberal democrats, and the politically indifferent.

Figure 8.3 reveals that, in every age group, those with a high school education are more supportive of *nonliberal democracy* than those without a high school education or a college education. It also shows that age and support for *nonliberal democracy* have an inverse relationship among both the high school- and college-educated groups: As age goes up in each of these two groups, support for *nonliberal democracy* goes down. Therefore, of the nine segments of the Confucian population defined by age and education, young people with only a high school education are the segment most supportive of *nonliberal democracy*, whereas old people with a college education are the least supportive. More than twice as many from the former group as the latter are nonliberal democrats (39% vs. 17%).

The most important result in Figure 8.3 concerns the negative relationship between age and support for *nonliberal democracy* among the two better educated segments. This consistently negative relationship, especially among the college educated, runs counter to what is expected from the neo-modernization theory of democratization, which holds that younger people are more likely than older people to uphold the self-expression values of freedom, equality, and participation and thus are the least likely to embrace nonliberal democracy (Inglehart and Welzel 2005). Instead, this negative relationship confirms the theory of indigenization advocated by Samuel P. Huntington (1996, 93): "As Western influence recedes, young aspiring leaders cannot look to the West to provide them with power and wealth. They have to find the means of success within their own society, and hence they have to accommodate the values and culture of that society."

Figure 8.4 shows that the relationships between age and nonliberal democratic support among *the college educated* vary throughout the region. In all countries except Singapore, these two variables are consistently negatively associated with each other; each step up in an age group is associated with a decrease in support for *nonliberal democracy*. Consequently, supporters of *nonliberal democracy* are most numerous among the youngest of the three age cohorts and least numerous among the oldest. Only in nondemocratic Singapore are nonliberal democrats most numerous among the oldest cohort. This finding linking younger age with greater support for nonliberal democracy seems to be a notable Confucian exception.

Which segments of the Confucian Asian population are most and least supportive of *liberal democracy*? Which segments are the most and least *politically indifferent*? To address these questions in terms of education and income, I constructed a 5-point socioeconomic resources index by combining the variables of education and income, each of which is

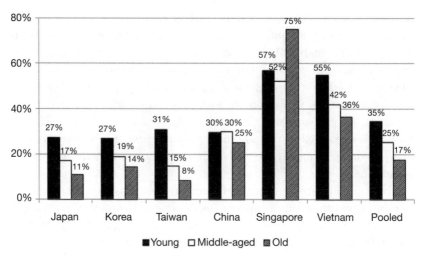

FIGURE 8.4. Age and Support for Nonliberal Democracy among the College Educated. *Source:* 2005–8 Asian Barometer Surveys.

measured on a 3-point scale. On this index, the lowest score of 1 indicates a combination of less than a high school education with low income, whereas the highest score of 5 indicates a combination of a college education with high income. For each point on this 5-point socioeconomic resources scale, Figure 8.5 shows the percentages of liberal democrats and the politically indifferent.

As expected from the separate analyses of education and income presented in Table 8.4, support for *liberal democracy* increases considerably and steadily with each advance in socioeconomic resources. In contrast, *political indifference* decreases considerably and steadily with each socioeconomic advance. As a result, liberal democrats are least numerous among the socioeconomically poorest and are most numerous among the most socioeconomically well-to-do. The latter, those with a college education and a high income, are more than four times more supportive of liberal democracy than the former, those with a low income and without a high school education (14% vs. 52%). In contrast, the politically indifferent are least numerous among the well-to-do and most numerous among the poor and uneducated. Nearly four times as many well-to-do individuals than poor individuals chose not to articulate a preference for regime structure and/or policy process (47% vs. 13%).

When percentages of liberal democrats and the politically indifferent are considered together, two contrasting patterns of citizen reactions to

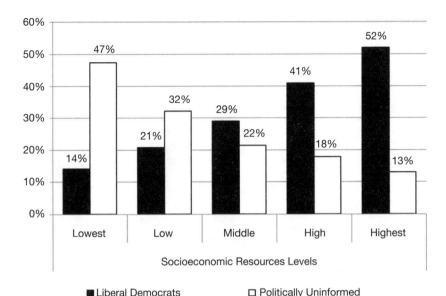

FIGURE 8.5. Supporters of Liberal Democracy and Politically Indifferent People by Levels of Socioeconomic Resources. *Source:* 2005–8 Asian Barometer Surveys.

democratic change emerge. In one pattern, seen with the two groups with the lowest levels of socioeconomic resources, the politically indifferent outnumber supporters of liberal democracy. In the other pattern, seen with the two groups with the highest levels of socioeconomic resources as well as the mid-level group, liberal democrats outnumber the indifferent. In historically Confucian Asia today, liberal democrats are concentrated into the most modern segment of the population, whereas the politically indifferent are concentrated into the least modern segment. This finding renders definitive support for the modernization theory, which links socioeconomic modernization with the increasing popularity of liberal democracy. It also suggests that an increasing number of Confucian Asians will be attracted to the virtues of liberal democracy as they become more educated and more affluent.

Confucianism and Support for Liberal and Nonliberal Democracy

Does Confucian Asia still remain a region with more nonliberal than liberal democrats because of the legacies of Confucianism that emphasize the rule of paternalistic meritocracy? In a preliminary attempt to explore

TABLE 8.5. *Support for Liberal and Nonliberal Democracy by Levels of Attachment to Political Confucianism*

A. Nonliberal Democracy

Country	Levels of Confucian Attachment					(*eta*)
	0	1	2	3	4	
Japan	18.6%	17.8%	26.6%	36.0%	43.9%	(0.18)*
Korea**	14.9	20.1	28.6	44.2	–	(0.24)*
Taiwan	11.1	24.9	28.5	37.0	38.1	(0.14)*
China	12.5	20.9	29.4	32.1	30.9	(0.07)*
Singapore	15.8	46.8	54.5	66.8	74.0	(0.24)*
Vietnam	42.9	47.3	50.6	57.7	54.2	(0.08)*
Pooled	18.4	26.5	35.2	47.6	52.8	(0.20)*

B. Liberal Democracy

Country	Levels of Confucian Attachment					(*eta*)
	0	1	2	3	4	
Japan	72.0%	65.5%	49.8%	33.0%	19.5%	(0.31)*
Korea**	67.5	57.2	48.0	29.1	–	(0.28)*
Taiwan	66.7	53.8	47.4	32.7	17.1	(0.25)*
China	50.0	38.1	24.8	17.3	4.5	(0.27)*
Singapore	73.7	34.5	26.2	13.7	5.7	(0.33)*
Vietnam	42.9	25.6	16.7	11.2	6.0	(0.23)*
(Pooled)	67.4	52.1	38.6	20.6	7.7	(0.38)*

* Significant at the 0.05 level.
** Korea did not ask all four questions tapping attachment to paternalistic meritocracy.
Source: 2005–8 Asian Barometer Surveys.

this question, I analyzed the bivariate relationships between attachment to the Confucian political legacies and support for liberal and nonliberal democracy. As discussed in Chapter 4, I first measured each of these two principles – meritocracy and paternalism – on a 3-point scale. Then I combined the resulting two 3-point scales into one 5-point index tapping attachment to the Confucian model of paternalistic meritocracy. For each and all of the six Confucian countries, Table 8.5 reports the percentages supportive of liberal democracy for each level of attachment on the 5-point scale. It also reports *eta* coefficients, which estimate the magnitude of their bivariate relationships.

Table 8.5a shows, that in every country, a higher level of Confucian attachment is always or nearly always accompanied by a higher percentage of nonliberal democrats. In all six countries, people are least supportive of nonliberal democracy when they are fully detached from political Confucianism. In four countries – Japan, Korea, Taiwan, and Singapore – they are most supportive of nonliberal democracy when they remain fully attached to political Confucianism. Between these two extreme levels of Confucian attachment there is a considerable gap in each country in nonliberal democratic support, ranging from 11 percentage points in Vietnam to 58 percentage points in Singapore. When all six countries are pooled together, moreover, there is a clear pattern of steadily increasing support for nonliberal democracy with a greater attachment to political Confucianism – from a low of 18 percent being supportive at the lowest level of attachment to Confucianism to a high of 53 percent being supportive at the highest level of attachment. This finding is strong evidence for the claim that Confucianism orients people to the nonliberal mode of democratic governance.

Table 8.5b shows the relationship between Confucianism and liberal democracy. Its most notable finding is the uniformity of the consistently negative relationship between the two variables throughout the entire region. In all six countries, whether democratic or nondemocratic, greater attachment to Confucianism is always accompanied by significantly less support for liberal democracy. Consequently, in every country, those fully detached from the Confucian model of paternalistic meritocracy are the most supportive of liberal democracy, whereas those fully attached to the model are the least supportive of it. In every country the difference in levels of support for liberal democracy based on attachment to Confucianism is statistically significant.

In Japan and Taiwan, the two democratic countries in which all four questions tapping Confucianism were asked, those who are fully detached from Confucianism are more than three times more likely to support liberal democracy than those who remain fully attached to it. In communist Vietnam, liberal democrats are more than seven times more numerous among the fully detached than the fully attached. In China and Singapore, the fully detached are more than ten times more supportive of liberal democracy than the fully attached. When all five countries are pooled together, the fully detached from Confucianism are more than eight times as likely as the fully attached to be liberal democrats (67% vs. 8%). This finding suggests that Confucianism powerfully deters ordinary citizens in historically Confucian Asia from embracing liberal democracy.

The bivariate analyses presented here suggest that Confucianism is capable of performing two divergent roles simultaneously in the process of democratization in Confucian Asia: It encourages people to favor non-liberal democracy, and it deters them from embracing liberal democracy. Let us now determine which of these two roles is performed more effectively by attachment to Confucianism. This question can be explored by comparing the *eta* coefficients reported in Tables 8.5a and 8.5b. In every country, the coefficient estimating the magnitude of the relationship between Confucianism and support for liberal democracy is significantly larger than the one estimating its relationship with support for nonliberal democracy. When all six countries are pooled together, the magnitude of the former is nearly two times larger than that of the latter (.38 vs. .20). This indicates that Confucianism is much more instrumental in driving East Asians away from liberal democracy than in driving them toward nonliberal democracy.

Sources of Popular Support for Liberal and Nonliberal Democracy

Why do so many people in Confucian Asia prefer nonliberal democracy to liberal democracy? Do they do so mainly because they remain attached to the political legacies of Confucianism? Or is the main reason that the nondemocratic regimes in which they live discourage them from learning about the virtues of liberal democracy? To explore these and other questions concerning the sources of support for nonliberal and liberal democracy, I performed multiple classification analysis (MCA) on support for attachment to Confucianism and the five other clusters of variables discussed earlier: socialization, modernization, democratic learning, regime performance, and social capital; each cluster was measured in terms of two variables. I considered twelve independent variables and estimated the independent impact of each independent variable on the dependent variables of liberal and nonliberal democratic support (see Table 8.6). I also estimated the extent to which all of the independent variables predicted each dependent variable jointly. Table 8.6 reports estimates of two statistical coefficients: *beta*, and R^2.

According to the *beta* coefficients, each of the six theoretical clusters has at least one variable with a significant impact on support for democracy, either liberal or nonliberal. Five of the twelve variables representing the six different theoretical clusters have a significant impact on both liberal and nonliberal democratic orientations: Those five variables are education, the type of political system, the cognitive capacity

TABLE 8.6. *Sources of Support for Nonliberal and Liberal Democracy* (MCA estimates)

Predictors	Support for Democracy	
	Liberal Democracy	Nonliberal Democracy
Socialization		
Gender	.07*	.01
Age	.03	.04
Modernization		
Education	.09*	.08*
Income	.04	.03
Democratic Learning		
Resident Regime	.27*	.23*
Conceptual Knowledge	.08*	.09*
Regime Performance		
Politics	.06*	.09*
Economy	.02	.02
Social Capital		
Trust	.05*	.02
Association	.00	.00
Confucianism		
Paternalistic Meritocracy	.23*	.16*
Hierarchical Collectivism	.02	.03
(R^2)	(.24)	(.15)

* Significant at the 0.05 level.
Source: 2005–8 Asian Barometer Surveys.

to define democracy,[3] satisfaction with regime performance,[4] and attachment to the Confucian legacies of paternalistic meritocracy. Two more, gender and trust, have an impact only on liberal democratic orientations. The remaining five variables – age, income, assessments of the economy,[5] associational membership, and Confucian hierarchical culture – have no significant independent effect on support for democracy.

[3] A 3-point index is constructed by the number of answers to open-ended (Q91) and closed-ended (Q92) questions, which tap, respectively, the meaning of democracy and the essentiality of its four properties.

[4] Q93 asked respondents to rate on a 4-point scale the extent to which they were satisfied or dissatisfied with the way democracy works in their country.

[5] A 5-point index is constructed by the number of positive answers to four questions (Q1–2 and Q4–5) tapping, respectively, the current situation of the national and household economies and their changes during the past five years.

Contrary to what is claimed in the literature, these five variables seem to affect democratic orientations only indirectly by affecting other variables.

The finding that gender and interpersonal trust have a significant independent effect only on support for liberal democracy indicates that orientations toward liberal democracy, as compared to nonliberal democracy, are more closely tied to certain population segments. When the effects of all other variables have been statistically removed, the two genders react to nonliberal democracy very similarly (46% vs. 46%), but males are significantly more supportive of liberal democracy than are females (36% vs. 30%). Likewise, people who trust others and those who do not are not much different in supporting nonliberal democracy (47% vs. 44%), but the former are significantly more supportive of liberal democracy than the latter (36% vs. 31%). This finding suggests that the factors that significantly influence citizen reactions to democracy vary according to its types, liberal and nonliberal.

As known in the literature on democratic support, levels of education and cognitive capacity have a significant independent impact on democratic support, either liberal or nonliberal, and political indifference. According to results of the MCA analysis that controlled for all other variables statistically, the college educated lead those without any formal education in supporting liberal democracy by 13 percentage points (40% vs. 27%). They also lead the uneducated in supporting nonliberal democracy by 6 percentage points (42% vs. 36%). Similarly, supporters of liberal and nonliberal democracy are significantly more numerous among those who understand the meaning of democracy than among those who do not. Evidently, higher education and cognitive capacity create more democrats primarily by transforming the politically indifferent into some form of democrat. The two variables, however, do not seem to be at all successful in transforming nonliberal democrats into liberal democrats.

Unlike education and the ability to define democracy, which produce a greater number of liberal and nonliberal democrats at the same time, democratic regime experience contributes significantly to the embrace of liberal democracy and to the rejection of nonliberal democracy. For each of the three types of regimes – old democracy, new democracy, and nondemocracy – Figure 8.6 reports the percentages supporting liberal and nonliberal democracy after the effects of all other factors considered have been adjusted for statistically. These adjusted percentages of liberal democrats increase sharply from a low of 21 percent for nondemocratic Singapore and Vietnam to 49 percent for the oldest democracy of Japan

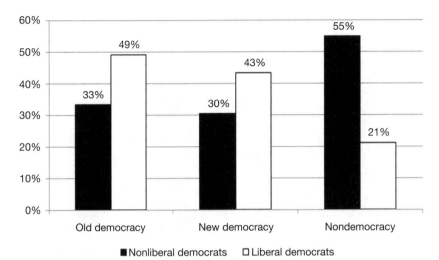

FIGURE 8.6. Adjusted Percentages of Nonliberal and Liberal Democrats by the Types of Resident Regime. *Source:* 2005–8 Asian Barometer Surveys.

(China is excluded from this analysis because its citizens were not asked the questions on family income and associational membership).

In contrast, the percentages of nonliberal democrats significantly decrease from 55 percent in authoritarian Vietnam and Singapore to 30 percent in the new democracies of Korea and Taiwan. In all three democratic countries, liberal democrats outnumber nonliberal democrats even when all other eleven variables have been controlled for statistically. In the two authoritarian countries of Singapore and China, nonliberal democrats outnumber liberal democrats. The preponderance of liberal democrats over nonliberal democrats only among those who live under democratic rule renders strong support for the theory of democratic learning that holds that people become fonder of democracy after experiencing democratic politics.

People who give positive assessments of their regime's performance are also more likely to turn away from nonliberal democracy and toward liberal democracy. In contrast, negative assessments of the government's performance turn people toward nonliberal democracy and away from liberal democracy. Figure 8.7 shows a consistently positive relationship between satisfaction with regime performance and the adjusted percentage of liberal democrats and a consistently negative relationship between performance satisfaction and the adjusted percentage of nonliberal democrats. By specifying the exact effect that citizens' assessments

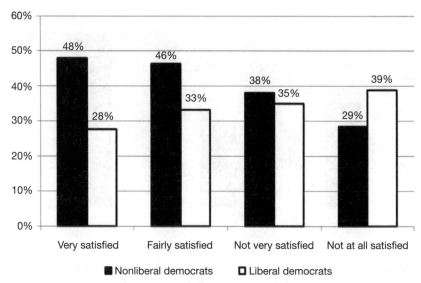

FIGURE 8.7. Adjusted Percentages of Nonliberal and Liberal Democrats by Assessments of Regime Performance. *Source:* 2005–8 Asian Barometer Surveys.

of regime performance have on their reactions to liberal and nonliberal democracy, this finding contributes to the refinement of the existing performance-based theory of democratic support (Bratton et al. 2005; Rose et al. 1998).

In contrast to the positive independent effects that living under a democratic regime and satisfaction with its performance have on support for liberal democracy, attachment to the political legacies of Confucianism have a significantly negative independent effect on support for liberal democracy and a significantly positive independent effect on support for nonliberal democracy. As shown in Figure 8.8, the adjusted percentages of liberal democrats decrease steadily at each higher level of attachment to Confucian political legacies, dropping sharply from a high of 55 percent to a low of 19 percent. In contrast, the adjusted percentages of nonliberal democrats increase steadily at each higher attachment level, increasing from a low of 29 percent to a high of 54 percent.

Among those who remain fully attached to political Confucianism, a majority (54%) supports nonliberal democracy, and a minority (19%) supports liberal democracy. Among those who are fully detached from political Confucianism, however, a majority (55%) supports liberal democracy, and a minority (29%) supports nonliberal democracy. This finding supports the claim that *Confucianism is incompatible with liberal*

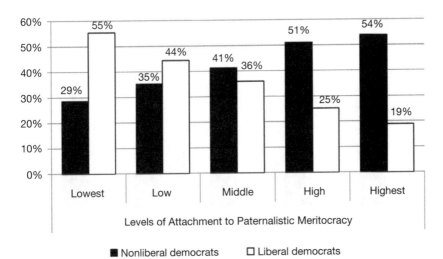

FIGURE 8.8. Adjusted Percentages of Nonliberal and Liberal Democrats by Levels of Attachment to Paternalistic Meritocracy. *Source:* 2005–8 Asian Barometer Surveys.

democracy but compatible with nonliberal democracy. It also suggests that detachment from Confucianism is essential to the growth of liberal democratic political culture in Confucian Asia.

Does attachment to Confucianism reduce support for liberal democracy regardless of the type of regime in which people live? Does it also bolster support for nonliberal democracy regardless of regime type? Figures 8.9 and 8.10 explore these questions by comparing the independent effects of attachment to Confucianism on liberal and nonliberal democratic support across the groups of democratic and nondemocratic countries. For both groups of countries, the percentages of nonliberal democrats increase steadily and sharply with increases in the level of Confucian attachment, from 18 to 41 percent in democratic countries and 35 to 65 percent in nondemocratic countries. In contrast, the adjusted percentages of liberal democrats decrease steadily and sharply with increases in the level of attachment to Confucianism, from 70 to 18 percent in democracies and 54 to 6 percent in nondemocracies.

These figures show that attachment to Confucianism has the same effect on residents of democracies and nondemocracies: Regardless of the type of political system in which people live, attachment to Confucian political traditions deters them from embracing liberal democracy while encouraging them to favor nonliberal democracy. This reinforces

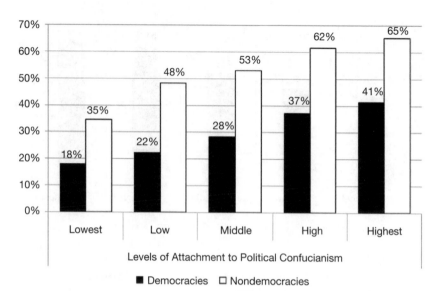

FIGURE 8.9. The Independent Effect of Political Confucianism on Support for Nonliberal Democracy in Democracies and Nondemocracies. *Source:* 2005–8 Asian Barometer Surveys.

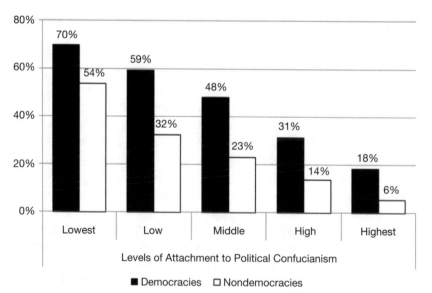

FIGURE 8.10. The Independent Effect of Political Confucianism on Support for Liberal Democracy in Nondemocratic and Democratic Countries. *Source:* 2005–8 Asian Barometer Surveys.

the Incompatibility Thesis, which posits that Confucian political values are prevalent throughout the region of East Asia and are in all settings incompatible with liberal democracy.

To identify the most powerful influences on support for liberal and nonliberal democracy, I compared the magnitude of *beta* coefficients reported in Table 8.6. Of all the variables with a significant independent effect on democratic support, the type of regime in which people live constitutes the most powerful influence on both liberal and nonliberal democratic support, with *beta* coefficients of .27 and .23, respectively. The variable with the next most significant impact is attachment to the Confucian legacies of paternalistic meritocracy, with *beta* coefficients of .23 for liberal democracy and .16 for nonliberal democracy.

Attachment to Confucianism affects citizen reactions to both liberal and nonliberal democracy more than two times more powerfully than the two variables of educational attainment and positive assessments of regime performance, which the literature reports to be very powerful influences on democratic support. A Confucian political heritage, which emphasizes paternalism and meritocracy, still remains a powerful force in the process of cultural democratization in Confucian Asia. A comparison of its two *beta* coefficients, however, indicates that attachment to political Confucianism is more instrumental in preventing the liberalization of authoritarian political orientations than in fostering or sustaining affinity for a nonliberal mode of governance.

Finally, it should be noted that Confucianism as a way of life, as opposed to as a political heritage, has no significant direct independent effect on support for either liberal or nonliberal democracy. Figure 8.11 compares the adjusted percentages supporting liberal and nonliberal democracy for each of the four types of culture discussed in Chapter 3. According to the grid-group theory, Confucianism represents a culture of hierarchical collectivism, which is less conducive to the development of democratic political culture than that of competitive individualism or egalitarianism. As this theory contends, upholders of hierarchical collectivism and competitive individualism among the historically Confucian Asian population are, respectively, least and most supportive of liberal democracy and most and least supportive of nonliberal democracy. Specifically, upholders of a hierarchical culture trail those of individualism in supporting liberal democracy by 7 percentage points (22% vs. 29%) but lead them in supporting nonliberal democracy by 6 percentage points (47% vs. 41%; see Figure 8.11). These percentage differences,

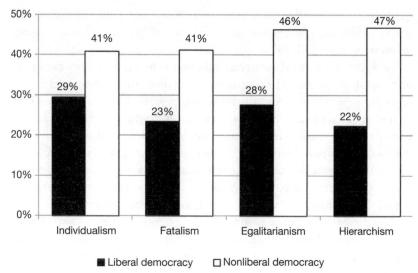

FIGURE 8.11. Adjusted Levels of Support for Nonliberal and Liberal Democracy by Four Types of Culture. *Source:* 2005–8 Asian Barometer Surveys.

however, amount to only one-fifth of those between the levels of attachment to Confucian political legacies, which clearly indicates that Confucianism affects the process of cultural democratization primarily through its political, not cultural, heritage.

Summary and Conclusions

There is a growing consensus among scholars and politicians that the democratization of authoritarian rule is not complete with the inauguration of competitive elections and multiparty systems alone. This political "hardware" must be joined with political "software," which is the overwhelming majority acceptance of democratic institutions and processes along with a rejection of all alternatives. Without such a majority of fully committed democratic citizens, countries in democratic transition are not likely to become complete or consolidated democracies; instead, they are likely to hobble along as "broken-back" democracies (Rose and Shin 2001).

To understand the process of democratization taking place among the mass citizenry, an increasing number of international and national public opinion surveys have recently been conducted in Asia and all other regions of the world. To date, studies based on these surveys have been concerned exclusively with the extent to which ordinary citizens prefer democracy to its alternatives at the regime level; the studies have neglected to determine whether the citizens who embrace democracy as the preferred regime are also in favor of their governments using the democratic method to formulate and implement policies. Consequently, little is known about how fully or firmly people are committed to democracy. Much less is known about how and why their support for democracy varies across its different manifestations, liberal and nonliberal, as suggested by advocates of the Incompatibility Thesis.

To fill this gap in the study of democratic citizenship and culture, I analyzed how the mass publics of Confucian Asian countries react to democracy and its alternatives not only as a regime structure but also as a political process. Considering their regime and process orientations together, I identified four distinct types of democratic and nondemocratic citizens among the Confucian Asian population: supporters of nondemocracy, supporters of nonliberal democracy, supporters of liberal democracy, and the politically indifferent. To test the thesis that Confucianism is incompatible with liberal democracy, I examined the independent effect of Confucian political orientations on support for liberal and nonliberal democracy.

These typological analyses of the Asian Barometer Surveys reveal that, in all six Confucian countries, large majorities embrace democracy as the preferred type of political regime. In every country, however, a majority of those who support democracy at the regime level do not embrace democracy as the preferred method or process of daily governance. As a result, liberal democrats, those who embrace democracy at both the regime and political process levels, do not constitute a majority in any of the six countries. Only in the three democratic countries analyzed – Japan, Korea, and Taiwan – do they constitute a near majority or plurality. In the three nondemocratic countries analyzed– China, Singapore, and Vietnam– liberal democrats form small minorities of less than 20 percent, and they are outnumbered by supporters of nonliberal democracy, who, although they support democracy at the regime level, prefer to be governed by a nondemocratic method.

In the region as a whole, moreover, there are more supporters of nonliberal democracy than those of liberal democracy. Also notable is the finding that in historically Confucian Asia today, there are more politically indifferent people than supporters of liberal democracy. Perhaps the most telling finding is that a very small minority of about 11 percent of the historically Confucian Asian population is *unqualified* in its embrace of democracy as the preferred regime structure and as the preferred policy process.

The overall commitment of mass citizenries to democracy in historically Confucian Asia as a whole, although not particularly encouraging to democratic supporters, compares favorably with what is found in the non-Confucian region of East Asia. Yet, their democratic commitment is very shallow in depth, although broad in scope. For example, more people express qualified than unqualified support for liberal democracy by refusing to endorse it fully at both the regime and process levels (18% vs. 11%). The distribution of supporters of liberal democracy is also highly uneven across the countries, as well as from one population segment to another within each country. In a nutshell, support for democracy, especially liberal democracy, remains, by and large, underdeveloped. Given that such support is one of the two fundamental requisites for full democratic citizenship – the other, also underdeveloped, being cognitive awareness of what is a democracy – the mass publics in Confucian Asia have a long road to travel before becoming effective democratic citizens.

In Confucian Asia today, two powerful forces work separately and jointly to deter its people from reorienting themselves toward the new practices of liberal democracy and away from the old practices of authoritarian or nonliberal politics. More powerfully than any of the other major factors, living under an authoritarian regime keeps Confucian Asians favorably oriented to authoritarian and nonliberal practices and discourages them from embracing those of liberal democracy. Consequently, majorities of the college educated in all three nondemocratic countries reject liberal democracy, while their counterparts in all three democratic countries embrace it. Similarly, the college educated in nondemocracies remain more supportive of nonliberal democracy than liberal democracy. Evidently, in these nondemocratic countries, the failure to establish democratic rule is the most powerful deterrent to the development of a democratic culture and the emergence of democratic citizens. As the theory of democratic learning suggests, people in Confucian Asia have to experience democratic rule to become fully democratic citizens.

However, just experiencing democratic rule is not enough to develop liberal democratic support, as is clear when one considers that majorities of citizens in Japan, Korea, and Taiwan still refuse to embrace democracy fully, even after living in a democracy for decades. Although some demographic characteristics, including education level, influence the level of support for democracy, a major influence is the area's Confucian heritage. As does living in an authoritarian regime, attachment to the Confucian principles of good government – paternalism and meritocracy – motivates East Asians to favor the age-old practices of authoritarian rule while discouraging them from embracing those of democratic rule. In both democratic and nondemocratic countries, attachment to political Confucianism is the most powerful bane limiting the embrace of liberal democracy and the most powerful boon for promoting nonliberal democracy. It is from one-and-a half times to five times more powerful than factors tapping any other theoretical cluster, including modernization and regime performance.

Our finding that Confucianism is one of the most powerful influences on the underdevelopment of democratic citizenship in Confucian Asia runs counter to what has been reported in previous public opinion research (Blondel and Inoguchi 2006; Chang et al. 2005; Dalton and Ong 2006; Dalton and Shin 2006; Fetzer and Soper 2007; S. Kim 2010; Nathan and Chen 2004; Park and Shin 2006; Welzel 2011). This finding offers credible support for the Incompatibility Thesis, which emphasizes the incompatibility of Confucianism with liberal democracy.

As expected from the thesis (Huntington 1991, 1996; Zakaria 1994, 1997, 2003), attachment to Confucian values undermines the development of liberal democratic political culture by discouraging ordinary citizens from embracing liberal democracy while encouraging them to support nonliberal democracy, which has even been called Asian-style democracy. Furthermore, the same values encourage some to prefer authoritarian or hybrid rule, which is called a nonliberal form of democracy (J. Chan 2007, 181). Clearly, Confucianism plays more important roles in the process of cultural democratization than has been claimed in the debate over the Asian Values Thesis.

Although a preference for nonliberal democracy over liberal democracy is a major obstacle to the development of fully democratic citizenship in Confucian Asia, it is not the only one. Also problematic is the fact that a plurality of people in Confucian Asia is indifferent concerning whether democracy or authoritarianism is best for their countries. In all six countries, the politically indifferent are many times more numerous than supporters of nondemocracy. In two countries, China and Vietnam, the indifferent are more than three times more numerous than liberal democrats. Moreover, in two countries, Japan and China, they are more numerous than supporters of nonliberal democracy. According to results of the MCA, which are not reported here, a lack of formal education is

the most powerful influence on this indifference. Evidently, being uninformed about authoritarian and democratic politics powerfully deters the
development of democratic citizenship in Confucian Asia.

Demographically, politically indifferent people are heavily concentrated among the least educated and poor segments of the population,
findings that support the theory that indifference stems from lack of
knowledge. Supporters of liberal democracy are most heavily concentrated in the best educated and most affluent population segments, which
are also the segments that are the least indifferent. In contrast, supporters of nonliberal democracy are most numerous among young middle-
income people with a high school education. From these findings, it
is evident that advances in socioeconomic modernization in Confucian
Asia are likely to reduce the population of politically indifferent people,
but whether such modernization will create more liberal or nonliberal
democrats seems to depend on other demographic variables. Contrary to
the neo-modernization theory, which links socioeconomic modernization
to the emergence of liberal political values (Inglehart and Welzel 2005),
socioeconomic modernization in Confucian Asia is most likely to expand
the family of nonliberal democrats among young people in their 20s
and 30s.

Among the six countries, Singapore is the only country in which a
substantial majority of young people and the college educated supports
nonliberal democracy while rejecting liberal democracy. Taiwan is the
only country where the youngest age cohort is nearly two times more
supportive of nonliberal democracy than the oldest cohort. Vietnam is
the only country where the youngest age cohort is as much or more
politically indifferent as the two older cohorts. Vietnam is also the only
country where people become more supportive of nonliberal democracy
than liberal democracy with socioeconomic advances, including a greater
level of education and income. China is the only country where people
with a college education are more than two times more supportive of
nonliberal democracy than those without a high school education.[6] Korea
is the only country where people become less supportive of nonliberal
democracy with a higher level of education but more supportive of it
with a higher income. Korea is also the only country in which more than
40 percent of females are supportive of liberal democracy. Japan has the

---

[6] Support for nonliberal democracy among the middle class in East Asia is often attributed
to the fact that they benefited from socioeconomic development under decades of authoritarian rule. For further detail, see Bell et al. 1996.

greatest gender gap not only in supporting liberal democracy but also in remaining politically indifferent. Only in Japan do more than two times as many females as males choose not to give a preferred regime and process. Only in China is more than half the population indifferent about those choices. These many differences illustrate that Confucian countries are not alike in reacting to the forces of socioeconomic modernization and political modernization.

Finally, these findings call into question the notion that political support, either democratic or authoritarian, is a reflection of deep-seated values. Contrary to what Easton (1975) and others (Kornberg and Clarke 1983) have suggested, traditional values are not impervious to change; instead they grow and decline in response to a variety of forces, including learning more about democracy-in-principle and democracy-in-practice and the perceived quality of regime performance. These results are an important piece of evidence supporting the theory of democratic learning, which claims that the different reactions citizens have to democratic regime change are as much an outcome as a cause of democratic practice (Muller and Seligson 1994).

PART V

FINAL THOUGHTS

9

Reassessing the Confucian Asian Values Debate

Today, historically Confucian East Asia represents a region of democratic underdevelopment. Are Confucian cultural legacies the force preventing the powerful third wave of global democratization from sweeping most countries in Confucian East Asia? Have these legacies also prevented new and old democracies in the region from becoming well-functioning liberal democracies, as proponents of the Asian Values Thesis have argued? The research reported on in this book sought to explore these and other related questions concerning the prevalence and dissemination of Confucian legacies, as well as their connection to democratic and authoritarian politics from the perspective of the mass citizenry.

To this end, I began with a broad conceptualization of Confucianism and democracy, describing each as a multidimensional phenomenon. Defining Confucianism as a system of political and social ethics, I considered the proper modes of both social living and political governance that Confucianism advocates for the achievement of *datong shehui*, a community of grand harmony. Furthermore, I regarded Confucianism as a phenomenon covering the region of East Asia identified as historically Confucian East Asia and rejected the equation of Confucian values with Asian values, which the Asian Values Thesis has often implied.

As with the Confucian notion of citizenship, I also broadly defined democracy, considering it a community of mutual caring and considered citizens engaged in civic affairs and committed to democratic politics. In studying citizens' democratic commitment, I examined both *affective* orientations of democratic support – or how citizens feel about democracy – and *cognitive* orientations of democratic knowledge – or what citizens know or think about democracy. For a more balanced account of cultural democratization in Confucian East Asia than what is found in the literature, I also identified and analyzed the distinct *patterns* in which citizens understand democracy and react to it both as an ideal and as a work in progress.

In this final chapter, I first highlight the most notable findings reported in earlier chapters and then evaluate the central claims and counterclaims surrounding the Asian Values Thesis in view of these findings. I then recast the thesis in the framework of Harry Eckstein's (1966) congruence theory and examine its limitations as a theory of democratic underdevelopment in view of the recent fine-tunings of Eckstein's theory. Finally, I examine the implications of this study's findings for three pairs of prominent competing theories of cultural democratization.

The Prevalence of Confucian Legacies

Is the region of historically Confucian East Asia still devoted to the moral values and norms that Confucius, Mencius, and other early Confucians advocated for building *datong shehui*? If so, is this region more broadly and deeply attached to those values and norms than are historically non-Confucian East Asia and other regions of the world? The Asian Values Thesis debate assumes that the Confucian legacies continue to have a unique impact on the residents of Confucian East Asia. If this assumption were proved false, and residents of Confucian East Asian countries were found to be unattached to Confucian legacies or no more attached than their peers in other regions, then attributing their region's democratic underdevelopment to those legacies would be an error.

How broadly and deeply do the contemporary mass publics of the historically Confucian East Asia region uphold the legacies of Confucian political and social ethics? Which of the legacies do they uphold most broadly and deeply? Across the region are Confucian East Asians more united or divided in upholding those legacies? If they are divided, what are the fault lines separating them? To address these questions, I analyzed the attachment that ordinary citizens of these countries have to the social and the political legacies identified in the Asian Values debate as most incompatible with the ideals and practices of liberal democracy. The social legacies are hierarchal collectivism, familism, and communitarianism; the political legacies are paternalism and elitism.

Hierarchal collectivism refers to a way of life that emphasizes strong group affiliation and strict conformity to norms and rules that define one's place in life. This particular way of life does not have a preferred status among citizens in the historically Confucian East Asia region; as a whole, less than one-third of the citizens (28%) are of this cultural type. Only in three – China, Taiwan, and Vietnam – of the five countries surveyed by the World Values Surveys is hierarchism more preferred than the three other cultural types: egalitarianism, individualism, and fatalism. Further, contrary to what is assumed in the Asian Values Thesis, hierarchical collectivism, which early Confucians prescribed for the good life, is not a trait unique to historically Confucian East Asia. In fact, it is far more prevalent in other non-Western regions, such as Africa and the Middle East.

The Confucian legacy of paternalistic elitism represents a political means of building *datong shehui*. Paternalistic elitism differs from democracy in that it represents a government *for* the people but not *by* the people. Here again, only in three countries – China, Singapore, and Vietnam – are majorities attached, at least somewhat, to the Confucian political principles of paternalism and elitism. Those fully attached to both principles constitute a minority of about two-fifths (39%) in the region, although a solid majority of three-fifths (62%) is partially attached to at least one of them. However, paternalistic meritocracy is more prevalent in non-Confucian East Asia than in Confucian East Asia.

Communitarianism holds that a harmonious community can be achieved only when citizens prioritize the good of their communities over individual rights and freedom (Bell 2010). To reach the ultimate goal of building *datong shehui*, Confucianism advocates a model of communitarian civic life, which emphasizes a cooperative spirit and engagement in civic life. This model contrasts strikingly with the liberal model of civic life, which encourages citizens to compete in the public arena for their own, individual best interests. In all six countries surveyed by the Asian Barometer Surveys (ABS), upholders of the Confucian model are more prevalent than those of the liberal model. Yet those fully attached to the Confucian model constitute majorities only in the three nondemocratic countries. As with the norms of hierarchical relations and paternalistic meritocracy, Confucian civic norms are not confined to historically Confucian Asia.

Of all the principles Confucius and his followers advocated for ethical living, familism reigns supreme. This value is so important because it governs family life, the cornerstone of Confucian culture. In all six Confucian East Asia countries, an overwhelming majority of about nine-tenths (87%) are attached, at least somewhat, to familism. This principle has broader support than any other Confucian legacy, and its support varies little across the countries. However, in no country do those fully attached to familism form a majority. Like the other Confucian legacies discussed earlier, familism is not a deeply ingrained cultural legacy in Confucian East Asia, although it is broadly embraced. Nor is it confined to the region: There are very similar patterns of attachment to and detachment from the norms of familism in non-Confucian East Asia.

The analyses of four defining legacies of Confucianism – hierarchical culture, paternalistic meritocracy, communitarianism, and familism – suggest four points about their prevalence and influence on democratization:

In historically Confucian East Asia today, popular attachment to Confucianism is miles wide but only inches deep: Most of the population reports attachment, but a shallow attachment, to Confucian legacies. Even in the wake of socioeconomic and political transformations, majorities in all of the region's countries remain at least partially attached to what Confucius and his followers taught about the good life and good government more than two millennia ago. In striking contrast, none of the legacies draws unqualified support from a majority of the Confucian Asian population.

In the region, people are less attached to Confucianism as a model of conduct or way of life than as a source for politics or a system of government. They are less attached to the social norms of civic life than those of family life. It appears that socioeconomic modernization, which affects how people go about their lives, has been a more powerful force than democratization in eroding Confucian social legacies. In addition, socioeconomic modernization has affected the public sphere of life more powerfully than the private sphere.

Historically Confucian East Asia is no longer a single cultural zone in regard to the mass public's commitment to the legacies of Confucian social and political ethics. The region is divided into two cultural subregions: in one, there is broad, although not deep, support for Confucian legacies; in the other, support is neither broad nor deep. Because these two cultural subregions fall roughly along the lines separating authoritarian and democratic regimes – and because both the authoritarian and democratic regimes have similar Confucian legacies – this finding of two cultural subregions also suggests that nondemocratic rule promotes continued orientation toward the Confucian model, whereas democratic rule promotes a turning away from it.

None of the Confucian legacies analyzed in this study constitutes a unique set of cultural characteristics found only in historically Confucian East Asia, where the teachings of Confucius and his followers served as the ideological and institutional foundations of political and social life. Certainly, the finding that these legacies are equally or more prevalent in other non-Western regions indicates that it is unsound to attribute the lack of democratization in Confucian East Asia exclusively to Confucian legacies, as the Asian Values Thesis does. It also suggests that some of the values long considered "Confucian" might be better labeled as "non-Western traditional values."

Confucian Influences on Democratic Citizenship

To transform age-old authoritarian rule into a fully functioning democracy, citizens have to embrace democracy fully, which requires much more than lip service to democracy as an abstract ideal. It involves developing an accurate understanding of the nature of democratic rule and its differences from authoritarian rule. A full embrace of democracy also requires a willingness to take part in civic affairs and to fulfill one's responsibility to the community in collaboration with other fellow citizens. The first dimension of *democratic commitment* deals with knowledge of democracy and affinity for its ideals and practices. The second dimension of *civic engagement* deals with associational activity and civic-mindedness. This study analyzed how Confucian legacies are linked with each of these two fundamental dimensions of democratic citizenship.

Not all Confucian legacies considered to be incompatible with democratic politics have a significant effect on each important component of citizenship, and not every significant impact that does exist is negative, as proponents of the Asian Values Thesis claim. These proponents, for example, have argued that the norms of familism deter people from extending trust outside the intimate circle of family members and relatives. In contrast, opponents of the thesis have argued that the norms of Confucian communitarianism urge people to engage actively in the realm of civic life, which Alexis de Tocqueville (1835/2000) once characterized as "an engine of democracy."

Although the study found significant direct effects of Confucian civic norms on the breadth of informal and formal associations, the norms of familism, together with communitarianism, contribute significantly to interpersonal trust and tolerance, two foundational components of democratic civic life. This finding, linking the two Confucian social norms to the making of civic-minded citizens, supports the Confucian tenet that "filial piety and fraternal duty are the roots of humanness" (*Analects* 1:2) and that family relations serve as the foundation for social life (*Analects* 2:7). This finding also confirms the counterclaim of the Asian Values Thesis that Confucianism contains the seeds of democratic politics. In addition, it disputes Francis Fukuyama's (1995a, 56) claim that Confucian familism is a sort of amoral familism that limits the extension of trust to those outside the family and thereby hinders economic development.

However, the legacies of Confucian social ethics do contribute significantly to the development of hybrid or nonliberal misconceptions of democracy. For example, of the four types of culture considered – hierarchal, individual, egalitarian, and fatalist – Confucian hierarchal culture is the one most often associated with a misconception of the distinctive characteristics of democracy and its alternatives, even when the influences of socialization and modernization variables have been statistically removed. As a result, a misconception of democracy as a hybrid regime is most prevalent among upholders of Confucian culture.

The political legacies of Confucianism, like its social legacies, remain a significant influence on the way in which people conceive of democracy and government. Specifically, attachment to paternalistic meritocracy contributes significantly to understanding democracy in substantive terms, and it has an equal negative effect on understanding democracy in procedural terms. Further, those attached to paternalistic meritocracy are very reluctant to understand democracy merely in liberal terms. *Authentic liberal democratic conceivers*, who equate democracy exclusively with freedom and who prioritize freedom as its most essential characteristic, constitute a very small minority (6%) of the Confucian East Asian population. Moreover, these democratic conceivers are significantly less numerous in historically Confucian East Asia than in non-Confucian East Asia (6% vs. 11%). Undoubtedly, such lack of liberal conceptions of democratic politics has a lot to do with the Confucian legacy of good government that prioritizes economic well-being.

Equally notable is the finding that the legacies of Confucian ethics neither orient people away from the democratic system of government nor toward its authoritarian alternatives, at least at the abstract, regime level. Most people in Confucian East Asia desire to live in a democracy, rather than in an authoritarian regime, regardless of their attachment level to Confucian legacies. Even among those who are strongly attached to those legacies, a large majority of nearly four-fifths (79%) prefer to live in a democracy, in contrast to a very small minority (2%) who prefer to live in an authoritarian regime. Contrary to what is expected from the central claim of the Asian Values Thesis – that Confucianism is incompatible with democracy – attachment to Confucian legacies turns out to be compatible with democratic regime preferences and incompatible with authoritarian regime preferences.

When people are attached to the legacies of paternalistic meritocracy, however, they feel differently about the two different types of democratic systems: They are favorably disposed toward nonliberal democracy, characterized by a democratic regime structure and an authoritarian mode of governance, and unfavorably disposed toward liberal democracy, characterized by a democratic regime structure and a democratic mode of governance. In the minds of people in Confucian East Asia, therefore, it is a nonliberal democratic system, not an authoritarian political system, which is most compatible with Confucianism. Moreover, it is liberal democracy, not electoral or delegative democracy, which is incompatible with Confucian legacies (Karl 2000; O'Donnell 1994).

Finally, it should be noted that attachment to Confucian political legacies constitutes one of the two most powerful forces shaping regime orientations. They shape both cognitive and affective orientations to democracy more powerfully than either of the two core components of socioeconomic modernization: education and income. Specifically, the political legacies of paternalistic meritocracy have more than twice as much influence over liberal and nonliberal democratic orientations as does each of the two socioeconomic resources. To put it differently, Confucianism detracts from liberal democratic support more powerfully than the two resources that promote it. Because attachment to Confucian legacies is a very powerful force, this finding indicates that Confucian legacies are capable of offsetting the liberalizing effect of socioeconomic modernization on cultural democratization. It also suggests that liberal democracy is not likely to become the only political game in Confucian East Asia in the near future.

Unlike Confucian political traditions, however, attachment to Confucian social legacies has no significant effect on democratic orientations, either liberal or nonliberal, although Confucian hierarchal culture, as compared to the three other types of culture, is least likely to foster liberal democratic orientations and most likely to foster nonliberal democratic orientations. This suggests that the Confucian way of life, featuring hierarchism and collectivism, affects popular reactions to democracy indirectly by orienting people toward the Confucian notion of good government featuring paternalism and meritocracy.

When considered as a whole, Confucian legacies cannot be judged as deterring the general process of cultural democratization (i.e., building a nation of democratic citizens). Instead their effects represent a mixed bag. Confucian political legacies seem to be inimical to the particular process of orienting citizens to liberal democracy in which individual freedom and interests matter above those of the community. In contrast, its social legacies are compatible with the process of orienting citizens toward communitarian democracy in which individual members cooperate with each other instead of competing against each other.

Equally notable is the finding that in all three nondemocratic countries in Confucian East Asia today, only a few citizens are both informed about democratization and demand democratic regime change, and these *authentic democratic transformers* are overwhelmingly outnumbered by those who misunderstand democratization and mistakenly support authoritarian rule as democracy.[1] In all three democratic countries in the region, only a few citizens are unconditionally committed to liberal democratic reform, and these *committed liberal democratic reformers* are overwhelmingly outnumbered by supporters of nonliberal democratic rule, many of whom are rediscovering and adopting the traditional values of Confucianism in response to powerful waves of modernization and globalization.[2]

As long as citizens with such nonliberal political orientations remain an overwhelming majority – especially among the young generation with

---

[1] In authoritarian Confucian East Asia today, only 3 percent are truly dissatisfied democrats, who are capable of distinguishing democracy from its alternatives and would be interested in supporting the democratization of their authoritarian regime. In all three countries including Singapore, moreover, these democrats, who are likely to play the role of *authentic democratic reformers*, constitute less than 5 percent of the adult population. Even among the next generation of political leaders (i.e., college-educated young people), they form a nearly identical minority of 6 percent. In addition, their proportions vary little from 3 percent in Vietnam and 4 percent in China to 8 percent in Singapore.

[2] In democratic Confucian Asia today, less than 1 percent (0.6%) of citizens are unconditionally committed to the expansion and deepening of their limited liberal democracies into fully liberal democratic regimes. The proportions of these committed reformers vary little across the three countries, ranging from less than 1 percent in Japan and Taiwan to about 2 percent in Korea. More notably, in all three countries, less than 2 percent of college-educated young people are unqualified in their commitment to the building of a fully liberal democracy. The next generation of political leaders in these countries therefore does not appear at all poised to demand further democratization in their countries; in fact, they appear even less committed than the current generation of political leaders.

a college education – Confucian East Asia is likely to remain, in the assessment of Western liberal democrats, a region of disappointing democratic development for many years to come. To East Asians who remain deeply ingrained in the virtues of Confucianism, however, their country's resistance to the current wave of global democratization may appear as an exciting opportunity to avoid the deeply flawed liberal model of the Western democracy and to establish instead a new, innovative political system that combines the best of Confucian and democratic ideals of good government.

Reassessing the Asian Values Thesis

The Asian Values Thesis maintains that the political and social legacies of Confucianism are incompatible with the norms, values, and structures of democratic politics and are instead compatible with those of authoritarian politics. Supporters of this thesis thus conclude that a democratic system of government is unsuitable for historically Confucian East Asia, where it is assumed that ordinary people and their leaders remain attached to Confucian ethical norms and values. Using the survey findings presented in this book, I first evaluate these claims of the thesis empirically. Then I recast the thesis in the framework of Harry Eckstein's (1966) congruence theory, examining the Asian Values Thesis's limitations as a theory of democratic underdevelopment in light of the recent fine-tunings of Eckstein's theory.

As a theory of democratic underdevelopment, the Asian Values Thesis bases its claim of an incompatibility between a Confucian heritage and full democratization on three highly dubious premises. The first premise is that Confucianism constitutes a well-unified or coherently integrated system of thought, in which all of its components are mutually supportive of one another. The second premise is that the key components of Confucianism are all pro-authoritarian and antidemocratic and thus consistently or uniformly negative in their effect on democratic politics. The third premise is that all Confucian legacies influence democratic politics, but none are influenced by it. Confucianism is therefore considered exclusively exogenous to democracy, and the two phenomena are not endogenous to each other.

As discussed in detail in Chapter 2, Confucianism does not represent a well-integrated system of *exclusively authoritarian* social and political ethics. Instead, it is one of many multivocal systems of political doctrines and social ethics (Stepan 2000). Being loosely structured, it consists of many conflicting elements. On religious and spiritual matters, for example, Confucius told his students not to "serve the spirits" (*Analects* 11:12), while preaching the virtue of practicing ancestor worship (*Analects* 1:11). As suggested in the following passages, he even emphasized the importance of understanding the spirit of Heaven: "Without understanding the ordinance of Heaven, it is impossible to become a superior man" (*Analects* 20:3); "Wealth and honor depend upon Heaven" (*Analects* 7:5).

Contrary to what is expected from the thesis, moreover, some key norms of interpersonal relationships, such as familism and communitarianism, are found to contribute to, rather than detract from, democratic citizenship. Other Confucian norms such as meritocracy and paternalism are found to be compatible with a popular preference for nonliberal democracy. As discussed earlier, democracy, not its authoritarian alternatives, is the most preferred system of government among residents of Confucian East Asia, even among those who are unqualified in their commitment to Confucian norms of paternalistic meritocracy. In the minds of people in Confucian East Asia today, it is clear that the legacies of Confucian political and social ethics are not uniformly detrimental to the development of democratic citizenship, as is assumed in the Asian Values Thesis. Some norms have a neutral effect on the embrace of democracy as a regime, whereas other norms actually encourage the development of civic-mindedness.

Equally significant is the finding that Confucian legacies and democratic political practices have a reciprocal and highly dynamic relationship, in which each influences the other. Attachment to the Confucian principles of ethical meritocracy and paternalistic government motivates people to prefer nonliberal democracy over liberal democracy. A continued experience of democratic rule, however, motivates people to dissociate themselves from those Confucian political principles, whereas a continued experience of authoritarian rule discourages them from doing so. In the real world of mass politics, Confucianism and democratic politics affect each other both positively and negatively. This finding conflicts with the Asian Value Thesis, which portrays the relationship between Confucian legacies and democratization as unidirectional and stagnant. The survey findings indicating such highly complex and dynamic reciprocal relationships between the two phenomena directly challenge two of the thesis's fundamental premises: (1) Confucianism is exogenous to democratic politics, and (2) its effect on democracy is always negative.

Theoretically, the central claim of the Asian Values Thesis can be recast as that of the congruence theory advocated by political scientist Harry

Eckstein (1966). Congruence theory assumes that a match, or congruence, between social norms and values on the one hand and political values and structure on the other is *functional* to stable democratic rule, and a mismatch, or incongruence, is *dysfunctional* to it. Therefore when prevailing social values are incongruent or in conflict with the values underlying the political structure, the regime cannot endure for an extended period of time, much less experience any further growth.

Advocates of the Asian Values Thesis agree with this assumption of congruence theory, holding that the only viable systems of government in a given society are those that are compatible with its dominant cultural values. It dismisses all other types of government as unsuitable for that society. In the belief that all Confucian legacies are incompatible with democratic politics, those advocates have dismissed democracy as unsuitable for all the countries in culturally Confucian East Asia.

When viewed through the lens of congruence theory, which Eckstein and others (Dalton and Shin 2006; Inglehart and Welzel 2005; Mattes and Bratton 2007) formulated as a cultural theory of democratic development, the Asian Values Thesis, as a model of democratization, is deeply flawed on conceptual and theoretical grounds. Conceptually, it is flawed because it is based on a misconception of democratization or democratic development. Theoretically, it is flawed because it fails to take into account the positive role that nondemocratic values and their incongruence with democratic structure plays in the process of democratization.

Conceptually, both advocates and critics of the Asian Values Thesis are concerned exclusively with the problems of maintaining the stability of democratic political order by preventing its reversion to authoritarian rule. Consequently, they fail to consider the problems faced by transforming nondemocracies into democracies and deepening and expanding limited democracies into fully democracies. As widely known in the voluminous literature on the third wave of democratization, democratization is a multiphased phenomenon, and the stability of the democratic polity is not always the most coveted goal that democratic reformers pursue (Haerpfer et al. 2009; Huntington 1991; Karl 2005; McFaul 2002; Rose and Shin 2001; Shin 1994; Welzel 2009).

Theoretically, a democratic polity cannot achieve stability solely with adherence of its citizens to the cultural values that are considered intrinsic to its functioning or with the dissociation of the citizenry from nondemocratic values. Other competing values also play an important balancing role in promoting democratic development (Almond and Verba 1963;

Wildavsky 1993). For this reason, the congruence theory incorporates the two conflicting notions of congruence and disparities in specifying and prescribing a stable democratic political system.

While the cultural values most often associated with democracy sustain its institutions, competing cultural values keep those institutions in check. This is why Eckstein characterized a democratic culture as a culture of "balanced disparities." For the same reason, Gabriel Almond and Sidney Verba (1963) emphasize the role of a mixed and balanced culture, which consists of parochial, subject, and participant orientations in democratic development. Likewise, Aaron Wildavsky (1993) characterizes democracy as "a coalition of cultures" including those of hierarchism, individualism, and egalitarianism. Ignoring all the important contributions that various norms and values not normally associated with democracy can make to democratic politics, both proponents and opponents of the Asian Values Thesis have dismissed those values and norms as inimical to its development.

Moreover, in analyzing the relationship between culture and democracy, proponents and opponents of the thesis are alike in failing to note that, even in the world of democratic polities, an incongruence or a gap often develops between the level of democracy supplied by institutions and the level demanded by the citizenry (Inglehart and Welzel 2005; Mattes and Bratton 2007; Norris 2011; Rose and Shin 2001; Shin 2008). When demand outstrips supply, this form of democratic incongruence does not deter the process of democratization, as assumed in the Asian Values Thesis. Instead, it contributes to the process.

In the last decade, a new generation of researchers has put forth a new democratic supply and demand model, in which a democratic deficit or incongruence does not cause the breakdown of democratic rule. Instead, it supports the further democratization of limited democratic rule by bringing about institutional reform (Inglehart and Welzel 2005; Rose, Mishler, and Haerpfer 1998; Shin 2008; Welzel and Klingemann 2008). When democratic demand and supply are in congruence or in equilibrium at a low level, moreover, democracy is known to remain "broken-back" (Rose and Shin 2001). In the world of newly emerging democracies, therefore, democratic progress is more likely to take place when democratic structure and culture are more incongruent than congruent. The failure to consider the potentially positive role of such incongruence is another major limitation of the Asian Values Thesis as a cultural theory of democratic development.

Furthermore, Amartya Sen (1999) and Francis Fukuyama (1995b) have challenged the Asian Values Thesis's claim that the norms and values Confucius and other early Confucians advocated for the building of a harmonious community called *datong shehui* are uniquely Asian. These critics have pointed out that harmony, order, paternalism, reciprocity, and family values, which in the thesis have been promoted as uniquely Asian, are also valued in other parts of the world. Furthermore, they have argued that freedom and equality, the two core values of democracy, are universal values superseding country and race and that these liberal values are respected in all societies, regardless of the level of their culture and socioeconomic modernization.

To construct a sound empirical framework, it is first necessary to examine whether there are values and patterns of behavior that cut across the Asian countries and their people. One group of Asian Values Thesis critics, which includes Amartya Sen (1999) and William de Bary (1998a), points out that Asia is a vast continent with a great deal of diversity in languages, racial makeup, and religious beliefs. In religions alone, the region is the birthplace of Buddhism, Christianity, Taoism, Hinduism, Islam, and Shintoism. Even within the region of historically and culturally Confucian East Asia, these critics note more differences than similarities in cultural legacies and value orientations. In view of such diversity, they argue that there is no set of common values encompassing the entire continent or its subregion called East Asia.

Another group of critics does recognize the existence of values common throughout the entire region of Asia or East Asia (Emmerson 1995; Levine 2007; Mauzy 1997; M. Thompson 2001). Yet they argue that those values are not distinctively Asian or Confucian. The Confucian values stressing the importance of authority, consensus, harmony, and order, for example, are valued in the West and all other regions as well (Friedman 1994). On the basis of these observations, these critics of the Asian Values Thesis claim that there are no quintessentially Asian values that are uniquely and pervasively shared only among the entire population of Asia or East Asia and that therefore can be responsible for Asia's unique response to the third wave of democratization.

There are two serious limitations with these arguments put forth by critics of the Asian Values Thesis. First, these critiques fail to take into account that values are a multidimensional phenomenon consisting both of preference, which is a simple matter of desire, and priority, which goes past desire to demand (Inglehart 1977, 1997). Of these two dimensions, these critics examined the Asian Values Thesis exclusively from the perspective of citizens' value preferences and thus completely overlooked the prioritization of those preferences among the Confucian Asian population.

Second, the critics failed to recognize that how people prioritize their values varies considerably across different societies because this prioritization depends on what Abraham Maslow (1943) called the hierarchy of human needs, which, as discussed in Chapter 4, has its roots in the Confucian conception of human nature. As suggested in the following passage from Mencius (6A:15; see also 6A:12), people even within the same society prioritize their values differently: "He who is guided by the interests of the parts of his person that are of greater importance is a great man; he who is guided by the interests of the parts of his person that are of smaller importance is a small man."[3]

As Donald K. Emmerson (1995) correctly observes, there is, by and large, little difference across various regions in what people desire or prefer for the quality of their own life and their society's. Just as people in Confucian East Asia value order, peace, familism, freedom, and equality, so do Africans and Europeans. The priorities given to these values, however, vary considerably according to the cultural values into which people have been socialized (Schwartz 1992; van Deth and Scarbrough 1995; see also Dalton 2008; Inoguchi 2007; Nevitte 1996). They also vary a great deal according to the types of culture in which people live and the level of socioeconomic resources that they command individually and collectively (Inglehart 1977, 1997; Inglehart and Norris 2003; Inglehart and Welzel 2005). The differences in their value priorities motivate them to engage in different patterns of thinking and behavior.

In Chapter 1, I identified and highlighted some of these values and behavioral patterns that are associated with Confucianism, and the subsequent survey analyses found distinctive patterns of democratic conceptions. People in historically Confucian East Asia do not value the liberal democratic core value of freedom as much as their counterparts in the West do (Shin 1999, 61). Even compared to their peers in non-Confucian Southeast Asia, people in historically Confucian East Asia rank political freedom as less essential, while ranking economic welfare as a more essential component of democracy. These differences in value priorities do have significant implications for the building of democracy in culturally Confucian East Asia.

To date, both advocates and critics of the Asian Values Thesis have failed to understand the essential components of democratic culture and the role these components play in the process of democratization. Further

---

[3] According to Mencius (6A:13), moreover, people can avoid the act of "unthinking to the highest degree" only when the person gets his or her priorities right.

they have failed to understand the distinctive value orientations among the Confucian East Asian population and the impact of those orientations on the preferred type of democratic regime. Confucianism contains both pro-democratic values and authoritarian values, and the conflict between them should not be assumed to create instability; instead, it should be recognized that this conflict can "energize" and expand limited democracy into full democracy.

Theoretical Implications

In the literature on cultural democratization, there are three prominent sets of competing theories. A first set concerns the relative importance of early socialization and adult learning as an influence on mass orientations to democracy. Whereas socialization theories of political learning emphasize the importance of learning during an early period of childhood or adolescence, institutional learning theories emphasize adult relearning in response to changing circumstances regardless of early socialization (Mishler and Rose 2002).

A second set of competing theories concerns the direction of the relationship between cultural values and democratic politics (Muller and Seligson 1994). Cultural theories, such as the Asian Values Thesis, cast cultural values as an independent variable, with the dependent variable being the reactions that the publics of former authoritarian states have to the forces of democratization. Institutional learning theories, in contrast, cast the practices of democratic politics as the independent variable, with the dependent variable being the transformation of authoritarian cultural values into democratic ones (Anderson and Dodd 2005; Peffley and Rohrschneider 2003; Rohrschneider 1999).

A third, final pair of theories offers two conflicting views concerning the consequences of socioeconomic modernization on cultural change; the views differ in whether those consequences are negative or positive. Whereas modernization theories emphasize socioeconomic modernization's contribution to the liberalization and secularization of traditional authoritarian values (Inglehart and Welzel 2005), indigenization theories emphasize its contribution to the revival and strengthening of traditional values (Huntington 1996). In this section, I evaluate the competing claims of these theories based on this study's findings about Confucian East Asia.

In Confucian Asia, people are exposed to Confucianism as a way of life from early childhood. Their attachments formed during this early socialization may contrast sharply with their adult experience of democratic or authoritarian rule, which is measured by the type of regime in which they live. How do these two types of contrasting life experiences compare with each other as an influence shaping democratic support? It is necessary to address this question to evaluate the claims of the two competing theories of early socialization and institutional learning.

In orienting Confucian East Asians away from liberal democracy and toward nonliberal democracy, early exposure to the age-old tradition of paternalistic meritocracy is far more instrumental than how citizens assess the performance of their regime or how they understand democracy. Early exposure to Confucianism, however, matters far less significantly than the particular type of regime experienced during adulthood. Gender and age, which are most often used to measure early socialization, also matter much less than regime assessments and democratic knowledge. From these conflicting findings, it is difficult to determine whether it is early socialization or adult learning that matters more in the process of democratization taking place among individual citizens. What is clear from the findings, however, is that learning is a lifetime process integrating what was learned in the past with what is currently being learned (Mishler and Rose 2002).

In addition to shaping popular reactions to liberal and nonliberal democracy, the experience of democratic politics is found to affect how people react to Confucian legacies. In terms of all the Confucian political and social legacies I analyzed, upholders of Confucianism are far less prevalent in democratic than nondemocratic countries even when levels of their socioeconomic resources are controlled. Attachment to Confucianism is less prevalent in an old democracy than new democracies. The type of regime in which people in Confucian Asia live significantly affects their adherence to Confucian political and social ethics. In addition, the duration of democratic experience also affects their commitment to Confucianism significantly by reducing popular attachment to its legacies.

Institutional learning theory postulates that people are likely to become supporters of democracy after experiencing democratic politics. In contrast, cultural theory postulates that people are unlikely to support democracy as long as they remain attached to nondemocratic values such as paternalistic meritocracy. Obviously, there is a bidirectional relationship between culture and democratic politics; neither of these two competing theories offers a full and balanced account of the contours and dynamics of that relationship. In Confucian East Asia, therefore, the two theories have to be considered together to understand just how culture and regime experience affect each other in the process of democratization.

Do Confucian East Asians dissociate themselves from traditional Confucian ethical norms when exposed to a modern way of life, which brings with it greater income and education? Or does such exposure lead to greater "indigenization" of traditional Confucian values? As expected from neo-modernization theory, this analysis found that people in Confucian East Asia were less willing to abide by Confucian norms of hierarchal collectivism and paternalistic meritocracy if they had achieved a higher level of education. Greater affluence, in contrast, was positively associated with a greater willingness to abide by the norms of hierarchal collectivism and to conceive of democracy as a hybrid or nonliberal regime. With increased education, people in China and Vietnam become more supportive of nonliberal democracy and less supportive of liberal democracy. Yet, supporters of nonliberal democracy are more numerous in highly modernized Singapore than in China and Vietnam, the two least modernized countries in the region. Evidently, some indigenization of traditional Confucian values is taking place in response to the rapid modernization of society; however, not all Confucian values are finding equal favor in this Confucian revival (Shi forthcoming).

When considered together, these findings suggest that, in the context of Confucian East Asia, education and income – the two key components of socioeconomic modernization – have divergent consequences on the liberalization of traditional values and the democratization of political orientations. These findings also suggest that exposure to the same force of modernization entails different consequences in different countries in the region. In short, the indigenization and the liberalization of traditional Confucian ethics are both currently taking place in the region.

References

Ackerly, Brooke A. 2005. "Is Liberalism the Only Way Toward Democracy?" *Political Theory* 33:547–76.

Alagappa, Muthiah. 2004. *Civil Society and Political Change in Asia: Expanding and Contracting Democratic Space.* Stanford, CA: Stanford University Press.

Alesina, Alberto and Paola Giuliano. 2011. "Family Ties and Political Participation." *Journal of the European Economic Association* (published online).

Almond, Gabriel A. and Sidney Verba. 1963. *The Civic Culture: Political Attitudes and Democracy in Five Nations.* Princeton, NJ: Princeton University Press.

Ames, Roger T. and Henry Rosemont. 1998. *The Analects of Confucius: A Philosophical Translation.* New York: Random House.

Anderson, Leslie and Lawrence Dodd. 2005. *Learning Democracy: Citizen Engagement and Electoral Choice in Nicaragua, 1990–2001.* Chicago: University of Chicago Press.

Andrew, Frank, James Morgan, John Sonquist, and Laura Klein. 1973. *Multiple Classification Analysis.* Ann Arbor: Institute for Social Research, University of Michigan.

Asian Barometer. 2011. "ABS WAVE 3: Frequency Distribution Tables." Taipei: National Taiwan University.

Bachnik, Jane. 2007. "Tatemae/Honne." In *Blackwell Encyclopedia of Sociology,* edited by George Ritzer. London: Blackwell (published online).

Badescu, Gabriel and Eric Uslaner. 2003. *Social Capital and the Transition to Democracy.* London: Routledge.

Bai, Tongdong. 2008. "A Mencian Version of Limited Democracy." *Res Publica* 14:19–34.

Banfield, Edward C. 1958. *Moral Basis of a Backward Society.* Glencoe, IL: Free Press.

Barber, Benjamin R. 1984. *Strong Democracy: Participatory Politics for a New Age.* Berkeley: University of California Press.

Barnes, Samuel H. and Janos Simon. 1998. *The Postcommunist Citizen*. Budapest: Erasumus Foundation.

Barr, Michael D. 2000. *Lee Kuan Yew: The Beliefs behind the Man*. Washington, DC: Georgetown University Press.

Bauer, Joanne R. and Daniel A. Bell. (eds.). 1999. *The East Asian Challenge for Human Rights*. New York: Cambridge University Press.

Baviskar, Siddhartha and Mary Fran T. Malone. 2004. "What Democracy Means to Citizens – and Why It Matters." *European Review of Latin American and Caribbean Studies* 76:3–23.

Bell, Daniel A. 1996. "Democracy in Confucian Societies: The Challenge of Justification." In *Towards Illiberal Democracy in Pacific Asia*, edited by Daniel A. Bell, David Brown, Kanishka Jayasuriya, and David M. Jones. New York: MacMillan, 17–40.

———. 2006. *Beyond Liberal Democracy: Political Thinking for an East Asian Context*. Princeton, NJ: Princeton University Press.

———. (ed.). 2008a. *Confucian Political Ethics*. Princeton, NJ: Princeton University Press.

———. 2008b. *China's New Confucianism: Politics and Everyday Life in a Changing Society*. Princeton, NJ: Princeton University Press.

———. 2008c. "Being Confucian: Why Confucians Needn't Be Old, Serious and Conservative." *Government and Opposition* 43:111–29.

———. 2008d. "A Visit to a Confucian Academy." *Dissent*, September 22.

———. 2009a. "Confucianism in Chinese Academia." *China Beat*. Retrieved from http://thechinabeat.blogspot.com/2009/07/confucianism-in-chinese-academia.htm.

———. 2009b. "Toward Meritocratic Rule in China?: A Response to Professors Dallmayr, Li, and Tan." *Philosophy East and West* 59:554–60.

———. 2010. "Communitarianism." In *The Stanford Encyclopedia of Philosophy*, edited by Edward N. Zalta. Stanford, CA: Metaphysics Research Lab (online publication).

Bell, Daniel A., David Brown, Kanishka Jayasuriya, and David M. Jones. 1996. *Towards Illiberal Democracy in Pacific Asia*. New York: MacMillan.

Bell, Daniel A. and Chaibong Hahm. (eds.). 2003. *Confucianism for the Modern World*. New York: Cambridge University Press.

Bermeo, Nancy. 2003. *Ordinary People in Extraordinary Times: The Citizenry and the Breakdown of Democracy*. Princeton, NJ: Princeton University Press.

Berthrong, John. 1998. *Transformations of the Confucian Way*. Boulder, CO: Westview Press.

Blondel, Jean and Takashi Inoguchi. 2006. *Political Culture in Asia and Europe*. New York: Routledge.

Bobo, Lawrence and Frederick Licari. 1989. "Education and Political Tolerance." *Public Opinion Quarterly* 53:285–308.

Boix, Carles and Daniel N. Posner. 1998. "Social Capital: Explaining Its Origins and Effects on Government Performance." *British Journal of Political Science* 28:686–93.

Boix, Carles and Susan C. Stokes. 2003. "Endogenous Democratization." *World Politics* 55:517–49.

Booth, John and Mitchell Seligson. 2009. *The Legitimacy Puzzle in Latin America*. New York: Cambridge University Press.

Borgida, Eugene, Christopher Michael Federico, and John Lawrence Sullivan. (eds.). 2009. *The Political Psychology of Democratic Citizenship*. New York: Oxford University Press.

Bratton, Michael, Robert Mattes, and E. Gyimah-Boadi. 2005. *Public Opinion, Democracy, and Market Reform in Africa*. Cambridge: Cambridge University Press.

Brennan, Andrew and Ruiping Fan. 2007. "Autonomy and Interdependence: A Dialogue between Liberalism and Confucianism." *Journal of Social Philosophy* 38:511–35.

Bunce, Valerie. 2000. "Comparative Democratization: Big and Bounded Generalizations." *Comparative Political Studies* 33:703–34.

_____. 2003. "Rethinking Recent Democratization: Lessons from the Postcommunist Experience." *World Politics* 55:167–92.

Burnell, Peter J. and Peter Calvert. (eds.). 2004. *Civil Society in Democratization*. London: Routlege.

Camp, Roderic. (ed.). 2001. *Citizen Views of Democracy in Latin America*. Pittsburgh: University of Pittsburgh Press.

Canache, Damarys. 2006. "Measuring Variance and Complexity in Citizens' Understanding of Democracy." Presented at the LAPOP-UNDP Workshop: Candidate Indicators for the UNDP Democracy Support Index (DSI), Vanderbilt University.

Carothers, Thomas. 2002. "The End of the Transition Paradigm." *Journal of Democracy* 13:5–21.

Chambers, Simone and Will Kymlicka. 2001. *Alternative Conceptions of Civil Society*. Princeton, NJ: Princeton University Press.

Chan, Joseph. 1999. "A Confucian Perspective on Human Rights for Contemporary China." In *The East Asian Challenge for Human Rights*, edited by Joanne R. Bauer and Daniel A. Bell. New York: Cambridge University Press, 212–37.

_____. 2003. "Giving Priority to the Worse Off: A Confucian Perspective on Social Welfare." In *Confucianism for the Modern World*, edited by Daniel A. Bell and Chaibong Hahm. Princeton, NJ: Princeton University Press, 236–53.

_____. 2004. "Exploring the Non-Familial in Confucian Political Philosophy." In *The Politics of Affective Relations: East Asia and Beyond*, edited by Chaehak Hahm and Daniel A. Bell. Lanham, MD: Lexington Books, 61–74.

_____. 2007. "Democracy and Meritocracy: Toward a Confucian Perspective." *Journal of Chinese Philosophy* 34:179–93.

_____. 2008a. "Confucian Attitudes toward Ethical Pluralism." In *Confucian Political Ethics*, edited by Daniel A. Bell. Princeton, NJ: Princeton University Press, 113–38.

_____. 2008b. "Territorial Boundaries and Confucianism." In *Confucian Political Ethics*, edited by Daniel A. Bell. Princeton, NJ: Princeton University Press, 61–84.

Chan, Wing-tsit. (trans.). 1963. *A Sourcebook in Chinese Philosophy*. Princeton, NJ: Princeton University Press.

Chang, Yu-tzung and Yun-han Chu. 2007. "Traditionalism, Political Learning and Conceptions of Democracy in East Asia." In *Asian Barometer Working Paper Series No. 39*. Taipei: National Taiwan University.

Chang, Yu-tzung, Yun-han Chu, and Chong-Min Park. 2007. "Authoritarian Nostalgia in Asia." *Journal of Democracy* 18:66–80.

Chang, Yu-Tzung, Yun-han Chu, and Frank Tsai. 2005. "Confucianism and Democratic Values in Three Chinese Societies." *Issues & Studies* 41:1–33.

Chen, Albert H. Y. 2007. "Is Confucianism Compatible with Liberal Constitutional Democracy?" *Journal of Chinese Philosophy* 34:195–216.

Cheng, Chung-ying. 2002. "Confucianism: Twentieth Century." In *Encyclopedia of Chinese Philosophy*, edited by Antonio S. Cua. London: Routledge, 160–72.

Cheng, Stephen K. K. 1990. "Understanding the Culture and Behavior of East Asians: A Confucian Perspective." *Australian and New Zealand Journal of Psychiatry* 24:510–15.

Cheng, Tun-jen. 2003. "Political Institutions of the Malaise of East Asian New Democracies." *Journal of East Asian Studies* 3:1–41.

Cheung, Tak Sing, Hoi Man Chan, Kin Man Chan, Ambrose Y.C. King, Chi Yue Chiu, and Chung Fang Yang. 2006. "How Confucian are Contemporary Chinese? Construction of an Ideal Type and its Application to Three Chinese Communities." *European Journal of East Asian Studies* 5:157–80.

Cho, Hein. 1997. "The Historical Origin of Civil Society in Korea." *Korea Journal* 37:24–41.

Chu, Yun-han, Larry Diamond, Andrew Nathan, and Doh C. Shin. (eds.). 2008. *How East Asians View Democracy*. New York: Columbia University Press.

Chu, Yun-han and Min-hua Huang. 2010. "Solving an Asian Puzzle," *Journal of Democracy* 21:114–21.

Cima, Ronald J. 1987. *Vietnam: A Country Study*. Washington, DC: U.S. Government Printing Office.

Clark, Elizabeth Spiro. 2000. "Why Elections Matter." *Wilson Quarterly* 23:27–40.

Cohen, Jean L. and Andrew Arato. 1992. *Civil Society and Political Theory*. Cambridge, MA: MIT Press.

Collcutt, Martin. 1991. "The Legacy of Confucianism in Japan." In *The East Asian Region: Confucian Heritage and Its Modern Adaptation*, edited by Gilbert Rozman. Princeton, NJ: Princeton University Press, 111–54.

Collier, David and Robert Adcock 1999. "Democracy and Dichotomies: Pragmatic Approaches to Choices about Concept," *Annual Review of Political Science* 2:537–65.

Collier, David and Steven Levitsky. 1997. "Democracy with Adjectives: Conceptual Innovation in Comparative Research." *World Politics* 49:430–51.

Collier, Ruth Berins. 1999. *Paths toward Democracy: The Working Class and Elites in Western Europe and South America*. New York: Cambridge University Press.

Collins, Michael. 2008. "China's Confucius and Western Democracy." *Contemporary Review* 290:161–72.

Compton, Robert W. 2000. *East Asian Democratization: Impact of Globalization, Culture, and Economy*. Westport, CT: Praeger.

Confucius. 1979. *The Analects.* Translated by D. C. Lau. New York: Penguin Books.

Converse, Philip E. 1964. "The Nature of Belief Systems in Mass Publics." In *Ideology and Discontent*, edited by David Apter. New York: Free Press, 206–71.

———. 1969. "Of Time and Partisan Stability." *Comparative Political Studies* 2:139–71.

Coppedge, Michael, Angel Alvareza, and Claudia Maldonado. 2008. "Two Persistent Dimensions of Democracy: Contestation and Inclusiveness." *Journal of Politics* 70:632–47.

Corby, Denis. 2011, July 25. "Russian Winter and Arab Spring," *New York Times* Online.

Coughlin, Richard M. and Charles Lockhart. 1988. "Grid-Group Theory and Political Ideology," *Journal of Theoretical Politics* 10:33–58.

Creel, H. G. 1949. *Confucius and the Chinese Way.* New York: Harper and Brothers.

Croissant, Aurel. 2004. "From Transition to Defective Democracy: Mapping Asian Democratization." *Democratization* 11:156–78.

Crowell, Todd. 2005, November 16. "The Confucian Renaissance." *Asia Times Online*, Hong Kong.

Dahl, Robert A. 1971. *Polyarchy: Participation and Opposition.* New Haven, CT: Yale University Press.

———. 1982. *Dilemmas of Pluralist Democracy.* New Haven, CT: Yale University Press.

———. 1989. *Democracy and Its Critics.* New Haven, CT: Yale University Press.

———. 1997. "Development and Democratic Culture." In *Consolidating the Third Wave Democracies: Regional Challenges*, edited by Larry Diamond, Marc F. Plattner, Yun-han Chu, and Hung-mao Tien. Baltimore: Johns Hopkins University Press, 34–9.

———. 1998. *On Democracy.* New Haven, CT: Yale University Press.

Dahrendorf, Ralf. 1990. *Reflections on the Revolution in Europe.* New York: Times Books.

Dallmayr, Fred. 2004. "Confucianism and the Public Sphere: Five Relationships plus One?" In *The Politics of Affective Relations: East Asia and Beyond*, edited by Chae-hak Hahm and Daniel A. Bell. Lanham, MD: Lexington Books, 41–60.

———. 2009. "Exiting Liberal Democracy: Bell and Confucian Thought." *Philosophy East and West* 59:524–30.

Dalton, Russell. 1999. "Political Support in Advanced Industrial Democracies." In *Critical Citizens*, edited by Pippa Norris. New York: Oxford University Press, 57–78.

———. 2007. *The Good Citizen: How a Younger Generation is Reshaping American Politics.* Washington, DC: CQ Press.

———. 2008. *Citizen Politics: Public Opinion and Political Parties in Advanced Industrial Democracies.* Washington, DC: Congressional Quarterly Press.

Dalton, Russell and Nhu-Ngoc T. Ong. 2006. "Authority Orientations and Democratic Attitudes: A Test of the 'Asian Values' Hypothesis." In *Citizens,*

Democracy and Markets around the Pacific Rim, edited by Russell Dalton and Doh Chull Shin. New York: Oxford University Press, 97–112.

Dalton, Russell and Doh C. Shin. (eds.). 2006. *Citizens, Democracy and Markets around the Pacific Rim*. New York: Oxford University Press.

Dalton, Russell, Doh C. Shin, and Willy Jou. 2007. "Understanding Democracy: Data from Unlikely Places." *Journal of Democracy* 18:142–56.

Dawson, Miles Menander. 1942. *The Basic Teachings of Confucius*. New York: New Home Library.

———. 2005. *The Ethics of Confucius*. New York: Cosmos.

Dawson, Richard E. and Kenneth Prewitt. 1969. *Political Socialization*. Boston: Little, Brown, and Co.

de Bary, Wm. Theodore. 1991. *The Trouble with Confucianism*. Cambridge, MA: Harvard University Press.

———. 1998a. *Asian Values and Human Rights: A Confucian Communitarian Perspective*. Cambridge, MA: Harvard University Press.

———. 1998b. "Confucianism and Human Rights in China," In *Democracy in Asia*, edited by Marc Plattner and Larry Diamond. Baltimore: Johns Hopkins University Press, 42–54.

de Bary, Wm. Theodore and Weiming Tu. 1998. *Confucianism and Human Rights*. New York: Columbia University Press.

de Tocqueville, Alexis. 2000 [1835–1840]. *Democracy in America*. Chicago: University of Chicago Press.

Delli Carpini, Michael. 2009. "The Psychology of Civic Learning." In *The Political Psychology of Democratic Citizenship*, edited by Eugene Borgida, Christopher M. Federico, and John L. Sullivan. New York: Oxford University Press, 23–52.

Dent, Christopher M. 2008. *East Asian Regionalism*. London: Routledge.

Deuchler, Martina. 1992. *The Confucian Transformation of Korea: A Study of Society and Ideology*. Cambridge, MA: Council on East Asian Studies, Harvard University.

———. 2002. "The Practice of Confucianism: Ritual and Order in Choson Dynasty," In *Rethinking Confucianism: Past and Present in China, Japan, Korea, and Vietnam*, edited by Benjamin A. Elman, John B. Duncan, and Herman Ooms. Los Angeles: UCLA Asia Institute, 292–334.

Diamond, Larry. 1994. "Rethinking Civil Society: Toward Democratic Consolidation." *Journal of Democracy* 5:4–17.

———. 1997. "Cultivating Democratic Citizenship: Education for a New Century of Democracy in the Americas." *Social Studies* 88:244–51.

———. 1999. *Developing Democracy: Toward Consolidation*. Baltimore: Johns Hopkins University Press.

———. 2001. "How People View Democracy: Findings from Public Opinion Surveys in Four Regions." Presented in Stanford Seminar on Democratization, Stanford University.

———. 2008a. *The Spirit of Democracy: The Struggle to Build Free Societies throughout the World*. New York: Times Books.

———. 2008b. "Democratic Rollback: The Resurgence of the Predatory State." *Foreign Affairs* 87:36–48.

———. 2011. "East Asia and the Receding Tide of the Third Wave of Democracy." Presented at an international Conference on "Democracy in East Asia and Taiwan in Global Perspective" held in National Taiwan University, Taiwan on August 24–25.

Doan, Phan Dai. 2002. "Some Distinctive Features of Confucianism in Vietnam." In *Confucianism in Vietnam*. Ho Chi Minh City: Vietnam National University and Ho Chi Minh City Publishing House, 66–9.

Doan, Tran Van. 2002. "The Ideological Essence of Vietnamese Confucianism." In *Confucianism in Vietnam*. Ho Chi Minh City: Vietnam National University and Ho Chi Minh City Publishing House, 75–96.

Douglas, Mary. 1978. *Cultural Bias* (occasional paper). London: Royal Anthropological Institute.

———. 1999. "Four Cultures: The Evolution of a Parsimonious Model." *GeoJournal* 47:411–15.

Douglas, Mary and Steven Ney. 1998. *Missing Persons: A Critique of Missing Persons*. Berkeley: University of California Press.

Downs, Anthony. 1957. *An Economic Theory of Democracy*. New York: Addison Wesley.

Duong, Dung N. 2003. "An Exploration of Vietnam Confucian Spirituality: The Idea of the University of Three Teaching." On *Confucian Spirituality* vol. 2, edited by Tu Weiming and Mary Evelyn Tucker. New York: Crossroad Publishing, 289–319.

Dupont, Alan. 1996. "Is There An Asian Way?" *Survival* 38:13–33.

Easton, David. 1965. *A System Analysis of Political Life*. New York: Wiley and Sons.

———. 1975. "A Reassessment of the Concept of Political Support." *British Journal of Political Science* 5:435–57.

Easton, David and Jack Dennis. 1969. *Children in the Political System: Origins of Political Legitimacy*. New York: McGraw-Hill.

Ebrey, Patricia. 1991. "The Chinese Family and the Spread of Confucian Values." In *The East Asian Region: Confucian Heritage and Its Modern Adaptation*, edited by Gilbert Rozman. Princeton, NJ: Princeton University Press, 45–83.

Eckstein, Harry. 1966. *A Theory of Stable Democracy*. Princeton, NJ: Princeton University Press.

Eckstein, Harry, Frediric Fleron, Erik Hoffmann, and William Reisinger. 1998. *Can Democracy Take Root in Post-Soviet Russia?* New York: Rowman & Littlefield.

Economist. 2007. "Confucius Makes a Comeback," May 19.

Economist Intelligence Unit. 2010, March 15. "Democracy Index 2010 Democracy in Retreat." Retrieved from http://graphics.eiu.com/PDF/Democracy_Index_2010_web.pdf.

Edwards, Bob, Michael W. Foley, and Mario Diani. 2001. *Beyond Tocqueville: Civil Society and the Social Capital Debate in Comparative Perspective*. Boston: Tufts University Press.

Ellis, Richard and Michael Thompson. (eds.). 1997. *Culture Matters: Essays in Honor of Aaron Wildavsky*. Boulder, CO: Westview Press.

Elman, Benjamin A. 2002. "Introduction." In *Rethinking Confucianism: Past and Present in China, Japan, Korea, and Vietnam*, edited by Benjamin A. Elman, John B. Duncan, and Herman Ooms. Los Angeles: UCLA Asia Institute, 1–29.

Emmerson, Donald K. 1995. "Singapore and the 'Asian Values' Debate." *Journal of Democracy* 6:95–105.

Englehart, Neil A. 2000. "Rights and Culture in the Asian Values Argument: The Rise and Fall of Confucian Ethics in Singapore." *Human Rights Quarterly* 22:548–68.

Evans, Geoffrey and Stephen Whitefield. 1995. "The Politics and Economics of Democratic Commitment: Support for Democracy in Transition Societies." *British Journal of Political Science* 25:485–514.

Evans, Peter B. 1995. *Embedded Autonomy*. Princeton, NJ: Princeton University Press.

Fails, Matthew and Heather Pierce. 2010. "Changing Mass Attitudes and Democratic Deepening." *Political Research Quarterly* 63:174–89.

Fan, Maureen. 2007. "Confucius Making a Comeback in Money-Driven China." *Washington Post*, July 24.

Fan, Ruiping. 2004. "Is a Confucian Family-Oriented Civil Society Possible?" In *The Politics of Affective Relations: East Asia and Beyond*, edited by Chae-hak Hahm and Daniel A. Bell. Lanham, MD: Lexington Books, 75–96.

Fetzer, Joel S. and J. Christopher Soper. 2007. "The Effect of Confucian Values on Support for Democracy and Human Rights in Taiwan." *Taiwan Journal of Democracy* 3:143–54.

Fingarette, Herbert. 1972. *Confucius – the Secular as Sacred*. New York: Harper Torchbook.

———. 1983. "The Music of Humanity in the Conversations of Confucius." *Journal of Chinese Philosophy* 10:331–56.

Fishkin, James S. 2009. *When the People Speak: Deliberative Democracy and Public Consultation*. New York: Oxford University Press.

Fox, Russell Arben. 1997. "Confucian and Communitarian Responses to Liberal Democracy." *Review of Politics* 59:561–92.

Freedom House. 2010. "Freedom in the World." Retrieved from http://www.freedomhouse.org/template.cfm?page=15.

———. 2011. "Freedom of Press 2010 Survey Release." Retrieved on May 3, 2011, from http://freedomhouse.org/template.cfm?page=668.

Freeman, Michael. 1996. "Human Rights, Democracy and 'Asian Values.'" *Pacific Review* 9:352–66.

Friedman, Edward. 1994. "Democratization: Generalizing East Asian Experiences." In *The Politics of Democratization: Generalizing East Asian Experiences*, edited by Edward Friedman. Boulder, CO: Westview Press, 19–60.

Fuchs, Dieter. 1999. "The Democratic Culture of United Germany." In *Critical Citizens*, edited by Pippa Norris. New York: Oxford University Press, 123–45.

Fuchs, Dieter, Giovanna Guidorossi, and Palle Svensson. 1995. "Support for the Democratic System." In *Citizens and the State*, edited by Hans-Dieter Klingemann and Dieter Fuchs. New York: Oxford University Press, 323–53.

Fuchs, Dieter and Edeltraud Roller. 2006. "Learned Democracy? Support of Democracy in Central and Eastern Europe." *International Journal of Sociology* 36:70–96.

Fukuyama, Francis. 1995a. *Trust: The Social Virtues and the Creation of Prosperity.* New York: Free Press.

———. 1995b. "Confucianism and Democracy," *Journal of Democracy* 6:20–33.

———. 2011. "The Historical Pattern of Political Development in East Asia." Presented at an international Conference on "Democracy in East Asia and Taiwan in Global Perspective" held in National Taiwan University, Taiwan on August 24-25.

Galston, William A. 2002. *Liberal Pluralism: The Implications of Value Pluralism for Political Theory and Practice.* New York: Cambridge University Press.

Gastil, John. 1992. "Why We Believe in Democracy: Testing Theories of Attitude Functions and Democracy." *Journal of Applied Social Psychology* 22:423–40.

Geddes, Barbara. 1999. "What Do We Know about Democratization after Twenty Years?" *Annual Review of Political Science* 2:115–44.

Gibson, James L. 2001. "Social Networks, Civil Society, and the Prospects for Consolidating Russia's Democratic Transition." *American Journal of Political Science* 45:51–68.

———. 2006. "Enigmas of Intolerance: Fifty Years after Stouffer's Communism, Conformity, and Civil Liberties." *Perspectives on Politics* 4:21–34.

Gibson, James L. and Amanda Gouws. 2005. *Overcoming Intolerance in South Africa: Experiments in Democratic Persuasion.* New York: Cambridge University Press.

Gold, Tom. 1996. "Civil Society in Taiwan: Confucian Dimension." In *Confucian Traditions in East Asian Modernity*, edited by Tu Weiming. Cambridge, MA: Harvard University Press, 244–58.

Greenstadt, Gunnar. 1999. "A Political Cultural Map of Europe: A Survey Approach." *GeoJournal* 47:463–75.

Griffith, Ernest S., John Plamenatz, and J. Roland Pennock. 1956. "Cultural Prerequisites to a Successfully Functioning Democracy: A Symposium." *American Political Science Review* 50:101–37.

Habermas, Jürgen. 1989. *The Structural Transformation of the Public Sphere: An Inquiry into a Category of Bourgeois Society.* Translated by Thomas Burger. Cambridge, MA: MIT Press.

Haboush, Jahyun Kim. 1991. "The Confucianization of Korean Society." In *The East Asian Region: Confucian Heritage and Its Modern Adaptation*, edited by Gilbert Rozman. Princeton, NJ: Princeton University Press, 84–110.

———. 2002. "Gender and the Politics of Language in Chosun Korea." In *Rethinking Confucianism: Past and Present in China, Japan, Korea, and Vietnam*, edited by Benjamin A. Elman, John B. Duncan, and Herman Ooms. Los Angeles: UCLA Asia Institute, 220–57.

Haerpfer, Christian W., Patrick Bernhagen, Ronald F. Inglehart, and Christian Welzel. (eds.). 2009. *Democratization.* New York: Oxford University Press.

Hahm, Chae-hak and Daniel A. Bell. (eds.). 2004. *The Politics of Affective Relations: East Asia and Beyond.* Lanham, MD: Lexington Books.

Hahm, Chaibong. 2001. "Why Asia Values?" *Korea Journal* 41:265–74.

_____. 2004. "The Ironies of Confucianism." *Journal of Democracy* 15:93–107.

Hahn, Jeffrey. 1991. "Continuity and Change in Russian Political Culture." *British Journal of Political Science* 21:393–421.

Hall, David L. and Roger T. Ames. 1987. *Thinking through Confucius*. Albany: State University of New York Press.

_____. 1995. *Thinking through the Narratives of Chinese and Western Cultures*. Albany: State University of New York Press.

_____. 1999. *The Democracy of the Dead: Dewey, Confucius, and the Hope for Democracy in China*. Chicago: Open Court.

_____. 2003. "A Pragmatist Understanding of Confucian Democracy." In *Confucianism for the Modern World*, edited by Daniel A. Bell and Chaibong Hahm. New York: Cambridge University Press, 124–60.

Halman, Loek, Ronald Inglehart, Jaime Diez-Medrano, Ruud Luijkx, Alejandro Moreno, and Miguel Basanez. 2007. *Changing Values and Beliefs in 85 Countries: Trends from the Values Surveys from 1981 to 2004*. Leiden: Brill.

He, Baogang. 2010. "Four Models of the Relationship between Confucianism and Democracy." *Journal of Chinese Philosophy* 37:18–33.

Heath, Anthony, Stephen Fisher, and Shawna Smith. 2005. "The Globalization of Public Opinion Research." *Annual Review of Political Science* 8:297–333.

Herr, Ranjoo Seodu. 2010. "Confucian Democracy and Equality." *Asian Philosophy* 20:261–82.

Hira, Anil. 2007. *An East Asian Model for Latin America*. New York: Ashgate.

Hiroshi, Watanabe. 1996. "'They are the Same as the Ancient Three Dynasties': The West as Seen through Confucian Eyes in Nineteenth Century Japan." In *Confucian Traditions in East Asian Modernity: Moral Education and Economic Culture in Japan and the Four Mini-Dragons*, edited by Tu Weiming. Cambridge, MA: Harvard University Press. 119–31.

Ho, Norman. 2009. "Unlikely Bedfellows? Confucius, the CCP, and the Resurgence of Guoxue." *Harvard International Review* 31:28–32.

Hofferbert, Richard I. and Hans–Dieter Klingemann. 1999. "Remembering the Bad Old Days: Human Rights, Economic Conditions, and Democratic Performance in Transitional Regimes." *European Journal of Political Research* 36:155–74.

Hong, Gui-Young. 2004. "Emotions in a Culturally Constituted Relational World." *Culture and Psychology* 1:33–58.

Hood, Steven J. 1998. "The Myth of Asian-Style Democracy." *Asian Survey* 38:853–66.

Hooghe, Marc and Dietlind Stolle. 2003. *Generating Social Capital: Civil Society and Institutions in Comparative Perspective*. New York: Palgrave Macmillan.

Howard, Marc Morjé. 2003. *The Weakness of Civil Society in Post-Communist Europe*. New York: Cambridge University Press.

Hsiung, James C. 1986. *Human Rights in East Asia: A Cultural Perspective*. New York: Pergamon House.

Hsu, Francis L. K. 1998. "Confucianism in Comparative Context." In *Confucianism and the Family*, edited by Walter H. Slote and George A. De Vos. Albany: State University of New York Press, 53–71.

Hsu, Leonard Shihlien. 1975. *The Political Philosophy of Confucianism: An Interpretation of the Social and Political Ideas of Confucius, His Forerunners, and His Early Disciples*. London: Curzon Press.

Hu, Shaohua. 1997. "Confucianism and Western Democracy." *Journal of Contemporary China* 6:347–63.

Hu, Weixi. 2007. "On Confucian Communitarianism." *Frontiers of Philosophy in China* 2:475–87.

Huang, Chun-Chieh. 1997. "A Confucian Critique of Samuel P. Huntington's *Clash of Civilizations*." *East Asia* 16:147–56.

Huber, Evelyne, Dietrich Rueschemeyer, and John D. Stephens. 1997. "The Paradoxes of Contemporary Democracy: Formal, Participatory, and Social Dimensions." *Comparative Politics* 29:323–42.

Huntington, Samuel P. 1991. *The Third Wave: Democratization in the Late Twentieth Century*. Norman: University of Oklahoma Press.

———. 1996. *The Clash of Civilizations and the Remaking of World Order*. New York: Touchstone.

Huy, Nguyen Ngoc. 1998. "The Confucian Incursion into Vietnam." In *Confucianism and the Family*, edited by Walter H. Slote and George A. De Vos. Albany: State University of New York Press, 91–103.

Hwang, Kwang-Kuo. 1998. "Two Moralities: Reinterpreting the Findings of Empirical Research on Moral Reasoning in Taiwan." *Asian Journal of Social Psychology* 1:211–38.

———. 2001. "The Deep Structure of Confucianism: A Social Psychological Approach." *Asian Philosophy* 11:179–204.

Im, Hyug Baeg. 2004. "Faltering Democratic Consolidation in South Korea: Democracy at the End of the 'Three Kims' Era." *Democratization* 11:179–98.

Inglehart, Ronald. 1977. *The Silent Revolution: Changing Values and Political Styles among Western Public*. Princeton, NJ: Princeton University Press.

———. 1997. *Modernization and Postmodernization*. Princeton, NJ: Princeton University Press.

Inglehart, Ronald and Pippa Norris. 2003. *Rising Tide: Gender Equality and Cultural Change around the World*. New York: Cambridge University Press.

Inglehart, Ronald and Christian Welzel. 2005. *Modernization, Cultural Change, and Democracy*. New York: Cambridge University Press.

Inoguchi, Takashi. 2007. "Clash of Values across Civilizations." In *The Oxford Handbook of Political Behavior*, edited by Russell Dalton and Hans-Dieter Klingemann. New York: Oxford University Press, 240–58.

Izvorski, Ivailo. 2010. "Why Has Developing East Asia Led the Global Economic Recovery?" Retrieved from http://blogs.worldbank.org.

Jackman, Robert W. and Ross A. Miller. 1998. "Social Capital and Politics." *Annual Review of Political Science* 1:47–73.

Johnson, Chalmers A. 1982. *MITI and the Japanese Miracle: The Growth of Industrial Policy, 1925–1975*. Stanford, CA: Stanford University Press.

Jowitt, Kenneth. 1992. *New World Disorder: The Leninist Extinction*. Berkeley: University of California Press.

Kang, Jung In. 1999. "Confucianism and Democracy in East Asia: A Critique of Samuel P. Huntington's Third Wave." *Korea Journal* 39:315–37.

Kang, Nam-Soon. 2004. "Confucian Familism and Its Social/Religious Embodiment in Christianity: Reconsidering the Family Discourse from a Feminist Perspective." *Asian Journal of Theology* 18:168–89.

Kang, Xiaoguang. 2006. "Confucianization: A Future in the Tradition." *Social Research* 73:77–120.

Karatnycky, Adrian and Peter Ackerman. 2005. *How Freedom is Won: From Civic Resistance to Durable Democracy*. New York: Freedom House.

Karl, Terry L. 2000. "Electoralism: Why Elections Are Not Democracy." In *The International Encyclopedia of Elections*, edited by Richard Rose. Washington, DC: CQ Press, 95–6.

———. 2005. *From Democracy to Democratization and Back: Before Transitions from Authoritarian Rule*. Center for Democracy, Development, and the Rule of Law, Working Paper No. 45. Stanford, CA: Stanford University.

Kaufmann, Daniel, Aart Kraay, and Massimo Mastruzzi. 2007. *Governance Matters 2007: Worldwide Governance Indicators for 1996–2006*. Washington, DC: World Bank Institute.

Keane, John. 1999. *Civil Society: Old Images, New Visions*. Stanford, CA: Stanford University Press.

Kim, Choong-Ryeol. 2010. "Is the 21st Century the Era of the East?: On How to Cope with the Major Proposition of the New Century." *Procedia-Social and Behavioral Sciences* 2:7181–4.

Kim, Dae Jung. 1994. "Is Culture Destiny? The Myth of Asia's Anti-Democratic Values." *Foreign Affairs* 73:189–94.

Kim, So Young. 2010. "Do Asian Values Exist? Empirical Tests of the Four Dimensions of Asian Values." *Journal of East Asian Studies* 10:315–44.

Kim, Sungmoon. 2008. "Filiality, Compassion, and Confucian Democracy." *Asian Philosophy* 18:279–98.

———. 2010. "Confucian Citizenship: Against Two Greek Models." *Journal of Chinese Philosophy* 37:438–56.

———. 2011. "The Virtue of Incivility: Confucian Communitarianism beyond Docility." *Philosophy & Social Criticism* 37:25–48.

Kim, Sunhyuk. 2000. *The Politics of Democratization in Korea: The Role of Civil Society*. Pittsburgh: University of Pittsburgh Press.

Kim, Terri. 2009. "Confucianism, Modernities and Knowledge: China, South Korea and Japan." In *International Handbook of Comparative Education*, edited by Robert Cowen and Andreas M. Kazamias. Dordrecht: Springer, 857–72.

Kim, Yung-Myung. 1997. "'Asian-Style Democracy': A Critique from East Asia." *Asian Survey* 37:1119–34.

King, Ambrose Y. C. 1996. "State Confucianism and its Transformation." In *Confucian Traditions in East Asian Modernity*, edited by Tu Weiming. Cambridge MA: Harvard University Press, 228–43.

Klingemann, Hans-Dieter. 1999. "Mapping Political Support in the 1990s: A Global Analysis." In *Critical Citizens*, edited by Pippa Norris. New York: Oxford University Press, 31–56.

Koh, Byong-Ik. 1996. "Confucianism in Contemporary Korea." In *Confucian Traditions in East Asian Modernity*, edited by Tu Weiming. New York: Cambridge University Press, 191–201.

Kornberg, Allan and Harold D. Clarke. 1983. *Political Support in Canada: The Crisis Years*. Durham, NC: Duke University Press.

Kumar, Krishan. 1993. "Civil Society: An Inquiry into the Usefulness of an Historical Term." *British Journal of Sociology* 44:375–95.

Kuo, Eddie C. Y. 1996. "Confucianism as Political Discourse in Singapore." In *Confucian Traditions in East Asian Modernity: Moral Education and Economic Culture in Japan and the Four Mini-Dragons*, edited by Tu Weiming. Cambridge, MA: Harvard University Press, 294–309.

Lagos, Marta. 2001. "Between Stability and Crisis in Latin America." *Journal of Democracy* 12:137–45.

Lam, Joy. 2008. *China's Revival of Confucianism*. Los Angeles: U.S.–China Institute, University of Southern California.

Langdon, Kenneth P. 1969. *Political Socialization*. New York: Oxford University Press.

Lee, Jong-Rong and Michael Hsiao. 2010. "Familism, Social Capital, and Civic Culture: A Multifaceted Test of Survey Data in Eleven Asian Societies." Presented at AsiaBarometer Workshop, Tokyo, December 19.

Lee, Kuan Yew. 1998. *The Singapore Story: Memoirs of Lee Kuan Yew*. Singapore: Prentice Hall.

Lee, Seung-Hwan. 2001. "'Asian Values' and Confucian Discourse." *Korea Journal* 41:198–212.

Lee, Teng-hui. 2006. "Confucian Democracy: Modernization, Culture, and the State in East Asia." *Harvard International Review* 21:16–18.

Lee, Thomas H. C. 2000. *Education in Traditional China: A History*. Leiden: Brill.

Levine, Stephen. 2007. "Asian Values and the Asia Pacific Community: Shared Interests and Common Concerns." *Politics and Policy* 35:102–35.

Lewis, J. David and Andrew Weigert. 1985. "Trust as a Social Reality." *Social Forces* 63:967–85.

Li, Chenyang. 1997. "Confucian Value and Democratic Value." *Journal of Value Inquiry* 31:183–93.

———. 1999. *The Tao Encounters the West: Explorations in Comparative Philosophy*. Albany: State University of New York Press.

———. 2006. "The Confucian Ideal of Harmony." *Philosophy East and West* 56:583–603.

———. 2008a. "The Confucian Concept of Ren and the Feminist Ethics of Care: A Comparative Study." In *Confucian Political Ethics*, edited by Daniel A. Bell. Princeton, NJ: Princeton University Press, 175–97.

———. 2008b. "The Philosophy of Harmony in Classical Confucianism." *Philosophy Compass* 3:423–35.

———. 2009. "Where Does Confucian Virtuous Leadership Stand?" *Philosophy East and West* 59:531–6.

Lijphart 1999. *Patterns of Democracy: Government Forms and Performance in Thirty-Six Countries*. New Haven, CT: Yale University Press.

Lingle, Christopher. 1997. *The Rise and Decline of the Asian Century: False Starts on the Path to the Global Millennium.* London: Ashgate Publishing.

Linz, Juan J. 1990. "Transitions to Democracy." *Washington Quarterly* 13:143–62.

Linz, Juan J. and Alfred Stepan. 1996. *Problems of Democratic Transition and Consolidation: Southern Europe, South America, and Post-Communist Europe.* Baltimore: Johns Hopkins University Press.

Lipset, Seymour Martin. 1959. "Some Social Requisites of Democracy: Economic Development and Political Legitimacy." *American Political Science Review* 53:69–105.

Liu, Shu-Hsien. 2007. "Democratic Ideal and Practice: A Critical Reflection." *Journal of Chinese Philosophy* 34:257–75.

Lockhart, Charles. 2001. "Using Grid-Group Theory to Explain Distinctive Japanese Political Institutions." *East Asia* 19:51–83.

Lomasky, Loren E. 2002. "Classical Liberalism and Civil Society." In *Alternative Conceptions of Civil Society*, edited by Simone Chambers and Will Kymlicka. Princeton, NJ: Princeton University Press, 50–69.

Lu, Zhaolu. 2001. "Fiduciary Society and Confucian Theory of Xin – on Tu Wei-Ming's Fiduciarity Proposal." *Asian Philosophy* 11:85–101.

MacIntyre, Alasdair. 1984. *After Virtue: A Study in Moral Theory.* Notre Dame, IN: University of Notre Dame Press.

Madsen, Richard. 2002. "Confucian Conceptions of Civil Society." In *Alternative Conceptions of Civil Society*, edited by Simone Chambers and Will Kymlicka. Princeton, NJ: Princeton University Press, 190–205.

———. 2008. "Conceptions of Civil Society." In *Confucian Political Ethics*, edited by Daniel A. Bell. Princeton, NJ: Princeton University Press, 3–19.

Mahbubani, Kishore. 1995. "The Pacific Way." *Foreign Affairs* 74:100–11.

Maslow, Abraham H. 1943. *Motivation and Personality.* New York: Harper.

Mattes, Robert. 2007. "Public Opinion Research in Emerging Democracies." In *The Sage Handbook of Public Opinion Research*, edited by Wolfgang Donsbach and Michael W. Traugott. London: Sage Publications, 113–22.

Mattes, Robert and Michael Bratton. 2007. "Learning about Democracy in Africa: Awareness, Performance, and Experience." *American Journal of Political Science* 51:192–217.

Mauzy, Diane K. 1997. "The Human Rights and 'Asian Values' Debate in Southeast Asia: Trying to Clarify the Key Issues." *Pacific Review* 10:210–36.

McClosky, Herbert and John Zaller. 1984. *The American Ethos: Public Attitudes toward Capitalism and Democracy.* Cambridge, MA: Harvard University Press.

McDonough, Peter, Samuel Henry Barnes, and Antonio López Pina. 1998. *The Cultural Dynamics of Democratization in Spain.* Ithaca, NY: Cornell University Press.

McFaul, Michael. 2002. "The Fourth Wave of Democracy and Dictatorship: Noncooperative Transitions in the Postcommunist World." *World Politics* 54:212–44.

McIntosh, Mary and Martha Abele. 1993. "The Meaning of Democracy in a Redefined Europe." Presented at the annual meeting of the American Association for Public Opinion. St. Charles, IL.

Mencius. 1970. *Mencius*. Translated by D. C. Lau. New York: Penguin Books.

Miller, Arthur H., Vicki L. Hesli, and William M. Reisinger. 1997. "Conceptions of Democracy among Mass and Elite in Post-Soviet Societies." *British Journal of Political Science* 27:157–90.

Miller, Geoffrey. 2006. "The Asian Future of Evolutionary Psychology." *Evolutionary Psychology* 4:107–19.

Mishler, William and Richard Rose. 1996. "Trajectories of Fear and Hope – Support for Democracy in Post-Communist Europe." *Comparative Political Studies* 28:553–81.

_____. 2001. "What Are the Origins of Political Trust?" *Comparative Political Studies* 34:30–62.

_____. 2002. "Learning and Re-Learning Regime Support: The Dynamics of Post-Communist Regimes." *European Journal of Political Research* 41: 5–36.

_____. 2005. "What Are the Political Consequences of Trust?" *Comparative Political Studies* 38:1050–78.

Mo, Jongryn. 2003. "The Challenge of Accountability: The Censorate." In *Confucianism for the Modern World*, edited by Daniel A. Bell and Chaibong Hahm. New York: Cambridge University Press, 54–68.

Moody, Peter R. 1996. "Asian Values." *Journal of International Affairs* 50:166–92.

Moreno, Alejandro. 2001. "Democracy and Mass Belief Systems in Latin America." In *Citizen Views of Democracy in Latin America*, edited by Roderic Camp. Pittsburgh: University of Pittsburgh Press, 27–50.

Mueller, John E. 2001. *Capitalism, Democracy, and Ralph's Pretty Good Grocery*. Princeton, NJ: Princeton University Press.

Muller, Edward N. and Mitchell A. Seligson. 1994. "Civic Culture and Democracy: The Question of Causal Relationships." *American Political Science Review* 88:635–52.

Mungello, D. E. 1991. "Confucianism in the Enlightenment: Antagonism and Collaboration between the Jesuits and the Philosophes." In *China and Europe: Images and Influences in Sixteenth to Eighteenth Centuries*, edited by Thomas H. C. Lee. Hong Kong: Chinese University Press, 99–127.

Munro, Donald J. 1969. *The Concept of Man in Early China*. Stanford, CA: Stanford University Press.

Murthy, Viren. 2000. "The Democratic Potential of Confucian Minben Thought." *Asian Philosophy: An International Journal of the Philosophical Traditions of the East* 10:33–47.

Nakane, Chie. 1970. *Japanese Society*. Berkeley: University of California Press.

Nathan, Andrew and Tse-Hsien Chen. 2004. *Traditional Social Values, Democratic Values, and Political Participation*. Asian Barometer Working Paper No. 23. Taipei: National Taiwan University.

Neher, Clark D. 1994. "Asian Style Democracy." *Asian Survey* 34:949–61.

Nevitte, Neil. 1996. *The Decline of Deference: Canadian Value Change in Cross National Perspective.* Peterborough, Canada: Broadview.

Newton, Kenneth. 2001. "Trust, Social Capital, Civil Society, and Democracy." *International Political Science Review* 22:201–14.

———. 2006. "Political Support: Social Capital, Civil Society and Political and Economic Performance." *Political Studies* 54:846–64.

Ng, Rita Mei Ching. 2009. "College and Character: What Did Confucius Teach Us about the Importance of Integrating Ethics, Character, Learning, and Education?" *Journal of College and Character* 10:1–7.

Ng, Rita Mei-Ching. 2009. "The Confucian Model of Self-Cultivation: Lessons for the West." Presented at the annual meeting of the International Communication Association, New Orleans.

Nie, Norman H., Jane Junn, and Kenneth Stehlik-Barry. 1996. *Education and Democratic Citizenship in America.* Chicago: University of Chicago Press.

Nisbett, Richard. 2003. *The Geography of Thought: How Asians and Westerners Think Differently... and Why.* New York: Free Press.

Norris, Pippa. (ed.). 1999. *Critical Citizens: Global Support for Democratic Governance.* New York: Oxford University Press.

———. 2002. *Democratic Phoenix: Reinventing Political Activism.* New York: Cambridge University Press.

———. 2011. *Democratic Deficit: Critical Citizens Revisited.* New York: Cambridge University Press.

Nosco, Peter. 2008. "Confucian Perspectives on Civil Society and Government." In *Confucian Political Ethics*, edited by Daniel A. Bell. Princeton, NJ: Princeton University Press, 20–45.

Nuyen, A. T. 2000. "Confucianism, the Idea of Min-pen and Democracy." *Copenhagen Journal of Asian Studies* 14:130–51.

———. 2002. "Confucianism and the Idea of Citizenship." *Asian Philosophy: An International Journal of the Philosophical Traditions of the East* 12:127–39.

Nylan, Michael. 2008. "Boundaries of the Body and Body Politics in Early Confucian Thought." In *Confucian Political Ethics*, edited by Daniel A. Bell. Princeton, NJ: Princeton University Press, 85–110.

O'Donnell, Guillermo. 1994. "Delegative Democracy." *Journal of Democracy* 5:55–69.

O'Donnell, Guillermo, Philippe C. Schmitter, and Laurence Whitehead. 1986. *Transitions from Authoritarian Rule: Tentative Conclusions about Uncertain Democracies.* Baltimore: Johns Hopkins University Press.

O'Dwyer, Shaun. 2003. "Democracy and Confucian Values." *Philosophy East and West* 53:39–63.

Orces, Diana. 2008. "Problems of Political Tolerance in the Americas." Retrieved from http://sitemason.vanderbilt.edu/files/lzeoz6/Orces.pdf.

Ottemoeller, Dan. 1998. "Popular Perceptions of Democracy: Elections and Attitudes in Uganda." *Comparative Political Studies* 31:98–124.

Park, Chong-Min and Doh Chull Shin. 2006. "Do Asian Values Deter Popular Support for Democracy in South Korea?" *Asian Survey* 46:341–61.

Paxton, Pamela. 2002. "Social Capital and Democracy: An Interdependent Relationship." *American Sociological Review* 67:254–77.

———. 2007. "Association Memberships and Generalized Trust: A Multilevel Model across 31 Countries." *Social Forces* 86:47–76.

Peffley, Mark and Robert Rohrschneider. 2003. "Democratization and Political Intolerance in Seventeen Countries." *Political Research Quarterly* 56:243–57.

Pertierra, Raul. 1999. "Introduction: Special Focus on Asian Ways: Asian Values Revisited." *SOJOURN: Journal of Social Issues in Southeast Asia* 14:275.

Pharr, Susan. 2000. "Officials' Misconduct and Public Distrust: Japan and the Trilateral Democracies." In *Disaffected Democracies: What's Troubling the Trilateral Countries?*, edited by Susan J. Pharr and Robert D. Putnam. Princeton, NJ: Princeton University Press, 173–201.

Putnam, Robert D. 1993. *Making Democracy Work: Civic Traditions in Modern Italy*. Princeton, NJ: Princeton University Press.

———. 2000. *Bowling Alone: The Collapse and Revival of American Community*. New York: Simon and Schuster.

Putnam, Robert and Khristin Goss 2002. "Introduction," in *Democracies in Flux: Evolution of Social Capital in Contemporary Society*. New York: Oxford University Press.

Pye, Lucian. 1968. *The Spirits of Chinese Politics: A Psychocultural Study of Authority Crisis in Political Development*. Cambridge, MA: MIT Press.

———. 1985. *Asian Power and Politics: The Cultural Dimensions of Authority*. Cambridge, MA: Harvard University Press.

———. 1999. "Civility, Social Capital, and Civil Society: Three Powerful Concepts for Explaining Asia." *Journal of Interdisciplinary History* 29:763–82.

Rappa, Antonio and Sor-hoon Tan. 2003. "Political Implications of Confucian Familism." *Asian Philosophy: An International Journal of the Philosophical Traditions of the East* 13:87–102.

Rawls, John. 1993. *Political Liberalism*. New York: Columbia University Press.

Realo, Anu, Jüri Allik, and Brenna Greenfield. 2008. "Radius of Trust." *Journal of Cross-Cultural Psychology* 39:447–62.

Reilly, Benjamin. 2008. *Democracy and Diversity: Institutional Engineering in the Asia-Pacific*. Oxford: Oxford University Press.

Robinson, Michael. 1991. "Perceptions of Confucianism in Twentieth-Century Korea." In *The East Asian Region: Confucian Heritage and Its Modern Adaptation*, edited by Gilbert Rozman. Princeton, NJ: Princeton University Press, 204–25.

Robinson, Richard. 1996. "The Politics of 'Asian Values.'" *Pacific Review* 9:309–27.

Rohrschneider, Robert. 1999. *Learning Democracy: Democratic and Economic Values in Unified Germany*. New York: Oxford University Press.

Rose, Richard and William Mishler. 1994. "Mass Reaction to Regime Change in Eastern Europe." *British Journal of Political Science* 24:159–82.

Rose, Richard and William Mishler. 2002. "Comparing Regime Support in Nondemocratic and Democratic Countries." *Democratization* 2:1–20.

Rose, Richard, William Mishler, and Christian Haerpfer. 1998. *Democracy and its Alternatives*. Baltimore: Johns Hopkins University Press.

Rose, Richard and Doh C. Shin. 2001. "Democratization Backwards: The Problem of Third-Wave Democracies." *British Journal of Political Science* 31:331–54.

Rosemont, Henry. 2008. "Civil Society, Government, and Confucianism: A Commentary." In *Confucian Political Ethics*, edited by Daniel A. Bell. Princeton, NJ: Princeton University Press, 46–58.

Rosenberg, Shawn. 2007. *Deliberation, Participation and Democracy: Can the People Govern?* New York: Palgrave Macmillan.

Rozman, Gilbert. (ed.). 1991a. *The East Asian Region: Confucian Heritage and its Modern Adaptation*. Princeton, NJ: Princeton University Press.

———. 1991b. "Introduction: The East Asian Region in Comparative Perspective." In *The East Asian Region: Confucian Heritage and Its Modern Adaptation*, edited by Gilbert Rozman. Princeton, NJ: Princeton University Press, 3–42.

———. 1991c. "Comparisons of Modern Confucian Values in China and Japan." In *The East Asian Region: Confucian Heritage and Its Modern Adaptation*, edited by Gilbert Rozman. Princeton, NJ: Princeton University Press, 157–203.

———. 2002. "Can Confucianism Survive in an Age of Universalism and Globalization?" *Pacific Affairs* 75:11–37.

———. 2003. "Center-Local Relations: Can Confucianism Boost Decentralization and Regionalism?" In *Confucianism for the Modern World*, edited by Daniel A. Bell and Chaibong Hahm. New York: Cambridge University Press, 181–200.

Sander, Thomas H. and Robert D. Putnam. 2010. "Still Bowling Alone?: The Post-9/11 Split." *Journal of Democracy* 21:9–16.

Sartori, Giovanni. 1995. "How Far Can Free Government Travel?" *Journal of Democracy* 6:101–11.

Scarpari, Maurizio. 2003. "The Debate on Human Nature in Early Confucian Literature." *Philosophy East and West* 53:323–39.

Schedler, Andreas and Rudolfo Sarsfield. 2007. "Democrats with Adjectives." *European Journal of Political Research* 45:637–59.

Scher, Roger 2010. "China: Would Machiavelli Be Proud?" *The Economist*, September 9.

Schmitter, Philippe C. and Terry Lynn Karl. 1991. "What Democracy Is... and Is Not." *Journal of Democracy* 2:75–88.

Schwartz, Benjamin Isadore. 1985. *The World of Thought in Ancient China*. Cambridge, MA: Harvard University Press.

Schwartz, Shalom. 1992. "Universals in the content and structure of values: Theoretical Advances and Empirical Test in 20 Countries." In *Advances in Experimental Social Psychology*, edited by M. Zanna. Orlando, FL: Academic Press, 1–65.

Selle, Per. 1991. "Culture and the Study of Politics." *Scandinavian Political Studies* 14:97–124.

Sen, Amartya. 1999. "Human Rights and Asian Values: What Lee Kuan Yew and Le Feng Do Not Understand about Asia." *New Republic* 217:33–41.

Sharma, Bhavna. 2008. *Voice, Accountability and Civic Engagement. Overseas Development Institute.* London: United Nations Development Programme.

Sheehan, Neil. 1989. *A Bright Shining Lie: John Paul Vann and America in Vietnam.* New York: Vintage Books.

Shi, Tian Jian. forthcoming. *A Theory of Culture: China and Taiwan as Test Cases.* New York: Cambridge University Press.

Shils, Edward. 1996. "Reflections on Civil Society and Civility in the Chinese Intellectual Tradition." In *Confucian Traditions in East Asian Modernity: Moral Education and Economic Culture in Japan and the Four Mini-Dragons,* edited by Tu Weiming. Cambridge, MA: Harvard University Press, 38–71.

Shin, Doh C. 1994. "On the Third Wave of Democratization: A Synthesis and Evaluation of Recent Theory and Research." *World Politics* 47:135–70.

———. 1999. *Mass Politics and Culture in Democratizing Korea.* New York: Cambridge University Press.

———. 2007. "Democratization: Perspectives from Global Citizenry." In *The Oxford Handbook of Political Behavior,* edited by Russell Dalton and Hans-Dieter Klingemann. New York: Oxford University Press, 259–282.

———. 2008. "The Third Wave in East Asia: Comparative and Dynamic Perspectives." *Taiwan Journal of Democracy* 4:91–131.

———. 2011. "Is Democracy the Only Political Game Worth Playing in Korea? Exploring Citizen Attitudes toward Democracy Legitimacy." Presented at a workshop on "East Asian Perspectives on Political Legitimacy" held in the University of Hong Kong on August 18–20.

Shin, Doh C., Myung Chey, and Kwang-Woong Kim. 1989. "Cultural Origins of Public Support for Democracy in Korea." *Comparative Political Studies* 22:217–38.

Shin, Doh C. and Takashi Inoguchi. 2009. "The Quality of Life in Confucian Asia: From Physical Welfare to Subjective Well-Being." *Social Indicators Research* 92:183–90.

Shin, Doh C. and Peter McDonough. 1999. "The Dynamics of Popular Reactions to Democratization in Korea." *Journal of Public Policy* 19:1–32.

Shin, Doh C. and Chong-Min Park. 2005. "Assessing the Shifting Qualities of Democratic Citizenship." *Democratization* 12:202–22.

Shin, Doh C. and Jason Wells. 2005. "Is Democracy the Only Game in Town?" *Journal of Democracy* 16:88–101.

Shun, Kwong-loi and David B. Wong. (eds.). 2004. *Confucian Ethics: A Comparative Study of Self-Autonomy and Community.* New York: Cambridge University Press.

Simon, Janos. 1998. "Popular Conceptions of Democracy in Postcommunist Europe." In *The Postcommunist Citizen,* edited by Samuel H. Barnes and Janos Simon. Budapest: Erasmus Foundation, 70–116.

Slote, Walter H. and George A. De Vos. (eds.). 1998. *Confucianism and the Family.* Albany: State University of New York Press.

Sniderman, Paul M., Philip E. Tetlock, James M. Glaser, Donald Philip Green, and Michael Hout. 1989. "Principled Tolerance and the American Mass Public." *British Journal of Political Science* 19:25–45.

Stepan, Alfred. 2000. "Religion, Democracy, and the 'Twin Tolerations.'" *Journal of Democracy* 11:37–57.

Stevenson, William and James W. Stigler. 1992. *Learning Gap: Why Our Schools Are Failing and What We Can Learn from Japanese and Chinese Education.* New York: Touchstone.

Subramaniam, Surain. 2000. "The Asian Values Debate: Implications for the Spread of Liberal Democracy." *Asian Affairs* 27:19–35.

Sullivan, John L., James Pierson, and George E. Marcus. 1982. *Political Tolerance and American Democracy.* Chicago: University of Chicago Press.

Sullivan, John L. and John E. Transue. 1999. "The Psychological Underpinnings of Democracy: A Selective Review of Research on Political Tolerance, Interpersonal Trust, and Social Capital." *Annual Review of Psychology* 50: 625–50.

Sun, Anna. 2009. "Counting Confucians in East Asia: Sociological Investigation." Presented at the International Conference on East Asian Confucianism. Rutgers University, New Brunswick, NJ.

Sztompka, Piotr. 1991. "The Intangibles and Imponderables of the Transition to Democracy." *Studies in Comparative Communism* 24:295–311.

Talisse, Robert B. 2005. "Liberalism, Pluralism, and Political Justification." *Harvard Review of Philosophy* 13:57–72.

Tamaki, Taku. 2007. "Confusing Confucius in Asian Values? A Constructivist Critique." *International Relations* 21:284–304.

Tamney, Joseph. 1991. "Confucianism and Democracy." *Asian Profile* 19:399–411.

Tan, Hwee Hoon and Dave Chee. 2005. "Understanding Interpersonal Trust in a Confucian-Influenced Society." *International Journal of Cross Cultural Management* 5:197–212.

Tan, Sor-hoon. 2003a. *Confucian Democracy: A Deweyan Reconstruction.* Albany: State University of New York Press.

———. 2003b. "Can There Be a Confucian Civil Society?" In *The Moral Circle and the Self: Chinese and Western Approaches*, edited by Kim Chong Chong, Sor-hoon Tan, and C. L. Ten. Chicago: Open Court, 193–208.

———. 2007. "Confucian Democracy as Pragmatic Experiment: Uniting Love of Learning and Love of Antiquity." *Asian Philosophy: An International Journal of the Philosophical Traditions of the East* 17:141–66.

———. 2009. "Beyond Elitism: A Community Ideal for a Modern East Asia." *Philosophy East and West* 59:537–53.

Tao, Julia and Andrew Brennan. 2003. "Confucian and Liberal Ethics for Public Policy: Holistic or Atomistic?" *Journal of Social Philosophy* 34:572–89.

Tavits, Margit. 2006. "Making Democracy Work More? Exploring the Linkage between Social Capital and Government Performance." *Political Research Quarterly* 59:211–25.

Theiss-Morse, Elizabeth and John R. Hibbing. 2005. "Citizenship and Civic Engagement." *Annual Review of Political Science* 8:227–49.

Thompson, Dennis F. 1970. *The Democratic Citizen: Social Science and Democratic Theory in the Twentieth Century.* New York: Cambridge University Press.

Thompson, Mark R. 2001. "Whatever Happened to Asian Values?" *Journal of Democracy* 12:154–65.

Thompson, Michael. 2008. *Organising and Disorganising: A Dynamic and Nonlinear Theory of Institutional Emergence and Its Implications.* Devon, UK: Triarchy Press.

Thompson, Michael, Richard J. Ellis, and Aaron Wildavsky. 1990. *Cultural Theory.* Boulder, CO: Westview Press.

Thurston, Anne. 1996. "Taiwan the Little Island That Could," *Wilson Quarterly* 20 (summer).

Tilly, Charles. 1996. *Citizenship, Identity, and Social History.* New York: Cambridge University Press.

Tran, Thi Phuong Hoa. 2009. *Franco-Vietnamese Schools and the Transition from Confucian to a New Kind of Intellectuals in the Colonial Context of Tonkin.* Harvard Yenching Institute Working Paper Series. Cambridge, MA: Harvard University.

Tu, Weiming. 1984. *Confucian Ethics Today: The Singapore Challenge.* Singapore: Federal Publications.

———. 1985. *Confucian Thought: Selfhood as Creative Transformation.* Albany: State University of New York Press.

———. 1986. *Confucianism in a Historical Perspective.* Singapore: Institute of East Asian Philosophies.

———. 1993. "Confucianism." In *Our Religions: The Seven World Religions Introduced by Preeminent Scholars from Each Tradition*, edited by Arvind Sharma. San Francisco, CA: HarperOne, 141–227.

———. 1994. "Embodying the Universe: A Note on Confucian Self-Realization." In *Self as Person in Asian Theory and Practice*, edited by Roger T. Ames, Wimal Dissanayake, and Thomis P. Kasulis. Albany: State University of New York Press, 177–86.

———. 1996a. "Confucian Traditions in East Asian Modernity." *Bulletin of the American Academy of Arts and Sciences* 50:12–39.

———. (ed.). 1996b. *Confucian Traditions in East Asian Modernity: Moral Education and Economic Culture in Japan and the Four Mini-Dragons.* Cambridge, MA: Harvard University Press.

———. 1996c. "Epilogue." In *Confucian Traditions in East Asian Modernity: Moral Education and Economic Culture in Japan and the Four Mini-Dragons*, edited by Tu Weiming. Cambridge, MA: Harvard University Press, 343–9.

———. 1998a. "Confucius and Confucianism." In *Confucianism and the Family*, edited by Walter H. Slote and George A. De Vos. Albany: State University of New York Press, 3–36.

———. 1998b. "Family, Nation, and the World: The Global Ethic as the Modern Confucian Quest." *Social Semiotics* 8:283–96.

———. 1998c. "Probing the 'Three Bonds' and 'Five Relationships' in Confucian Humanism." In *Confucianism and the Family*, edited by Walter H. Slote and George A. De Vos. Albany: State University of New York Press, 121–36.

———. 1999. *Humanity and Self-Cultivation: Essays in Confucian Thought.* Boston: Cheng & Tsui.

————. 2000. "Implications of the Rise of 'Confucian' East Asia." *Daedalus* 129:195–218.

————. 2002. "Confucianism and Liberalism." *Dao* 2:1–20.

Tucker, Mary Evelyn. 2003. "Introduction." In *Confucian Spirituality*, edited by Tu Weiming and Mary Evelyn Tucker. New York: Crossroad Publishing Company, 1–35.

Tusalem, Rollin F. 2007. "A Boon or a Bane? The Role of Civil Society in Third- and Fourth-Wave Democracies." *International Political Science Review* 28:361–86.

UNESCO. 2003. "Declaration of Principles on Tolerance." Paris: UNESCO.

Uslaner, Eric. 2002. *The Moral Foundation of Trust*. New York: Cambridge University Press.

Van Deth, Jan W. 2007. "Norms of Citizenship." In *The Oxford Handbook of Political Behavior*, edited by Russell Dalton and Hans-Dieter Klingemann. New York: Oxford University Press, 402–34.

Van Deth, Jan W., Marco Maraffi, Kenneth Newton, and Paul Whiteley. 1999. *Social Capital and European Democracy*. New York: Routledge.

Van Deth, Jan W. and Elinor Scarbrough. 1995. *The Impact of Values*. Oxford: Oxford University Press.

Wade, Robert. 1990. *Governing the Market: Economic Theory and the Role of the Government in East Asian Industrialization*. Princeton, NJ: Princeton University Press.

Wang, Zhengxu. 2008. *Democratization in Confucian East Asia: Citizen Politics in China, Japan, Singapore, South Korea, Taiwan, and Vietnam*. Amherst, NY: Cambria Press.

Wang, Zhengxu and Ern-Ser Tan. 2006. "Self-Expression, 'Asian Values,' and Democracy: East Asia in Global Perspective." In *Citizens, Democracy, and Markets around the Pacific Rim*, edited by Russell Dalton and Doh C. Shin. New York: Oxford University Press, 50–72.

Warren, Mark E. 1999. *Democracy and Trust*. New York: Cambridge University Press.

————. 2000. *Democracy and Association*. Princeton, NJ: Princeton University Press.

Weatherley, Robert. 1999. *The Discourse of Human Rights in China: Historical and Ideological Perspectives*. New York: Palgrave.

Weil, Frederick D. 1994. "Political Culture, Political Structure, and Democracy." In *Research on Democracy and Society: Political Culture and Political Structure, Vol. 2*, edited by Frederick D. Weil and Mary Gautier. Greenwich, CT: JAI Press, 65–115.

————. 2007. "Are Levels of Democracy Affected by Mass Attitudes? Testing Attainment and Sustainment Effects on Democracy." *International Political Science Review* 28:397–424.

Welzel, Christian. 2009. "Theories of Democratization." In *Democratization*, edited by Christian W. Haerpfer, Patrick Bernhagen, Ronald F. Inglehart, and Christian Welzel. New York: Oxford University Press, 74–90.

————. 2011. "The Asian Values Thesis Revisited: Evidence from the World Values Survey." *Japanese Journal of Political Science* 13:1–31.

Welzel, Christian and Hans-Dieter Klingemann. 2008. "Evidencing and Explaining Democratic Congruence: The Perspective of 'Substantive' Democracy." *World Values Research* 1:57–90.

Whitehead, Laurence. 2002. *Democratization: Theory and Experience.* New York: Oxford University Press.

Whitmore, John K. 1984. "Social Organization and Confucian Thought in Vietnam." *Journal of Southeast Asian Studies* 15:296–306.

Wildavsky, Aaron. 1987. "Choosing Preferences by Constructing Institutions: A Cultural Theory of Preference Formation." *American Political Science Review* 81:4–21.

———. 1993. "Democracy as a Coalition of Cultures." *Society* 31:80–3.

Wong, John. 1996. "Promoting Confucianism for Socioeconomic Development: The Singaporean Experience." In *Confucian Traditions in East Asian Modernity*, edited by Tu Weiming. Cambridge, MA: Harvard University Press, 277–93.

Woo-Cumings, Meredith. (ed.). 1999. *The Developmental State.* Ithaca, NY: Cornell University Press.

World Bank. 2000. *East Asia: Recovery and Beyond.* Washington, DC: World Bank.

———. 1993. *The East Asian Miracle: Economic Growth and Public Policy.* Washington, DC: World Bank.

Xu, Keqian. 2006. "Early Confucian Principles: The Potential Theoretic Foundation of Democracy in Modern China." *Asian Philosophy: An International Journal of the Philosophical Traditions of the East* 16:135–48.

Yamagishi, Toshio and Toko Kiyonari. 2000. "The Group as the Container of Generalized Reciprocity." *Social Psychology Quarterly* 63:116–32.

Yamashita, Samuel Hideo. 1997. "Confucianism and the Japanese, 1904–1945." In *Confucian Traditions in East Asian Modernity: Moral Education and Economic Culture in Japan and the Four Mini-Dragons*, edited by Tu Weiming. Cambridge, MA: Harvard University Press, 132–54.

Yao, Xinzhong. 1999. "Confucianism and its Modern Values: Confucian Moral, Educational and Spiritual Heritages Revisited." *Journal of Beliefs & Values: Studies in Religion & Education* 20:30–40.

———. 2000. *An Introduction to Confucianism.* New York: Cambridge University Press.

———. 2001. "Who is a Confucian Today? A Critical Reflection on the Issues Concerning Confucian Identity in Modern Times." *Journal of Contemporary Religion* 16:313–28.

Yu, Dan. 2009. *Confucius from the Heart: Ancient Wisdom for Today's World.* New York: Macmillan.

Yum, June Ock. 1988. "The Impact of Confucianism on Interpersonal Relationships and Communication Patterns in East Asia." *Communication Monographs* 55:374–88.

Yung, Betty. 2010. "Can Confucianism Add Value to Democracy Education?" *Procedia: Social and Behavioral Sciences* 2:1919–26.

Zakaria, Fareed. 1994. "Culture is Destiny: A Conversation with Lee Kuan Yew." *Foreign Affairs* 73:109–26.

_____. 1997. "The Rise of Illiberal Democracy." *Foreign Affairs* 76:22–43.

_____. 2003. *The Future of Freedom: Illiberal Democracy at Home and Abroad*. New York: W. W. Norton and Company.

Zhang, Tong and Barry Schwartz. 1997. "Confucius and the Cultural Revolution: A Study in Collective Memory." *International Journal of Politics, Culture, and Society* 11:189–212.

Zmerli, Sonja and Kenneth Newton. 2008. "Social Trust and Attitudes toward Democracy." *Public Opinion Quarterly* 72:706–24.

Index

359